Boards and Wards

A Review for

USMLE Steps 2 & 3

Boards and Wards

A Review for

USMLE Steps 2 & 3

Carlos Ayala, MD
Clinical Fellow in Surgery
Harvard Medical School
Resident in Otolaryngology
Harvard Otolaryngology Residency Program
Boston, Massachusetts

Brad Spellberg, MD
Resident in Internal Medicine
Harbor-UCLA Medical Center
Torrance, California

b

**Blackwell
Science**

©2000 by Carlos Ayala and Brad Spellberg

Blackwell Science, Inc.

Editorial Offices:
Commerce Place, 350 Main Street, Malden, Massachusetts 02148, USA
Osney Mead, Oxford OX2 0EL, England
25 John Street, London WC1N 2BS, England
23 Ainslie Place, Edinburgh EH3 6AJ, Scotland
54 University Street, Carlton, Victoria 3053, Australia
Other Editorial Offices:
Blackwell Wissenschafts-Verlag GmbH, Kurfürstendamm 57, 10707 Berlin, Germany
Blackwell Science KK, MG Kodenmacho Building, 7-10 Kodenmacho Nihombashi, Chuo-ku, Tokyo 104, Japan

Distributors:

The Americas
Blackwell Publishing
c/o AIDC
P.O. Box 20
50 Winter Sport Lane
Williston, VT 05495-0020
(Telephone orders: 800-216-2522;
fax orders: 802-864-7626)

Outside The Americas and Australia
Blackwell Science, Ltd.
c/o Marston Book Services, Ltd.
P.O. Box 269
Abingdon, Oxon OX14 4YN, England
(Telephone orders: 44-01235-465500;
fax orders: 44-01235-465555)

Australia
Blackwell Science Pty, Ltd.
54 University Street
Carlton, Victoria 3053
(Telephone orders: 03-9347-0300;
fax orders: 03-9349-3016)

All rights reserved. No part of this book may be reproduced in any form or by any electronic or mechanical means, including information storage and retrieval systems, without permission in writing from the publisher, except by a reviewer who may quote brief passages in a review.

Acquisitions: Joy Denomme
Development: Marlo Harris
Production: Erin Whitehead
Manufacturing: Lisa Flanagan
Cover Design: Juan Carlos Morales, Madison Design
Typeset by Best-set Typesetter Ltd., Hong Kong
Printed and bound by Braun-Brumfield, Inc.
Printed in the United States of America
01 02 5 4 3

The Blackwell Science logo is a trade mark of Blackwell Science Ltd., registered at the United Kingdom Trade Marks Registry

Library of Congress Cataloging-in-Publication Data
Boards and wards: a review for USMLE steps 2 & 3 / edited by Carlos Ayala and Brad Spellberg.
    p. cm.
  ISBN 0-632-04493-4
  1. Medicine–Examinations, questions, etc. I. Ayala, Carlos, MD. II. Spellberg, Brad.
  [DNLM: 1. Clinical Medicine. WB 18.2 B662 2000]
  R834.5.B63 2000
  616'.0076—dc21   99-049379

Figure Credits

Drs. Ayala and Spellberg and Blackwell Science, Inc., wish to thank the following authors for contributing figures to *Boards and Wards*:

- Peter Armstrong, Martin L. Wastie (Figures 1-16, 1-17, 2-13, 2-14, 2-15, 5-1, 7-2, 7-3, 10-1, 10-3 through 10-10, and 10-15 borrowed from *Diagnostic Imaging, 4e*, ©1998 Blackwell Science)
- John Axford (Figures 1-1, 1-10, 1-12 through 1-15, 1-18 through 1-23, 1-25, 3-5, 3-7, 8-1 and Plates 1 through 22 borrowed from *Medicine*, ©1996 Blackwell Science)
- Dale Berg (Figure 1-3 borrowed from *Advanced Clinical Skills and Physical Diagnosis*, ©1999 Blackwell Science)
- Geoffrey Chamberlain (Figures 3-10 and 3-11 from *Lecture Notes on Obstetrics, 7e*, ©1996 Blackwell Science)
- Alfred Cuschieri, Thomas P.J. Hennessy, Roger M. Greenhalgh, David I. Rowley, Pierce A. Grace (Figures 2-2 and 2-8 borrowed from *Clinical Surgery*, ©1996 Blackwell Science)
- Harold Ellis, Sir Roy Calne, Christopher Watson (Figures 1-11 and 2-1 borrowed from *Lecture Notes on General Surgery, 9e*, ©1998 Blackwell Science)
- N.C. Hughes-Jones, S.N. Wickramasinghe (Figures 1-26 through 1-30 from *Lecture Notes on Haematology, 6e*, ©1996 Blackwell Science)
- Bruce James, Chris Chew, Anthony Bron (Figures 9.2 through 9.9 and Plates 23 through 30 from *Lecture Notes on Ophthalmology, 8e*, ©1997 Blackwell Science)
- P.R. Patel (Figures 1-7, 1-8, 1-24, 2-4, 2-6, 2-9, 2-10, 2-11, 2-12, 2-18, 2-19, 2-20, 5-2, and 10-11 through 10-14 borrowed from *Lecture Notes on Radiology*, ©1998 Blackwell Science)

Dedication

Dedicated to my wife, Teresa, and to all those who strive to be caring, compassionate physicians.

Carlos Ayala, MD

I dedicate this book to all those interns manning the front lines of our hospitals, and to all those MS IVs who will soon know their pain.

Brad Spellberg, MD

TABLE OF CONTENTS

Contributors

Carlos Ayala, MD
Clinical Fellow in Surgery
Harvard Medical School
Resident in Otolaryngology
Harvard Otolaryngology Residency Program
Boston, Massachusetts

Pedro Cheung, MD
Resident in Family Medicine
Kaiser Permanente
Orange County, California

Eric Daniels, MD
Resident Physician, Department of Surgery
University of California, Los Angeles School of Medicine
Los Angeles, California

Michael Gentry, MD
Resident in Radiology
University of California, Los Angeles School of Medicine
Los Angeles, California

Griselda Gutierrez, MD
Resident in Obstetrics and Gynecology
Harbor-UCLA Medical Center
Torrance, California

Charles Lee, MD
Resident in Psychiatry
University of California, San Francisco
San Francisco, California

Beatriz Mares, MD
Resident in Pediatrics
Oakland Children's Hospital
Oakland, California

Joseph Rosales, MD
Resident in Internal Medicine
Saint Mary's Medical Center
Long Beach, California

Ming-Sing Si, MD
Resident in General Surgery
UC Irvine Medical Center
Irvine, California

Brad Spellberg, MD
Resident in Internal Medicine
Harbor-UCLA Medical Center
Torrance, California

List of Tables

LIST OF ALGORITHMS

ABBREVIATIONS KEY

↑ (↑↑)	Increases/High (markedly increases/Very high)
↓ (↓↓)	Decreases/Low (markedly decreases/Very low)
→	Causes/Leads to/Analysis shows
1°/2°	Primary/Secondary
BP	Blood pressure
Bx	Biopsy
CA	Carcinoma
CN	Cranial nerve
CNS	Central nervous system
CXR/X-ray	Chest x-ray/X-ray
Dx/DDx	Diagnosis/Differential diagnosis
ETOH	Ethyl alcohol
dz	Disease
HA	Headache
HTN	Hypertension
Hx/FHx	History/Family history
ICP	Intracranial pressure
I&D	Incision and drainage
infxn	Infection
IVIG	Intravenous immunoglobulin
N or Nml	Normal
PE	Physical exam or Pulmonary embolus
pt(s)	Patient(s)
Px	Prognosis
Si/Sx/aSx	Sign/Symptom/Asymptomatic
subQ	Subcutaneous
Tx	Treatment/Therapy
Utz	Ultrasound

Preface

Scutted-out medical students and exhausted interns have no time to waste studying for the USMLE Steps 2 and 3 exams. That's where we come in. Our book is authored by house staff, like you, training in each of the major fields of medicine tested on the USMLE exams: Internal Medicine, Surgery, Obstetrics-Gynecology, Pediatrics, Family Medicine, Psychiatry, Neurology, Dermatology, and Radiology. However, in contrast to most review texts, we have targeted each chapter toward clinicians *who are not going into that field of medicine*. Thus, Family Medicine is written for surgeons, Obstetrics-Gynecology is written for psychiatrists, Internal Medicine is written for pediatricians, and so on.

None of you surgeons out there want to spend the five minutes you have before nodding off to sleep "learning" Dermatology for the USMLE Step 2 or 3 exam! Rather, you need a concise review, broad in content but lacking extensive detail, to jar your memory of testable concepts you long ago learned and forgot. Don't waste your precious waking hours pouring over voluminous review texts! Remember, sleep when you can sleep. During those few minutes before dozing off in the call room, use a text written by colleagues and designed to help you breeze through subjects you have little interest in and have forgotten most of, but in which you need the most review. Like you, we know and live by the old axiom: study 2 months for the USMLE Step 1 exam, 2 days for the Step 2 exam, and bring a number 2 pencil to the Step 3 exam!

We welcome any feedback you may have about *Boards and Wards*. Please feel free to contact the authors with your comments or suggestions.

Boards and Wards
c/o Blackwell Science, Inc.
Commerce Place
350 Main Street
Malden, MA 02148

1. Internal Medicine

Joe Rosales

Carlos Ayala

Brad Spellberg

Cardiology

I. Hypertension (HTN)

Definition = BP ≥ 140/90 measured on 3 separate days

A. CAUSES

  1. 95% of all HTN is idiopathic, called **"essential HTN"**

  2. Most of 2° HTN causes can be divided into 3 organ systems & drugs

TABLE 1-1   Causes of Secondary Hypertension

Cardiovascular	• Aortic regurgitation causes **wide pulse pressure** • Aortic coarctation causes HTN in arms with ↓ **BP in legs**
Renal	• **Glomerular dz commonly presents with proteinuria** • **Renal artery stenosis causes refractory HTN** in older men (atherosclerosis) or young women (fibromuscular dysplasia) • Polycystic kidneys
Endocrine	• Hypersteroidism, typically **Cushing's & Conn's syndromes, which cause HTN with hypokalemia** (↑ aldosterone) • Pheochromocytoma causing episodic autonomic symptoms • Hyperthyroidism causing **isolated systolic HTN**
Drug Induced	• Oral contraceptives, glucocorticoids, phenylephrine, NSAIDs

B. MALIGNANT HYPERTENSION

  1. Defined as severe hypertension with resultant neurologic defect

  2. Si/Sx = mental status changes (e.g., obtundation), ↑ ICP (papilledema), oliguria/anuria, left heart strain, myocardial infarction, or chest pain, focal neural deficits

  3. **This is a medical emergency & immediate therapy is needed**

  4. Tx = nitroprusside or nifedipine, **but do NOT lower BP by more than $\frac{1}{4}$ at first or pt will stroke out, target = systolic pressure of 160 mm Hg**

C. HYPERTENSION TREATMENT

  1. Lifestyle modifications first line in pts without comorbid dz

   a. Weight loss, exercise, quitting alcohol & smoking can each significantly lower BP independently—salt restriction may help

   b. ↓ fat intake to ↓ risk of coronary artery dz (CAD); HTN is a cofactor

  2. Medications

1

TABLE 1-2   Medical Treatment of Hypertension

Indications	1) Failure of lifestyle modifications after 6 mo to 1 yr 2) Immediate use necessary if comorbid organ disease present (e.g., stroke, angina, renal disease) 3) Immediate use in emergent or urgent hypertensive states (e.g., neurologic impairment, ↑ ICP)
First-line drugs	
No comorbid dz	**Diuretic or β-blocker** (proven to ↓ mortality)
Diabetes	**ACE inhibitors** (proven to ↓ vascular & renal dz)
↓ ejection fraction	**ACE inhibitors** (proven to ↓ mortality)
Myocardial infarction	**β-blocker & ACE inhibitor** (proven to ↓ mortality)
Osteoporosis	**Thiazide diuretics** (↓ Ca^{2+} excretion)
Prostatic hypertrophy	**α-blockers** (treat HTN & BPH concurrently)
Contraindications	
β-blockers	**Chronic obstructive pulmonary dz**, due to bronchospasm
β-blockers (relative)	**Diabetes**, due to alteration in insulin/glucose homeostasis & blockade of autonomic response to hypoglycemia
β-blockers	**Hyperkalemia**, due to risk of ↑ serum K levels
ACE inhibitors	**Pregnancy**, due to teratogenicity
ACE inhibitors	**Renal artery stenosis**, due to precipitation of acute renal failure (GFR dependent on angiotensin-mediated constriction of efferent arteriole)
ACE inhibitors	**Renal failure (creatinine > 1.5)**, due to hyperkalemia morbidity
K^+ sparing diuretics	**Renal failure (creatinine > 1.5)**, due to hyperkalemia morbidity
Diuretics	**Gout**, due to causation of hyperuricemia
Thiazides	**Diabetes**, due to hyperglycemia

II. Ischemic Heart Disease (Coronary Artery Disease)

A. RISK FACTORS FOR CORONARY ARTERY DISEASE
  1. **Major risk factors (memorize these!!!)**
     a. Diabetes (may be the most important)
     b. Smoking
     c. Hypertension
     d. Hypercholesterolemia **(total cholesterol-HDL ratio > 5.0)**
     e. Family history
  2. Minor risk factors: obesity, age, lack of estrogen (males or postmenopausal women not on estrogen replacement), homocystinuria
  3. Smoking is the #1 preventable risk factor
  4. Diabetes probably imparts the greatest risk of all of them
  5. Unlike diabetic microvascular dz (e.g., retinopathy, etc.) **there is no evidence that tight glucose control can diminish onset of CAD**

B. STABLE ANGINA PECTORIS
  1. Caused by atherosclerotic CAD, supply of blood to heart < demand
  2. Si/Sx = precordial pain radiating to left arm, jaw, back, etc., relieved by rest & nitroglycerin, EKG → **ST depression & T-wave inversion**
  3. **Classic Sx often not present in elderly & diabetics (neuropathy)**
  4. Dx = clinical, based on Sx, CAD risks, confirm CAD with angiography

5.

TABLE 1-3   Angina Treatment

Acute	Sublingual NTG • Usually acts in 1–2 min • May be taken up to 3 times q3–5 minute intervals • If doesn't relieve pain after 3 doses, pt may be infarcting
Chronic prevention	• Long-acting nitrates effective in prophylaxis • β-blockers ↓ myocardial O_2 consumption in stress/exertion • Aspirin to prevent platelet aggregation in atherosclerotic plaque • Quit smoking! (2 years after quitting, MI risk = nonsmokers) • ↓ LDL levels, ↑ HDL with diet (↓ saturated fat intake more important than actual cholesterol intake), ↑ exercise, ↑ fiber intake, stop smoking, lose weight, HMG-CoA reductase inhibitors • Folate lowers homocysteine levels, but there is controversy over role of ↑ homocysteine in MI, so role of folate Tx is unclear
Endovascular intervention	*Percutaneous Transluminal Coronary Angioplasty (PTCA)* • Indicated with failure of medical management • Morbidity less than surgery but has up to 50% restenosis rate • Stent placement reduces restenosis rate to 20–30% • Platelet gpIIB/IIIA inhibitors (e.g., ReoPro) may also ↓ restenosis rate
Surgery	• Procedure is coronary artery bypass graft (CABG) • Indications = failure of medical Tx, 3 vessel CAD, or 2 vessel dz in diabetes • Comparable mortality rates with PTCA after several years, except in diabetic patients who do better with CABG

C. UNSTABLE ANGINA (USA)

1. Sx similar to stable angina but occur more frequently with less exertion and **may occur at rest**
2. USA is caused by transient clotting of atherosclerotic vessels, clot spontaneously dissolves before infarction occurs
3. EKG during episode usually shows ST depression or flattening of T wave; if ST segment elevation follows, pt is progressing to infarction
4. Labs = cardiac enzymes (CK-MB, troponins) usually negative
5. Tx must be aggressive to prevent infarction, hospitalization is indicated
    a. Immediate IV heparin & aspirin (ASA) to stabilize clotting, pt should continue with ASA after discharge
    b. Nitroglycerin increases O_2 delivery to myocardium
    c. β-blockers decrease myocardial O_2 demand
    d. Once stabilized, pt should undergo evaluation (e.g., exercise stress testing) for risk stratification, usually followed by medical management, PTCA or CABG

D. MYOCARDIAL INFARCT

1. Infarct usually 2° to acute thrombosis in atherosclerotic vessel
2. Si/Sx = crushing substernal pain, as per angina, but not relieved by rest, ⊕ diaphoresis, nausea/vomiting, tachycardia or bradycardia, dyspnea
3. Dx = 2 out of 3 criteria
    a. **EKG → ST elevation & Q waves** (See Figure 1-1)
    b. Enzymes: troponin I or CK-MB & myoglobin—**troponin I rises faster (4 hr) & is more specific & as sensitive as CK-MB**
    c. Appropriate signs & symptoms with risk factors
4. Tx = reestablish vessel patency
    a. Medical Tx = thrombolysis within 6 hr of the infarct: by using **TPA + heparin** (first line) or streptokinase
    b. PTCA may be more effective, can open vessels mechanically or with local administration of thrombolytics
    c. CABG is longer-term Tx, rarely used for acute process
5. Adjuvant medical therapies
    a. **#1 priority is aspirin! (proven to ↓ mortality)**
    b. **#2 priority is β-blocker (proven to ↓ mortality)**
    c. Statin drugs to lower cholesterol are essential (**LDL must be < 100 postinfarct,** proven to ↓ mortality)
    d. Heparin should be given for 48 hr postinfarct **if tPA was used to lyse the clot** (heparin has no proven benefit if streptokinase was used or if no lysis was performed)
    e. O₂ & morphine for pain control
    f. Nitroglycerin to reduce both pre- & afterloads
    g. ACE inhibitors are excellent late- & long-term therapy, ↓ afterload & prevent remodeling
    h. Exercise strengthens heart, develops collateral vessels, ↑ HDL
    i. STOP SMOKING!!!!!!!!!!!!!!!!!

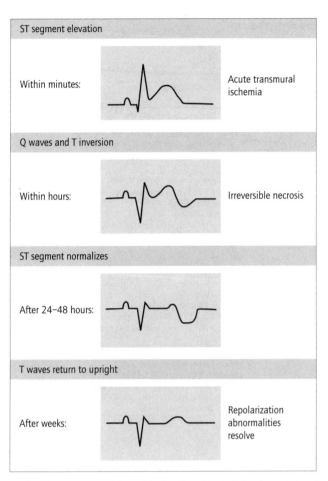

FIGURE 1-1   The changing pattern of the EKG in the affected leads during the evolution of a myocardial infarction.

III. Selected Arrhythmias

A.

TABLE 1-4   Basic Heart Blocks (See Figure 1-2)

TYPE	CHARACTERISTICS	PX & TX
1°	• EKG → PR interval > 0.20 seconds • All atrial impulses conducted • May occur in normal individuals due to ↑ vagal tone	Px good, no intervention required
2° Mobitz type I	• Mobitz type I or Wenckebach block • **EKG → PR intervals progressively ↑ from beat to beat** until they become so long the beat is dropped • Following the dropped beat, PR interval resets to baseline & begins to progressively lengthen again • May also occur in normal people or pts taking drugs (e.g., β-blockers, digoxin, Ca-blockers)	Px good, Tx = stop offending drugs if symptomatic
2° Mobitz type II	• Mobitz type II block • **EKG → PR interval fixed at > 0.20 seconds & there is a fixed ratio of dropped beats** • Usually due to block with the His bundle system	Px = poor, ↑ risk progression to 3° Tx = ventricular pacemaker
3°	• Complete heart block • **EKG → absolutely no relationship between P-P intervals & QRS intervals** • Si/Sx = dyspnea, syncope, cannon A waves in jugular veins (See Figure 1-3), wide pulse pressure, may be aSx	Tx = permanent ventricular pacemaker

B. **ATRIAL FIBRILLATION (A-FIB)** (See Figure 1-4)
1. Most common chronic arrhythmia
2. Etiologies include heart dz (e.g., valvular), surgery, pulmonary dz, toxicity (e.g., thyrotoxicosis, alcohol intoxication or withdrawal)
3. Pulse is **irregularly irregular, classic descriptor of a-fib**
4. Si/Sx = chest discomfort/palpitations, hypotension/syncope, tachycardia
5. Complications = diffuse embolization, often to brain, of atrial mural thrombi
6. Tx
   a. Rate control with β-blockers, digoxin (not acutely), Ca-blockers (e.g., verapamil & diltiazem)
   b. Convert to normal rhythm (cardioversion) with drugs or electricity
      1) Drug = IV procainamide (first line), sotalol, or amiodarone
      2) Electrical → shocks of 100–200J followed by 360J
   c. All pts with a-fib lasting > 24 hr should be anticoagulated with Coumadin for 3 wk before electrical cardioversion to prevent embolization during cardioversion

C. MULTIFOCAL ATRIAL TACHYCARDIA (MFAT)
1. Multiple concurrent pacemakers in the atria, also an irregularly irregular rhythm, usually found in pts with COPD
2. **EKG → tachycardia with ≥ 3 distinct P waves present in 1 rhythm strip** (note: if the pt has ≥ 3 distinct P waves but is not tachycardic, rhythm = wandering pacemaker)
3. Tx = verapamil; also treat underlying condition

D. SUPRAVENTRICULAR TACHYCARDIA (SVT) (See Figure 1-4)
1. SVT is a grab-bag of tachyarrhythmias originating "above the ventricle"
2. Pacer can be in atrium or at AV junction, & multiple pacers can be active at any one time (multifocal atrial tachycardia)
3. DDx = ventricular tachycardia; differentiation of SVT from ventricular tachycardia requires careful EKG analysis as they cannot be distinguished clinically
4. Presence of P waves on EKG & narrow QRS (< 0.12 s) suggests SVT, but can be very difficult to distinguish if pt also has a bundle branch block
5. Tx depends on etiology
   a. Correct electrolyte imbalance, ventricular rate control (digoxin, Ca^{2+}-channel blocker, β-blocker, adenosine) & electrical cardioversion in unstable pts
   b. Attempt carotid massage in pts with paroxysmal SVT

E. VENTRICULAR TACHYCARDIA (V-TACH) (See Figure 1-4)
1. Defined as ≥ 3 consecutive premature ventricular contractions (PVCs)
2. Sustained V-tach lasts minimum of 30 sec, requires immediate intervention due to risk of onset of v-fib (see below)
3. If hypotension or no pulse is coexistent → defibrillate and treat as V-fib
4. Tx depends on symptomatology
   a. If hypotension or no pulse is coexistent → emergency electrical defibrillation, 200–300–360J
   b. If asymptomatic first line Tx is lidocaine, which can convert rhythm to normal

F. VENTRICULAR FIBRILLATION (V-FIB) (See Figure 1-4)
1. Si/Sx = syncope, severe hypotension, sudden death
2. **Emergent electric countershock is the primary therapy** (very rarely precordial chest thump is effective), converts rhythm 95% of the time (200–300–360J)
3. Second line Tx is lidocaine
4. Without Tx, natural course = total failure of cardiac output → death

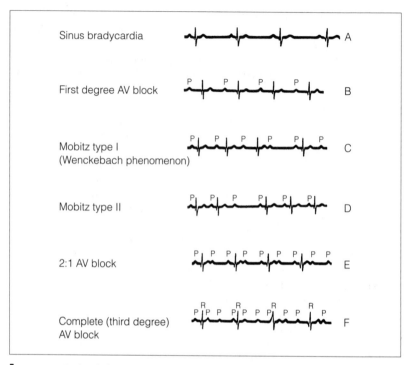

FIGURE 1-2   Bradyarrhythmias.

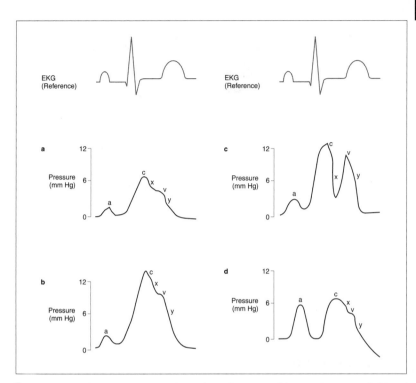

FIGURE 1-3   Jugular venous pressure tracing. (a) Normal: *a* wave, atrial contraction; *c* wave, bulging of tricuspid cusps into the right atrium at the beginning of each systole; *x* descent, relaxation of the right atrium; *v* wave, volume of blood that enters the right atrium during ventricular systole; *y* descent, rapid flow of blood into the right ventricle upon opening of the tricuspid valve. (b) Right ventricular failure: overall increase in jugular venous pulsations and merging of *c* and *v* waves. (c) Tricuspid regurgitation: overall increase in pressure and marked increase in the magnitude of the *x* descent, resulting in separate *c* and *v* waves. (d) Canon *a* waves: marked increase in *a* wave intensity with no increase in jugular venous pulsations (found in AV dissociation).

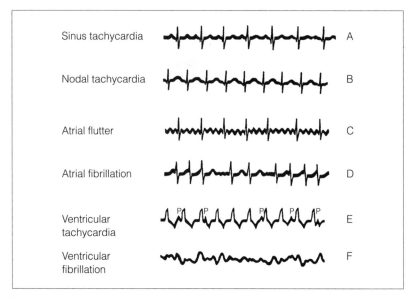

Sinus tachycardia .... A

Nodal tachycardia .... B

Atrial flutter C

Atrial fibrillation .... D

Ventricular tachycardia .... E

Ventricular fibrillation .... F

FIGURE 1-4   Tachydysrhythmias.

IV. Congestive Heart Failure

A. ETIOLOGIES & DEFINITION

1. Causes = valve dz, MI (acute & chronic), HTN, anemia, pulmonary embolism, cardiomyopathy, thyrotoxicosis, endocarditis
2. Definition = cardiac output insufficient to meet systemic demand, can have right, left, or both-sided failure

B. SIGNS & SYMPTOMS & DIAGNOSIS

1. Left-sided failure Si/Sx due to ↓ cardiac output & ↑ cardiac pressures = **exertional dyspnea, orthopnea, paroxysmal nocturnal dyspnea,** cardiomegaly, rales, S3 gallop, renal hypoperfusion → ↑ aldosterone production → Na retention → ↑ total body fluid → worse heart failure
2. Right-sided failure Si/Sx due to blood pooling "upstream" from R-heart = ↑ jugular venous pressure, dependent edema, hepatic congestion with transaminitis, atrial fibrillation, fatigue, weight loss, cyanosis
3. Atrial fibrillation common in CHF, ↑ risk of embolization
4. Dx = echocardiography that reveals ↓ cardiac output

C. TREATMENT

1. **ACE inhibitors (first line for CHF)** & β-blockers
2. Digitalis used in pts with a-fib, as the drug's cholinomimetic effects protect ventricular rate by slowing AV nodal conduction
3. **Only ACE inhibitors proven to improve survival, digitalis & diuretics palliate symptoms but have not been shown to increase survival (probably due to arrhythmia side effects)**

4. Beware of giving loop/thiazide diuretics with digitalis—diuretics → hypokalemia that can induce lethal digitalis toxicity
   a. Digitalis toxicity presents as **supraventricular tachycardia with AV block**, & can cause **yellow vision**
   b. Tx acutely with antidigitalis FAB antibodies as well as correction of underlying potassium deficit
5. Coumadin first line, aspirin second line anticoagulant [see *Circulation*, 1996 93:1262–1277)
6. Definitive Tx = cardiac transplant, left ventricular assist device can palliate pt until matched heart becomes available

V. Cardiomyopathy

TABLE 1-5   Cardiomyopathy

	DILATED	**HYPERTROPHIC**	**RESTRICTIVE**
Cause	Ischemic, infectious (HIV, Coxsackie virus, Chagas' disease), metabolic, drugs (alcohol, doxorubicin, AZT)	Genetic myosin disorder	Amyloidosis, scleroderma, hemochromatosis, glycogen storage dz, sarcoidosis
Si/Sx	R & L heart failure, a-fib, S3 gallop, mitral regurgitation **Systolic dz**	Exertional syncope, angina, EKG → LVH **Diastolic dz**	Pulmonary HTN, S4 gallop, EKG → ↓ QRS voltage **Diastolic dz**
Px	30% survival at 5 yr	5% annual mortality usually due to sudden death	30% survival at 5 yr
Tx	Stop offending agent, once cardiomyopathy onsets, Tx similar to CHF	• β-blockers & Ca blockers • Surgical excision of myocardium if Sx severe • Dual-chamber pacing with implantable defibrillator	None

VI. Valvular Diseases

A. MITRAL VALVE PROLAPSE (MVP)
1. Seen in 7% of population, in vast majority is a benign finding in young people which is aSx & eventually disappears
2. **Murmur: pathologic prolapse → late systolic murmur with midsystolic click (Barlow's syndrome)**, predisposing to regurgitation
3. Dx = clinical, confirm with echocardiography
4. Tx not required

B. MITRAL VALVE REGURGITATION (MVR)
1. Seen in severe MVP, rheumatic fever, papillary muscle dysfunction (often 2° to MI) & endocarditis
2. Results in dilation of left atrium (LA), ↑ in LA pressure, leading to pulmonary edema/dyspnea
3. See below, Section VIII.A for physical findings

4. Dx = clinical, confirm with echocardiography

5. Tx = ACE inhibitors, vasodilators, diuretics, consider surgery in severe dz

C. MITRAL STENOSIS

1. Almost always due to prior rheumatic fever

2. Decreased flow across the mitral valve leads to left atrial enlargement (LAE) & eventually to right heart failure

3. Si/Sx = dyspnea, orthopnea, hemoptysis, pulmonary edema, a-fib

4. See below, Section VIII.A for physical findings

5. Dx = clinical, confirm with echocardiography

6. Tx

    a. β-blockers to slow HR

    b. Digitalis to slow ventricle in pts with a-fib

    c. Anticoagulants for embolus prophylaxis

    d. Surgical valve replacement for uncontrollable dz

    e. **NEVER give ⊕ inotropic agents for mitral stenosis as are given for other ↓ cardiac output dzs**

D. AORTIC REGURGITATION (AR)

1. Seen in endocarditis, rheumatic fever, VS defect (children), congenital bicuspid aorta, 3° syphilis, aortic dissection, Marfan's syndrome, trauma

2. **There are 3 murmurs in AR** (see below, Section VIII.A)

3. AR has numerous classic signs

    a. **Water-Hammer pulse** = wide pulse pressure presenting with forceful arterial pulse upswing with rapid fall-off

    b. **Traube's sign** = pistol-shot bruit over femoral pulse

    c. **Corrigan's pulse** = unusually large carotid pulsations

    d. **Quincke's sign** = pulsatile blanching & reddening of fingernails upon light pressure

    e. **de Musset's sign** = head bobbing caused by carotid pulsations

    f. **Muller's sign** = pulsatile bobbing of the uvula

    g. **Duroziez's sign** = to-&-fro murmur over femoral artery heard best with mild pressure applied to the artery

4. Dx = clinical, confirm by echocardiography

5. Tx

    a. ↓ afterload with ACE inhibitors or vasodilators (e.g., hydralazine)

    b. Antibiotic prophylaxis prior to procedures (e.g., dental work)

    c. Consider valve replacement if dz is fulminant or refractory to drugs

E. AORTIC STENOSIS (AS)

1. Frequently congenital, also seen in rheumatic fever, mild degenerative calcification = aortic sclerosis that is a normal part of aging

2. Obstructive hypertrophic subaortic stenosis (OHSS)

    a. Also called "hypertrophic obstructive cardiomyopathy"

    b. Ventricular septum hypertrophies inferior to the valve

    c. Stenosis due to septal wall impinging upon anterior leaflet (rarely posterior leaflet) of mitral valve during systole

3. **Si/Sx = classic triad of syncope, angina, exertional dyspnea**

4. Dx = clinical, confirm by echocardiography

5. Tx is surgery for all symptomatic pts who can tolerate it
   a. Either mechanical or bioprosthesis required, pt anticoagulated chronically after surgery
   b. Use balloon valvuloplasty of aortic valve for poor surgical candidates
   c. Tx with digitalis effective only in mild dz
   d. Patients need endocarditis prophylaxis prior to procedures
   e. **NEVER give AS patients β-blockers or afterload reducers (vasodilators & ACE inhibitors)—peripheral vasculature is maximally constricted to maintain BP, so administration of such agents will cause pt to go into shock**

F. TRICUSPID & PULMONARY VALVES

1. Both undergo fibrosis in carcinoid syndrome
2. Endocarditis prophylaxis required prior to procedures (e.g., dental work)
3. Tricuspid stenosis → **diastolic rumble easily confused with mitral stenosis, differentiate from MS by ↑ loud with inspiration** (see below, Section VIII.A)
4. Tricuspid regurgitation → holosystolic murmur (see below, Section VIII.A), look for jugular & hepatic systolic pulsations
5. Pulmonary stenosis → dz of children, or in adults with carcinoid syndrome, with midsystolic ejection murmur
6. Pulmonary regurgitation → develops 2° to pulmonary HTN, endocarditis, or carcinoid syndrome, due to valve ring widening, **Graham Steell murmur** = diastolic murmur at left sternal border, mimicking AR murmur
7. Tx for stenosis = balloon valvuloplasty, valve replacement rarely done

G. ENDOCARDITIS

1. Acute endocarditis caused by *Staphylococcus aureus, Streptococcus pneumoniae, Neisseria gonorrhoeae*
2. Subacute disease (slower onset, symptoms less severe) caused by *Enterococcus, S. viridans, Staph. epidermidis*
3. Marantic endocarditis is due to cancer seeding of heart valves during metastasis, very poor Px, malignant emboli → cerebral infarcts
4. Culture negative endocarditis (**HACEK**): *Hemophilus parainfluenzae, Actinobacillus, Cardiobacterium, Eikenella, Kingela kingai*
5. SLE causes **Libman-Sacks endocarditis,** may be due to autoantibody damage of valves—usually endocarditis is aSx, but murmur can be heard
6. Si/Sx = splenomegaly, **splinter hemorrhages** in fingernails, **Osler's nodes** (painful red nodules on digits), **Roth spots** (retinal hemorrhages with clear central areas), **Janeway lesions** (dark macules on palms/soles), conjunctival petechiae, brain/kidney/splenic abscesses → focal neuro findings/hematuria/abdominal or shoulder pain
7. Dx based upon the Duke criteria

TABLE 1-6   Duke Criteria for Endocarditis Diagnosis*

Major criteria	1) ⊕ blood cultures (×2) of common organisms
	2) ⊕ echocardiogram or onset of new murmur (transesophageal should be used, as transthoracic only 50–60% sensitive)
Minor criteria	1) Presence of predisposing condition (i.e., valve abnormality)
	2) Fever > 38°C
	3) Embolic disease (e.g., splenic, renal, hepatic, cerebral)
	4) Immunologic phenomena (i.e., Roth spots, Osler's nodes)
	5) ⊕ blood culture × 1 or rare organisms cultured

*80% specific if 2 major or 1 major + 3 minor, or 5 minor criteria are met.

8. Tx = prolonged antibiotics, 4–6 wk typically required (new research indicates sometimes 2 wk can be used for certain organisms)
9. Tailor antibiotics to blood cultures, ampicillin/sulbactam (if resistant to penicillin) + aminoglycoside often used
10. Surgery required for severe heart disease or large, expanding abscesses

H. RHEUMATIC FEVER/HEART DISEASE
1. Presents usually in 5–15-year-olds after group A Strep infection
2. Dx = Jones criteria (2 major & 1 minor)
3. Major criteria (**mnemonic: J♥NES**)
    a. Joints (migratory polyarthritis), responds to NSAIDs
    b. ♥carditis (pancarditis, Carey-Coombs murmur = middiastolic)
    c. Nodules (subcutaneous)
    d. Erythema marginatum (serpiginous skin rash)
    e. Sydenham's chorea (face, tongue, upper-limb chorea)
4. Minor criteria = fever, ↑ ESR, arthralgia, long EKG PR interval
5. In addition to Jones criteria, need evidence of prior strep infection by either culture or ⊕ antistreptolysin O (ASO) antibody titers
6. Tx = penicillin

VII. Pericardial Disease

A. PERICARDIAL FLUID
1. Pericardial effusion can result from any disease causing systemic edema
2. Hemopericardium is blood in the pericardial sac, often 2° to trauma, metastatic cancer, viral/bacterial infections
3. Both can lead to cardiac tamponade
    a. **Classic Beck's triad: distant heart sounds, distended jugular veins, hypotension**
    b. **Look for pulsus paradoxus, which is ≥ 10 mm Hg fall in BP during inspiration**
    c. EKG shows **electrical alternans**, which is beat-to-beat alternating height of QRS complex
4. Dx = clinical, confirm with echocardiography
5. Tx = immediate pericardiocentesis in tamponade, otherwise treat the underlying condition & allow the fluid to resorb

B. PERICARDITIS
1. Caused by bacterial, viral, or fungal infections, also in generalized serositis 2° to rheumatoid arthritis (RA), SLE, scleroderma, uremia
2. Si/Sx = retrosternal pain relieved when sitting up, often following URI, not affected by activity or food, listen for pleural friction rub
3. **EKG → ST elevation in all leads**, also see PR depression
4. Dx = clinical, confirm with echocardiography
5. Tx = NSAIDs for viral, antimicrobial agents for more severe dz, pericardiectomy reserved for recurrent dz

VIII. Murmurs

A.

TABLE 1-7   Summary of Major Murmurs*

DISEASE	MURMUR	PHYSICAL EXAM
Mitral stenosis	**Diastolic apical rumble** & opening snap	Feel for RV lift 2° to RVH
Mitral valve prolapse	**Late systolic murmur with midsystolic click (Barlow's syndrome)**	Valsalva → click earlier in systole, murmur prolonged
Mitral regurgitation	High-pitched **apical blowing holosystolic murmur radiate to axilla**	Laterally displaced PMI, systolic thrill
Tricuspid stenosis	**Diastolic rumble** often confused with MS	**Murmur louder with inspiration**
Tricuspid regurgitation	High-pitched **blowing holosystolic** murmur at left sternal border	**Jugular & hepatic pulsations, murmur louder with inspiration**
Aortic stenosis (AS)	**Midsystolic crescendo-decrescendo murmur at second right interspace, radiates to carotids & apex, with S_4 due to atrial kick,** systolic ejection click	**Pulsus parvus et tardus =** peripheral pulses are weak & late compared to heart sounds, systolic thrill second interspace
Aortic sclerosis	Peaks earlier in systole than AS	None
Aortic regurgitation	**3 murmurs:** • **Blowing early diastolic** at aorta & LSB • **Austin Flint = apical diastolic rumble** like mitral stenosis but no opening snap • Midsystolic flow murmur at base	Laterally displaced PMI, **wide pulse pressure, pulsus bisferiens** (double-peaked arterial pulse): see text for classic eponym physical findings
Hypertrophic subaortic stenosis	Systolic murmur at apex & left sternal border that is poorly transmitted to carotids	**Murmur increases with standing & Valsalva**

*The authors thank Dr. J. Michael Criley & Dr. Richard D. Spellberg for assistance with creation of this table.

B.

TABLE 1-8   Physical Exam Differential Diagnosis for Murmurs*

TIMING	POSSIBLE DISEASE: DIFFERENTIATING CHARACTERISTICS			
Midsystolic ("Ejection")	**Aortic stenosis/ sclerosis:** crescendo-decrescendo, second right interspace	**Pulmonic stenosis:** second left interspace, EKG → RVH	**Any high flow state → "flow murmur": aortic regurgitation** (listen for other AR murmurs), **A-S defect** (fixed split S_2), **anemia, pregnancy, adolescence**	
Late Systolic	**Aortic stenosis:** worse dz → later peak	**Mitral valve prolapse:** apical murmur	**Hypertrophic subaortic stenosis:** murmur louder with Valsalva	
Holosystolic	**Mitral regurgitation:** radiates to axilla	**V-S defect:** diffuse across precordium	**Tricuspid regurgitation:** louder with inspiration	
Early Diastolic	**Aortic regurgitation:** blowing aortic murmur		**Pulmonic regurgitation:** Graham Steell murmur	
Middiastolic	**Mitral stenosis:** opening snap, no change with inspiration	**Aortic regurgitation** (Austin Flint murmur): apical, resembles MS	**A-S defect:** listen for fixed split S_2, diastolic rumble	**Tricuspid stenosis:** louder with inspiration
Continuous	**Patent ductus:** machinery murmur loudest in back	**Mammary souffle:** harmless, heard in pregnancy due to ↑ flow in mammary artery	**Coarctation of aorta:** upper/lower extremity pulse discrepancy	**A-V fistula**

*The authors thank Dr. J. Michael Criley & Dr. Richard D. Spellberg for assistance with creation of this table.

Pulmonary

I. Hypoxemia

A. DIFFERENTIAL DIAGNOSIS

TABLE 1-9   Five Mechanisms of Hypoxemia

CAUSE	PCO$_2$	PA-aO$_2$*	EFFECT OF O$_2$	DLCO	Tx
↓ FIO$_2$	Nml	Nml	⊕	Nml	O$_2$
Hypoventilation	↑	Nml	⊕	Nml	O$_2$
Diffusion impairment	Nml	↑	⊕	↓	O$_2$
V/Q Mismatch	↑/Nml	↑	⊕	Nml	O$_2$
Shunt	↑/Nml	↑	—	Nml	Reverse cause

* PAO$_2$ - PaO$_2$ gradient (PA-aO$_2$) ≡ PO$_2$ in Alveoli minus PO$_2$ in arteries.
Normal gradient = 10, ↑ by 5–6 per decade above age 50.

$$PAO_2 = FIO_2(P_{breath} - P_{H_2O}) - (PaCO_2/R)$$
At sea level: FIO$_2$ = .21, P$_{H_2O}$ = 47, P$_{breath}$ = 760: **PAO$_2$ = 150 − (PaCO$_2$/R)**
PaCO$_2$ is measured by lab analysis of arterial blood, R = .8

B. CAUSES
1. Low inspired FIO$_2$ most often caused by high altitude
2. Hypoventilation
   a. Can be due to hypopnea (↓ respiratory rate) or ↓ vital capacity
   b. Hypopnea causes = CNS dz (e.g., narcotics, trauma, infection, etc.)
   c. ↓ vital capacity causes = chest wall neuromuscular dz (e.g., amyotrophic lateral sclerosis, kyphoscoliosis, etc.), airflow obstruction (e.g., sleep apnea), or any parenchymal lung dz
3. Diffusion impairment causes = ↑ diffusion path (fibrosis) or ↓ blood transit time through lung (↑ cardiac output, anemia)
4. V/Q inequality causes = pulmonary embolism, parenchymal lung disease
5. R-L shunt causes = pulmonary edema, pneumonia, atelectasis, atrial & ventricular septal defects, & chronic liver disease

C. PRESENTATION
1. Symptoms = tachycardia (very sensitive; primary compensation for hypoxia is to increase tissue blood flow), dyspnea/tachypnea, feeling of "inability to breathe enough" (dyspnea) usually precedes increase in breaths per minute
2. Si = crackles & rales present in some pulmonary parenchymal disorders, clubbing/cyanosis (not just in lung dz, but can be correlated to long-term hypoxemic states)

D. TREATMENT

1. Requires Tx for hypoxemia along with correction of underlying disorder
2. ↑ FIO_2 → ↑ PaO_2 & ↑ hemoglobin O_2 saturation
3. Give O_2 by nasal cannula (NC), face mask, CPAP, intubation, tracheostomy
   a. General rule, 1 L/min O_2 ↑ FIO_2 by 3% (e.g., giving pt 1 L/min O_2 → FIO_2 = 24%)
   b. Nasal cannula cannot administer > 40% FIO_2 even if flow rate is > 7 L/min
   c. Face mask ↑ maximum FIO_2 to 50–60%, nonrebreather face mask ↑ maximum FIO_2 to > 60%
   d. CPAP = tightly-fitting face mask connected to generator that creates continuous positive pressure, can ↑ maximum FIO_2 to 80%
   e. Intubation/tracheostomy ↑ maximum FIO_2 to 100%
4. **Note that ↑ FIO_2 will not improve hypoxemia caused by R-L shunt!** (because alveoli are not ventilated & blood will not come in close contact with O_2)
5. Oxygen toxicity seen with FIO_2 > 50–60% for longer than 48 hr, presents with neurologic dz & ARDS-like findings
6. Cannot just rely on O_2 supplementation, must also Tx underlying cause
7. High-altitude hypoxemia is self-limiting & stabilizes in weeks to months

HYPOXEMIA[a]

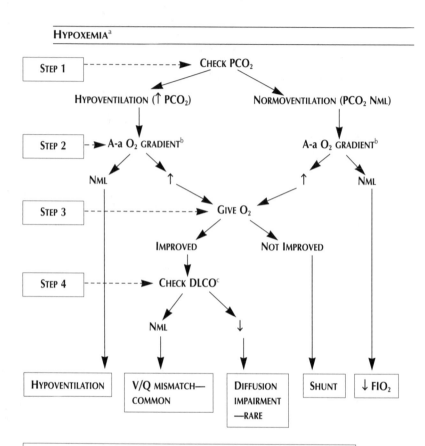

[a] The authors thank Dr. Arian Torbati for his assistance with this algorithm.
[b] A-a O_2 gradient = difference in alveolar and arterial O_2 concentrations.
[c] DLCO = diffusion limited carbon monoxide, a measurement of diffusion capacity.

II. Chronic Obstructive Pulmonary Disease (COPD)

↓ **FEV/FVC** & Nml/↑ TLC

(Forced expiratory volume at 1 min/Forced vital capacity & total lung capacity)

TABLE 1-10   Diagnosis and Treatment of Obstructive Lung Disease

DISEASE	CHARACTERISTICS	TX
Emphysema (Pink puffer)	• **Dilation of air spaces with alveolar wall destruction** • **Smoking is by far the most common cause**, α-1-antitrypsin deficiency causes **panacinar** disease • Si/Sx = hypoxia, hyperventilation, barrel chest, **classic pursed lips breathing**, ↓ breath sounds • CXR → loss of lung markings & **lung hyperinflation** • Dx = clinical	• Ambulatory O_2 including home O_2 • Stop smoking!!! • Bronchodilators • Steroid pulses for acute desaturations
Chronic bronchitis (Blue bloater)	• Defined as **expectoration on most days during ≥3 consecutive months for ≥2 consecutive years** • Si/Sx = as per emphysema but **hypoxia is more severe**, plus pulmonary hypertension with right ventricular hypertrophy, distended neck veins, hepatomegaly • Dx clinical, confirmed by lung biopsy → ↑ Reid index (gland layer is >50% of total bronchial wall thickness)	As per emphysema, use of antibiotics very controversial
Asthma	• Bronchial hyperresponsiveness → **reversible bronchoconstriction** due to smooth muscle contraction • Usually starts in childhood, in which case it often resolves by age 12, can start in adulthood • Acute asthma attacks are the most common cause of pediatric ER visits • Si/Sx = episodic dyspnea & **expiratory wheezing, reversible with bronchodilation** • Dx = ≥ 10% ↑ in FEV with bronchodilator therapy • Status asthmaticus (refractory attack lasting for days, can cause death) is a major complication	• Albuterol/atrovent inhalers are mainstay • Add inhaled steroids for improved long-term control • Pulse with steroids for acute attacks • Intubate as needed to protect airway
Bronchiectasis	• Permanent abnormal dilation of bronchioles commonly due to cystic fibrosis, chronic infxn (often tuberculosis, fungal infxn, or lung abscess), or obstruction (e.g., tumor) • Si/Sx = foul breath, purulent sputum, hemoptysis, CXR → **tram-track lung markings**, CT → thickened bronchial walls with dilated airways • Dx = clinical with radiologic support	• Ambulatory O_2 • Aggressive antibiotic use for frequent infections • Consider lung transplant for long-term cure

III. Restrictive Lung Disease

Nml/↑ FEV/FVC & ↓ TLC

TABLE 1-11   Diagnosis and Treatment of Restrictive Lung Disease

DISEASE	CHARACTERISTICS	TX
↓ Lung tissue	• Causes = atelectasis, airway obstruction (tumor, foreign body), surgical excision	• Ambulate pt • Incentive spirometer to encourage lung expansion • Remove foreign body/tumor
Parenchymal disease	• Causes = inflammatory (e.g., vasculitis & sarcoidosis), idiopathic pulmonary fibrosis, chemotherapy (the **B's, b**usulfan & **b**leomycin), amiodarone, radiation, chronic infections (TB, fungal), & toxic inhalation (e.g., asbestos & silica) • Dx = clinical, biopsy to rule out infection	• Antibiotics for chronic infection • Steroids for vasculitis, sarcoidosis, & toxic inhalations
Interstitial fibrosis	• Chronic injury caused by asbestos, oxygen toxicity, organic dusts, chronic infection (e.g., TB, fungi, CMV, idiopathic pulmonary fibrosis & collagen-vascular dz) • **CXR → "honeycomb" lung**	• Ambulatory O_2 • Steroids for collagen-vascular dz • Add PEEP to reduce FIO_2 for O_2 toxicity
Extrapulmonary disease	• Neuromuscular dz (e.g., multiple sclerosis, kyphoscoliosis, amyotrophic lateral sclerosis, Guillain-Barré, spinal cord trauma) • ↑ diaphragm pressure (e.g., pregnancy, obesity, ascites)	Supportive

Pleural effusion	• ↑ fluid in the pleural space, transudative or exudative
	• Transudate
	   ◊ **Low protein content** due to ↓ oncotic pressure
	   ◊ causes = CHF, nephrotic syndrome, hepatic cirrhosis
	• Exudate
	   ◊ High protein content due to ↑ hydrostatic pressure
	   ◊ Causes = malignancy, pneumonia ("parapneumonic effusion"), collagen-vascular dz, pulmonary embolism
		Thoracentesis (see below)

TABLE 1-12   Lab Analysis of Pleural Effusions

STUDY	TRANSUDATE	EXUDATE
Effusion protein	≤3.0 g/dL (≤0.5 of serum)	>3.0 g/dL* (>0.5 of serum)
Effusion LDH	≤200 IU/L (≤0.6 of serum)	>200 IU/L* (>0.6 of serum)
Specific gravity	≤1.015	>1.015
pH	≥7.2	<7.2 → parapneumonic effusion
Gram's stain	No organisms	ANY organism → parapneumonic
Cell count	WBC ≤1000	WBC >1000 (lymphocytes → TB)
Glucose	≥50 mg/dL	<50 mg/dL → infxn, neoplasm, collagen-vascular dz (≤10 → RA)
Amylase	↑ in pancreatitis, esophageal rupture, malignancy	
RF	Titer > 1 : 320 → virtually pathognomonic for RA (pH often <7.2)	
ANA	Titer > 1 : 160 → highly indicative for SLE (pH often >7.4)	

*Either of these findings rules out transudative effusion, rules in exudative effusion.

IV. Pulmonary Vascular Disease

A. PULMONARY EDEMA & ACUTE RESPIRATORY DISTRESS SYNDROME (ARDS) (See Figure 1-5)
   1. Si/Sx = dyspnea, tachypnea, resistant hypoxia, diffuse alveolar infiltrate
   2. Differential for pulmonary edema
      a. **If pulmonary capillary wedge pressure < 12 = ARDS**
      b. **If pulmonary capillary wedge pressure > 15 = cardiogenic**
   3. Tx = O_2, diuretics, positive end-expiratory pressure (PEEP) ventilation
   4. Purpose of PEEP
      a. Helps prevent airway collapse in a failing lung
      b. ↑ functional residual capacity (maintain lung volume) & ↓ shunting
      c. Expands alveoli for better diffusion

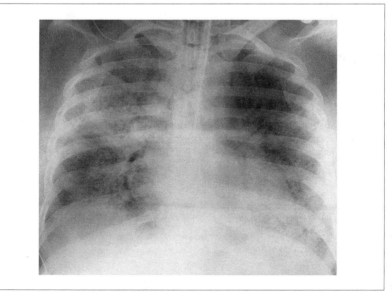

FIGURE 1-5   Adult respiratory distress syndrome (ARDS). There is widespread consolidation of the lungs. This patient had suffered extensive trauma to the limbs.

B. PULMONARY EMBOLISM (PE)

1. 95% of emboli are from leg deep venous thrombi (DVT)
2. Si/Sx = swollen, painful leg, sudden dyspnea/tachypnea, tachycardia, hemoptysis—
   are often no Sx at all, most emboli are clinically silent
3. Risk factors = **Virchow's triad = endothelial cell trauma, stasis, hypercoagulable
   states** (nephrosis, DIC, tumor, postpartum amniotic fluid exposure, antithrombin III
   deficiency, protein C or S deficiency, factor V Leiden deficiency, oral contraceptives,
   smoking)
4. PE can cause lung infarctions
   a. 75% occur in lower lobes
   b. **Classic CXR finding is "Hampton's hump,"** a wedge-shaped opacification at
      distal edges of lung fields
5. EKG findings
   a. Classically (but rarely) → S wave in I, Q in III, inverted T III ($S_I Q_{III} T_{III}$)
   b. **Most common finding is simply sinus tachycardia**
6. Dx = leg Utz to check for DVT, **spiral CT of chest & V/Q scan best to rule out PE,**
   & pulmonary angiography (gold standard)
7. Tx = prevention with heparin, IVC filter, or Coumadin, use tPA thrombolysis in
   massive PE or hemodynamic compromise

C. PULMONARY HYPERTENSION

1. Defined as pulmonary pressure $\geq \frac{1}{4}$ systemic (should be 1/8)
2. Can be active (1° pulmonary dz) or passive (2° to heart dz)
   a. 1° dz includes idiopathic pulmonary HTN (rare, occurs in young women), COPD
      & interstitial restrictive diseases
   b. 2° dz seen in any heart disease, **commonly seen in HIV**
3. Si/Sx: loud S_2, tricuspid regurgitation, audible crackles, ↓ breath sounds, pulsatile
   liver, EKG → right atrial enlargement, CXR → large hilar shadow
4. Dx = clinical, confirm with heart catheterization
5. Tx = home O_2 and try prostaglandins

V. Respiratory Tract Cancers

A. EPIDEMIOLOGY

1. **#1 cause of cancer deaths & second most frequent cancers**
2. Can only be seen on x-rays if > 1 cm in size, by that time they have usually already
   metastasized, **so x-rays not a good screening tool**
3. Si/Sx = cough, hemoptysis, hoarseness (recurrent laryngeal nerve paralysis), weight
   loss, fatigue, recurrent pneumonia

B. PARENCHYMAL LUNG CANCERS

1. Diseases & characteristics

TABLE 1-13   Parenchymal Lung Cancers

CANCER	CHARACTERISTICS
Adenocarcinoma	• **Most frequent lung CA in nonsmokers** • **Presents in subpleura & lung periphery** • Presents in preexisting scars, "scar cancer" • Carcinoembryonic antigen (CEA) ⊕, used to follow Tx, not for screening due to ↓ specificity
Bronchoalveolar carcinoma	• Subtype of adenocarcinoma **not related to smoking** • **Presents in lung periphery**
Large cell carcinoma	• **Presents in lung periphery** • Highly anaplastic, undifferentiated cancer • Poor prognosis
Squamous cell carcinoma	• **Central hilar masses arising from bronchus** • **Strong link to smoking**
Bronchogenic carcinoma	• **Causes hypercalcemia due to secretion of PTHrp** (parathyroid hormone related peptide)
Small cell (Oat cell) carcinoma	• **Usually has central hilar location** • **Often already metastatic at Dx, very poor Px** • **Strong link to smoking (99% are smokers)** • Causes numerous endocrine syndromes ◊ ACTH secretion (cushingoid) ◊ Secretes ADH, causing SIADH
Bronchial carcinoid tumors	• Carcinoid syndrome = serotonin (5-HT) secretion • **Si/Sx = recurrent diarrhea, skin flushing, asthmatic wheezing & carcinoid heart dz** • Dx by ↑ 5-HIAA metabolite in urine • Tx = methysergide, a 5-HT antagonist
Lymphangio-leiomyomatosis	• Neoplasm of lung smooth muscle → cystic obstructions of bronchioles, vessels & lymph • **Almost always seen in menstruating women** • Classic presentation = **pneumothorax** • Tx = progesterone or lung transplant

2. Tx differs from small cell vs. non-small cell lung CA
   a. Small cell → radiation & chemotherapy
   b. Non-small cell CA
      1) Local disease → lung resection +/– radiation
      2) Metastatic disease → radiation + chemotherapy

C. OTHER CANCER SYNDROMES
   1. **Superior sulcus tumor (pancoast tumor)** (See Figure 1-6)
      a. **Horner's syndrome** (ptosis, miosis, anhydrosis) by damaging the sympathetic cervical ganglion in the lower neck
      b. **Superior vena cava syndrome** = obstructed SVC → facial swelling, cyanosis & dilation of veins of head & neck
   2. Small cell carcinoma can cause a **myasthenia gravis-like condition known as the Lambert-Eaton syndrome** due to induction of Abs to tumor that cross-reacts with presynaptic Ca channel
   3. Renal cell CA metastatic to lung can cause 2° polycythemia by ectopic production of erythropoietin

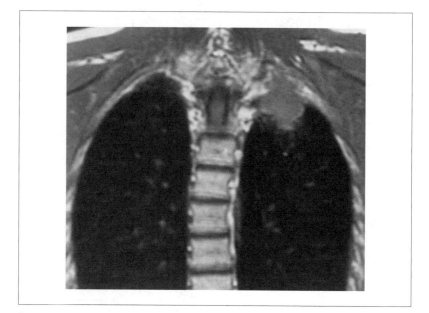

FIGURE 1-6   Pancoast's tumor. This carcinoma of the lung can be seen invading the root of the neck on this coronal MRI scan (T1-weighted).

VI. Mediastinal Tumors

TABLE 1-14   Mediastinal Tumors (See Figure 1-7)

ANTERIOR[a]	MIDDLE	POSTERIOR[b]
Thymoma	Lymphoma	Neuroblastoma
Thyroid tumor	Pericardial cyst	Schwannoma
Teratoma	Bronchial cyst	Neurofibroma
Terrible lymphoma		
Tx = excision for all, add radiation/chemotherapy as needed		

[a] The four T's.
[b] Neural tumors.

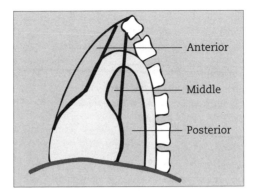

FIGURE 1-7   Mediastinal compartments.

VII. Tuberculosis (See Figure 1-8)

A. PRIMARY TB
1. Classically affects lower lobes (bacilli deposited in dependent portion of lung during inspiration)
2. Usually asymptomatic
3. **Classic radiologic finding is "Ghon complex"** = calcified nodule at primary focus ⊕ calcified hilar lymph nodes

B. SECONDARY (REACTIVATION) TB
1. Reactivates in **apical lung** due to ↑ oxygen tension in upper lobes
2. Si/Sx = insidious fevers, night sweats, weight loss, cough, hemoptysis
3. Risk factors = HIV, imprisonment, homelessness, malnourishment

C. MILIARY (DISSEMINATED) TB
1. Hematogenous **dissemination involving any organ**, often the liver, spleen, bone, kidneys, pericardium, spine, meninges
2. Presents in any patient with immune deficiency
3. Classic syndromes
   a. Pott's dz = TB of spine, presents with multiple compression fractures
   b. Scrofula = TB causing massive cervical lymphadenopathy
   c. Gastroenteritis with profuse diarrhea & colitis

D. DIAGNOSIS
1. Criteria for purified protein derivative (PPD) skin test
   a. > 15 mm induration at 48 hr in low-risk pts
   b. > 10 mm induration at 48 hr in high-risk pts
   c. > 5 mm induration in HIV pts, or close contact with infected person
   d. Negative PPD does NOT rule out Dx of tuberculosis
      1) Pt may be anergic, place a control to rule this out (particularly common in AIDS patients)
      2) Even with ⊕ control (i.e., pt not anergic), up to 50% of pts with disseminated TB have negative PPD at time of Dx—may convert to PPD⊕ after Tx begun

2. CXR
    a. Look for Ghon complex (calcified primary focus) indicating prior dz
    b. Look for active nodular/cavitating lesions, particularly in apical lung fields for active disease
3. Sputum
    a. Acid fast stain for rapid diagnosis, lower yield
    b. Culture for higher yield, can take weeks to grow TB

E. TREATMENT
1. Isoniazid prophylaxis
    a. Give to all new PPD converters < 35 yr
    b. Due to risk of hepatotoxicity, do not give to new PPD converters > 35 yr **unless they are high-risk populations (e.g., HIV, close contact with active disease, immunosuppressed, etc.)**
2. Active TB
    a. Combinations of **RIPES** drugs (and side effects)
        Rifampin (hepatotoxic)
        Isoniazid (hepatotoxic and neuropathy)
        Pyrazinamide (hepatotoxic)
        Ethambutol (optic neuritis → color vision changes)
        Streptomycin (renal and ototoxic)

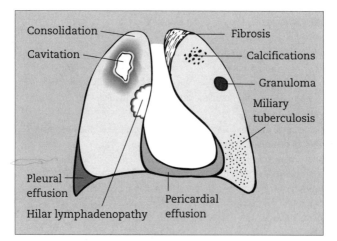

FIGURE 1-8   Manifestations of pulmonary tuberculosis.

VIII. Pneumonia

TABLE 1-15   Pneumonia

ORGANISM	CHARACTERISTICS	TX
Bacterial Pneumonia		
Streptococcus pneumoniae	Children, elderly, immunosuppressed pts, acute onset with rigors, can rapidly progress, #1 cause of CAP[a] (70%)	PCN first line, 10% resistant
Hemophilus	H. influenzae causes 10% CAP[a], same patients as S. pneumoniae	Cephalosporin
Moraxella catarrhalis	Causes 5% CAP[a], common in COPD & immunosuppressed	Bactrim
Staphylococcus aureus	2° infects after influenza virus, commonly → pleural effusion	Oxacillin[b]
Gram-negative rods	Often nosocomial infections	Cephalosporin
Pseudomonas	Often in cystic fibrosis, commonly nosocomial, cavitates, rapid antibiotic resistance (use 2 antibiotics!)	Piperacillin + gentamicin
Klebsiella	Seen in alcoholics, diabetics, nosocomial, classically sputum is "currant jelly" bloody red, antibiotic resistant	Cephalosporin + gentamicin
Anaerobes	Aspiration pneumonia seen in loss of consciousness, dementia, alcoholic → abscess, foul sputum, dz in dependent lung lobes	Metronidazole/ clindamycin
Atypical Pneumonia		
Mycoplasma pneumoniae	Classically young adults (college), causes 10% of CAP*, after 2–4 wk incubation → tracheobronchitis & nocturnal cough	Doxycycline, azithromycin
Legionella pneumophila	Seen in alcoholic, transplant pts, COPD, malignancy, diabetes, water exposure (e.g., air conditioner): 25% lethal with Tx, classic Si/Sx = hyponatremia, CNS changes, LDH > 700, diarrhea	Azithromycin, ofloxacin
Chlamydia pneumoniae	Seen in elderly pts, Sx = sore throat, hoarse voice, sinusitis	Azithromycin, levofloxacin
Chlamydia psittaci	Contracted from birds (often parrots), bird may show signs of illness also (e.g., ruffled feathers)	Doxycycline
Coxiella burnetii	Called "Q-fever," contracted from farm animals (e.g., cattle, goats), inhalation or ingestion of milk, etc.	Tetracycline
Francisella tularensis	Found in hunters, butchers, etc., classically contracted from rabbits, but other animals & ticks as well	Streptomycin
Actinomyces israelii	50% → empyema, crosses tissue planes (e.g., pericardium, spine), look for sinus tract drainage through anterior chest wall	Penicillin (6–12 mo)
Nocardia asteroides	Gram-positive acid fast aerobe, mimics TB, Si/Sx = fever, night sweats, **eosinophilia**, seen in AIDS as opportunistic infection	Bactrim
Fungal Pneumonia		
Pneumocystis carinii	Insidious onset of dry cough/dyspnea, bilateral infiltrates, not pleural effusions (very rare), Dx → sputum silver stain, ↑ LDH: AIDS pts with CD4 <200 get prophylaxis with Bactrim (See Figure 1-9)	Bactrim
Coccidioides immitis	"San Joaquin Valley Fever," major risks = travel to SW desert (e.g., California, Arizona, New Mexico, Texas), imprisonment, ↑ incidence after earthquakes, Filipinos & blacks have ↑ rate disseminated dz, Dx best by sputum cytology → budding yeast	Amphotericin (ampB) or fluconazole (flucon)

TABLE 1-15   *Continued*

ORGANISM	CHARACTERISTICS	TX
Histoplasma	Exposure to Ohio/Mississippi River valleys, bat or bird dung	AmpB/flucon
Aspergillus	Seen in neutropenic pts, CXR → "fungus-ball" with cavitation	AmpB/itracon[c]
Cryptococcus	Seen in AIDS patients or any immunosuppressed	AmpB/flucon
Viral Pneumonia		
Influenza	Presents in patients >65 yr, can be deadly in them	Amantadine
Hantavirus	Children/young adults exposed to SW desert rodents, 50% fatal with Tx, 3–6 day prodromal fever & myalgias → acute ARDS	Supportive (intubation)
Other	RSV, adenovirus, parainfluenza, less severe than influenza	Supportive

[a] CAP = community-acquired pneumonia.
[b] Vancomycin if resistant to oxacillin.
[c] Itracon = itraconazole.

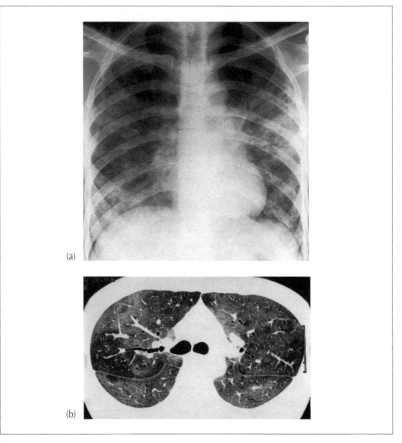

(a)

(b)

FIGURE 1-9   *Pneumocystis carinii* pneumonia in a patient with AIDS showing (a) typical widespread low-density air space shadowing on chest x-ray; (b) high-resolution CT in another patient with similar but less advanced changes.

Gastroenterology and Hepatology

I. Gastroesophageal Disease

A. CHRONIC (NONEROSIVE) GASTRITIS (ATROPHIC GASTRITIS)
1. Type A (fundal) = autoimmune (pernicious anemia, thyroiditis, etc.)
2. Type B (antral) due to *Helicobacter pylori (H.p.)*, NSAIDs, herpes, CMV
3. NSAIDs are #1 cause of chronic gastritis (in antrum, not fundus)
4. Si/Sx = usually aSx, may cause pain, nausea/vomiting, anorexia, upper GI bleeding manifested as coffee grounds emesis or hematemesis
5. Dx = upper endoscopy
6. *H.p.* infxn Dx by urease breath test, can screen with serum IgG test (less expensive but less sensitive & does not indicate **active** infection), can confirm with endoscopic Bx
7. Tx depends on etiology
   a. Tx *H.p.* gastritis with proton pump inhibitor +2 antibiotics (tetracycline + clarithromycin or Flagyl) + bismuth compound
   b. If drug induced, stop offending agent (usually NSAIDs), add sucralfate, H2 blocker, or proton pump inhibitor
   c. Pernicious anemia Tx = vitamin B_{12} replenishment
   d. Stress ulcer (especially in ICU setting), Tx with sucralfate or H2 blocker IV infusion

B. GASTRIC ULCERS (GU)
1. *H.p.* found in 70% of GU, 10% caused by ulcerating malignancy
2. **As opposed to duodenal ulcers, GUs are NOT caused by acid hypersecretion—** patients with GU have low-to-normal acid secretion, may have ↓ mucosal protection from acid
3. Si/Sx = gnawing/burning pain in midepigastrium, **worse with food intake**, if ulcer erodes into artery can cause hemorrhage & peritonitis, may be guaiac positive
4. Dx = endoscopy with Bx to confirm not malignant, *H.p.* testing as above
5. Tx = mucosal protectors (e.g., bismuth, sucralfate, misoprostol), H2 blockers or proton pump inhibitors & antibiotics for *H.p.*

II. Small Intestine

A. DUODENAL ULCER (DU)
1. Almost all DU pts have ↑ acid production, 80% have ↑ nocturnal secretion
2. *H.p.* found in 90% of duodenal ulcers
3. Smoking & excessive alcohol intake ↑ risk for peptic ulcer
4. Sx/Si = burning or gnawing epigastric pain 1–3 hr postprandial, **relieved by food/antacids**, pain typically awakens patient at night, melena
5. Dx = endoscopy, barium swallow if endoscopy unavailable
6. Tx = as for GU above, quit smoking
7. Sequelae
   a. Upper GI bleed
      1) Usually see hematemesis, melena, or (rarely) hematochezia if briskly bleeding ulcer

   2) Dx with endoscopy

   3) Tx = endoscopic coagulation or sclerosant, surgery rarely necessary

   b. Perforation

      1) Change in pain pattern is suspicious for perforation

      2) Plain abd films may show free air, can perform UGI series with water-soluble contrast (barium contraindicated)

      3) Tx is emergency surgery

B. CROHN'S DISEASE (INFLAMMATORY BOWEL DISEASE)

   1. A GI inflammatory disease that may be infectious in nature

   2. Affects any part of GI from mouth to rectum, but usually the intestines

   3. Si/Sx = abdominal pain, diarrhea, malabsorption, fever, stricture causing obstruction, fistulae, see below for extraintestinal manifestations

   4. Dx = colonoscopy with biopsy of affected areas → transmural, **noncaseating granulomas, cobblestone mucosal morphology, skip lesions, creeping fat on gross dissection is pathognomonic**

   5. Tx

      a. Sulfasalazine (5-ASA), better for colonic dz but also helps in small bowel

      b. Steroids for acute exacerbation, but no effect on underlying dz

      c. Immunotherapy (azathioprine & mercaptopurine) – useful in pts with unresponsive dz

      d. Newest Tx is antitumor necrosis factor antibody [see *N Engl J Med*, 1997, 337:1029–1035], which appears promising from clinical trials

C. CARCINOID SYNDROME

   1. APUDoma (**a**mine **p**recursor **u**ptake & **d**ecarboxylate)

   2. Occurs most frequently in the appendix

   3. Carcinoid results from liver mets that secrete serotonin (5-HT)

   4. Si/Sx = flushing, watery diarrhea & abdominal cramps, bronchospasm, right-sided heart valve lesions

   5. Dx = ↑ levels of urine 5-HIAA (false ⊕ seen if eat lots of bananas)

   6. Tx = somatostatin & methysergide

III. Large Intestine

A. ULCERATIVE COLITIS (UC) (INFLAMMATORY BOWEL DISEASE)

   1. An idiopathic autoinflammatory disorder of the colon

   2. Always starts in rectum & spreads proximal

   3. If confined to rectum = ulcerative proctitis, a benign subtype

   4. Si/Sx = bloody diarrhea, colicky abdominal pain, can progress to generalized peritonitis, watch for toxic megacolon!

   5. Dx = colonoscopy with biopsy → crypt abscess with numerous PMNs, friable mucosal patches that bleed easily

   6. Tx depends on site & severity of dz

      a. Distal colitis → topical mesalamine & corticosteroids

      b. Moderate colitis (above sigmoid) → oral steroids, mesalamine & sulfasalazine

      c. Severe colitis → IV steroids, cyclosporine & surgical resection if unresponsive

      d. Fulminant colitis (rapidly progressive) → broad-spectrum abx

   7. Comparison of inflammatory bowel disease (IBD)

TABLE 1-16   Comparison of Inflammatory Bowel Disease

	ULCERATIVE COLITIS	CROHN'S DISEASE
Infectious etiology?	No	Likely
Location	Isolated to colon	Anywhere in GI tract
Lesions	Contiguously proximal from colon	Skip lesions, disseminated
Inflammation	Limited to mucosa/submucosa	Transmural
Neoplasms	Very high risk for development	Lower risk for development
Fissures	None	Extend through submucosa
Fistula	None	Frequent: can be enterocutaneous
Granulomas	None	Noncaseating are characteristic
Extraintestinal manifestations	Seen in both: • Arthritis, iritis, erythema nodosum, pyoderma gangrenosum • Sclerosing cholangitis = chronic, fibrosing, inflammation of biliary system leading to cholestasis & portal hypertension	

IV. Liver

A. JAUNDICE—VISIBLE WHEN SERUM BILIRUBIN EXCEEDS 2 MG/DL
1.

TABLE 1-17   Congenital Hyperbilirubinemia

SYNDROME	CHARACTERISTICS	TX
Gilbert's	• Mild defect of glucuronyl transferase in 5% of population • Si/Sx = ↑ serum **unconjugated bilirubin** → jaundice in stressful situations, completely benign	None required
Crigler-Najjar	• Genetic deficiency of glucuronyl transferase → ↑ serum **unconjugated bilirubin** • Type 1 = severe, presents in neonates with markedly ↑ bilirubin levels → death from kernicterus by age 1 • Type 2 = mild, pts suffer no severe clinical deficits	Phenobarbitol
Dubin-Johnson	• ↑ **conjugated bilirubin** due to defective bilirubin excretion • Si/Sx = jaundice, liver turns black, no serious clinical deficits	None required
Rotor	• ↑ **conjugated bilirubin** similar to Dubin-Johnson • Defect is in bilirubin storage, not excretion	None required

2. Hemolytic Anemias
   a. Excess production → ↑ unconjugated bilirubin
   b. Si/Sx = as per any anemia (weakness, fatigue, etc.), others depend on etiology of hemolytic anemia [see Hematology section]
   c. Dx = ⊕ Coombs' test, ↓ haptoglobin, ⊕ urine hemosiderin
   d. Tx depends on etiology [see Hematology section]
3. Intrahepatic cholestasis (hepatocellular)
   a. May be due to viral hepatitis or cirrhosis
   b. May be due to drug-induced hepatitis (acetaminophen, methotrexate, oral contraceptives, phenothiazines, INH, fluconazole)

c. Dx = ↑ transaminases, liver biopsy to confirm hepatitis
d. Tx = cessation of drugs, or supportive for viral infection
4. Extrahepatic
   a. Myriad causes include choledocholithiasis (but not cholelithiasis), CA of biliary system or pancreas, cholangitis, biliary cirrhosis
   b. Primary biliary cirrhosis
      1) An autoimmune disorder usually seen in women
      2) Si/Sx = jaundice, pruritus, hypercholesterolemia, **antimitochondrial antibody test is 90% sensitive**
      3) Dx = clinical ⊕ serology, confirm with biopsy
      4) Tx = liver transplant, otherwise supportive
   c. Secondary biliary cirrhosis results from long-standing biliary obstruction due to any cause (e.g., cholangitis)
   d. Si/Sx of acquired jaundice = acholic stools (pale), urinary bilirubin, fat malabsorption, pruritus, ↑ serum cholesterol, xanthomas
   e. Dx may require abdominal CT or endoscopic retrograde cholangiopancreaticoduodenoscopy (ERCP) to rule out malignancy or obstruction of bile pathway
   f. Tx depends on etiology

B. HEPATITIS
1. General Si/Sx = jaundice, abdominal pain, diarrhea, malaise, fever, ↑ AST & ALT
2.

TABLE 1-18   Hepatitis Diagnosis and Treatment

TYPE	CHARACTERISTICS	TX
Fulminant	• Complication of acute hepatitis, progresses over less than 4 wk • Can be 2° to viral hepatitis, drugs (INH), toxins & some metabolic disorders like Wilson's dz • Dx = falling prothrombin levels & hepatic encephalopathy	Urgent liver transplant
Viral	• Hepatitis A → fecal-oral transmission, transient influenza-like illness • Hepatitis B & C → blood transmission, B also sex & vertical → chronic hepatitis • 5–10% of HBV & >50% of HCV infxn → chronic • Dx = serologies & ↑ ALT & AST—ratio ≅ 1:1 (See Figure 1-10) ◊ HBV surface antigen = active infection ◊ anti-HBV surface antibody = immunity ◊ anti-HBV core antibody = immunity ◊ HBV e antigen = highly infectious ◊ HCV antibody = exposure, not immune	Interferon-α +/– lamivudine for HBV (New Engl J Med) 1997, 339:61–8), Interferon-α +/– ribavirin for HCV (New Engl J Med 1998, 339:1485–1492 & 1493–1499)—both ↓ risk of chronic infxn
Granulomatous	• Causes = TB, fungal (e.g., Coccidioides, Candida, Aspergillus), sarcoidosis, brucella, rickettsia, syphilis, leptospirosis • Dx = liver biopsy	Antibiotics, prednisone for sarcoidosis

TABLE 1-18 *Continued*

TYPE	CHARACTERISTICS	TX
Alcoholic	• Most common form of liver disease in US • Si/Sx = as per other hepatitis with specific alcohol signs = palmar erythema, Dupuytren's contractures, spider angiomas, gynecomastia • Dx = clinical, ↑ AST & ALT, with AST:ALT = 2:1 is highly suggestive	Cessation of alcohol can reverse dz if early in course, otherwise → cirrhosis & only Tx is transplant
Autoimmune	• Type I occurs in young women, ⊕ ANA, ⊕ anti–smooth muscle Ab • Type II occurs mostly in children, linked to Mediterranean ancestry, ⊕ anti-liver-kidney-muscle (anti-LKM) antibody • Si/Sx as for any other hepatitis	Tx = prednisone +/– azathioprine

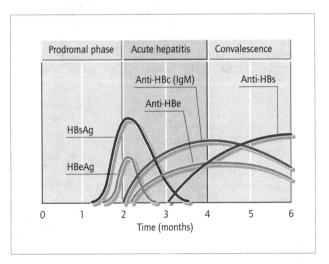

FIGURE 1-10 Time course of events leading to acute hepatitis B infection.

C. CIRRHOSIS

1. Most commonly due to alcoholism, also to chronic viral hepatitis
2. Si/Sx = purpura & bleeding & ↑ PT/PTT, jaundice, ascites 2° to ↓ albumin & portal hypertension, spontaneous bacterial peritonitis, encephalopathy, asterixis
   a.

TABLE 1-19 Ascites Differential Diagnosis

	PORTAL HYPERTENSION	NO PORTAL HYPERTENSION
Serum/ascites albumin gradient	> 1.1 g/dL	< 1.1 g/dL
Causes	Cirrhosis, alcoholic hepatitis, Budd-Chiari, liver metastases (mets), CHF	Pancreatic dz, nephrosis, TB, peritoneal mets, idiopathic
Other labs	Ascites total protein > 2.5 → heart dz Ascites total protein ≤ 2.5 → liver dz	Amylase ↑ in pancreatic dz

b. Spontaneous bacterial peritonitis
   1) Usually low protein ascites with no Sx of infxn
   2) Dx = ascitic fluid with absolute neutrophil count of >250 or ⊕ Gram's stain/culture of ascitic fluid
   3) Common organisms include *E. coli, Klebsiella, Enterococcus* & *S. pneumoniae*
   4) Tx = third-generation cephalosporins
c. Encephalopathy
   1) Due to ↑ levels of toxins, likely related to ammonia, but ammonia levels do not correlate well with encephalopathy
   2) Characterized by asterixis (flapping tremor of the wrist upon flexion) & altered mental status
   3) Tx of encephalopathy is to lower ammonia levels
      a) Lactulose metabolized by bacteria, acidifies the bowel, $NH_3 \rightarrow NH_4^+$, which cannot be absorbed
      b) Neomycin kills bacteria making NH_3 in gut
      c) Sodium benzoate binds NH_3 in blood & causes it to be excreted as hippurate via kidney
d. Delirium tremens (DTs)
   1) EtOH withdrawal time course—**time from last drink**
      a) Within 12 hr, pt has headache, malaise, irritable
      b) **24–48 hr, seizures develop**, ⊕ resting tremor
      c) **72 hr autonomic instability (↑↑ BP/HR), delirium**
   2) DTs → agitation, delirium, confusion, **auditory & tactile hallucinations** (bugs crawling on skin), **generalized seizures that can be lethal, hypertension/tachycardia**
e. Treatment of inpatient alcoholics
   1) IV thiamine & B_{12} supplements to correct deficiency (very common), also **must give thiamine before IV glucose or will precipitate Wernicke's encephalopathy**
   2) Give IV glucose, fluids & electrolytes
   3) Correct any underlying coagulopathy
   4) Benzodiazepine for prevention & Tx of delirium tremens

D. HEPATIC ABSCESS

1. Caused by (in order of frequency in the US) bacteria, parasites (usually amebic) or fungal
2. Bacterial abscesses usually result from direct extension of infection from gallbladder, hematogenous spread via the portal vein from appendicitis of diverticulitis, or via the hepatic artery from distant sources such as from a pneumonia or bacterial endocarditis
3. Organisms in pyogenic hepatic abscesses are usually of enteric origin (e.g., *E. coli, K. pneumoniae, Bacteroides* & *Enterococcus*)
4. Si/Sx = high fever, malaise, rigors, jaundice, epigastric or RUQ pain & referred pain to the right shoulder
5. Labs → leukocytosis, anemia, ↑ alkaline phosphatase
6. Dx = Utz or CT scan

7. Tx
    a. IV ampicillin/gentamicin/Flagyl, or mezlocillin/Flagyl
    b. Percutaneous or surgical drainage
    c. For amebic abscesses (caused by *Entamoeba histolytica*) use Flagyl
8. Complications = intrahepatic spread of infxn, sepsis & abscess rupture
9. Mortality of hepatic abscesses is 15%, higher with coexistent malignancy

E. PORTAL HYPERTENSION
1. Defined as portal vein pressure >12 mm Hg (normal = 6–8 mm Hg)
2. Si/Sx = ascites, hepatosplenomegaly, variceal bleeding, encephalopathy
3. Can be presinusoidal, intrahepatic, or postsinusoidal in nature

TABLE 1-20   Causes of Portal Hypertension

PREHEPATIC	INTRAHEPATIC		POSTHEPATIC
• Portal vein thrombosis • Splenomegaly • Arteriovenous fistula	• Cirrhosis • Schistosomiasis • Massive fatty change • Nodular regenerative hyperplasia	• Idiopathic portal hypertension • Granulomatous dz (e.g., tuberculosis, sarcoidosis)	• Severe right-sided heart failure • Hepatic vein thrombosis (Budd-Chiari syndrome) • Constrictive pericarditis • Hepatic veno-occlusive disease

4. Dx = endoscopy & angiography (variceal bleeding), & Utz (dilated vessels) (See Figure 1–11)
5. Tx
    a. Acute variceal bleeding controlled by sclerotherapy
    b. If continued bleeding, use Sengstaken-Blakemore tube to tamponade bleeding
    c. Pharmacotherapy = IV infusion of vasopressin or Octeotride
    d. Long term → propranolol once varices are identified (↓ bleeding but long-term survival is variable)
    e. Decompressive shunts—most efficacious way of stopping bleeding
    f. **Indication for liver transplant is end-stage liver disease, not variceal bleeding**
6. **Budd-Chiari syndrome**
    a. Rarely congenital, usually acquired thrombosis occluding hepatic vein or hepatic stretch of inferior vena cava
    b. Associated with hypercoagulability (e.g., polycythemia vera, hepatocellular or other CA, pregnancy, etc.)
    c. Sx = acute onset of abdominal pain, jaundice, ascites
    d. Hepatitis quickly develops, leading to cirrhosis & portal hypertension
    e. Dx = right upper quadrant ultrasound
    f. Tx = clot lysis or hepatic transplant
    g. Px poor, less than 1/3 pts survive at 1 yr

SYSTEMIC SHUNTS IN PORTAL HYPERTENSION

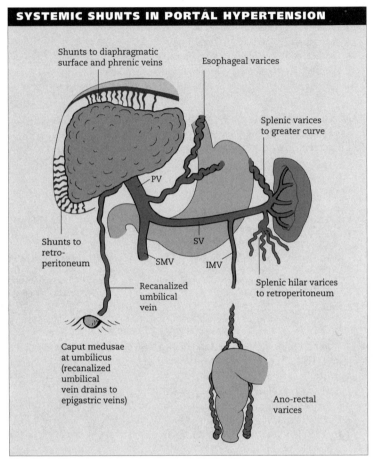

Shunts to diaphragmatic surface and phrenic veins

Esophageal varices

Splenic varices to greater curve

PV

Shunts to retro-peritoneum

SV

SMV   IMV

Recanalized umbilical vein

Splenic hilar varices to retroperitoneum

Caput medusae at umbilicus (recanalized umbilical vein drains to epigastric veins)

Ano-rectal varices

FIGURE 1-11   The sites of occurrence of portal-systemic communications in patients with portal hypertension. PV = portal vein; SMV = superior mesenteric vein; IMV = inferior mesenteric vein; SV = splenic vein.

7. Veno-occlusive disease (VOD)
   a. Occlusion of hepatic venules (not large veins)
   b. Associated with graft vs. host disease, chemotherapy & radiation therapy
   c. Px = 50% mortality at 1 yr
   d. Tx = hepatic transplant, sometimes is self-limiting

Nephrology

I. Renal Tubular and Interstitial Disorders

A. DRUG-INDUCED INTERSTITIAL NEPHRITIS

1. Amphotericin, aminoglycosides, radiocontrast dyes cause direct toxicity
2. Penicillin, sulfonamides, diuretics & NSAIDs cause hypersensitivity
3. Si/Sx = pyuria, maculopapular rash, eosinophilia, proteinuria, hematuria, oliguria, flank pain, fever, eosinophiluria—**eosinophiluria is rare, but is pathognomonic for hypersensitivity TIN or atheroembolic dz**
4. Dx = clinical, improvement following withdrawal of offending drug can help confirm Dx, but sometimes the dz can be irreversible
5. Tx = removal of underlying cause, consider corticosteroids for allergic dz

B. ACUTE RENAL FAILURE (ARF)

1. Rapid $\uparrow$ azotemia ($\uparrow$ creatinine & BUN), +/– oliguria ($\equiv$ <500 mL/day urine)
2. Causes = 1) prerenal (hypoperfusion), 2) postrenal (obstruction), 3) renal
3. Prerenal failure caused by volume depletion, heart failure, liver failure, sepsis, heatstroke (myoglobinuria), burns & bilateral renal artery stenosis
4. Postrenal ARF due to obstruction $2°$ to BPH, bladder/pelvic tumors, calculi
5. Intrinsic renal causes = acute tubular necrosis (most common, see below), others include nephrotoxin exposure & renal ischemia
6. Si/Sx = hyperkalemia $\rightarrow$ arrhythmias, oliguria, metabolic acidosis
7. Dx

TABLE 1-21   Laboratory Characteristics of Acute Renal Failure

TEST/INDEX	PRERENAL	POSTRENAL	RENAL
Urine osmolality	**>500**	<350	<350
Urine Na	**<20**	>40	>20
FE_{Na}*	<1%	>4%	>2%
BUN/Creatinine	>20	>15	**<15**

*FE_{Na} = (U/P sodium) / (U/P creatinine).

   a. Urinary eosinophils suggest allergic nephriti or atheroembolic dz
   b. **RBC casts virtually pathognomonic for glomerulonephritis**
8. Tx
   a. IV fluids to maintain urine output, diurese to prevent volume overload
   b. Closely monitor electrolyte abnormalities
   c. Indications for dialysis: recalcitrant volume overload status, critical electrolyte abnormalities, unresponsive metabolic acidosis, toxic ingestion, uremia

C. ACUTE TUBULAR NECROSIS (ATN)

1. Most common cause of ARF, falls into the intrinsic renal category
2. ATN causes = renal ischemia $2°$ to sepsis, trauma, hemorrhage, crush injury or rhabdomyolysis $\rightarrow$ myoglobinuria, direct toxins (e.g., heavy metal)

3. 3 phases of injury: 1) prodromal, 2) oliguric, 3) postoliguric
4. Tx = resolution of precipitating cause, IV fluids to maintain urinary output, monitor electrolytes, diurese as needed to prevent fluid overload

D. RENAL TUBULE FUNCTIONAL DISORDERS

1. Renal tubular acidosis (RTA)

TABLE 1-22   Renal Tubular Acidosis*

TYPE	CHARACTERISTIC	URINARY pH
Type I	• **Distal tubular defect** of urinary H^+ gradient	**Urine pH > 5.5**
Type II	• **Proximal tubule failure** to resorb HCO_3	Urine pH > 5.5 early, then → <5.5 as acidosis worsens
Type IV	• ↓ **Aldosterone** → hyperkalemia & hyperchloremia • Usually due to ↓ secretion (**hyporeninemic hypoaldosteronism**), seen in diabetes, interstitial nephritis, NSAID use, ACE inhibitors & heparin • Also due to aldosterone resistance, seen in urinary obstruction & sickle cell dz	**Urine pH < 5.5**

*There is no RTA III for historical reasons.

2. Diabetes insipidus (DI)
   a. ↓ ADH secretion (central) or ADH resistance (nephrogenic)
   b. Si/Sx = polyuria, polydipsia, nocturia, urine specific gravity <1.010, urine osmolality (U_{osm}) ≤ 200, serum osmolality (S_{osm}) ≥ 300
   c. Central DI
      1) 1° (idiopathic) or 2° (acquired via trauma, infarction, granulomatous infiltration, fungal or TB infection of pituitary)
      2) Tx = DDAVP (ADH analogue) nasal spray
   d. Nephrogenic DI
      1) 1° dz is X-linked, seen in infants, may regress with time
      2) 2° dz in sickle cell, pyelonephritis, nephrosis, amyloid, multiple myeloma, drugs (aminoglycoside, lithium, demeclocycline)
      3) Tx = ↑ water intake, sodium restriction
   e. **Dx = water deprivation test**
      1) Hold all water, administer vasopressin
      2) Central DI: U_{osm} after deprivation no greater than S_{osm}, but ↑ ≥ 10% after vasopressin given
      3) Nephrogenic DI: U_{osm} after deprivation no greater than S_{osm}, & vasopressin does not ↑ U_{osm}
3. Syndrome of inappropriate antidiuretic hormone (SIADH)
   a. Etiologies
      1) CNS dz: trauma, tumor, Guillain-Barré, hydrocephalus
      2) Pulmonary dz: pneumonia, tumor, abscess, COPD
      3) Endocrine dz: hypothyroidism, Conn's syndrome

4) Drugs: NSAIDS, antidepressants, chemotherapy, diuretics, phenothiazine, oral hypoglycemics

b. Dx = hyponatremia with U_{osm} >300 mmol/kg

c. Tx = usually self-limiting, otherwise give normal saline, demeclocycline for resistant cases—**beware of central pontine myelinolysis with rapid correction of hyponatremia**

E. CHRONIC RENAL FAILURE

1. Always associated with azotemia of renal origin
2. Uremia = biochemical & clinical syndrome of the following characteristics
   a. Azotemia
   b. Acidosis due to accumulation of sulfates, phosphates, organic acids
   c. Hyperkalemia due to inability to excrete K^+ in urine
   d. Fluid volume disorder (early can't concentrate urine, late can't dilute)
   e. Hypocalcemia due to lack of vitamin D production
   f. Anemia due to lack of EPO production
   g. Hypertension 2° to activated renin-angiotensin axis
3. Si/Sx = anorexia, nausea/vomit, dementia, convulsions, eventually coma, bleeding due to platelet dysfunction, fibrinous pericarditis
4. Dx = renal Utz → small kidneys in chronic dz, anemia from chronic lack of EPO, diffuse osteopenia
5. Tx = salt & water restriction, diuresis to prevent fluid overload, dialysis to correct acid-base or severe electrolyte disorders

II. Glomerular Diseases

A. NEPHROTIC SYNDROME

1. Si/Sx = proteinuria >3.5 g/day, generalized edema (anasarca), lipiduria with hyperlipidemia, marked ↓ albumin, hypercoagulation
2. Dx of type made by renal biopsy
3. General Tx = protein restriction, salt restriction & diuretic therapy for edema, HMG-CoA reductase inhibitor for hyperlipidemia
4.

TABLE 1-23 Nephrotic Glomerulopathies

DISEASE	CHARACTERISTICS
Minimal change disease (MCD)	• Classically seen in young children • Tx = prednisone, disease is very responsive, Px is excellent
Focal segmental glomerulosclerosis	• Clinically similar to MCD, but occurs in adults with refractory HTN • Usually idiopathic, but heroin, HIV, diabetes, sickle cell are associated • Idiopathic typically presents in young, hypertensive black males • Tx = prednisone + cyclophosphamide, dz is refractory, Px poor

TABLE 1-23   *Continued*

DISEASE	CHARACTERISTICS

Membranous glomerulonephritis	• Most common primary cause of nephrotic syndrome in adults
	• Slowly progressive disorder with ↓ response to steroid treatment seen
	• Causes of this disease are numerous
	  ◊ Infections include HBV, HCV, syphilis, malaria
	  ◊ Drugs include gold salts, penicillamine (note, both used in RA)
	  ◊ Occult malignancy
	  ◊ SLE (10% of patients develop)
	• Tx = prednisone +/– cyclophosphamide, 50% → end-stage renal failure

Membranoproliferative glomerulonephritis	• Disease as 2 forms
	  ◊ Type I often slowly progressive
	  ◊ Type II more aggressive, often have an autoantibody against C3 convertase "C3 nephritic factor" → ↓ serum levels of C3
	• Tx = prednisone +/– plasmapheresis or interferon-α, Px very poor

Systemic diseases	See Table 1-24

5.

TABLE 1-24   Systemic Glomerulonephropathies

DISEASE	CHARACTERISTIC NEPHROPATHY

Diabetes	• Most common cause of end-stage renal disease in US
	• Early manifestation is microalbuminuria
	  ◊ ACE inhibitors ↓ progression to renal failure if started early
	  ◊ Strict glycemic & hypertensive control also ↓ progression
	• Biopsy shows pathognomonic Kimmelstiel-Wilson nodules
	• As dz progresses only Tx is renal transplant

HIV	• Usually seen in HIV acquired by intravenous drug abuse • Presents with focal segmental glomerulonephritis • Early Tx with antiretrovirals may help kidney disease
Renal amyloidosis	• Dx → birefringence with Congo Red stain • Tx = transplant, dz is refractory & often recurrent
Lupus	
Type I	No renal involvement
Type II	• **Mesangial disease** with focal segmental glomerular pattern • Tx not typically required for kidney involvement
Type III	• **Focal proliferative disease** • Tx = aggressive prednisone +/– cyclophosphamide
Type IV	• **Diffuse proliferative disease**, the most severe form of lupus nephropathy • Presents with a combination of nephrotic/nephritic disease • Classic LM → wire-loop abnormality • Tx = prednisone + cyclophosphamide, transplant may be required
Type V	• **Membranous disease**, indistinguishable from other 1° membranous GNs • Tx = consider prednisone, may not be required

B. NEPHRITIC SYNDROME
1. Results from diffuse glomerular inflammation
2. Si/Sx = acute onset hematuria (smoky-brown urine), ↓ GFR resulting in azotemia (↑ BUN & creatinine), oliguria, hypertension & edema

3.

TABLE 1-25 Nephritic Glomerulonephropathies

DISEASE	CHARACTERISTICS
Poststreptococcal (Postinfectious) Glomerulonephritis (PSGN/PIGN)	• Prototype of nephritic syndrome (acute glomerulonephritis) • Classically follows infection with group A β-hemolytic streptococci (*S. pyogenes*), but can follow infxn by virtually any organism, viral or bacterial • Lab → urine red cells & casts, azotemia, ↓ serum C3, ↑ ASO titer • **Immunofluorescence → coarse granular IgG or C3 deposits** • Tx typically not needed, dz usually self-limiting

Crescentic (rapidly progressive) glomerulonephritis	• Nephritis progresses to renal failure within weeks or months
	• May be part of PIGN or other systemic diseases
	• Goodpasture's disease
	  ◊ **Disease causes glomerulonephritis with pneumonitis**
	  ◊ **90% pts present with hemoptysis**, only later get glomerulonephritis
	  ◊ Peak incidence in men in mid-20s
	  ◊ **Classic immunofluorescence → smooth, linear deposition of IgG**
	• Tx = prednisone & plasmapheresis, minority → end-stage renal dz

Berger's disease (IgA nephropathy)	• **Most common worldwide nephropathy** • Due to IgA deposition in the mesangium • Si/Sx = recurrent hematuria with low-grade proteinuria • Whereas PIGN presents weeks after infection, **Berger's presents concurrently or within several days of infection** • 25% of pts slowly progress to renal failure, otherwise harmless • Tx = prednisone for acute flares, will not halt dz progression
Henoch-Schönlein purpura (HSP)	• Also an IgA nephropathy, but almost always presents in children • Presents with abdominal pain, vomiting, hematuria & GI bleeding • **Classic physical finding = "palpable purpura" on buttocks & legs in kids** • Often follows respiratory infection • Tx not required, dz is self-limiting
Multiple myeloma	↑ production of light chains → tubular plugging by Bence-Jones proteins • 2° hypercalcemia also contributes to development of "myeloma kidney" • Myeloma cells can directly invade kidney parenchyma • Defect in normal antibody production leaves pt susceptible to chronic infections by encapsulated bacteria (e.g., *E. coli*) → chronic renal failure • Tx is directed at underlying myeloma

C.

TABLE 1-26 Urinalysis in Primary Glomerular Diseases

	NEPHROTIC SYNDROME	NEPHRITIC SYNDROME	CHRONIC DISEASE
Proteinuria	↑↑↑↑	+/–	+/–
Hematuria	+/–	↑↑↑↑	+/–
Cells	—	⊕ RBCs ⊕ WBCs	+/–
Casts	**Fatty casts**	RBC & granular casts	Waxy & pigmented granular casts
Lipids	Free fat droplets, oval fat bodies	—	—

III. Renal Artery Stenosis (RAS)

A. PRESENTATION
1. **Classic dyad = sudden hypertension with low K⁺** (pt not on diuretic)
2. Causes are atherosclerotic plaques & fibromuscular dysplasia
3. Screening Dx = oral captopril induces ↑ renin
4. Dx confirmed with angiography
5. Tx = surgery vs. angioplasty

IV. Urinary Tract Obstruction

A. GENERAL CHARACTERISTICS
1. Most common causes in children are congenital
2. Most common causes in adults are BPH & stones
3. Obstruction → urinary stasis → ↑ risk of UTI

B. NEPHROLITHIASIS
1. Calcium pyrophosphate stones
   a. 80–85% stones, are **radiopaque**, associated with hypercalciuria
   b. Hypercalciuria can be idiopathic or due to ↑ intestinal calcium absorption, ↑ 1° renal calcium excretion, or hypercalcemia
   c. **50% associated with idiopathic hypercalciuria**
   d. Tx = vigorous hydration, loop diuretics if necessary
2. Ammonium magnesium phosphate stones ("struvite stones")
   a. Second most common form of stones, are **radiopaque**
   b. Most often due to urease⊕ *Proteus* or *Staph. saprophyticus*
   c. Can form large staghorn or struvite calculi
   d. Tx = directed at underlying infection
3. Uric acid stones
   a. 50% of pts with stones have hyperuricemia
   b. 2° to gout or ↑ cell turnover (leukemia, myeloproliferative dz)
   c. Stones are **radiolucent**
   d. Tx = alkalinize urine, treat underlying disorder
4. Si/Sx of stones = urinary colic = sharp, 10/10 pain, often described as the worse pain in the pt's life, radiates from back → anterior pelvis/groin
5. Tx = vigorous hydration, loop diuretics as needed

V. Tumors of the Kidney

A. RENAL CELL CARCINOMA
1. Most common renal malignancy, occurs in male smokers aged 50–70
2. **Hematogenously disseminates by invading renal veins or the vena cava**
3. Si/Sx = hematuria, palpable mass, flank pain, fever, 2° polycythemia
4. Tx = resection, systemic interleukin-2 immunotherapy, poor Px

B. WILMS' TUMOR
1. Most common renal malignancy of childhood, incidence peaks at 2–4 yr
2. Si/Sx = palpable flank mass (often huge)

3. Can be part of **WAGR** complex = **W**ilms' tumor, **A**niridia, **G**enitourinary malformations, mental motor **R**etardation
4. **Also associated with hemihypertrophy of the body**
5. Tx = nephrectomy plus chemotherapy &/or radiation

Endocrinology

I. The Hypothalamic Pituitary Axis

A. PROLACTINOMA

1. Si/Sx = headache, diplopia, CN III palsy, impotence, amenorrhea, gynecomastia, galactorrhea, ↑ androgens in females → virilization
2. **50% cause hypopituitarism, caused by mass effect of the tumor**
3. Dx = MRI/CT confirmation of tumor
4. Tx
   a. First line = dopamine agonist (e.g., bromocriptine)
   b. Large tumors or refractory → transsphenoidal surgical resection
   c. Radiation therapy for nonresectable macroadenomas

B. ACROMEGALY

1. Almost always due to pituitary adenoma secreting growth hormone
2. Childhood secretion prior to skeletal epiphyseal closure → gigantism
3. If secretion begins after epiphyseal closure → acromegaly
4. Si/Sx = adult whose glove, ring, or shoe size acutely ↑, coarsening of skin/facial features, prognathism, voice deepening, joint erosions, peripheral neuropathies due to nerve compression
5. Dx = ↑ insulin-like growth factor 1 &/or MRI/CT confirmation of neoplasm
6. Tx = surgery or radiation to ablate the enlarged pituitary, octreotide (somatostatin analogue) second line for refractory tumors

II. Diabetes

A. TYPE I DIABETES

1. Autoinflammatory destruction of pancreas → insulin deficiency
2. Si/Sx = polyphagia, polydipsia, polyuria, weight loss in child or adolescent, can lead to diabetic ketoacidosis (DKA) when pt is stressed (e.g., infection)
3. Dx = see type II below for criteria
4. Tx = **insulin replacement required—oral hypoglycemics will not work!**
5. Complication of type I diabetes = diabetic ketoacidosis (DKA)
6. Sx/Si of DKA = **Kussmaul hyperpnea** (slow & deep breaths), **abdominal pain, dehydration, ⊕ anion gap**, urine/blood ketones, hyperkalemia, hyperglycemia, *Mucor* sinusitis = rapidly fatal fungal infxn seen in DKA
7. DKA Tx
   a. **1° Tx = FLUIDS!!!**
   b. **2° = K⁺ & insulin**
   c. **3° = add glucose to insulin drip if pt becomes normoglycemic**—insulin is given to shut down ketogenesis, NOT to ↓ glucose, so insulin must be given until ketones are gone despite normal glucose!

B. TYPE II DIABETES

1. Peripheral insulin resistance—a metabolic dz, not autoinflammatory!
2. Usually adult onset, not ketosis prone, often strong FHx
3. Si/Sx
   a. Acute = dehydration, polydipsia/-phagia/-uria, fatigue, weight loss
   b. Subacute = infections (yeast vaginitis, *Mucor*, *S. aureus* boils)
   c. Chronic (See Figure 1-12)
      1) Macrovascular = stroke, coronary artery disease
      2) Microvascular = retinitis, nephritis
      3) Neuropathy = ↓ sensation, paresthesias, glove-in-hand burning pain, autonomic insufficiency
4. Dx of any diabetes (type I or II)
   a. Random plasma glucose over 200 with symptoms or
   b. Fasting glucose over 125 twice or
   c. 2-hr oral glucose tolerance test glucose >200 with or without Sx
5. Tx
   a. Oral hypoglycemics first line for mild to moderate hyperglycemia
      1) Metformin is first line, unknown mechanism, watch for GI upset and lactic acidosis
      2) Sulfonylureas (e.g., glyburide, glipizide), ↑ β-cell insulin secretion
      3) Troglitazone improves insulin mediated signaling to cell—use is controversial due to reports of fulminant hepatic failure
   b. Dz refractory to oral hypoglycemics requires insulin
   c. Diet & nutrition education
   d. ACE inhibitors slow progression of nephropathy
6. Monitoring: glycosylated hemoglobin A1c (HgA1c)
   a. Because of serum half-life of hemoglobin, HgA1c is a marker of the prior 3 mo of therapeutic regimen
   b. **Tight glucose control has been shown to reduce complications & mortality in IDDM & NIDDM**, thus HgA1c is a crucial key tool to follow efficacy & compliance of diabetic Tx regimens
   c. HgAlC of <8 is recommended
7. Complication = hyperosmolar hyperglycemic nonketotic coma (HHNK)
   a. 2° to hypovolemia, precipitated by acute stress (e.g., infxn, trauma)
   b. Glucose often >1000 mg/dL, no acidosis, ⊕ renal failure & confusion
   c. Tx = rehydrate (may require 10 L), mortality approaches 50%

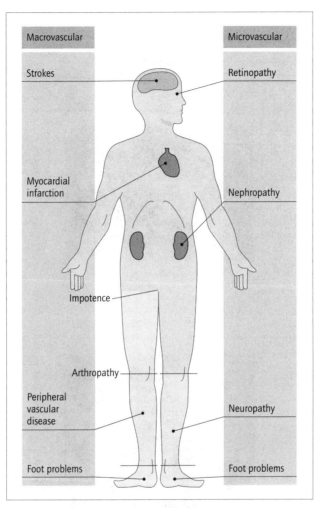

Macrovascular	Microvascular
Strokes	Retinopathy
Myocardial infarction	Nephropathy
Impotence	
Arthropathy	
Peripheral vascular disease	Neuropathy
Foot problems	Foot problems

FIGURE 1-12   Macro- and microvascular complications of DM.

III. Adrenal Disorders

A. CUSHING'S SYNDROME

1. Usually iatrogenic (cortisol Tx) or due to pituitary adenoma = Cushing's disease, rarely due to adrenal hyperplasia, ectopic ACTH/CRH production
2. Si/Sx = **buffalo hump** (See Figure 1-13), **truncal obesity** (See Figure 1-14), **moon facies**, **striae** (See Figure 1-15), hirsutism, hyperglycemia, hypertension, purpura, amenorrhea, impotence, acne
3. Dx = 24 hr urine cortisol & high dose dexamethasone suppression test

4. Tx
  a. Excision of tumor with postop glucocorticoid replacement
  b. Mitotane (adrenolytic), ketoconazole (inhibits P450), metyrapone (blocks adrenal enzyme synthesis), or aminoglutethimide (inhibits P450) for nonexcisable tumors

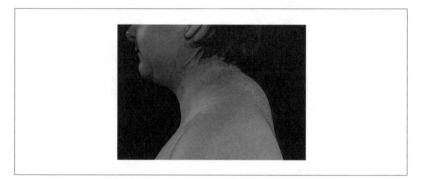

Figure 1-13   Buffalo hump.

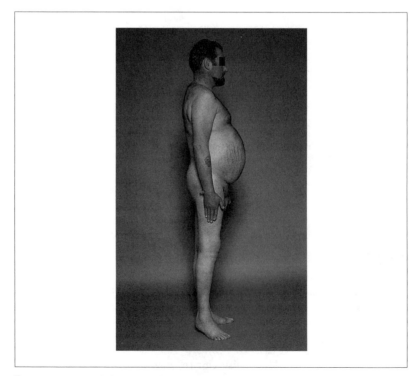

Figure 1-14   Truncal obesity with abdominal striae.

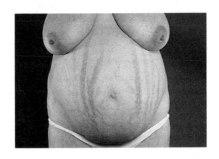

FIGURE 1-15   Abdominal striae.

B. ADRENAL INSUFFICIENCY
1. Can be 1° (Addison's disease) or 2° (↓ ACTH production by pituitary)
2. Addison's disease
   a. Causes = autoimmune (most common), granulomatous disease, infarction, HIV, DIC (Waterhouse-Friderichsen syndrome)
   b. **Waterhouse-Friderichsen** = hemorrhagic necrosis of adrenal medulla during the course of meningococcemia
   c. Si/Sx = fatigue, anorexia, nausea/vomit, constipation, diarrhea, salt craving (pica), hypotension, **hyponatremia, hyperkalemia**
   d. **Dx = hyperpigmentation, ↑ACTH, ↓cortisol response to ACTH**
3. 2° Dz → **NO hyperpigmentation, ↓ ACTH**, ↑ cortisol response to ACTH
4. Acute adrenal crisis
   a. Due to stress (e.g., surgery or trauma), usually in setting of treated chronic insufficiency or withdrawal of Tx
   b. Can occur in pituitary apoplexy (infarction)
5. Tx = cortisol replacement, ↑ replacement for times of illness or stress—**must taper replacement off slowly to allow HPA axis to restore itself**

C. ADRENAL CORTICAL HYPERFUNCTION
1. 1° hyperaldosteronism = Conn's syndrome
   a. Adenoma or hyperplasia of zona glomerulosa
   b. Si/Sx = **HTN, ↑Na, ↑Cl, ↓ K, alkalosis**, ↓ renin (feedback inhibition)
   c. Dx = ↑ aldosterone, ↓ renin, CT → adrenal neoplasm
   d. Tx = excision of adenoma—bilateral hyperplasia → spironolactone; bilateral adrenalectomy should NOT be performed
2. 2° hyperaldosteronism
   a. Due to increased renin production 2° to renal ischemia (e.g., CHF, shock, renal artery stenosis), cirrhosis, or tumor
   b. Dx = ↑ renin (renin levels differentiate 1° vs. 2° hyperaldosteronism)
   c. Tx = underlying cause, β-blocker or diuretic for hypertension

D. ADRENAL MEDULLA
1. Pheochromocytoma
   a. Si/Sx = hypertension (episodic or chronic), **diaphoresis, palpitations**, tachycardia, headache, nausea/vomit, flushing, dyspnea, diarrhea

b. **Rule of 10**: 10% malignant, 10% bilateral, 10% extra-adrenal (occurs in embryologic cells that reactivate outside the adrenal gland)

c. Dx = ↑ urinary catecholamines, CT scan of adrenal showing neoplasm

d. Tx

    1) Surgical excision after preop administration of α-blockers

    2) Ca^{2+} channel blockers for hypertensive crisis

    3) Phenoxybenzamine or phentolamine (α-blockers) for inoperable disease

IV. Gonadal Disorders

A. MALE GONADAL AXIS [SEE OB-GYN FOR FEMALE AXIS]

TABLE 1-27   Differential Diagnosis of Male Gonadal Disorders

DISEASE	CHARACTERISTICS	TX
Klinefelter's syndrome	• XXY chromosome inheritance, variable expressivity • Often not Dx until puberty when ↓ virilization is noted • Si/Sx = tall, eunuchoid, with small testes & gynecomastia, ↓ testosterone, ↑ LH/FSH from lack of feedback • **Dx = buccal smear analysis for presence of Barr bodies**	Testosterone supplements
XYY syndrome	• Si/Sx = may have mild mental retardation, severe acne, ↑ incidence of violence & antisocial behavior • Dx = karyotype analysis	None
Testicular feminization syndrome	• Defect in the dihydrotestosterone receptor → female external genitalia with sterile, undescended testes • Si/Sx = appear as females but are sterile & the vagina is blind-ended, testosterone, estrogen & LH are all ↑ • Dx = H&P, genetic testing	None
5-α-reductase deficiency	• Si/Sx = ambiguous genitalia until puberty, then a burst in testosterone overcomes lack of dihydrotestosterone → external genitalia become masculinized, **testosterone & estrogen are normal** • Dx = genetic testing	Testosterone supplements

B. HYPOGONADISM OF EITHER SEX

TABLE 1-28   Genetic Hypogonadism

DISEASE	CHARACTERISTICS	TX
Congenital adrenal hyperplasia (CAH)	• Defects in steroid synthetic pathway causing either virilization of females or failure to virilize males • 21-α-hydroxylase deficiency causes 95% of all CAH • Severe dz presents in infancy with ambiguous genitalia & salt loss (2° to ↓↓ aldosterone) • Less severe variants → minimal virilization & salt loss, & can have Dx delayed for several years	Tx = replacement of necessary hormones
Prader-Willi syndrome	• Paternal imprinting (only gene from dad is expressed) • Si/Sx = presents in infancy with floppy baby, **short limbs**, obesity due to gross hyperphagia, nasal speech, retardation, **classic almond-shaped eyes with strabismus** • Dx = clinical or genetic analysis	None

TABLE 1-28 *Continued*

DISEASE	CHARACTERISTICS	TX
Laurence-Moon-Biedl syndrome	• Autosomal recessive inheritance • Si/Sx = obese children, **normal craniofacies**, may be retarded, **are not short, have polydactyly** • Dx = clinical or genetic	None
Kallmann's syndrome	• Autosomal dominant hypogonadism with anosmia (can't smell) • Due to ↓ production/secretion of GnRH by hypothalamus • Dx by lack of circulating LH & FSH	Pulsatile GnRH → virilization

V. Thyroid

A. HYPERTHYROIDISM

1. Causes = Grave's dz, Plummer's dz, adenoma, subacute thyroiditis
2. Si/Sx of hyperthyroidism = tachycardia, **isolated systolic hypertension**, tremor, a-fib, anxiety, diaphoresis, weight loss with increased appetite, insomnia/**fatigue**, diarrhea, **exophthalmus, heat intolerance**
3. Grave's disease
   a. Diffuse toxic goiter, causes 90% of US hyperthyroid cases
   b. Seen in young adults, & is 8x more common in females than males
   c. **Si/Sx include 2 findings only seen in hyperthyroid due to Grave's: infiltrative ophthalmopathy & pretibial myxedema**
   d. **Infiltrative ophthalmopathy** = exophthalmus not resolving when thyrotoxicosis is cured, due to autoantibody-mediated damage
   e. **Pretibial myxedema**
      1) Brawny, pruritic, nonpitting edema usually on the shins
      2) Often spontaneously remits after months to years
   f. Dx confirmed with thyroid stimulating immunoglobulin test
4. Plummer's disease (toxic multinodular goiter)
   a. Due to multiple foci of thyroid tissue that cease responding to T4 feedback inhibition, more common in older people
   b. Dx = multiple thyroid nodules felt in gland, confirm with radioactive iodine uptake tests → hot nodules with cold background
5. Thyroid adenoma due to overproduction of hormone by tumor in the gland
6. Subacute thyroiditis (giant cell or de Quervain's thyroiditis)
   a. Gland inflammation with spilling of hormone from the damaged gland
   b. **Presents with hyperthyroidism, later turns into hypothyroidism**
7. Tx for all
   a. Propylthiouracil or methimazole induces remission in 1mo to 2yr (up to 50% of time), lifelong Tx not necessary unless relapses
   b. Radioiodine is first line for Grave's: radioactive iodine is concentrated in the gland & destroys it, resolving the diffuse hyperthyroid state
   c. If the above fail → surgical excision (of adenoma or entire gland)
8. Thyroid storm is the most extreme manifestation of hyperthyroidism
   a. Due to exacerbation of hyperthyroidism by surgery or infection

b. Si/Sx = high fever, dehydration, cardiac arrhythmias, high output cardiac failure, coma & 25% mortality

c. Tx = high-dose β-blockers, ICU admission

B. HYPOTHYROIDISM

1. Causes include Hashimoto's & subacute thyroiditis
2. Si/Sx = **cold intolerance**, weight gain, **low energy**, husky voice, mental slowness, constipation, thick/coarse hair, puffiness of face/eyelids/hands (**myxedema**), prolonged relaxation phase of deep tendon reflexes
3. Hashimoto's disease
   a. Autoimmune lymphocytic infiltration of the thyroid gland
   b. **8:1 ratio in women to men,** usually between ages of 30 and 50
   c. **Dx confirmed by antithyroid peroxidase (TPO) antibodies**
   d. Tx = lifelong Synthroid
4. Subacute thyroiditis
   a. Seen following flu-like illness with sore throat & fevers
   b. Si/Sx = **jaw/tooth pain,** can be confused with dental dz, ↑ ESR
   c. Early on looks like hyperthyroidism as damaged gland spills T4
   d. Tx with aspirin, only with cortisol in very severe disease
   e. Usually self-limiting, resolves after weeks to months
5. Myxedema coma
   a. **The only emergent hypothyroid condition**—spontaneous onset or precipitated by cold exposure, infection, analgesia, sedative drug use, respiratory failure, or other severe illness
   b. Si/Sx = stupor, coma, seizures, hypotension, hypoventilation
   c. Tx = IV levothyroxine, cortisone, mechanical ventilation

VI.

TABLE 1-29   The Multiple Endocrine Neoplasia Syndromes

Type I (Wermer's syndrome)	**The 3(4) Ps: P**ituitary (**P**rolactinoma most common), **P**arathyroid, **P**ancreatoma
Type IIa (Sipple's syndrome)	Pheochromocytoma, medullary thyroid CA, parathyroid hyperplasia or tumor
Type IIb (Type III)	Pheochromocytoma, medullary thyroid CA, mucocutaneous neuromas, particularly of the GI tract

Musculoskeletal

I. Metabolic Bone Diseases

A. OSTEOPOROSIS

1. Due to **postmenopausal (↓estrogen)**, physical inactivity, high cortisol states (e.g., Cushing's, exogenous), hyperthyroidism, Ca^{2+} deficiency
2. Si/Sx = typically aSx until fracture occurs, particularly of hip & vertebrae
3. Dx = **DEXA scan** showing ↓ bone density compared to general population

4. Tx
  a. Estrogens are first line, only Tx shown to stimulate new bone growth
  b. Bisphosphonates are second line, like estrogen proven to ↓ risk of fracture & slow or stop bone degeneration
  c. Calcitonin particularly useful for treating bone pain but its effects wear off after chronic use
  d. Raloxifene & tamoxifen (selective estrogen receptor modulators) ↑ bone density but also ↑ risk for thromboembolism—role unclear currently
  5. **Every osteoporosis pt should take Ca to keep dietary intake ≥ 1.5 g/day**

B. RICKETS/OSTEOMALACIA
  1. Vitamin D deficiency in children = rickets, in adults = osteomalacia
  2. Si/Sx in kids (rickets) = **craniotabes** (thinning of skull bones), **rachitic rosary** (costochondral thickening looks like string of beads), **Harrison's groove** (depression along line of diaphragmatic insertion into rib cage), **Pigeon breast** = pectus carinatum (sternum protrusion)
  3. In adults the dz mimics osteoporosis
  4. Dx = x-ray → radiolucent bones, can confirm with vitamin D level
  5. Tx = vitamin D supplementation

C. SCURVY
  1. Vitamin C deficiency → ↓ osteoid formation
  2. Si/Sx = subperiosteal hemorrhage (painful), **bleeding gums**, multiple ecchymoses, osteoporosis, **"woody leg" from soft tissue hemorrhage**
  3. Dx = clinical
  4. Tx = Vitamin C supplementation

D. PAGET'S BONE DISEASE (OSTEITIS DEFORMANS)
  1. Idiopathic ↑ activity of both osteoblasts & osteoclasts, usually in elderly
  2. Si/Sx = **diffuse fractures & bone pain**, most commonly involves spine, pelvis, skull, femur, tibia, **high output cardiac failure, ↓ hearing**
  3. Dx = ↑↑ **alkaline phosphatase**, ⊕ bone scans, x-rays → sclerotic lesions
  4. Tx = bisphosphonates first line, calcitonin second line
  5. Complications = pathologic fractures, hypercalcemia & kidney stones, spinal cord compression in vertebral disease, osteosarcoma in long-standing disease

II. Nonneoplastic Bone Diseases

A. FIBROUS DYSPLASIA
  1. Idiopathic replacement of bone with fibrous tissue
  2. 3 types = a) monostotic, b) polystotic, c) McCune-Albright's
  3. McCune-Albright's syndrome
    a. Syndrome of hyperparathyroidism, hyperadrenalism & acromegaly
    b. **Dx = polystotic fibrous dysplasia, precocious puberty, café-au-lait spots** (See Color Plate 1)
  4. Tx = supportive

B. PYOGENIC OSTEOMYELITIS
  1. *S. aureus* most common cause, also *S. epidermidis* & *Strep. spp.*
  2. **Sickle cell patients get *Salmonella*, IV drug abusers get *Pseudomonas***

3. Si/Sx = painful inflammation of bone, striking skin changes include hyperpigmenta-tion, ulceration, erythema
4. Dx = **x-ray → periosteal elevation, can lag onset of dz by weeks**, MRI is gold stan-dard, can confirm with cultures of deep bone biopsy
5. Tx = 6–8 weeks of antibiotics, fluoroquinolones empirically, then narrow as cultures come back, surgical débridement as needed

III. Bone Tumors

1.

TABLE 1-30   Diagnosis[a] and Treatment of Primary Bone Neoplasms

TUMOR	PT AGE[b]	CHARACTERISTICS	TX
Osteochondroma	<25	• Benign, usually in males • Seen at distal femur & proximal tibia	Excision
Giant cell	20–40	• Benign, epiphyseal ends of long bones (>50% in knee) • X-ray → **soap bubble** sign • Often recurs after excision	Excision & local irradiation
Osteosarcoma	10–20	• #1 primary bone malignancy, in males • Seen at distal femur & proximal tibia • 2–3 fold ↑ alkaline phosphatase • **X-ray → Codman's triangle** = periosteal elevation due to tumor & **"sun-burst" sign** = lytic lesion with surrounding spiculated periostitis (See Figure 1-16)	Excision & local irradiation
Ewing's sarcoma	<15	• Young boys, metastasizes very early • Si/Sx mimic osteomyelitis (See Figure 1-16)	Chemotherapy

[a] Diagnoses all confirmed with bone biopsy.
[b] Peak age of onset.

2. Multiple myeloma
   a. Malignant clonal neoplasm of plasma cells producing whole Abs (e.g., IgM, IgG, etc.), light chains only, or very rarely no Abs (just ↑ B cells)
   b. Seen in pts >40, African Americans have 2 : 1 incidence
   c. **Si/Sx = bone pain worse with movement, lytic bone lesions on x-ray** (See Figure 1-17), pathologic fractures, **hypercalcemia**, renal failure, anemia, frequent infec-tions by encapsulated bacteria, ↓ **anion gap** (Abs positively charged, unseen cations make anion gap appear ↓)
   d. **Hyperviscosity syndrome** = stroke, retinopathy, CHF, **ESR > 100**
   e. **Bence-Jones proteinuria**
      1) **Urine dipsticks do NOT detect light chains**, can use sulfosalicylic acid test in lieu of dipstick to screen
      2) Dx = 24-hr urine collection → protein electrophoresis
      3) Light chain deposition causes renal amyloidosis
   f. Dx
      1) Serum/urine protein electrophoresis (SPEP/UPEP)
         a) Both → tall electrophoretic peak called "M-spike" due to ↑ Ab
         b) SPEP → M-spike if clones make whole Ab

      c) UPEP → spike if clones make light chains only

      d) **Either SPEP or UPEP will almost always be ⊕**

   2) Dx = ⊕ SPEP/UPEP & any of **1)**↑ plasma cells in bone marrow, **2)** osteolytic bone lesions, **3)** Bence-Jones proteinuria

 g. Tx

   1) Radiation given for isolated lesions, chemotherapy for metastatic dz

   2) Bone marrow transplantation may prolong survival

   3) Palliative care important for pain

 h. Px poor despite Tx

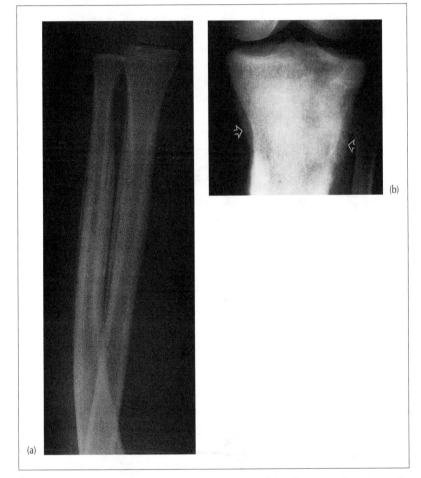

(a)

(b)

FIGURE 1-16   Different types of periosteal reactions. (a) Smooth lamellar periosteal reaction on the radius and ulna in a case of nonaccidental injury. (b) Spiculated (sunray) periosteal reaction in a case of osteogenic sarcoma (arrows). (c) Onion skin periosteal reaction in a case of Ewing's sarcoma (arrows). Here the periosteal new bone consists of several distinct layers. (d) Codman's triangle in a case of osteogenic sarcoma. At the edge of the lesion the periosteal new bone is lifted up to form a cuff (arrow).

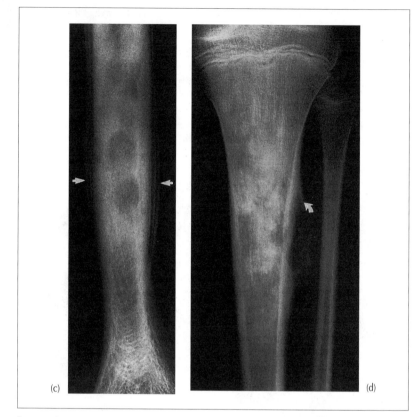

(c)

(d)

FIGURE 1-16 *Continued*

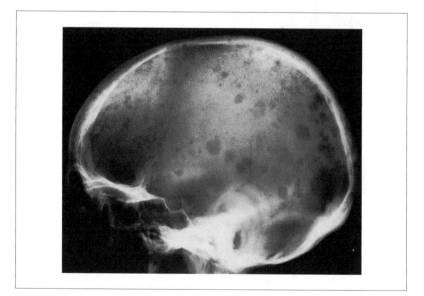

FIGURE 1-17 Myeloma.

IV. Arthropathies and Connective Tissue Disorders

A. RHEUMATOID ARTHRITIS (RA)
  1. Autoimmune dz of unknown etiology → **symmetric inflammatory arthritis**
  2. Female-male = 3:1, patients are commonly **HLA-DR4⊕**
  3. Si/Sx = **symmetric arthritis worse in morning** affecting knees, feet, metacarpopha-
     langeal (**MCP**) & proximal interphalangeal (**PIP**) joints, pleural effusions (serositis),
     anemia of chronic dz, flexion contractures → ulnar deviation of digits, subQ nodules
     (present in <50% of pts)
  4. Labs
     a. Rheumatoid factor (RF) = IgM anti-IgG
        1) Present in >70% of RA pts, but may appear late in dz course
        2) **Not specific for RA**, can be ⊕ in any chronic inflammatory state & may be
           present in 5–10% of healthy geriatric patients
     b. ESR is elevated in >90% cases, but is not specific for RA
  5. **Dx = clinical**, no single factor is sufficient
  6. Tx
     a. NSAIDs are first line, selective cyclooxygenase-2 inhibitors may be preferable
     b. Hydroxychloroquine second line, refractory pts → prednisone, gold salts, penicil-
        lamine, all of which cause severe side effects
     c. Newest Tx = recombinant receptor for tumor necrosis factor α (TNFα), recent
        trials show markedly improved Sx, even in refractory pts [see *N Engl J Med* 1997,
        337:141 & 1999, 340:253]

B. SYSTEMIC LUPUS ERYTHEMATOSUS
  1. Systemic autoimmune disorder, female-male = 9:1
  2. Si/Sx = fever, polyarthritis, skin lesions, splenomegaly, hemolytic anemia, thrombocy-
     topenia, serositis (e.g., pleuritis & pericarditis), Libman-Sacks endocarditis, renal dz,
     skin rashes, thrombosis, neurologic disorders
  3. Labs
     a. **Antinuclear antibody (ANA) sensitive (>98%) but not specific**
     b. **Anti-double-stranded-DNA (anti-ds-DNA) antibodies 99% specific**
     c. Anti-Smith (anti-Sm) antibodies are highly specific but not sensitive
     d. Anti-Ro antibodies are ⊕ in 50% of ANA negative lupus
     e. Antiribosomal P & antineuronal antibodies correlate with risk for cerebral
        involvement of lupus (lupus cerebritis)
     f. Antiphospholipid autoantibodies cause false-positive lab tests in SLE
        1) **SLE pts frequently have false ⊕ RPR/VDRL tests for syphilis**
        2) **SLE pts frequently have ↑ PTT (lupus anticoagulant antibody)**
           a) PTT is falsely ↑ because the lupus anticoagulant antibody binds to
              phospholipid that initiates clotting in the test tube
           b) **Despite the PTT test & the name lupus anticoagulant antibody, SLE
              patients are THROMBOGENIC, because antiphospholipid antibodies
              cause coagulation in vivo**
  4. Mnemonic for SLE diagnosis: **DOPAMINE RASH**
     a. **D**iscoid lupus = circular, erythematous macules with scales
     b. **O**ral aphthous ulcers (can be nasopharyngeal as well)
     c. **P**hotosensitivity

d. Arthritis (typically hands, wrists, knees)
e. Malar rash = classic butterfly macule on cheeks
f. Immunologic criteria = anti-ds-DNA, anti-Sm Ab, anti-Ro Ab, anti-La
g. Neurologic changes = psychosis, personality change, seizures
h. ESR rate ↑ (NOT 1 of the 11 criteria, but it is a frequent lab finding)
i. Renal disease → nephritic or nephrotic syndrome
j. ANA⊕
k. Serositis (pleurisy, pericarditis)
l. Hematologic dz = hemolytic anemia, thrombocytopenia, leukopenia
5. Drug-induced SLE
   a. Drugs = procainamide, hydralazine, Dilantin, sulfonamides, INH
   b. **Lab → antihistone antibodies**, differentiating from idiopathic SLE
6. Tx = NSAIDs, hydroxychloroquine, prednisone, cyclophosphamide depending on severity of dz
7. Px = variable, 10-yr survival is excellent, **renal dz is a poor Px indicator**

C. SJOGREN'S SYNDROME (SS)

1. An autoinflammatory disorder associated with **HLA-DR3**
2. Si/Sx = **classic triad of keratoconjunctivitis sicca** (dry eyes), **xerostomia** (dry mouth), **arthritis**, usually less severe than pure RA
3. Systemic Si/Sx = pancreatitis, fibrinous pericarditis, CN V sensory neuropathy, renal tubular acidosis, 40-fold ↑ in lymphoma incidence
4. Dx = Concomitant presence of 2 of the triad is diagnostic
5. Lab → ANA⊕, anti-Ro/anti-La Ab⊕ ("SSA/SSB Abs"), 70% are RF⊕
6. Tx = steroids, cyclophosphamide for refractory disease

D. BEHÇET'S SYNDROME

1. Multisystem inflammatory disorder that chronically recurs
2. Si/Sx = painful oral & genital ulcers, also arthritis, vasculitis, neurologic dz
3. Classic dermatologic Sx = **circinate balanitis** (serpiginous, moist plaques on glans penis) & **keratoderma blennorrhagicum** (crusting papules with central erosion, **looks like mollusk shell**)
4. Tx = prednisone during flare-ups

E. SERONEGATIVE SPONDYLOARTHROPATHY

1. Osteoarthritis
   a. **A noninflammatory arthritis** caused by joint wear & tear
   b. The most common arthritis, results in wearing away of joint cartilage
   c. Si/Sx = pain & crepitation upon joint motion, ↓ range of joint motion, can have radiculopathy due to cord impingement
   d. **X-ray → osteophytes (bone spurs) & asymmetric joint space loss**
   e. Physical exam → **Heberden's nodes** (DIP swelling 2° to osteophytes) & **Bouchard's nodes** (PIP swelling 2° to osteophytes)
   f. **Note: RA affects MCP & PIP joints, osteoarthritis affects PIP & DIP**
   g. Tx = NSAIDs, muscle relaxants, joint replacement (third line)
   h. **Isometric exercise to strengthen muscles around joint has been shown to improve Sx**
2. Ankylosing spondylitis
   a. Rheumatologic dz usually in **HLA-B27⊕** males (male-female = 3:1)

b. Si/Sx = sacroiliitis, spinal dz → complete fusion of adjacent vertebral bodies causing **"bamboo spine"** (See Figures 1-18 and 1-19), uveitis, heart block

c. **If sacroiliac joint is not affected, it is not ankylosing spondylitis!**

d. Dx = x-ray signs of spinal fusion & negative rheumatoid factor

e. Tx = NSAIDs & strengthening of back muscles

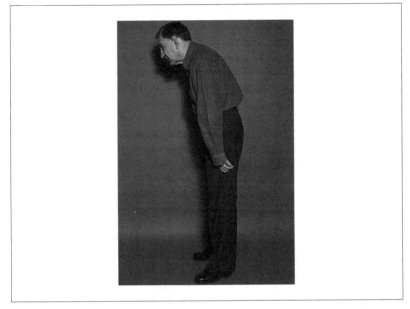

FIGURE 1-18   Spine. AS can cause a marked thoracic kyphosis with increased wall-to-tragus measurement.

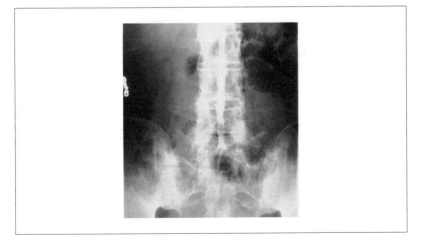

FIGURE 1-19   Radiograph of the lumbar spine (anteroposterior view). This patient has what is known as a "bamboo spine." There is syndesmophyte formation causing fusion of the vertebral bodies and there is also calcification of the interspinus ligament. The sacroiliac joints are also fused.

3. Reiter's syndrome
   a. Usually seen in males, **about 3/4 of these patients are HLA-B27⊕**
   b. Presents as nongonococcal **urethritis** (often chlamydial), **conjunctivitis, reactive arthritis** & **uveitis**
   c. Tx = erythromycin (for *Chlamydia* coverage) + NSAIDs for arthritis
4. Psoriatic arthritis
   a. Presents with **nail-pitting** & **DIP** joint involvement
   b. Occurs in up to 10% of patients with psoriasis
   c. Psoriatic flares may exacerbate arthritis, & vice versa
   d. Tx = UV light for psoriasis & gold/penicillamine for arthritis
5. Inflammatory bowel disease can cause seronegative arthritis
6. Disseminated gonococcal infection can cause **monoarticular** arthritis

F. SCLERODERMA (PROGRESSIVE SYSTEMIC SCLEROSIS = PSS)
1. Systemic fibrosis affecting virtually every organ, female-male = 4:1
2. Can be diffuse disease (PSS), or more benign CREST syndrome
3. **Si/Sx of CREST syndrome**
   a. **C**alcinosis = subcutaneous calcifications, often in fingers (See Figure 1-20)
   b. **R**aynaud's phenomenon, often the initial symptom (See Figure 1-21)
   c. **E**sophagitis due to lower esophageal sphincter sclerosis → reflux
   d. **S**clerodactyly = fibrosed skin causes immobile digits & rigid facies (See Figure 1-22)
   e. **T**elangiectasias occur in mouth, on digits, face & trunk (See Figure 1-23)
4. Other Sx = flexion contractures, biliary cirrhosis, lung/cardiac/renal fibrosis
5. Lab = ⊕ ANA in 95%, anti-Scl-70 has ↓ sensitivity but ↑ specificity, anticentromere is 80% sensitive for CREST syndrome
6. Dx = clinical
7. Tx = immunosuppressives for palliation, none are curative

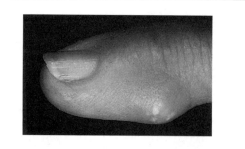

FIGURE 1-20   Subcutaneous and periarticular calcium deposits may occur and can be extremely painful.

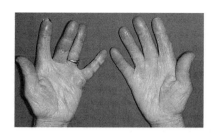

FIGURE 1-21   Raynaud's disease. Cyanosis of the fingers due to arterial vasoconstriction, which in this patient has resulted in an area of infarction of the left forefinger.

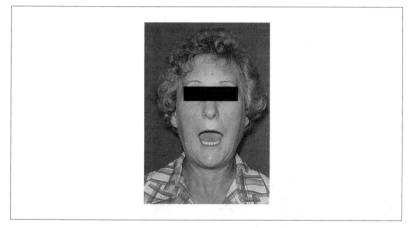

FIGURE 1-22   Scleroderma may cause thickening of the skin around the mouth and an inability to open the jaw fully.

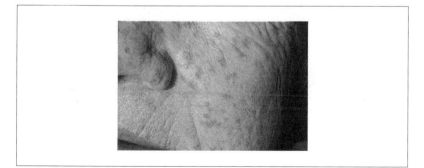

FIGURE 1-23   Telangiectasia in a patient with systemic sclerosis.

G. SARCOIDOSIS

1. Idiopathic, diffuse dz presenting in 20s to 40s, **African Americans are 3x more likely to develop than Caucasians**
2. Si/Sx = **50% of pts present with incidental finding on CXR & are aSx**, other presentations include fevers, chills, night sweats, weight loss, cough, dyspnea, rash, arthralgia, blurry vision (uveitis)
3. **CXR → bilateral hilar adenopathy** (See Figure 1-24)
4. Can affect ANY organ system
   a. CNS → CN palsy, classically CN VII (can be bilateral)
   b. **Eye → uveitis (can be bilateral), requires aggressive Tx**
   c. Cardiac → heart blocks, arrhythmias, constrictive pericarditis
   d. Lung → typically a restrictive defect
   e. GI → ↑ AST/ALT, CT → granulomas in liver, cholestasis
   f. Renal → nephrolithiasis due to hypercalcemia
   g. Endocrine → diabetes insipidus
   h. Hematologic → anemia, thrombocytopenia, leukopenia
   i. Skin → various rashes, including erythema nodosum
5. Dx is clinical, **noncaseating granulomas on biopsy is very suggestive**
6. Lab → 50% pts have ↑ angiotensin converting enzyme level
7. Tx = prednisone (first line), but 50% pts spontaneously remit, so only Tx if 1) eye/heart involved, 2) dz does not remit after months

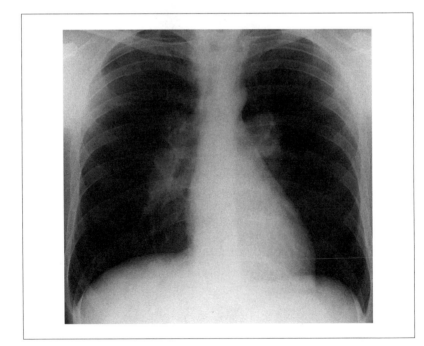

FIGURE 1-24   Bilateral hilar lymphadenopathy.

H. MIXED CONNECTIVE TISSUE DISEASE (MCTD)
1. Commonly onsets in women in teens & 20s
2. Si/Sx = overlapping SLE, scleroderma & polymyositis, but **characterized by ⊕ anti-U1 RNP antibody that defines the dz**
3. Dx = anti-U1RNP antibody
4. Tx = steroids, azathioprine

I. GOUT
1. **Monoarticular arthritis** due to urate crystal deposits in joint
2. **Gout develops after 20–30 yrs of hyperuricemia, often precipitated by sudden changes in serum urate levels** (gout in teens → 20s likely genetic)
3. **Most people with hyperuricemia never get gout**
4. ↑ production of uric acid can be genetic or acquired (e.g., alcohol, hemolysis, neoplasia, psoriasis)
5. Underexcretion of urate via kidney (<800 mg/dL urine urate) can be idiopathic or due to kidney dz, drugs (aspirin, diuretics, alcohol)
6. Si/Sx of gout = painful monoarticular arthritis affecting distal joints (often first metatarsophalangeal joint = **podagra** [See Figure1-25a]), **overlying skin erythema** (See Figure 1-25b)
7. Dx = **clinical triad of monoarticular arthritis, hyperuricemia, ⊕ response to colchicine** (see below), confirm with needle tap of joint → crystals
8. Acute Tx = colchicine & NSAIDs (not aspirin!)
9. Px = some people never suffer more than 1 attack, those that do → chronic tophaceous gout, with significant joint deformation (**classic rat-bite appearance to joint on x-ray**) & toothpaste-like discharge from joint
10. Maintenance Tx
    a. Do not start unless patient has more than 1 attack
    b. Over-producers → allopurinol (inhibits xanthine oxidase)
    c. Under-excreters → probenecid/sulfinpyrazone
    d. **Always start while pt still taking colchicine, because sudden ↓ in serum urate precipitates an acute attack**
11. Pseudogout
    a. Caused by calcium pyrophosphate dihydrate (CPPD) crystal deposition in joints & articular cartilage (chondrocalcinosis)
    b. Mimics gout very closely, seen in persons age 60 or older, often affects larger, more proximal joints.
    c. Can be 1° or 2° to metabolic dz (hyperparathyroidism, Wilson's dz, diabetes, hemochromatosis)
    d. Dx → microscopic analysis of joint aspirate
    e. Tx = colchicine & NSAIDs
12. Microscopy
    a. **Gout → needle-like negatively birefringent crystals** (See Color Plate 2)
    b. **"P"seudogout → "P"ositively birefringent crystals** (See Color Plate 3)

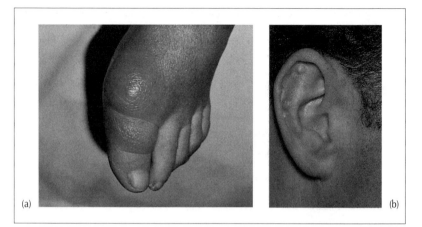

(a)   (b)

FIGURE 1-25   Gout. (a) Acute gouty arthritis affecting the big toe. This is extremely painful. (b) Urate crystal deposition in the cartilage of the ear.

V. Muscle Diseases

A. GENERAL
1. Diseases of muscle are divided into 2 groups: neurogenic & myopathic
2. Neurogenic diseases → **distal weakness, no pain, fasciculations present**
3. Myopathic diseases → **proximal weakness, ± pain, no fasciculations**

B. DUCHENNE'S MUSCULAR DYSTROPHY
1. **X-linked** lack of dystrophin
2. Si/Sx commence at 1 yr of age with **progressive proximal weakness & wasting,** ↑ CPK, **calf hypertrophy,** waddling gait, Gower's maneuver (pts pick themselves off the floor by using arms to help legs)
3. Tx = supportive
4. Px = death occurs in 10s–20s, most often due to pneumonia
5. Becker's dystrophy is similar but less severe disease

C. POLYMYOSITIS
1. Autoinflammatory dz of muscles & sometimes skin (dermatomyositis)
2. Female-male = 2:1, occurs in young children & geriatric populations
3. Si/Sx = symmetric weakness/atrophy of proximal limb muscles, muscle aches, dysphonia (laryngeal muscle weakness), dysphagia
4. Dermatomyositis presents with periorbital heliotropic red to purple rash
5. Dx = ANA⊕, ↑ creatine kinase, muscle biopsy → inflammatory changes
6. Tx = steroids, methotrexate or cyclophosphamide for resistant disease

D. MYASTHENIA GRAVIS (MG)
1. Autoantibodies block the postsynaptic acetylcholine receptor
2. Most common in women in 20s–30s or men in 50s–60s
3. **Associated with thymomas, thyroid & other autoimmune dz (e.g., lupus)**
4. Sx = **muscle weakness worse with use,** diplopia, dysphagia, proximal limb weakness, can progress to cause respiratory failure

5. Dx = trial of edrophonium → immediate ↑ in strength, confirm with electromyelography → repetitive stimulation ↓ action potential
6. DDx
    a. **Lambert-Eaton syndrome**
        1) AutoAb to **pre**synaptic Ca channels seen with small cell lung CA
        2) Differs from MG in that Lambert-Eaton → ↓ reflexes, autonomic dysfunction (xerostomia, impotence) & **Sx improve with muscle use (action potential strength ↑ with repeated stimulation)**
    b. Aminoglycosides worsen MG, or induce mild MG Sx in normal people
7. Tx = anticholinesterase inhibitors (e.g., pyridostigmine) first line
    a. Steroids, cyclophosphamide, azathioprine for ↑ severe dz
    b. Plasmapheresis temporarily alleviates Sx by removing the Ab
    c. Resection of thymoma can be curative

Hematology (See Figure 1-26)

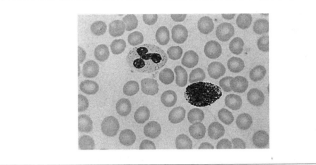

FIGURE 1-26   Normal blood films.

I. Anemia

A. MICROCYTIC ANEMIAS (≡ MCV <80)
1. **Result from ↓ hemoglobin (Hgb) production or impaired Hgb function**
2. Iron deficiency anemia
    a. **NOT a Dx, must find the cause of iron deficiency!!!**
    b. Epidemiology
        1) #1 anemia in the world, hookworms the #1 cause in the world
        2) ↑ incidence in women of childbearing age 2° to menses
        3) **In the elderly it is colon cancer until proven otherwise!**
        4) Dietary deficiency **virtually impossible in adults, seen in kids**
    c. Si/Sx = tachycardia, fatigue, pallor all from anemia, smooth tongue, brittle nails, esophageal webs & pica all from iron deficiency
    d. Dx = **↓ serum iron,** ↓ serum ferritin, **↑ total iron binding capacity (TIBC),** peripheral smear → target cells
    e. Tx = iron sulfate, should achieve baseline hematocrit within 2 mo

3. Sideroblastic anemia
   a. Ineffective erythropoiesis due to disorder of porphyrin pathway
   b. Etiologies = chronic alcoholism, drugs (commonly isoniazid), genetic
   c. Si/Sx as per any anemia
   d. Labs: ↑ **iron**, N/↑ TIBC, ↑ ferritin
   e. Dx = ringed sideroblasts on iron stain of bone marrow
   f. Tx = sometimes responsive to pyridoxine (vitamin B_6 supplements)
4. Lead poisoning
   a. Si/Sx = anemia, encephalopathy (worse in children), seizures, ataxic gait, **wrist/foot drops**, renal tubular acidosis
   b. Classic findings
      1) **Bruton's lines** = blue/gray discoloration at gumlines
      2) **Basophilic stippling of red cells (blue dots in red cells)**
   c. Dx = serum lead level
   d. Tx = chelation with dimercaprol (BAL) &/or EDTA
5. Thalassemias
   a. Hereditary dz of ↓ production of globin chains → ↓ Hgb production
   b. Differentiation through gel-electrophoresis of globin proteins
   c. α-Thalassemia (↓ α-globin chain synthesis, there are 4 α alleles)
      1) Seen commonly in Asians, less so in Africans & Mediterraneans
      2)

TABLE 1-31 α-Thalassemia

#ALLELES AFFECTED/DZ		CHARACTERISTIC	BLOOD SMEAR
4	Hydrops fetalis	Fetal demise, total body edema	Bart's β_4 Hgb precipitations
3	Hgb H disease	Precipitation of β-chain tetramers	Intraerythrocytic inclusions
2	α-Thalassemia minor	Usually clinically silent	Mild microcytic anemia
1	Carrier state	No anemia, asymptomatic	No abnormalities

   d. β-Thalassemia (↓ β-globin chain synthesis, there are 2 β alleles)
      1) Usually of Mediterranean or African descent
      2)

TABLE 1-32 β-Thalassemia

	THALASSEMIA MAJOR (β–/β–)	THALASSEMIA MINOR (β+/β–)
Si/Sx	Anemia develops at 6 mo old (due to switch from fetal γ Hgb to adult β), splenomegaly, frontal bossing due to extramedullary hematopoiesis, iron overload (2° to transfusions)	Typically asymptomatic carriers
Dx	**Electrophoresis** ↓↓↓ Hgb A, ↑ Hgb A2, ↑ **Hgb F**	**Electrophoresis** ↓ Hgb A, ↑ Hgb A2(γ), **N Hgb F**
Tx	Folate supplementation, splenectomy for hypersplenism, transfuse only for severe anemia	Avoid oxidative stress

6. Sickle cell anemia (See Figure 1-27)
   a. HgS tetramer polymerizes, causing sickling of deoxygenated RBCs
   b. Si/Sx
      1) Vaso-occlusion → pain crisis, myocardiopathy, infarcts of
        bone/CNS/lungs/kidneys & autosplenectomy due to splenic infarct →
        ↑susceptible to encapsulated bacteria
      2) **Intravascular hemolysis → gallstones in children or teens**
      3) ↑ risk of aplastic anemia from parvovirus B19 infections
   c. Dx = hemoglobin electrophoresis → HgS phenotype
   d. Tx
      1) O$_2$ (cells sickle when Hgb desaturates), transfuse as needed
      2) Hydroxyurea → ↓ incidence & severity of pain crises
      3) Pneumococcal vaccination due to ↑ risk of infection

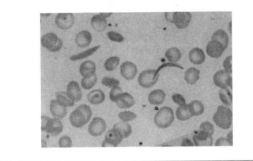

FIGURE 1-27   Sickle cell anemia.

B. MEGALOBLASTIC ANEMIAS (≡ MCV >100)
   1. **Results from ↓ DNA synthesis with normal RNA/protein synthesis**
   2. **Pathognomonic blood smear → hypersegmented neutrophils** (See Figure 1-28)
   3. Vitamin B$_{12}$ deficiency
      a. Pernicious anemia is most common cause
        1) Antibody to gastric parietal cells → ↓ production of intrinsic factor (necessary
          for uptake of B$_{12}$ in the terminal ileum)
        2) Accompanied by achlorhydria & atrophic gastritis
      b. Other causes = malabsorption due to gastric resection, resection of terminal
        ileum, or intestinal infection by *Diphyllobothrium latum*
      c. Si/Sx = megaloblastic anemia **with neurologic signs** = peripheral neuropathy,
        paresthesias, ↓ balance & position sense, **worse in legs**
      d. **Dx = ↑serum methylmalonic acid & ↑ homocysteine levels**—more sensitive than
        B$_{12}$ levels, which may or may not be ↓
      e. Tx = Vitamin B$_{12}$, high-dose oral Tx proven equivalent to parenteral
   4. Folic acid deficiency
      a. Folic acid derived from green, leafy vegetables ("foliage")

b. Causes = dietary deficiency (most common), pregnancy or hemolytic anemia (↑ requirements), methotrexate or prolonged Bactrim Tx (inhibits reduction of folate into tetrahydrofolate)

c. Si/Sx = megaloblastic anemia, no neurologic signs

d. Dx = **Nml serum methylmalonic acid but ↑ homocysteine levels**—more sensitive than folate levels, which may or may not be ↓

e. Tx = oral folic acid supplementation

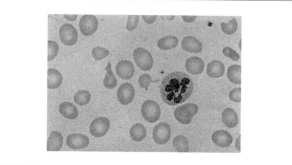

FIGURE 1-28   Hypersegmented neutrophil in severe pernicious anemia; also see ovalocytes.

C. NORMOCYTIC ANEMIAS
   1.

TABLE 1-33   Hypoproliferative Anemias

DISEASE	CHARACTERISTICS	TX
Anemia of renal failure	• ↓ erythropoietin production by kidney • Indicates chronic renal failure	Erythropoietin IM 3x per week
Anemia of chronic dz	• Seen in chronic inflammation (e.g., cancer, TB or fungal infxn, collagen-vascular dz) • Dx = ↓ **serum iron**, Nml/↑ ferritin, ↓**TIBC**	Tx underlying inflammatory dz, supportive
Aplastic anemia	• Bone marrow failure, usually idiopathic, or due to parvovirus B19 (especially in sickle cell), hepatitis virus, radiation, drugs (e.g., chloramphenicol) • Dx = bone marrow Bx → hypocellular marrow	BMT[a] for severe dz, ATG[b] & cyclosporin may help for mild dz

[a] BMT = bone marrow transplantation.
[b] ATG = antithymocyte globulin.

2.

TABLE 1-34   Hemolytic Anemias

DISEASE	CHARACTERISTICS	TX
Intrinsic Hemolysis (RBC defects)		
Spherocytosis	• Autosomal dominant membrane protein defect (fibrillin) → spherical, stiff RBCs trapped in the spleen • Si/Sx = childhood jaundice & gallstones, indirect hyperbilirubinemia, Coombs negative • Dx = clinical ⊕ peripheral smear → spherocytes	Folic acid, splenectomy for severe dz
Extrinsic Hemolysis		
Autoimmune hemolysis (IgG-mediated)	• Etiologies = idiopathic (most common), lupus, drugs (e.g., penicillin), leukemia, lymphoma • Si/Sx = rapid-onset, **spherocytes on blood smear**, ↑ indirect bilirubin, jaundice, **↓ haptoglobin, ↑ urine hemosiderin** • Dx = ⊕ direct Coombs' test	First line = prednisone +/– splenectomy, cyclophosphamide for refractory dz
Cold-agglutinin disease (IgM-mediated)	• Most commonly idiopathic, can due to *Mycoplasma pneumoniae* & mononucleosis (CMV, EBV infxns) • Si/Sx = anemia on exposure to cold or following URI • Dx = cold-agglutinin test & indirect Coombs' test	Prednisone for severe dz, supportive for mild
Mechanical destruction	• Causes = disseminated intravascular coagulation (DIC), thrombotic thrombocytopenic purpura (TTP), hemolytic-uremic syndrome (HUS) & artificial heart valve • Peripheral smear → schistocytes (See Figure 1-29)	Tx directed at underlying disorder

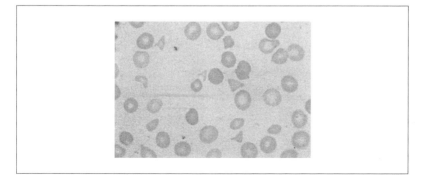

FIGURE 1-29   Schistocytes in patient with malfunctioning aortic valve.

II. Coagulation Disorders

A. THROMBOCYTOPENIA

1. Caused by splenic sequestration, stem-cell failure, or ↑ destruction
2. Si/Sx = bleeding time ↑ at counts < 50,000, clinically significant bleeds start at counts < 20,000, CNS bleeds occur when counts < 10,000
3. ↓ production seen in leukemia, aplastic anemia & alcohol (even minimal)
4.

TABLE 1-35   Causes of Platelet Destruction (Thrombocytopenia)

DISEASE	CHARACTERISTICS	TX
Idiopathic thrombocytopenic purpura (ITP)	• Autoantibody-mediated platelet destruction • **In children follows URI & is self-limiting, in adults it is chronic**	Steroids (first line), splenectomy (second line) or cyclophosphamide
Thrombotic thrombocytopenic purpura (TTP)	• Idiopathic dz, often seen in HIV, can be fatal • **Pentad** = hemolytic anemia, renal failure, thrombocytopenia, fever, neurologic dz	Plasma exchange or IVIG until dz abates, dz is fatal without Tx
Hemolytic-uremic syndrome (HUS)	• Usually in kids, often due to *E. coli* O157:H7 • Si/Sx = acute renal failure, bloody diarrhea & abdominal pain, seizures, **fulminant thrombocytopenia with hemolytic anemia**	Dialysis helps children, but adult Px is much poorer
Disseminated intravascular coagulation (DIC)	• Seen in adenocarcinoma, leukemia, sepsis, trauma • ↑ fibrin-split products, ↓ fibrinogen, ↑ PT/PTT	Directed at underlying cause
Drug-induced	• Causes = heparin, sulfonamides, valproate • Reverses within days of ceasing drug intake	Stop drug

5.

TABLE 1-36   Labs in Platelet Destruction

STUDY	AUTOANTIBODY	DIC	TTP/HUS
Blood smear	Microspherocytes	Schistocytes (+)	Schistocytes (+++)
Coombs' test	⊕	–	–
PT/PTT	Nml	↑↑↑	Nml/↑

B. INHERITED DISORDERS

1. von-Willebrand factor (vWF) deficiency
   a. **Most common inherited bleeding dz**
   b. Si/Sx = **episodic ↑ bleeding time & ecchymoses, normal PT/PTT**
   c. Dx = vWF levels & ristocetin-cofactor test
   d. Tx = DDAVP (↑ vWF secretion) or cryoprecipitate for acute bleeding
2. Hemophilia
   a. X-linked deficiency of factor VIII (hemophilia A) or autosomal recessive defect of factor IX (hemophilia B = Christmas disease)
   b. Si/Sx = hemarthroses (bleeding into joint), ecchymoses with minor trauma, ↑ **PTT, normal PT, normal bleeding time**

c. Dx = ↓ factor levels

d. Tx = recombinant factor VIII or factor IX concentrate

C. HYPERCOAGULABLE DISEASES

TABLE 1-37   Hypercoagulable Diseases

PRIMARY (INHERITED)	SECONDARY (ACQUIRED)	
Antithrombin III deficiency	Prolonged immobilization	L-asparaginase
Protein C deficiency	Pregnancy	Hyperlipidemia
Protein S deficiency	Surgery/Trauma	Anticardiolipin Ab
Factor V Leiden deficiency	Oral contraceptives	Lupus anticoagulant
Dysfibrinogenemia	Homocystinuria	DIC
Plasminogen (activator) deficiency	Malignancy (adenocarcinoma)	Vitamin K deficiency
Heparin cofactor II deficiency	Smoking	
Homocystinemia	Nephrotic syndrome	

III. Myeloproliferative Diseases

1. Caused by clonal proliferation of a myeloid stem cell → excessive production of mature, differentiated myeloid cell lines
2. All can transform into acute leukemias
3.

TABLE 1-38   Myeloproliferative Diseases

DISEASE	CHARACTERISTICS	TX
Polycythemia vera	• Rare, peak onset at 50–60 yr, male predominance • Si/Sx = headache, diplopia, retinal hemorrhages, stroke, angina, claudication (all due to vascular sludging), early satiety, splenomegaly, gout, **pruritus after showering, basophilia** • **5% progress to leukemia, 20% to myelofibrosis**	Phlebotomy, hydroxyurea to keep blood counts low
Essential thrombocythemia	• Si/Sx = platelet count >5 × 10^5 cells/μL, splenomegaly, ecchymoses • Dx = rule out 2° thrombocytosis (due to iron deficiency, malignancy, etc.) • 5% progress to myelofibrosis or acute leukemia	Platelet exchange (apheresis), hydroxyurea or anagrelide
Idiopathic myelofibrosis	• Typically affects patients ≥ 50 yr • Si/Sx = massive hepatosplenomegaly, blood smear → **teardrop cells** • Dx = hypercellular marrow on biopsy • Poor Px, median 5 yr before marrow failure	Supportive (splenectomy, antibiotics, allopurinol for gout)

Chronic myelogenous leukemia—see below.

4. Thrombocytosis potential causes mnemonic: **SHAPIRO**

a. **S**plenectomy

b. **H**odgkin's or other lymphoma

c. **A**cute bleed

d. **P**olycythemia vera, 1° thrombocytosis

e. **I**nfection

f. **R**heumatoid arthritis (collagen vascular disease)

g. **O**ccult malignancy

IV. Leukemias

A. ACUTE LYMPHOBLASTIC LEUKEMIA
1. **Peak age 3–4 yr**, most common neoplasm in children
2. Si/Sx = fever, fatigue, anemia, pallor, petechiae, infections
3. Lab → leukocytosis, anemia, ↓ platelets, marrow bx → ↑ blasts, peripheral blood blasts are **PAS +, CALLA +, TdT +**
4. Tx = chemotherapy: induction, consolidation, maintenance—CNS radiation or intrathecal chemotherapy during consolidation
5. Px = 80% cure in children (much worse in adults)

B. ACUTE MYELOGENOUS LEUKEMIA (AML)
1. **Most common leukemia in adults**
2. Si/Sx = fever, fatigue, pallor, petechiae, infections, lymphadenopathy
3. Lab → thrombocytopenia, peripheral blood & marrow bx → myeloblasts that are **myeloperoxidase +, Sudan Black +, Auer Rods +**
4. Tx
   a. Chemotherapy → induction, consolidation (no maintenance)
   b. All-trans retinoic acid used for a subtype of AML, causes differentiation of blasts, beware of onset of disseminated intravascular coagulation in these patients
5. Px = overall 30% cure, bone marrow transplant improves outcomes

C. CHRONIC MYELOGENOUS LEUKEMIA
1. Presents most commonly in the 50s, can be any age
2. Si/Sx = anorexia, early satiety, diaphoresis, arthritis, bone tenderness, leukostasis (WBC ≥ 1×10^5) → dyspnea, dizzy, slurred speech, diplopia
3. Labs → **Philadelphia chromosome** ⊕ (see below), **peripheral blood → cells of all maturational stages**, ↓ leukocyte alkaline phosphatase
4. Philadelphia (Ph) chromosome is pathognomonic, seen in > 90% of CML pts, due to translocation of *abl* gene from chromosome 9 to *bcr* on 22
5. Tx in chronic phase = chemotherapy to diminish WBC count
6. **Blast crisis = acute phase, invariably develops causing death in 3–6 mo, mean time to onset = 3–4 yr, only BMT can prevent**

D. CHRONIC LYMPHOCYTIC LEUKEMIA
1. Increasing incidence with age, causes 30% of leukemias in US
2. Si/Sx = organomegaly, hemolytic anemia, thrombocytopenia, blood smear & marrow → normal morphology lymphocytosis of blood & marrow, **lymphocytes almost always express CD5 protein**
3. **Tx = palliative, early therapy does NOT prolong life**
4. Other presentations of similar leukemias
   a. Hairy cell leukemia (B-cell subtype)
      1) Si/Sx = characteristic hairy cell morphology, pancytopenia
      2) Tx = interferon-α, splenectomy
   b. T-cell leukemias tend to involve skin, often present with erythematous rashes, some are due to human T-cell leukemia virus (HTLV)

Most Common Leukemias by Age:
Up to age 15 = ALL; age 15–39 = AML; age 40–59 = AML & CML;
60 & over = CLL

V. Lymphoma

A. NON-HODGKIN'S LYMPHOMA (NHL)

1. Commonly seen in HIV, often in brain, teenagers get in head & neck
2. Burkitt's lymphoma
   a. Closely related to Epstein-Barr virus (EBV) infections
   b. African Burkitt's involves jaw/neck, US Burkitt's involves abdomen
3. Cutaneous T-cell lymphoma (CTCL, mycosis fungoides)
   a. Si/Sx = often in elderly, diffuse scaly rash or erythroderma (total body erythema), precedes clinically apparent malignancy by years
   b. **Stained cells have cerebriform nuclei** (looks like cerebral gyri)
   c. Leukemic phase of this disease is called "Sézary syndrome"
   d. Tx = UV light therapy, consider systemic chemotherapy
4. Angiocentric T-cell lymphoma
   a. 2 subtypes = nasal T-cell lymphoma (lethal midline granuloma) & pulmonary angiocentric lymphoma (Wegener's granulomatosis)
   b. Si/Sx = large mass, biopsy often non-Dx due to diffuse necrosis
   c. Tx = palliative radiation therapy, Px very poor

B. HODGKIN'S LYMPHOMA

1. Occurs in a bimodal age distribution, young men & the elderly
2. EBV infection is present in up to 50% of cases
3. Si/Sx = **Pel-Epstein fevers** (fevers wax & wane over weeks), chills, night sweats, weight loss, pruritus, **Sx worsen with alcohol intake**
4. Reed-Sternberg (RS) cells seen on biopsy, **appear as binucleated giant cells ("owl eyes")** or **mononucleated giant cell (lacunar cell)** (See Figure 1-30)
5. Tx depends on clinical staging
   a. Stage I = 1 lymph node involved → radiation
   b. Stage II = ≥ 2 lymph nodes on same side of diaphragm → radiation
   c. Stage III = involvement on both sides of diaphragm → chemo
   d. Stage IV = disseminated to organs or extranodal tissue → chemo
   e. Chemo regimens
      1) MOPP = **m**eclorethamine, **o**ncovin (vincristine), **p**rocarbazine, **p**rednisone
      2) ABVD = **a**driamycin, **b**leomycin, **v**incristine, **d**acarbazine

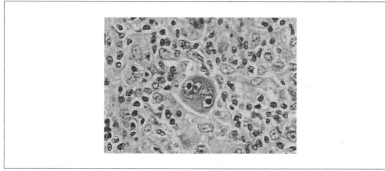

FIGURE 1-30   Reed-Sternberg cell in patient with Hodgkin's disease.

DETERMINATION OF PRIMARY ACID-BASE DISORDER

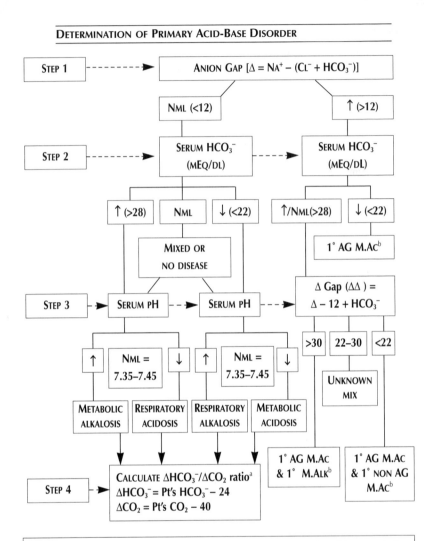

^{a} The $\Delta HCO_3^-/\Delta CO_2$ ratio determines the presence of mixed acid-base disorders. If the ratio is higher than predicted (CO_2 is lower than expected) there is an additional alkalotic process aside from the $1°$ disorder (a second acid-base disorder). Ratios lower than predicted indicate an additional acidotic process. Ratios as predicted indicate a pure $1°$ disorder.
- Metabolic Alkalosis: $\Delta HCO_3^-/\Delta CO_2$ ratio should be $1:0.7$
- Metabolic Acidosis: $\Delta HCO_3^-/\Delta CO_2$ ratio should be $1:1$
- Respiratory ratio depends on acute or chronic respiratory process (see table below)

	ACIDOSIS	ALKALOSIS
Acute	1	2
Chronic	3–4 (3.5)	5
Numbers represent ΔHCO_3^- per 10 change in CO_2		

^{b} AG = anion gap. M.Alk = metabolic alkalosis. M.Ac = metabolic acidosis.

METABOLIC ACIDOSIS

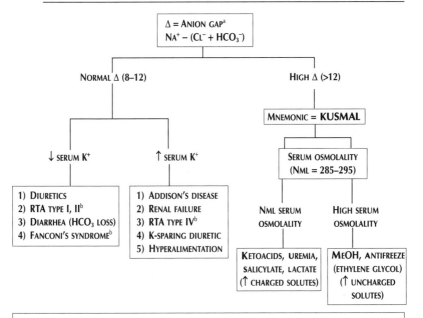

Check for compensation or the presence of a mixed disorder. Winter's formula predicts the CO_2 if there is compensation: $CO_2 = 1.5 * HCO_3^- + 8 \pm 2$. An informal check can be made by comparing the change in CO_2 and HCO_3 from normal (normal $CO_2 = 40$, normal $HCO_3 = 24$). For a compensated metabolic acidosis, CO_2 should decrease by 1 for every 1 the HCO_3^- decreases. If the CO_2 is higher than expected, there is an additional acidotic process occurring. If the CO_2 is lower than expected, there is an additional alkalotic process occurring.

[a] Calculate Δ in *all* patients, regardless of pH or HCO_3^-. Mixed acidosis and alkalosis can cancel each other out, causing neutral pH. Perform the following steps to search for a mixed disorder.
1) Calculate Δ: if $\Delta \geq 12$, the disorder is a 1° anion gap acidosis
2) Calculate $\Delta\Delta = [\Delta - 12 + HCO_3^-]$: if $\Delta\Delta \geq 31$, there is also a 1° metabolic alkalosis
     if $\Delta\Delta \leq 21$, there is also a 1° *non*anion gap acidosis
Example: A diabetic in ketoacidosis who is vomiting can have a 1° anion gap acidosis from the ketoacidosis and a 1° metabolic alkalosis from the vomiting. In this case, the $\Delta > 12$, the $\Delta\Delta \geq 31$. A diabetic with renal failure who presents with ketoacidosis can have a 1° anion gap and nonanion gap acidosis, with a $\Delta > 12$ and a $\Delta\Delta \leq 21$. Note that this patient may also be vomiting and either tachypneic or bradypneic from obtundation. Thus the patient may have three 1° metabolic acid-base disorders (1° AG acidosis, 1° nonAG acidosis, 1° metabolic alkalosis) and a respiratory disorder. In this case, the disorders must be discriminated clinically or by changes in status in response to therapy.
    Our thanks to Dr. Arian Torbati for his assistance with the $\Delta\Delta$ algorithm.
[b] See Section III.F for description of RTA and Fanconi's syndrome.

METABOLIC ALKALOSIS

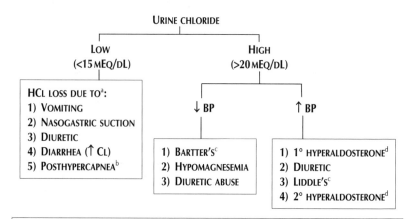

URINE CHLORIDE

LOW (<15 MEQ/DL)

HIGH (>20 MEQ/DL)

HCL LOSS DUE TO[a]:
1) VOMITING
2) NASOGASTRIC SUCTION
3) DIURETIC
4) DIARRHEA (↑ CL)
5) POSTHYPERCAPNEA[b]

↓ BP

↑ BP

1) BARTTER'S[c]
2) HYPOMAGNESEMIA
3) DIURETIC ABUSE

1) 1° HYPERALDOSTERONE[d]
2) DIURETIC
3) LIDDLE'S[c]
4) 2° HYPERALDOSTERONE[d]

Check for compensation or the presence of a mixed disorder by comparing the change in CO_2 and HCO_3 from normal (normal CO_2 = 40, normal HCO_3 = 24). For a compensated metabolic alkalosis, CO_2 should increase by 0.7 for every 1 the HCO_3^- increases. If the CO_2 is higher than expected, there is an additional acidotic process occurring. If the CO_2 is lower than expected, there is an additional alkalotic process occurring.

[a] These conditions are all known as "contraction alkaloses," or "chloride-responsive alkaloses." The contraction in extracellular volume creates a hypochloremic state. The kidney resorbs extra bicarbonate from the tubules due to the loss of chloride anion (tubules need a different anion to maintain electrical neutrality). Administration of chloride anion in the form of normal saline will correct the alkalosis.
[b] Patients who are hypercapnic undergo renal compensation, with resorption of extra bicarb from the tubules to offset the respiratory acidosis. When the hypercapnia is corrected (e.g., via intubation) the kidneys must adjust and resorb less bicarb. Until they adjust, the patient will have a posthypercapnic metabolic alkalosis.
[c] See Appendix B for Bartter's & Liddle's.
[d] 1° hyperaldosteronism is known as Conn's syndrome. See Endocrinology, Section III.D.1. 2° hyperaldosteronism can be caused by renal artery stenosis (see Nephrology, Section V), Cushing's syndrome (see Endocrine, Section III.B), congestive heart failure, and hepatic cirrhosis.

RESPIRATORY ACID-BASE DIFFERENTIAL

RESPIRATORY ALKALOSIS	RESPIRATORY ACIDOSIS
• CNS LESION	• MORPHINE/SEDATIVES
• PREGNANCY	• STROKE IN BULBAR AREA OF BRAIN STEM
• HIGH ALTITUDE	• ONDINE'S CURSE (CENTRAL SLEEP APNEA)
• SEPSIS/INFECTION	• COPD (EMPHYSEMA, ASTHMA, BRONCHITIS)
• SALICYLATE TOXICITY	• ADULT RESPIRATORY DISTRESS SYNDROME
• LIVER FAILURE	• CHEST WALL DISEASE (POLIO, KYPHOSCOLIOSIS,
• ANXIETY (HYPERVENTILATION)	MYASTHENIA GRAVIS, MUSCULAR DYSTROPHY)
• PAIN/FEAR (HYPERVENTILATION)	• OBESITY
• CONGESTIVE HEART FAILURE	• HYPOPHOSPHATEMIA (DIAPHRAGM REQUIRES
• PULMONARY EMBOLUS	LOTS OF ATP DUE TO HIGH ENERGY DEMAND)
• PNEUMONIA	• SUCCINYLCHOLINE (PARALYSIS FOR INTUBATION)
• HYPERTHYROIDISM	• PLEURAL EFFUSION
• COMPENSATION FOR A 1° ACIDOSIS	• PNEUMOTHORAX

Check for the presence of a mixed disorder by comparing the change in CO_2 and HCO_3 from normal (normal $CO_2 = 40$, normal $HCO_3 = 24$).

Acute respiratory acidosis: HCO_3^- increases by 1 for every 10 the CO_2 increases.
Acute respiratory alkalosis: HCO_3^- decreases by 2 for every 10 the CO_2 decreases.
Chronic respiratory acidosis: HCO_3^- increases by 3.5 for every 10 the CO_2 increases.
Chronic respiratory alkalosis: HCO_3^- decreases by 5 for every 10 the CO_2 decreases.

It's easy to remember the compensations by organizing them in the following table.

	ACIDOSIS	ALKALOSIS
Acute	1	2
Chronic	3–4 (3.5)	5
Change in HCO_3^- per 10 change in CO_2. Just remember = 1:2:3–4:5!		

As usual, if the CO_2 is higher than predicted, there is a mixed acidotic process. If the CO_2 is lower than predicted, there is a mixed alkalotic process.

EVALUATION OF HYPONATREMIA

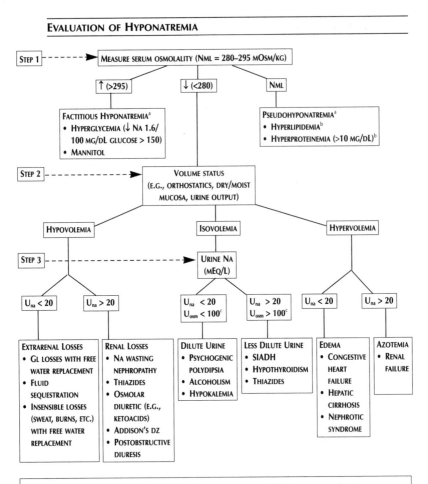

STEP 1 ┄┄┄▶ MEASURE SERUM OSMOLALITY (NML = 280–295 MOSM/KG)

↑ (>295)   ↓ (<280)   NML

FACTITIOUS HYPONATREMIA[a]
- HYPERGLYCEMIA (↓ NA 1.6/ 100 MG/DL GLUCOSE > 150)
- MANNITOL

PSEUDOHYPONATREMIA[a]
- HYPERLIPIDEMIA[b]
- HYPERPROTEINEMIA (>10 MG/DL)[b]

STEP 2 ┄┄┄▶ VOLUME STATUS
(E.G., ORTHOSTATICS, DRY/MOIST MUCOSA, URINE OUTPUT)

HYPOVOLEMIA   ISOVOLEMIA   HYPERVOLEMIA

STEP 3 ┄┄┄▶ URINE NA (MEQ/L)

$U_{na} < 20$ $U_{na} > 20$ $U_{na} < 20$ $U_{osm} < 100^c$ $U_{na} > 20$ $U_{osm} > 100^c$ $U_{na} < 20$ $U_{na} > 20$

EXTRARENAL LOSSES
- GI LOSSES WITH FREE WATER REPLACEMENT
- FLUID SEQUESTRATION
- INSENSIBLE LOSSES (SWEAT, BURNS, ETC.) WITH FREE WATER REPLACEMENT

RENAL LOSSES
- NA WASTING NEPHROPATHY
- THIAZIDES
- OSMOLAR DIURETIC (E.G., KETOACIDS)
- ADDISON'S DZ
- POSTOBSTRUCTIVE DIURESIS

DILUTE URINE
- PSYCHOGENIC POLYDIPSIA
- ALCOHOLISM
- HYPOKALEMIA

LESS DILUTE URINE
- SIADH
- HYPOTHYROIDISM
- THIAZIDES

EDEMA
- CONGESTIVE HEART FAILURE
- HEPATIC CIRRHOSIS
- NEPHROTIC SYNDROME

AZOTEMIA
- RENAL FAILURE

[a] Pseudohyponatremia is a lab artifact due to serum volume occupation by lipid or protein, resulting in an apparent decrease in the amount of Na per given volume of serum. Factitious hyponatremia is a true decrease in serum Na concentration (but normal total body Na) caused by glucose or mannitol osmotically drawing water into the serum.
[b] These disorders are characterized by ≥ 10 mOsm/kg gap between the calculated & and the measured serum osmolarity. Serum osmolarity is calculated by (2*Na) + (BUN/2.8) + (glucose/18). The gap is due to the presence of solutes detected by the lab but not accounted for in the osmolality calculation.
[c] U_{osm} = urine osmolality.

EVALUATION OF HYPERNATREMIA

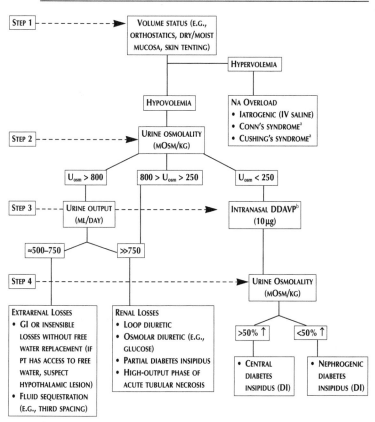

[a] See Endocrinology, Section III.B.1 and III.D.1 for Cushing's syndrome and Conn's syndrome.
[b] DDAVP = long-acting antidiuretic hormone analogue. Patients with central DI respond by successfully increasing the concentration of their urine by 50%. Patients with nephrogenic DI are unable to concentrate their urine in the presence of DDAVP. Patients with DI tend to be only mildly hypernatremic.

EVALUATION OF HYPOKALEMIA

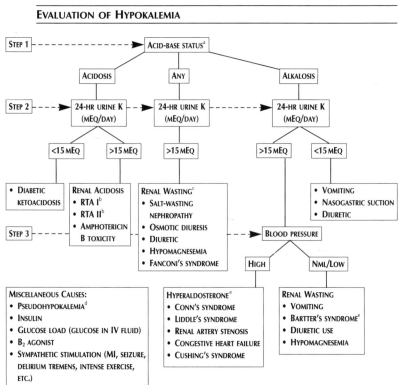

---

[a] Metabolic acidosis or alkalosis. Please see Acid-Base algorithms to determine acid-base status.
[b] RTA = Renal Tubular Acidosis. See Nephrology, Section III.F for a full description.
[c] Salt wasting nephropathies are tubulointerstitial disorders (e.g., pyelonephritis, renal medullary dz, acute tubular necrosis & allergic interstitial nephritis). For Fanconi's syndrome, see Nephrology, Section III.F.2.
[d] Pseudohypokalemia is seen in conditions with very high white blood cell counts (e.g., leukemia). The white cells take up potassium while they are sitting in the blood draw tube, creating spurious results.
[e] See Endocrinology, Sections III.B & D for Cushing's & Conn's syndromes, IV.C for congenital adrenal hyperplasia, Nephrology, Section V for renal artery stenosis, and Appendix B for Liddle's & Bartter's syndromes.

EVALUATION OF HYPERKALEMIA

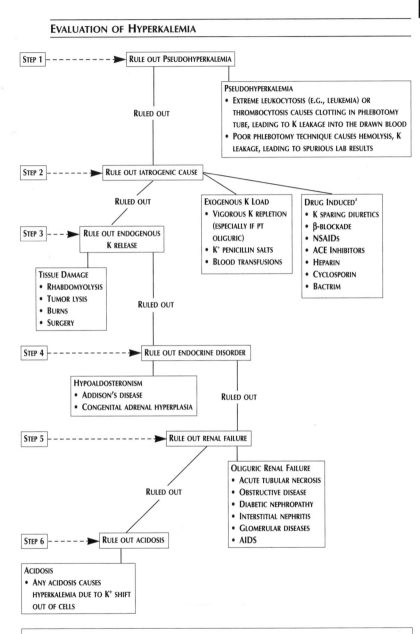

STEP 1 - - - - - - - - ▶ RULE OUT PSEUDOHYPERKALEMIA

PSEUDOHYPERKALEMIA
- EXTREME LEUKOCYTOSIS (E.G., LEUKEMIA) OR THROMBOCYTOSIS CAUSES CLOTTING IN PHLEBOTOMY TUBE, LEADING TO K LEAKAGE INTO THE DRAWN BLOOD
- POOR PHLEBOTOMY TECHNIQUE CAUSES HEMOLYSIS, K LEAKAGE, LEADING TO SPURIOUS LAB RESULTS

RULED OUT

STEP 2 - - - - - - ▶ RULE OUT IATROGENIC CAUSE

RULED OUT

EXOGENOUS K LOAD
- VIGOROUS K REPLETION (ESPECIALLY IF PT OLIGURIC)
- K$^+$ PENICILLIN SALTS
- BLOOD TRANSFUSIONS

DRUG INDUCED[a]
- K SPARING DIURETICS
- β-BLOCKADE
- NSAIDs
- ACE INHIBITORS
- HEPARIN
- CYCLOSPORIN
- BACTRIM

STEP 3 - - - ▶ RULE OUT ENDOGENOUS K RELEASE

TISSUE DAMAGE
- RHABDOMYOLYSIS
- TUMOR LYSIS
- BURNS
- SURGERY

RULED OUT

STEP 4 - - - - - - - - - ▶ RULE OUT ENDOCRINE DISORDER

HYPOALDOSTERONISM
- ADDISON'S DISEASE
- CONGENITAL ADRENAL HYPERPLASIA

RULED OUT

STEP 5 - - - - - - - - - - ▶ RULE OUT RENAL FAILURE

RULED OUT

OLIGURIC RENAL FAILURE
- ACUTE TUBULAR NECROSIS
- OBSTRUCTIVE DISEASE
- DIABETIC NEPHROPATHY
- INTERSTITIAL NEPHRITIS
- GLOMERULAR DISEASES
- AIDS

STEP 6 - - - - - ▶ RULE OUT ACIDOSIS

ACIDOSIS
- ANY ACIDOSIS CAUSES HYPERKALEMIA DUE TO K$^+$ SHIFT OUT OF CELLS

---

[a] **NSAIDs** = nonsteroidal anti-inflammatories, inhibit prostaglandins → ↓ renal perfusion → ↓ K delivery to nephron. **ACE inhibitors** block efferent arteriole constriction → ↓ GFR → ↓ K delivery to the nephron. **Heparin** blocks aldosterone production, while **cyclosporine** blocks aldosterone activity. **Bactrim** (trimethoprim) has K-sparing diuretic effect on tubules.

Internal Medicine Case Scenarios

A 52-year-old woman presents with progressive dyspnea and orthopnea for the past four months. Initially, symptoms presented only on exertion and she attributed them to lack of physical conditioning. Over the past month or so, however, she has been experiencing shortness of breath with little or no activity and sometimes even as she lies down in bed to sleep. She reports no dizziness or loss of consciousness, though she does feel the occasional palpitation. She has no personal history of heart disease but her father died at 73 of a myocardial infarction. Further review of systems was negative. Physical exam reveals a middiastolic murmur, loudest over the apex. Her radial pulse is slightly diminished in amplitude but has regular rhythm.

1. This history and physical exam is most consistent with:

   a) Mitral stenosis

   b) Bacterial endocarditis

   c) Aortic stenosis

   d) Tricuspid regurgitation

2. What would you expect to find on EKG?

   a) ST-segment elevation in the inferior leads (II, III, and aVF)

   b) Left-atrial enlargement

   c) ST-segment depression in the lateral leads (I and aVL)

   d) Irregularly irregular rhythm with P waves present

3. What else would you expect in this patient's history?

   a) Multivessel coronary artery disease

   b) Undiagnosed systemic lupus erythematosus

   c) Childhood history of pharyngitis

   d) A long pack-year history of smoking

4. What kind of arrhythmia is this patient in danger of developing?

   a) Ventricular fibrillation

   b) Atrial fibrillation

   c) Torsades des pointes

   d) Wolff-Parkinson-White syndrome

A 53-year-old man complains of weakness, lethargy, and occasional "pounding" in his heart. He is found to have a normocytic anemia and his stool is positive for occult blood. Two repeat tests for occult blood are also positive.

5. What is the next management step?

   a) Watch and wait—it is normal for middle-aged individuals to have heme ⊕ stools

   b) Tagged RBC scan to determine source of bleeding

   c) Colonoscopy—to look for possible polyps

   d) Upper endoscopy—searching for the probable gastric or duodenal ulcer

A 28-year-old woman is being treated for TB with INH, rifampin, pyrazinamide, and ethambutol.

6. What is the appropriate follow-up for this patient?

    a) Repeat mycobacterial culture every two weeks until negative

    b) Check transaminases and do vision exam every visit

    c) Repeat chest x-rays every visit

    d) No need for follow-up until drug course complete

A 22-year-old Caucasian female is seen for a routine pre-employment physical. The patient is without complaint and has a completely normal exam. She has no past medical history, no relevant family history, no known drug allergies, and does not take medications. You send her to the lab for routine blood tests and she then goes home. Several days later you receive her lab results and note that she is mildly anemic. The indices suggest a microcytic anemia. You phone her at home and ask her to come back to your office for a follow-up visit. Upon direct questioning, she indicates that her menses are regular, coming every month, and lasting about 5 days. They are not painful, and do not seem excessive.

7. The most appropriate course of action is:

    a) Schedule for flexible sigmoidoscopy, give iron replacement

    b) Refer to a gynecologist for further evaluation of menstrual blood loss

    c) Iron supplements plus erythropoietin

    d) Iron supplements plus vitamin B_{12}

    e) Check an iron panel, give iron supplements, follow-up in 2–3 months

The patient returns to see you in 3 months, and a STAT lab in the office reveals that she is still microcytic anemic. Her prior labs showed a low serum iron, low ferritin, and a high total iron binding capacity. On further questioning you learn that the patient had traveled to the Amazon basin the prior year on an archaeological expedition. She had lived in South America for more than 3 months over the summer, and had returned 6 months ago. You repeat a physical exam and finding nothing abnormal. The patient is guaiac negative, and you can find no source of ongoing blood loss. You also check a blood smear, and find no evidence of hemolysis (a finding confirmed by the normal bilirubin on her prior labs).

8. The most appropriate course of action is:

    a) Continue iron supplements for 3 more months

    b) Hemoglobin electrophoresis to screen for hemoglobinopathies

    c) Stool studies

    d) Colonoscopy

    e) Renal ultrasound

The patient's 60-year-old mother is also your patient, and comes to see you regarding increasing fatigue over the past 3 months. Her blood labs reveal that she also has a microcytic anemia. She takes a multivitamin every day, but no other medications, and has no significant past medical history. Her exam is completely normal, and she is guaiac negative. She is post-menopausal and has had no vaginal bleeding.

9. The most appropriate course of action is:

a) Colonoscopy

b) Stool studies

c) Renal ultrasound

d) Iron replacement for 3 months and then follow-up to make sure anemia is improved

e) Refer to dietitian

An 80-year-old male is admitted to the hospital from a nursing home for acute onset of altered mental status. The patient appeared disoriented upon waking this morning, and after vomiting several times was rushed to the hospital. He has had no fevers, chills, or diarrhea. He has a long history of diabetes controlled with oral hypoglycemics, coronary artery disease, and benign prostatic hypertrophy. He also has a large diabetic foot ulcer on his right sole. He has not been ill recently. On exam the patient is afebrile, but tachycardic with a blood pressure of 100/40, taking 30 breaths per minute. He appears in moderate respiratory distress. His neck veins are distended and he has bilateral rales halfway up the back. He has an apical heave and you hear an S_3. His extremity exam is notable for mild pedal edema. EKG reveals sinus tachycardia with occasional premature ventricular complexes, as well as ST elevation in leads V4 to V6. WBC count is 12,000. Chem 7 reveals Na = 136, K = 4.3, Cl = 105, HCO_3 = 22, BUN = 56, Creatinine = 2.3 (last recorded was 2 months earlier, measuring 1.4), glucose = 160. Urinalysis reveals 0 white cells, 8 red cells, negative protein, 1+ blood on dipstick, no ketones, gram-negative. Urine creatinine = 45, urine sodium = 15. Troponin is pending. CXR reveals bilateral, symmetric infiltrates consistent with pulmonary edema and an enlarged heart shadow.

10. What is the cause of this patient's acute decompensation?

a) Uremia

b) Urinary tract infection

c) Diabetic ketoacidosis

d) Pneumonia

e) Myocardial infarction

11. What is the cause of this patient's acute renal failure?

a) Hypoperfusion

b) Obstruction

c) Diabetic nephropathy

d) Urinary tract infection

e) Rhabdomyolysis

The patient is taken to the Cath lab for angioplasty. His left circumflex artery is 80% occluded, but there is no evidence of current thrombotic obstruction (i.e., the thrombus has already resolved). Balloon angioplasty with stent placement is performed. The patient tolerates the procedure well and is stable afterwards. In the coronary care unit he is persistently tachycardic, and overnight his blood cultures grow gram-negative rods. His morning BUN/Cr is 43/2.1. You give the patient a single dose of gentamicin for synergy, and then order a third-generation cephalosporin to cover the gram-negative rods. In the afternoon the patient's nurse calls you because the urine in his catheter bag is pink. STAT labs reveal a BUN/Cr of 63/3.0. Urinalysis shows 4 white cells, 68 red cells, 2+ blood, 1+ protein, ⊕ urine eosinophils. You stop the cephalosporin (the patient has received 1 dose) and switch the patient to ciprofloxacin.

12. What is the cause of the patient's worsening renal failure?

   a) Gentamicin toxicity

   b) Sepsis

   c) Atheroembolic disease

   d) Allergic interstitial nephritis

   e) Obstruction

A 36-year-old male is brought to the ER by ambulance after being found down in his apartment by a friend. The patient is unconscious, and was found lying in his own vomit, with a half-full whiskey bottle at his side. It is unclear how long he has been unconscious, since he was found on Tuesday morning after a 3-day weekend. The patient's friend told the paramedics that the patient has been a heavy drinker since he was in his teens. The patient is currently tachycardic with a BP of 160/80. He appears poorly nourished and poorly groomed. His pupils are mid-size and normoreactive. He has no evidence of cirrhosis on exam, but he does have marked hepatomegaly. His blood alcohol level is barely detectable and a STAT urine tox screen is negative. Shifting dullness cannot be appreciated, nor can a spleen be palpated. You are still waiting for the STAT CBC and full metabolic panel to come back.

13. Immediate therapy for this patient includes:

   a) naloxone

   b) 5% dextrose in normal saline at 100 cc/hr, then thiamine

   c) Thiamine, then 5% dextrose in normal saline at 100 cc/hr

   d) β-blocker

   e) Alcohol drip

The patient arouses within several hours. He is disoriented to place but he is able to carry on a conversation. He does not remember when his last drink was, but says he began binging on Friday afternoon. He confirms a long history of alcohol abuse, and says he has been through severe withdrawals several times in his life. The patient is not agitated and denies any hallucinations. He does appear somewhat tremulous. His heart rate and BP are 110 and 180/96.

14. Appropriate therapy at this time is:

   a) β-blocker

   b) Alcohol drip

   c) IV normal saline

   d) Antabuse

   e) Benzodiazepine

A 38-year-old female is rushed to the hospital after complaining of retrosternal, crushing chest pain while sitting at her desk at work. The patient is diaphoretic and complains of nausea. She describes the chest pain as 8 out of 10 in intensity, and it is not relieved by sublingual nitroglycerin. The patient has a history of a mild skin rash for which she has not sought medical attention. For the past several weeks she has been having intermittent fevers and muscle aches. She does not smoke, is not diabetic, and has no family history of cardiac disease, and is still menstruating. She has never before had chest pain or any sign of cardiac disease. She takes ibuprofen occasionally for her "bad knees." The patient is tachycardic to 108, with a blood pressure of 140/80. She is afebrile and breathing at 20 respirations per minute, and her oxygen saturation is 93% on room air, improving to 98% with 3 L oxygen by nasal cannula. She is a well-developed, non-obese female in acute distress. She has several coin-shaped hyperpigmented plaques on her face and neck. She has an apical mid-systolic murmur and a vigorous pleural rub on auscultation. Abdomen is flat, without hepatomegaly. Her spleen tip is palpable. Both of her knees and her right elbow are swollen and tender to the touch. EKG shows ST elevations and Q waves in II, III, and AVF, with diffuse T-wave inversions. Her troponin is pending. White blood count is 13,000, with a hemoglobin of 11 and platelets of 101. Chem 7 is normal except for a creatinine of 1.4. Liver panel reveals Total Bilirubin of 1.7, with a Direct Bilirubin of 0.4, but normal transaminases. PT/INR is normal but her PTT is prolonged. Albumin and total protein are normal. Urinalysis shows 0 white cells, 2 red cells, 2+ protein, and RBC casts. CXR shows small bilateral pleural effusions.

15. What is the underlying disorder?

   a) Marfan's syndrome

   b) Hyperthyroidism

   c) Factor V deficiency

   d) Systemic lupus erythematosus

   e) Subacute bacterial endocarditis

The patient is thrombolysed with streptokinase per protocol and stabilizes quickly. She is started on aspirin and a β-blocker and does well for the rest of the day. Her oxygen saturation improves somewhat, to 95% on room air. The next morning an echocardiogram confirms inferior wall dyskinesis. Shortly after the echocardiogram, the patient's nurse pages you to tell you that she is desaturating. You rush to her bedside and find her in moderate respiratory distress. Her oxygen saturation on room air is 87%, and improves only to 91% on 6 liters of nasal cannula O_2. She has become dyspneic and increasingly tachypneic, and complains of pleuritic chest pain. You order a stat CXR that shows the same bilateral pleural effusions with no interval change. The arterial blood gas, which you sent off before starting the patient on the nasal cannula, shows hypoxia and mild respiratory alkalosis. EKG reveals a broad S wave in lead I, with decreases in the ST elevations in the inferior leads.

16. What management steps would you take now?

   a) Face mask O_2 and antibiotics

   b) Spiral CT and heparin

   c) Check a troponin level

   d) Thoracentesis

   e) Morphine

A 46-year-old obese male is brought to the ER by paramedics after passing out on the street. No medical records are available. The patient is currently delirious and unable to provide any history. He is febrile to 101.5°F, and tachycardic to 116, with a blood pressure of 160/90. He is breathing at 12 per minute, with very deep inspirations. You note soft exudates and possibly flame hemorrhages bilaterally on funduscopic exam. His oral mucosa is dry and his neck veins are flat. Cardiac, respiratory, and extremity exams are unremarkable. Labs are as follows: Na = 146, K = 5.0, Cl = 104, HCO_3 = 13, BUN = 38, Cr = 1.6, glucose = 360. White count is 13,000, H & H are 14.6/48. Urinalysis reveals 0 white cells, 2 red cells, 3+ protein, +glucose, +ketones, urine sodium = 10, urine creatinine = 30. CXR is normal. EKG shows sinus tachycardia with no ST/T changes.

17. What is your diagnosis?

    a) Hypothyroidism

    b) Renal failure

    c) Stroke

    d) Myocardial infarction

    e) Diabetic ketoacidosis

After 2 hours of hydration, the patient becomes more alert and begins to complain of a severe headache. He keeps rubbing his maxillary prominence, and when you press your fingers over the maxillary sinus he literally jumps in pain.

18. What action do you take?

    a) Start po Bactrim

    b) Start IV amoxicillin/clavulanic acid

    c) Administer ibuprofen

    d) STAT head CT

    e) Slow the rate of the insulin drip

Answers

1. **a)** This patient complains of dyspnea and orthopnea, the hallmarks of valvular disease. Bacterial endocarditis (b) would have also presented with fevers or chills or other signs of infection. (NOTE: she is now at high risk for developing endocarditis in the future because of her valvular lesion.) The main clue lies in the quality of the murmur: first, it is a diastolic murmur, which rules out the systolic murmur of aortic stenosis (c). Also, the murmur was heard best over the apex of the heart, also known as the mitral auscultatory area.

2. **b)** Because of difficulty of blood flow through the stenosed mitral valve, blood will remain in the left atrium and enlarge it. ST-changes are more consistent with myocardial infarction (a) or ischemia (c). Irregularly irregular rhythm without P waves is consistent with atrial fibrillation, previously discounted by our physical examination!

3. **c)** Most patients with mitral stenosis have evidence of rheumatic heart disease, though few ever experience rheumatic fever. This infection is caused by group A Strep and usually occurs in childhood. Rheumatic heart disease is actually more common with cutaneous Strep infections, but can also occur with pharyngitis. Multivessel coronary artery disease (a) and smoking (d) would more likely cause ischemic heart disease. Lupus (b) manifests as pericarditis or Libman-Sacks endocarditis.

4. **b)** Enlargement of her right atrium may eventually cause conduction defects and irritation of the myocardium, leading to the development of alternate foci of excitation. This manifests itself as atrial fibrillation. V-Fib is usually seen in the context of ischemic heart disease, especially after myocardial infarction with ventricular involvement. Torsades is caused mostly by drugs or hypokalemia. Wolff-Parkinson-White syndrome refers to a specific arrhythmia where a conduction tract between the atria and ventricles allows the atrial impulse to bypass the A-V node and arrive at the ventricles; this has nothing causally to do with valvular disease.

5. **c)** Anemia in a middle-aged male is colon cancer until proven otherwise—especially if paired with definitely blood-positive stool! In this population, watching and waiting (a) is not advised. Tagged RBC scans (b) are more useful if bleeding is brisk (i.e., diverticular bleeding or A-V malformations). Upper endoscopy is indicated in upper GI bleeding, which usually presents as melena rather than occult blood. Colonoscopy also has the added benefit of being able to obtain a tissue sample for biopsy or removing any overt polyps.

6. **b)** INH, rifampin, and pyrazinamide are notoriously hepatotoxic (especially INH) and monthly transaminases are indicated in anyone receiving TB treatment. Elevation to three times normal requires discontinuation of current treatment and reevaluation. In addition, ethambutol can cause optic neuritis that is reversible on discontinuation of the drug. The best vision test is actually red–green color differentiation. There is no need to repeat mycobacterial culture every two weeks (a) because they take six to eight weeks to grow and therefore have no value as a means for following treatment. Repeat chest x-rays (c) are not useful because scarring and other tubercular changes may remain even months after the disease has been successfully treated. (d) just makes no sense.

7. **e)** The most likely cause of microcytic anemia in a young, otherwise healthy female is menstruation. The patient does not have to have menorrhagia or other gynecological disease to explain a mild anemia secondary to menses. The flexible sigmoidoscopy is not warranted in a young healthy person with no family history of an inherited familial polyposis. Erythropoietin is appropriate therapy for anemia of renal failure, which is usually normocytic and which is seen in older patients with a long history of kidney disease. Although vitamin B_{12} supplements cannot hurt, they are not indicated for a microcytic anemia. The most prudent course of action is to prescribe iron supplements and to confirm the

presumed iron deficiency by drawing a routine iron panel of blood tests. The patient should return to the doctor's office in several months to confirm that the iron supplements are treating her anemia.

8. **c)** The patient's iron panel confirms that she had an iron deficiency anemia. However, 3 months of iron supplements should have corrected a mild deficiency secondary to menses. Furthermore, her travel history is very important. The most common cause of iron deficiency anemia worldwide is intestinal parasite infection (i.e., hookworm). The patient lived for a prolonged period of time in an area where hookworm infections occur. Thus, checking her stool for ova and parasites is the next step. In a Caucasian female the probability of having a hemoglobinopathy is very low. As mentioned, colonoscopy and renal ultrasound (to detect chronic renal failure) are tests appropriate for older patients or patients with significant medical or family histories.

9. **a)** Iron deficiency anemia in an older patient is colon cancer until proven otherwise. This patient must have an appropriate test to visualize her large bowel.

10. **e)** The ST elevations on EKG are diagnostic of acute myocardial infarction, even without confirmation of cardiac enzymes (e.g., troponin). The BUN/Cr are not nearly high enough to consider uremia. There is no evidence of a UTI in this patient (should see pyuria), and there is no evidence that the patient is in ketoacidosis (normal anion gap, normal serum HCO_3, no urine ketones). Although pneumonia should be considered, the fact that the patient's neck veins are distended, he has a precordial heave and an S_3 on auscultation, he has pedal edema, and an enlarged heart shadow on CXR are all consistent with a diagnosis of pulmonary edema secondary to acute heart failure. Since myocardial infarction can precipitate acute congestive heart failure, pulmonary edema is the most likely cause for the bilateral infiltrates. Note that myocardial infarction can also cause altered mental status (i.e., delirium) and leukocytosis.

11. **a)** This patient is prerenal. The evidence for this is overwhelming: urine Na < 20, BUN/Cr > 20, and, particularly, the FeNa is < 1% (U_{na} * S_{Cr} / U_{cr} * S_{Na} = 15 * 2.3 / 136 * 45 = 0.56%). Furthermore, the patient is hypotensive due to pump failure, consistent with insufficient blood flow to the kidneys. The negative protein on urine dipstick makes diabetic nephropathy very unlikely, and in rhabdomyolysis the dipstick test for blood, which detects hemoglobin, should be markedly positive even if few RBCs are seen.

12. **c)** Although allergic interstitial nephritis is a concern, the fact that the patient received only 1 dose of the cephalosporin before the marked jump in creatinine mitigates against this possibility. A single dose of gentamicin is not likely responsible for the worsening renal failure, and the urine eosinophils are not consistent with this diagnosis. Urine eosinophils are specific for interstitial nephritis or atheroembolic disease. This patient, in particular, has a major risk factor for atheroembolic disease, having recently had a major intravascular procedure (the PTCA with stenting).

13. **c)** The concept addressed in this question is the need to administer thiamine to alcoholics before giving them any dextrose IV. Administration of dextrose will precipitate a Wernicke's encephalopathy in these patients unless thiamine is repleted beforehand. Alcohol drip is used in patients with methanol toxicity. The patient has no evidence of narcotic ingestion (note pupils and negative toxicology screen), so naloxone is not indicated. There is no indication for a β-blocker.

14. **e)** This patient must be treated for alcohol withdrawal and the presumed onset of delirium tremens (DTs). Remember that hallucinations and agitation are later markers of DTs (about 72 hours), and that autonomic instability and tremulousness are earlier markers (48 hours). The best treatment for DTs is prevention. The fact that this patient has had prior episodes of "severe withdrawals," combined with the persistent tachycardia and hypertension, should warn you that the onset of DTs is likely imminent.

15. **d)** This patient has 6 out of the 11 criteria for diagnosing SLE. She has a rash consistent with discoid lupus on her face and neck. She has large joint arthritis (knees). She has evidence of immunologic disease, as her prolonged PTT without apparent liver disease is consistent with the lupus anticoagulant. She has evidence of renal involvement, with elevated creatinine, 2+ protein on urinalysis, and RBC casts that are virtually pathognomonic for glomerular disease. She has serositis, as evidenced by a pleural rub on auscultation and pleural effusions, both of which are consistent with pleuritis. Finally, she has hematologic disease, with hemolytic anemia (hemoglobin of 11, elevated indirect bilirubin, splenomegaly). Furthermore, myocardial infarction in a young, otherwise healthy female with no known risk factors is highly suspicious for lupus, which causes a thrombogenic state (remember, the lupus anticoagulant is actually thrombogenic in vivo). Although bacterial endocarditis could explain joint swelling, serositis and a murmur, as well as intermittent fevers, it cannot account for the prolonged PTT, the myocardial infarction, or the discoid-like rash. None of the other diagnoses can account for the diverse array of signs and symptoms with which this patient presents. Of note, factor V Leiden deficiency increases the risk of venous but not arterial thrombosis, and thus does not increase the risk of myocardial infarction.

16. **b)** The sudden onset of hypoxia with pleuritic chest pain, particularly in a patient who is known to be hypercoagulable, should set off warning bells for pulmonary embolism. Remember the classic EKG findings (even though they are seen less often than sinus tachycardia) of $S_IQ_{III}T_{III}$; this patient already has a Q in III from her infarct, and now has a new onset deep S in I. The routine use of heparin in myocardial infarction is controversial unless tPA (but not streptokinase) has been used for thrombolysis; all patients who receive tPA should be heparinized (tPA creates a thrombogenic state immediately postclot lysis). Since this patient received streptokinase, heparin is not indicated for the infarct. However, heparin probably should have been started for the patient's lupus anticoagulant, and certainly should be started now that pulmonary embolism

is suspected. Spiral CT or V/Q scans are appropriate tests for assessing the probability of pulmonary embolism. Even if we suspected a new infarction (which is not evidenced on the EKG), checking a troponin level is not likely to be helpful, because we know it will be elevated from the prior day's infarct. Thoracentesis is not indicated; we already have the diagnosis of lupus pleuritis, so it will not be diagnostically useful, and since the pleural effusion has not changed in size, it is not responsible for the new onset hypoxia. Morphine will only exacerbate the hypoxia by slowing respirations.

17. **e)** This is a clear case of diabetic ketoacidosis. The patient's obesity and the findings on funduscopic exam (hemorrhages and exudates), as well as the proteinuria, glucosuria, and high blood glucose are all consistent with the diagnosis of diabetes. Furthermore the patient has an anion gap acidosis and ketones in his urine. The acute renal insufficiency is due to prerenal hypoperfusion (FeNa = 0.36%). There is no evidence of myocardial infarction on EKG, and the altered mental status is easily explained by the ketoacidosis, so the presence of a stroke does not have to be inferred. There is no evidence of hypothyroidism.

18. **d)** Patients with diabetic ketoacidosis should always be carefully evaluated for underlying infection. One dreaded infection seen specifically in ketoacidosis is *Mucor* sinusitis. Every diabetic ketoacidosis patient complaining of headache or sinus pain should be carefully evaluated to rule out this fungal infection. A head CT is the most accurate way to do this, and it should be ordered STAT because the primary treatment for *Mucor* is rapid and extensive surgical débridement. Antifungal agents are of limited utility.

2. Surgery

Ming-Sing Si
Eric Daniels

I. Fluid and Electrolytes

A. PHYSIOLOGY (See Figure 2-1)
1. 50–70% of lean body weight is water, most of it is in skeletal muscle
2. Total body water (TBW) is divided into extracellular (1/3) & intracellular (2/3) compartments
3. Extracellular water
   a. Comprises 20% of lean body weight
   b. 25% intravascular & 75% extravascular (interstitial)
4. Intracellular water comprises 40% of lean body weight

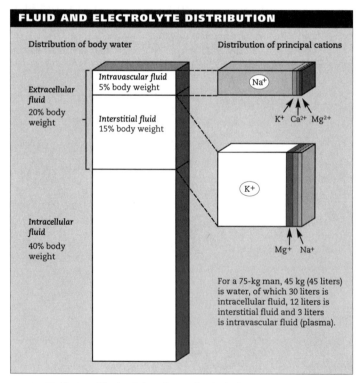

FLUID AND ELECTROLYTE DISTRIBUTION

Distribution of body water

Distribution of principal cations

Extracellular fluid
20% body weight

Intravascular fluid
5% body weight

Na^+

K^+ Ca^{2+} Mg^{2+}

Interstitial fluid
15% body weight

K^+

Intracellular fluid
40% body weight

Mg^+ Na^+

For a 75-kg man, 45 kg (45 liters) is water, of which 30 liters is intracellular fluid, 12 liters is interstitial fluid and 3 liters is intravascular fluid (plasma).

FIGURE 2-1   Distribution of fluid and electrolytes within the body.

B. FLUID MANAGEMENT
1. 3 for 1 rule   *every 1L lost blood, 3 L fluids given*
   a. By 1–2 hours after a 1 L infusion of isotonic saline or lactated Ringer's, only 300 mL remains in the intravascular compartment
   b. **Thus 3–4 times the vascular deficit should be administered** if isotonic crystalloid solutions are used for resuscitation
2. Colloid solutions (contain high molecular weight molecules, e.g., albumin, hetastarch & dextrans) stay in the intravascular space longer
3. Colloids are more expensive than crystalloids & are most useful in the edematous patient where, for instance, 100 mL of 1% albumin solution will be able to draw about 400 mL from the extravascular compartment, thus decreasing edema

C. HYDRATION OF SURGICAL PATIENTS
1. Pts are commonly NPO (Nothing Per Oral) & require IV fluid hydration
2. An uncomplicated pt without oral intake loses ≥1 L of fluid a day from sweat, urine, feces & respiration
3. Adequate fluid hydration is indicated by **urine output ≥$\frac{1}{2}$ cc/kg/hr (for typical patient ≥30 cc/hr)** & by measuring daily weight changes
4. Electrolytes should be replaced as necessary
   a. Salivary & colon secretions are high in K^+
   b. Stomach, ileum & bile secretions are high in Cl^-
   c. Salivary, ileum, pancreas & bile secretions are high in HCO_3^-

D. COMMON ELECTROLYTE DISORDERS

TABLE 2-1   Common Electrolyte Disorders

DISORDER	DDX	SI/SX	TX
↑ Na^+	• Fluid loss • Steroid use • Hypertonic fluids	• Lethargy, weakness, irritability • Can be severe → seizures & coma	• Normal saline IV • Correct 1/2 the deficit in first 24 hr & the second 1/2 over 2–3 days
↓ Na^+	• Copious bladder irrigation s/p TURP* • High output ileostomy • Adrenal insufficiency	• Severe (<115 mmol/L) → seizures, nausea, vomiting, stupor, or coma	• Water restriction • Hypertonic saline IV & loop diuretics
↑ K^+	• Acidosis • ↓ insulin • Leukocytosis • Burns • Crush injury	• Neuromuscular & cardiac sequelae (heart block, v-fib & asystole) • EKG → peaked T waves, flattened P waves, wide QRS, eventually a sinusoidal pattern	• Stabilize cardiac membranes with IV calcium gluconate • Glucose & insulin infusion • Albuterol & loop diuretics • Binding resins (Kayexalate) & dialysis longer term
↓ K^+	• Diarrhea, NG suction & vomiting • Diuretics, met. alk. • Cushing's, burns, β-agonists, ↓ Mg^{++}	• Ectopy, T-wave depression, prominent U waves • Also V-Tach & increased sensitivity to digoxin	• Oral supplements unless the patient is NPO • Infusion of K^+ over ≤ 10 mEq/hr • Correction of hypomagnesemia • K^+ sparing diuretics

TABLE 2-1   *Continued*

DISORDER	DDx	SI/SX	TX
↑ Ca⁺⁺	• Malignancy (#1 cause in inpatients) • Disorders involving bone, parathyroid, or kidneys	• Altered mental status, muscle weakness, ileus, constipation, nausea & vomiting • Nephrolithiasis • QT interval shortening	• Calcium restriction • Hydration & loop diuretics • Calcitonin, pamidronate • Dialysis
↓ Ca⁺⁺	• Acute pancreatitis • Blood transfusion • Parathyroid resection • ↓ Mg⁺⁺ • Renal failure	• Chvostek's & Trousseau's signs • Paresthesias, tetany, seizures, weakness & mental status changes • QT interval prolonged	• Calcium gluconate • Vitamin D supplement
↑ Mg⁺⁺	• Overzealous Mg⁺⁺ supplements in patients with renal failure	• Lethargy, weakness, ↓ deep tendon reflexes • Paralysis, ↓ BP & HR • Prolonged PR & QT intervals	• Calcium gluconate • Normal saline infusion with a loop diuretic • Dialysis
↓ Mg⁺⁺	• Diarrhea, malabsorption • Vomiting • Aggressive diuresis, alcoholism, chemoTx	• Torsades des pointes, • v-fib, atrial tach & atrial fib • Hyperreflexia & tetany • T wave & QRS widening PR & QT intervals prolonged	• MgSO₄
↑ Phos	• Usually iatrogenic • Rhabdomyolysis • Hypoparathyroid • Hypocalcemia	• Can cause soft-tissue calcification • Heart block	• Decrease dietary phosphorus • Aluminum hydroxide • Hydration & acetazolamide • Dialysis
↓ Phos	• Excessive IV glucose • Hyperparathyroidism • Osmotic diuresis	• Diffuse weakness & flaccid paralysis (all due to decreased ATP production)	• Potassium phosphate or sodium phosphate

*TURP = transurethral resection of prostate.

II. Blood Product Replacement

A. NORMAL HEMOSTASIS

1. Coagulation involves endothelium, platelets & coagulation factors
2. Endothelial damage allows platelets to bind to subendothelium, inducing platelet release of ADP, 5-HT, PDGF, which promote platelet aggregation
3. Initial thrombus stabilized by fibrin laid down by coagulation factors
4. Coagulation cascades
   a. The two coagulation pathways share factors I, II, V & X
   b. Extrinsic pathway
      1) Tissue thromboplastin (tissue factor) activates factor VII, which then activates factor X
      2) Measured in vitro by prothrombin time (PT)
   c. Intrinsic pathway

1) Factor XII → XI → IX → VIII, activated factor VIII causes activation of the common factor X

2) Measured in vitro by partial thromboplastin time (PTT)

d. Factor I = fibrin, which cross-links platelets to provide the tensile strength needed to stabilize the thrombus

5. Vitamin K is fat soluble, derived from leafy vegetables & colonic flora

   a. Cofactor for γ-carboxylation of factors II, VII, IX, X & the anticoagulation factors, proteins C & S, enables them to interact with Ca^{2+}

   b. Deficiency caused by malabsorption, prolonged parenteral feeding, prolonged oral antibiotics, or ingestion of oral anticoagulants

   c. First sign is prolonged PT, due to the short half-life of factor VII

B. PREOPERATIVE EVALUATION OF BLEEDING DISORDERS

1. Si/Sx = Hx or FHx of ↑ bleeding following minor cuts, dental procedures, menses, or past surgeries, ecchymoses or sequelae of liver dz

2. Ask about NSAID or herbal medicine intake the week of surgery

3. Bleeding time

   a. Evaluates platelet function

   b. ↑ bleeding time indicates quantitative or qualitative platelet dz

   c. Also ↑ in von Willebrand's dz & vasculitis

4. Thrombin time (TT)

   a. Measures the time to clot after the addition of thrombin, which is responsible for conversion of fibrinogen to fibrin

   b. ↑ TT may be due to ↑ fibrin, dysfibrinogenemia, DIC, or heparin

5. **Routine preoperative lab screening is not warranted without Si/Sx suggestive of underlying disorder**

C. TRANSFUSIONS

1. Packed red blood cells (pRBCs)

   a. Type & screen = pt's RBCs tested for A, B & Rh antigens & donor's serum screened for antibodies to common RBC antigens

   b. Cross-match = when the pt's serum checked for preformed antibodies against the donor's RBCs

   c. In trauma situations, type O negative blood is given while additional units are being typed & crossed

   d. **1 unit pRBCs should ↑ hemoglobin by 1 g/dL & ↑ hematocrit 3%**

   e. Complications

      1) Acute rejection

         a) Due to preformed antibodies against the donor RBCs

         b) Si/Sx = anxiety, flushing, tachycardia, renal failure, shock

         c) **The most common cause is clerical error**

         d) Recheck all paperwork & repeat cross-match

         e) Tx = stop transfusion, IV fluids to maintain urine output

      2) Infectious diseases

         a) HCV is by far the most common cause of hepatitis in pts who prior received transfusions, although risk of new HCV infection is now lower with blood bank screening

         b) Current risks

TABLE 2-2   Risk of Viral Infection from Blood Transfusions

DISEASE	ESTIMATED RISK*
Hepatitis B	1 case per 50,000 units transfused
Hepatitis C	1 case per 50,000 units transfused
HIV	1 case per 300,000 units transfused

*Mean estimates from *New Engl J Med* 1999, 340:438–47.

2. Platelet transfusions
  a. Pts do not bleed significantly until platelets <50,000/μL, so transfusion should be given only to maintain this level
  b. If pt is anticipated to experience severe blood loss intraoperatively or the pt is actively bleeding transfuse to maintain even higher
  c. Most common complication is alloimmunization
    1) Platelet counts fail to rise despite continued transfusion
    2) Caused by induction of antibodies against the donor's MHC type
    3) Single donor, HLA-matched platelets may overcome problem
3. Plasma component transfusion
  a. Plasma products do not require cross-matching but donor & recipient should be ABO compatible
  b. Fresh frozen plasma (FFP)
    1) Contains all the coagulation factors
    2) Used to correct all clotting factor deficiencies
  c. Cryoprecipitate is rich in factor VIII, fibrinogen & fibronectin

III. Perioperative Care

A. PREOPERATIVE CARE
1. All pts require detailed history & physical
2. Laboratory tests
  a. CBC for pts undergoing procedure that may incur large blood loss
  b. Electrolytes, BUN & creatinine in pts over 60yr or who have illnesses (e.g., diarrhea, liver & renal dz) or take medications (e.g., diuretics) that predispose them to electrolyte disorders
  c. UA in pts with urological Sx or those having urologic procedures
  d. PT & PTT in pts with bleeding diathesis, with liver disease, or who are undergoing neurosurgery or cardiac surgery
  e. Liver function tests in pts with liver disease
  f. CXR in pts with ↑ risk of pulmonary complications (e.g., obesity or thoracic procedures) & those with preexisting pulmonary problems
  g. EKG in males >40, females >50, or young pts with preexisting cardiac dz

B. PERIOPERATIVE REVIEW OF SYSTEMS
1. Neurological
  a. Cerebrovascular disease
    1) Strokes usually occur postop & are caused by hypotension or emboli from atrial fibrillation

2) Patients with a recent history of strokes should have their surgical procedure delayed 6 wk

3) Anticoagulation should stop 2 weeks prior to surgery if possible

2. Cardiovascular
   a. Most postop complications are cardiac related
   b. Goldman cardiac risk index stratifies the operative risk of noncardiac surgery pts & helps in the decision of pursuing further Dx testing
   c.

TABLE 2-3   Goldman Cardiac Risk Index

CONDITION	POINTS	CONCERN
S3 gallop, JVD	11	CHF
MI within 6 mo	10	Cardiac injury
Abnormal EKG rhythm	7	Diseased cardiac conduction
>5 PVCs/min	7	Cardiac excitability
Age > 70	5	Increased comorbidity
General poor health	3	Increased morbidity
Aortic stenosis	3	Left ventricular outflow obstruction
Peritoneal/thoracic/aortic surgery	3	Major surgery
Emergency	3	Emergency surgery
>26 points warrants life-saving procedures only due to ↑↑↑ risk of cardiac-related death		

3. Pulmonary
   a. Pulmonary complications rarely occur in healthy pts
   b. COPD is the most important & significant risk factor to consider
   c. Obesity, abdominal, & intrathoracic procedures predispose pts to pulmonary complications in the postoperative period
   d. Smoking Hx, independent of COPD, is also an important risk factor

4. Renal
   a. Postop acute renal failure → ≥50% mortality despite hemodialysis
   b. Chronic renal failure is a significant risk factor not only because of the ↑ risk of developing acute failure, but because of the associated metabolic disturbances & underlying medical conditions
   c. Azotemia, sepsis, intraoperative hypotension, nephrotoxic drugs & radiocontrast agents are risk factors for postoperative renal failure
   d. Preventive measures include expanding the intravascular volume with IV fluids & use of diuretics after administration of radiocontrast dye

5. Infection/Immunity
   a. Infection risk depends upon patient characteristics & surgery
   b. Advanced age, diabetes, immunosuppression, obesity, preexisting infection & preexisting illness all increase risk
   c. Surgical risk factors include GI surgery, prosthetic implantation, preoperative wound contamination & duration of the operation
   d. Prophylaxis

1) To prevent surgical wound infections, antibiotics should be administered before the skin incision is made
2) Appropriate choice of the antibiotics depends on the procedure
3) Give all patients with prosthetic heart valves antibiotic prophylaxis to prevent bacterial endocarditis

6. Hematologic
   a. Deep venous thrombosis (DVT) prevented by early ambulation & mechanical compression stockings
   b. Subcutaneous heparin may be substituted for compression stockings
   c. Pulmonary embolus should always be considered as a cause of postop acute onset dyspnea

7. Endocrinology
   a. Adrenal insufficiency
      1) Surgery creates stress for the body, normally the body reacts to stress by secreting more corticosteroids
      2) Response may be diminished in pts taking corticosteroids for ≥ 1 week preoperatively & pts with primary adrenal insufficiency
      3) Hence, for these patients, steroid replacement is needed, & **hydrocortisone is given before, during & after surgery to approximate the response of the normal adrenal gland.** If these measures are not taken, then adrenal crisis may occur.
      4) Adrenal crisis
         a) A life-threatening complication of adrenal insufficiency
         b) **Si/Sx = unexplained hypotension & tachycardia despite fluid & vasopressor administration**
         c) Tx = corticosteroids dramatically improve BP

C. FEVER

1. Intraoperative fever
   a. DDx = transfusion reaction, malignant hyperthermia, or prior infxn
   b. Malignant hyperthermia
      1) Triggered by several anesthetic agents, e.g., halothane, isoflurane & succinylcholine
      2) Tx = dantrolene, cooling measures, ICU monitoring
2. Postoperative fever
   a. **Mnemonic for causes: the 5 Ws**
      1) Wind (lungs)
      2) Water (urinary tract)
      3) Wound
      4) Walking (DVT)
      5) Wonder drug (drug reaction)
   b. Immediate postoperative fever includes atelectasis, *Streptococcus* & *Clostridium* wound infections & aspiration pneumonia
   c. 1–2 days postoperatively look for indwelling vascular line infection, aspiration pneumonia & infectious pneumonia
   d. Tx = encourage early postoperative ambulation, incentive spirometry use postoperatively, treat infections with appropriate antibiotics

IV. Trauma

A. GENERAL
1. Trauma is the major cause of death in those under age 40
2. Management broken into primary & secondary surveys

B. PRIMARY SURVEY = ABCDE
1. **A** = **A**irway
   a. All pts immobilized due to ↑ risk of spinal injury
   b. Maintain airway with jaw thrust or mandible/ tongue traction, protecting cervical spine
   c. If pt is likely to vomit, position them in a slightly lateral & head-down position to prevent aspiration
   d. If airway cannot be established, 2 large bore (14-gauge) needles can be inserted into the cricothyroid membrane
   e. Do not perform tracheotomy in the field or ambulance
   f. Unconscious patients need endotracheal (ET) tube!
2. **B** = **B**reathing
   a. Assess chest expansion, breath sounds, respiratory rate, rib fractures, sub-Q emphysema & penetrating wounds
   b. Life-threatening injuries to the lungs or thoracic cavity are:
      1) Tension pneumothorax → contralateral mediastinal shift, distended neck veins (↑ CVP), hypotension, ↓ breath sounds on 1 side & hyperresonance on the other side, Tx = immediate chest tube or 14-gauge needle puncture of affected side
      2) Open pneumothorax → Tx = immediate closure of the wound with dressings & placement of a chest tube
      3) Flail chest → caused by multiple rib fractures that form a free-floating segment of chest wall that moves paradoxically to the rest of the chest wall, resulting in an inability to generate sufficient inspiratory or expiratory pressure to drive ventilation, Tx = intubation with mechanical ventilation
      4) Massive hemothorax → injury to the great vessels with subsequent hemorrhage into the thoracic cavity, Tx = chest tube, surgical control of the bleeding site
3. **C** = **C**irculation
   a. 2 large bore IVs placed in upper extremities (if possible)
   b. For severe shock, place a central venous line
   c. O-negative blood on stand-by for any suspected significant hemorrhage
4. **D** = **D**isability
   a. Neurologic disability assessed by history, careful neurologic examination (Glasgow Coma Scale), laboratory tests (blood alcohol level, blood cultures, blood glucose, ammonia, electrolytes & urinalysis) & skull x-rays
   b. Loss of consciousness
      1) DDx = **AEIOU TIPS** = **A**lcohol, **E**pilepsy, **E**nvironment (temp), **I**nsulin(+/–), **O**verdose, **U**remia (electrolytes), **T**rauma, **I**nfection, **P**sychogenic, **S**troke
      2) Tx = Coma cocktail = dextrose, thiamine, naloxone & O_2
   c. ↑ ICP → HTN, bradycardia & bradypnea = Cushing's triad
   d. Tx = ventilation to keep $PaCO_2$ at 30–40 mm Hg, controlling fever, administration of osmotic diuretics (mannitol), corticosteroids & even bony decompression (burr hole)

5. **E** = Exposure
   a. Remove all clothes without moving pt (cut off if necessary)
   b. Examine all skin surfaces & back for possible exit wounds
   c. Ensure patient not at risk for hypothermia (small children)

C. SECONDARY SURVEY

1. Identify all injuries, examine all body orifices
2. Periorbital & mastoid hematomas ("raccoon eyes" & Battle's sign), hemotympanum & CSF otorrhea/rhinorrhea → basilar skull fractures
3. The Glasgow Coma Scale should be performed

TABLE 2-4   Glasgow Coma Scale

FINDING	POINTS	FINDING	POINTS
Eye Opening		**Motor Response**	
Spontaneous	4	To command	6
To voice	3	Localizes	5
To stimulation (pain)	2	Withdraws	4
No response	1	Abnormal flexion	3
Verbal Response		Extension	2
Oriented	5	No response	1
Confused	4		
Incoherent	3		
Incomprehensible	2		
No response	1		
GCS < 8 indicates severe neurologic injury, intubation must be performed to secure airway.			

4. Deaths from abdominal trauma are usually from sepsis due to hollow viscus perforation or hemorrhage if major vessels are penetrated
5. Diagnostic peritoneal lavage, abdominal Utz, or CT scan (if pt stable) suggests abdominal injury, if pt unstable Dx is by surgical laparotomy, Tx = surgical hemostasis
6. If blood noted at urethra perform retrograde urethrogram before placement of a bladder catheter, hematuria suggests significant retroperitoneal injury & requires CT scan for evaluation, take pt to OR for surgical exploration if unstable
7. Check for compartment syndrome of extremities, Si/Sx = tense, pale, paralyzed, paresthetic & painful extremity, Tx = fasciotomy

D. SHOCK

1.

TABLE 2-5   Differential Diagnosis of Shock

TYPE	CARDIAC OUTPUT	PULMONARY CAPILLARY WEDGE PRESSURE	PERIPHERAL VASCULAR RESISTANCE
Hypovolemic	↓	↓	↑
Cardiogenic	↓	↑	↑
Septic	↑	↓	↓

2.

TABLE 2-6   Correction of Defect in Shock

TYPE	DEFECT	FIRST-LINE TREATMENT
Hypovolemic	↓ preload	2 large bore IVs, crystalloid or colloid infusions [see Fluids and Electrolytes above], replace blood losses with the **3 for 1** rule = give 3 L of fluid per liter of blood loss
Cardiogenic	Myocardial failure	Pressors—dobutamine first line, can add dopamine &/or norepinephrine, supplemental O_2
Septic	↓ peripheral vascular resistance	Norepinephrine to vasoconstrict peripheral arterioles, prevent progression to multiple organ dysfunction syndrome (MODS), give IV antibiotics as indicated, supplemental O_2

3. Shock in trauma can be neurogenic or hypovolemic
4. Neurogenic due to blood pooling in splanchnic bed & muscle from loss of autonomic innervation
5. Tx = usually self-limiting, can be managed by placing pt in supine or Trendelenburg position

V. Burns

A. PARTIAL THICKNESS
1. 1° & 2° burns are limited to epidermis & superficial dermis
2. Si/Sx = skin is red, blistered, edematous, skin underneath blister is pink or white in appearance, very painful
3. Infection may convert to full-thickness burns

B. FULL THICKNESS
1. 3° & 4° burns affect all layers of skin & subcutaneous tissues
2. Si/Sx = skin is initially painless, dry, white, charred, cracked, insensate
3. 4° burns also involve muscle & bone
4. All full-thickness burns require surgical treatment
5. % of body surface area (BSA) affected (See Figure 2-2)

TABLE 2-7   Body Surface Area in Burns

Palm of hand	1%	Upper extremities*	9%
Head & neck*	9%	Lower extremities*	18%
Anterior trunk*	18%	Genital area*	1%
Posterior trunk*	18%		

*In adults.

FIGURE 2-2   Rule of nines.

6. Tx = resuscitation, monitor fluid status, remove eschars
   a. Consider any facial burns or burning of nasal hairs as a potential candidate for ARDS & airway compromise
   b. Fluid resuscitation
      1) Parkland formula = % BSA × weight (kg) ×4, formula used to calculate volume of crystalloid needed
      2) Give ½ of fluid in first 8 hr, remainder given over the next 16 hr
   c. CXR to r/o inhalation injury   ↗ not needed· unless infection⊕
   d. Labs → PT/PTT, CBC, type & cross, ABGs, electrolytes, UA
   e. Irrigate & débride wound, IV & topical antibiotics (silver sulfadiazine, mafenide, polysporin), tetanus prophylaxis & stress ulcer prophylaxis
   f. Transfer to burn center if pt is very young or old, burns >20% BSA, full-thickness burns >5% BSA, coexisting chemical or electrical injury, facial burns, or preexisting medical problems
   g. Make pt NPO until bowel function returns, pt will have extremely ↑ protein & caloric requirements with vitamin supplementation
   h. Excision of eschar to level of bleeding capillaries & split thickness skin grafts
   i. **Marjolin's ulcer = squamous cell carcinoma arising in an ulcer or burn**

VI. Neck Mass Differential

TABLE 2-8   Neck Mass Differential Diagnosis

DISEASE	CHARACTERISTICS	DX FINDINGS	TX
Congenital			
Torticollis	• Lateral deviation of head due to hypertrophy of unilateral sternocleidomastoid • Can be congenital, neoplasm, infection, trauma, degenerative disease, or drug toxicity (particularly D_2 blockers = phenothiazines)	Rock hard knot in the sternocleido-mastoid that is easily confused with the hyoid bone upon palpation	Muscle relaxants &/or surgical repair
Thyroglossal duct cyst	• **Midline** congenital cysts, which usually present in childhood	**Cysts elevate upon swallowing**	Surgical removal _sticking moves with out tongue_
Branchial cleft cyst	• **Lateral** congenital cysts, which usually do not present until adulthood, when they become infected or inflamed	**Do not elevate upon swallowing** Aspirate contains cholesterol crystals	Surgical excision
Cystic hygroma	• Occluded lymphatics, which usually present within first 2 years of life • **Lateral or midline**	Translucent, benign mass painless, soft & compressible	Surgical excision
Dermoid cyst	• **Lateral or midline** • Soft, fluctuant mass composed of an overgrowth of epithelium	**No elevation with swallowing**	Surgical excision
Carotid body tumor = paraganglioma	• Palpable mass at bifurcation of common carotid artery • Not a vascular tumor, but originate from neural crest cells in the carotid body within the carotid sheath • Rule of 10: 10% malignant, 10% familial, 10% secrete catecholamines _⌉ like pheo_	**Pressure on tumor can cause bradycardia & dizziness**	Surgical excision
Acquired-Inflammatory			
Cervical lymphadenitis	• Bilateral lymphadenopathy is usually viral, caused by EBV, CMV, or HIV • Unilateral is usually bacterial, caused by *S. aureus,* group A & B Strep Other Causes • Cat scratch fever (*Bartonella henselae*), transmitted via scratch of young cats • Scrofula due to miliary tuberculosis • *Actinomyces israelii* → sinuses drain pus containing "sulfur granules" • Kawasaki's syndrome • Hodgkin's lymphoma	Fine-needle aspirate & culture	Per cause: Viral → supportive, bacteria → IV antibiotics, Kawasaki's → _prevent endocarditis_ aspirin, Lymphoma → chemotherapy
Thyroid			
Goiter	• Enlargement of thyroid gland • Usually 2° to decreased iodine intake, inflammation or use of goitrogens	Fine-needle aspirate, TSH, T4 levels	Treat underlying condition

TABLE 2-8   *Continued*

DISEASE	CHARACTERISTICS	DX FINDINGS	TX

Malignancy (+mets)	• Papillary CA
	  ◊ **most common cancer of thyroid**
	  ◊ good Px, 85% 5-yr survival
	• Medullary CA
	  ◊ intermediate Px
	  ◊ **secretes calcitonin**, can use it to Dx
	    & follow dz
	• Follicular CA (can't dx with FNA)
	  ◊ has good Px
	  ◊ commonly metastasizes to bone &
	    lungs
	• Anaplastic CA
	  ◊ has terrible Px (0% survival at 5 yr)
		Fine-needle
		aspirate
			Surgical excision

VII. Surgical Abdomen (See Figure 2-3)

A. RIGHT UPPER QUADRANT (RUQ)

TABLE 2-9A   RUQ Differential Diagnosis

DISEASE	CHARACTERISTICS
Biliary colic	• Si/Sx = constant RUQ to epigastric pain • Utz → gallstones but no gallbladder wall thickening or pericholecystic fluid
Cholecystitis	• Si/Sx = fever, RUQ tenderness, **Murphy's sign** (inspiratory arrest upon deep palpation of RUQ) • Labs → moderate to severe leukocytosis, ↑ LFTs, ↑ bilirubin • Utz → gallstones, pericholecystic fluid, thickened gallbladder wall
Choledocholithiasis	• Si/Sx = RUQ pain worse with fatty meals, jaundice • Utz → common bile duct dilatation • Labs → ↑ LFTs, ↑ bilirubin
Pneumonia*	• Si/Sx = pleuritic chest pain & fever • CXR → infiltrate, labs → leukocytosis
Fitz-Hugh-Curtis syndrome*	• Syndrome of perihepatitis caused by ascending *Chlamydia* or *N. gonorrhoeae* salpingitis • Si/Sx = RUQ pain, fever, Hx or Si/Sx of salpingitis • Labs → leukocytosis but normal bilirubin & LFTs • Utz → normal gallbladder & biliary tree but fluid around the liver & gallbladder

Cholangitis	• Life threatening
	• Si/Sx
	  ◊ **Charcot's triad** = fever, jaundice & RUQ pain
	  ◊ **Reynolds' pentad**: add hypotension & mental status change
	• Labs → leukocytosis, blood Cx → enteric organisms, ↑ LFTs, ↑ bilirubin
	• Utz & CT → biliary duct dilatation from obstructing gallstones
	• Dx with ERCP or percutaneous transhepatic cholangiography (PTC)

Hepatitis*	• Si/Sx = RUQ pain/tenderness, jaundice, fever • Labs → ↑ LFTs, ↑ bilirubin, leukocytosis, ⊕ hepatitis virus serologies • Utz rules out other causes of RUQ pain

*Medical treatment indicated unless patient absolutely requires surgery for cure.

B. Right Lower Quadrant (RLQ)

Table 2-9b   RLQ Differential Diagnosis

Disease	Characteristics *periumbilical*
Appendicitis	• Si/Sx = RLQ pain/tenderness originally diffuse & then migrating to **McBurney's point** (1/3 the distance from the anterior superior iliac spine to the umbilicus), fever, diarrhea • Perform rectal exam to rule out retroperitoneal appendicitis • Labs → leukocytosis, fecalith on plain film or abdominal CT • Decision to take to OR based mostly on clinical picture
*Yersinia enterocolitis**	• Si/Sx = fever, diarrhea, severe RLQ pain make it hard to distinguish from appendicitis • Labs → leukocytosis, plain films negative for fecalith
Ectopic pregnancy	• Si/Sx = crampy to constant lower abdominal pain, vaginal bleeding, tender adnexal mass & menstrual irregularity • Labs → anemia, ↑ hCG, culdocentesis reveals blood
Salpingitis/ Tubo-ovarian abscess (TOA)	• Si/Sx = lower abdominal/pelvic pain (constant to crampy, sharp to dull), purulent vaginal discharge, cervical motion tenderness, adnexal mass • Labs → leukocytosis, wet smear → WBCs, endocervical Cx ⊕ for *N. gonorrhoeae* or *Chlamydia* • Utz → TOA. CT scan can help r/o appendicitis
Meckel's diverticulum	• **1-10-100** rule: 1–2% prevalence, 1–10 cm in length, 50–**100** cm proximal to ileocecal valve, or rule of 2's: **2% of the population, 2% are symptomatic (usually before age 2), remnants are roughly 2 in, found 2 ft from ileocecal valve & found 2x as common in males** • Si/Sx = GI bleed (melena, hematochezia), small bowel obstruction (intussusception, Littre's hernia), Meckel's diverticulitis (similar presentation to appendicitis) • *ectopic tissue* Nuclear medicine gastric scan to detect gastric mucosa present in 50% of Meckel's diverticula or tagged RBC scan to detect bleeding source
Ovarian torsion	• Si/Sx = acute onset, sharp unilateral lower abdominal/pelvic pain, pain may be intermittent due to incomplete torsion, pain related to change in position, nausea & fever present, tender adnexal mass • Utz & laparoscopy confirm Dx
Intussusception	• Most common in infants 5–10 mo • Si/Sx = infant crying with pulling legs up to abdomen, dark, red stool (**currant jelly**), vomiting, shock • Barium or air contrast enema → diagnostic "coiled spring" sign

*Medical treatment indicated unless patient absolutely requires surgery for cure.

C. LEFT UPPER QUADRANT (LUQ)

TABLE 2-9C   LUQ Differential Diagnosis

DISEASE	CHARACTERISTICS
Peptic ulcer*	• Si/Sx = epigastric pain relieved by food or antacids • Perforated ulcers present with sudden upper abdominal pain, shoulder pain & GI bleed • Labs → endoscopy or upper GI series
Myocardial infarction*	• Si/Sx = chest pain, dyspnea, diaphoresis, nausea • Labs → EKG, troponins, CK-MB
Splenic rupture	• Si/Sx = tachycardia, broken ribs, Hx of trauma, & hypotension • **Kehr's sign** = left upper quadrant pain & referred left shoulder pain • Labs → leukocytosis • X-ray → fractured ribs, medially displaced gastric bubble • CT scan of abdomen preferred method of Dx

*Medical treatment indicated unless patient absolutely requires surgery for cure.

D. LEFT LOWER QUADRANT (LLQ)

TABLE 2-9D   LLQ Differential Diagnosis

DISEASE	CHARACTERISTICS
Diverticulitis*	• Si/Sx = LLQ pain & mass, fever, urinary urgency • Labs → leukocytosis • CT scan & Utz → thickened bowel wall, abscess—do not do contrast enema
Sigmoid volvulus	• Si/Sx = elderly, chronically constipated patient, abdominal pain, distention, obstipation • X-ray → **inverted-U**, contrast enema → **bird's beak deformity**
Pyelonephritis*	• Si/Sx = high fever, rigors, costovertebral angle tenderness, Hx of UTI • Labs → pyuria & ⊕ urine culture
Ovarian torsion	• See RLQ above
Ectopic pregnancy	• See RLQ above
Salpingitis	• See RLQ above

*Medical treatment indicated unless patient absolutely requires surgery for cure.

E. MIDLINE

TABLE 2-9E Midline Differential Diagnosis

DISEASE	CHARACTERISTICS
Pancreatitis	• Si/Sx = severe epigastric pain radiating to the back, nausea/vomiting, signs of hypovolemia because of "third spacing," ↓ bowel sounds • In hemorrhagic pancreatitis, there are ecchymotic appearing skin findings in the flank (**Grey Turner's** sign) or periumbilical area (**Cullen's sign**) • Labs → leukocytosis, ↑ serum & urine amylase, ↑ lipase • X-ray → dilated small bowel or transverse colon adjacent to the pancreas, called **"sentinel loop"** ileus • CT → phlegmon, pseudocyst, necrosis, or abscess
Pancreatic pseudocyst	• Si/Sx = sequelae of pancreatitis, if pancreatitis Sx do not improve, may present with fever or shock in infected or hemorrhagic cases • CT & Utz → fluid-filled cystic mass
Abdominal aortic aneurysm (AAA)	• Si/Sx = usually aSx, rupture presents with back or abdominal pain & shock, compression on duodenum or ureters can cause obstructive Sx, palpable pulsatile periumbilical mass • X-ray (cross-table lateral films), Utz, CT & aortography reveal aneurysm
Gastroesophageal reflux disease*	• Si/Sx = position dependent (supine worse) substernal or epigastric burning pain, regurgitation, dysphagia, hoarse voice cough • Dx by barium swallow, manometric or pH testing & esophagoscopy
Myocardial infarction*	• See LUQ above
Peptic ulcer*	• See LUQ above
Gastroenteritis*	• Si/Sx = diarrhea, vomiting, abdominal pain, fever, malaise, headache • Labs → stool studies not usually indicated except in severe cases

*Medical treatment indicated unless patient absolutely requires surgery for cure.

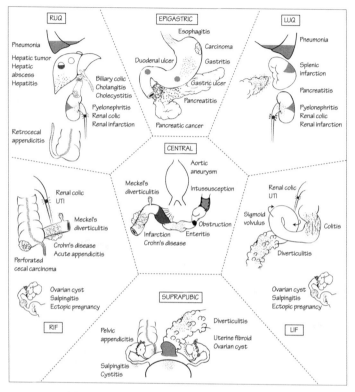

FIGURE 2-3   Acute abdominal pain.

F. TREATMENT

1. Generally all above surgical conditions will require **NPO, NG tube, IV fluids, cardiac monitoring**
2. IV antibiotics as needed
3. Surgery for hemostasis, & life-threatening conditions, consulting appropriate surgical service (O.B., pediatric surgery, etc.) as indicated

VIII. Esophagus

A. HIATAL HERNIA

1. The majority of patients with reflux have hiatal hernia (80%)
2. Si/Sx = same as GERD
3. Dx = barium swallow to identify anatomic variations
4. There are two types of hiatal hernias
   a. Type I
      1) Sliding hiatal hernia, is more common than the type II hernia
      2) It is the movement of the gastroesophageal junction & stomach up into the mediastinum
      3) Tx = medical as per GERD (see above) according to the degree of Sx present

b. Type II *(Paraesophageal)*
1) Herniation of the stomach fundus through the diaphragm parallel to the esophagus   *GE junction stays in abdomen*
2) Tx = mandatory surgical repair due to ↑ risk of strangulation

B. ACHALASIA

1. The most common motility disorder, affects 70% of pts with scleroderma
2. Loss of esophageal motility & failure of lower esophageal sphincter (LES) relaxation, may be caused by ganglionic degeneration or Chagas' disease, results in the dilatation of the proximal esophagus
3. Si/Sx = dysphagia of both solids & liquids, weight loss & repulsion of undigested foodstuffs that may produce a foul odor
4. May ↑ risk of esophageal CA because stasis promotes development of Barrett's esophagus
5. Dx
   a. Barium swallow → dilatation of the proximal esophagus with subsequent narrowing of the distal esophagus, studies may also reveal esophageal diverticula   *Bird's beak*
   b. Manometry → ↑ LES pressure & diffuse esophageal spasm
6. Tx
   a. Endoscopic dilation of LES with balloon cures 80% of pts
   b. Alternative is a myotomy with a modified fundoplication
   c. Surgical Tx may be used for palliation in patients with scleroderma, who may experience dysphagia or severe reflux

C. ESOPHAGEAL DIVERTICULA (ZENKER'S DIVERTICULUM)

1. Proximal diverticula are usually Zenker's
2. Pulsion diverticula involving only the mucosa, located between the thyropharyngeal & cricopharyngeus muscle fibers (condition associated with muscle dysfunction/spasms)
3. Si/Sx = dysphagia, regurgitation of solid foods, choking, left-sided neck mass & bad breath
4. Dx = clinically + barium swallow
5. Tx = myotomy of cricopharyngeus muscle & removal of diverticulum

D. ESOPHAGEAL TUMORS

1. Squamous cell carcinoma
   a. Most common esophageal cancer, alcohol & tobacco synergistically ↑ risk of development
   b. Most commonly seen in men in the sixth decade of life
2. Adenocarcinoma
   a. Seen in pts with chronic reflux → Barrett's esophagus = squamous to columnar metaplasia
   b. 10% of Barrett's patients will develop adenocarcinoma
3. Si/Sx for both = **dysphagia**, weight loss, hoarseness, tracheoesophageal fistula, recurrent aspiration & may include symptoms of metastatic disease
4. Dx = barium study demonstrates **classic apple-core lesion**, Dx confirmed with endoscopy with biopsy to confirm diagnosis, CT of abdomen & chest is also performed to determine extent of spread

5. Tx = esophagectomy with gastric pull-up or colonic interposition with or without chemotherapy/radiation
6. Px poor unless resected prior to spread (very rare); however, palliation should be attempted to restore effective swallowing

IX. Gastric Tumors

1. Benign tumors comprise <10% of all gastric tumors, most commonly are polyps & leiomyoma
2. Stomach CA most common after 50 yr, ↑ incidence in men
3. Linked to blood group A (suggesting genetic predisposition), immunosuppression & environmental factors
4. Nitrosamines, excess salt intake, low fiber intake, *H. pylori*, achlorhydria, chronic gastritis are all risk factors   Japan
5. Almost always adenocarcinoma, usually involves antrum, rarely fundus, aggressive spread to nodes/liver
6. Rarer gastric tumors = lymphoma & leiomyosarcoma
7. Several classic physical findings in metastatic gastric cancers
   a. **Virchow's node = large rock-hard supraclavicular node** (L)
   b. **Krukenberg tumor = mucinous, signet-ring cells that metastasize from gastric CA to bilateral ovaries, so palpate for ovarian masses in women**
   c. **Sister Mary Joseph sign = metastasis to umbilicus, feel for hard nodule there, associated with poor prognosis**
   d. **Blumer's shelf = palpable nodule superiorly on rectal exam, caused by metastasis of GI cancer**
8. Linitis plastica (leather bottle)
   a. Infiltrating, diffuse CA, invariably fatal within months
   b. **This is the most deadly form of gastric cancer**
9. Lymphoma causes 4% of gastric cancers, better Px than adenocarcinoma, associated with *H. pylori* infection
10. Si/Sx = weight loss, anemia, anorexia, GI upset
11. Dx = biopsy
12. Tx = mostly palliative, combination surgery & chemotherapy when tolerated
13. Px = about 5% survival at 5 yr   Chemo + RT dont work gastric CA except lymphoma

X. Hernia

A. INGUINAL HERNIAS

1. Most common hernia, more common in men
2. Direct type = viscera protrudes directly through abdominal wall at Hesselbach's triangle (inferior epigastric artery, rectus sheath & inguinal ligament), medial to inferior epigastric artery
3. Indirect type is more common (2/3 are indirect), pass lateral to inferior epigastric artery into spermatic cord covered by cremasteric muscle
4. Si/Sx = intermittent groin mass with bowel sounds that appear during Valsalva maneuvers
5. DDx = femoral hernias, which protrude below the inguinal ligament
6. Dx = physical exam, some unable to completely differentiate until surgery
7. Tx = surgical repair with mesh placement

B. FEMORAL HERNIAS
1. More common in women
2. Si/Sx = bulge above or below the inguinal ligament, ↑ risk of incarceration
3. Dx = clinical &/or surgical
4. Tx = surgical repair should not be delayed

C. VISCERAL HERNIAS
1. Cause intestinal obstruction
2. Si/Sx = as per bowel obstruction (e.g., obstipation, abdominal pain, etc.)
3. X-ray → no gas in rectum, distended bowel, air–fluid levels
4. DDx = other causes of bowel obstruction such as adhesions, external hernia, malignancy, etc.
5.

TABLE 2-10   Hernia Definitions

Combined (pantaloon)	Concurrent direct & indirect hernias
Sliding	Part of the hernia sac wall is formed by a visceral organ
Richter's	Part of the bowel is trapped in the hernia sac
Littre's	Meckel's diverticulum contained inside hernia
Reducible	Able to replace herniated tissue to its usual anatomic location
Incarcerated	Hernias that are not reducible
Strangulated	Incarcerated hernia with vascular compromise → ischemia
Incisional	Herniation through surgical incision, commonly 2° to wound infection

6. Dx = clinical or surgical
7. Tx = surgical repair if hernia is not reducible

XI. Hepatic Tumors

A. BENIGN TUMORS
1. Hemangioma is most common benign tumor of the liver
2. Hepatic adenoma incidence related to oral contraceptives
3. Adenomas may rupture → severe intraperitoneal bleed
4. Dx = Utz, CT scan
5. Tx = Surgery only indicated if danger of rupture, patient symptomatic, or large amount of liver involved

B. MALIGNANT TUMORS
1. Metastases are the most common malignant hepatic tumors
2. Hepatocellular CA is the most common 1° hepatic malignancy
   a. Note also called "hepatoma," incorrectly implying benign tumor (historical misnomer)
   b. Most common malignancy in the world, endemic in Southeast Asia & sub-Saharan Africa due to vertical transmission of HBV
   c. Associated with cirrhosis, HBV & HCV infection, alcoholism, hemochromatosis, Wilson's disease
   d. Si/Sx = weight loss, jaundice, weakness, dull & constant RUQ or epigastric pain, hepatomegaly, palpable mass or bloody ascites may also be present

e. Labs → ↑ serum alkaline phosphatase, ↑ bilirubin, ⊕ hepatitis B or C virus serologies, commonly causes ↑ α-fetoprotein (AFP) level

f. Dx = Utz or CT scan

g. Tx = surgical resection & its variations is the treatment modality that offers the greatest survival rates

3. Hemangiosarcoma

  a. Associated with toxic exposure to polyvinyl chloride, Thorotrast, & arsenic

  b. Dx = Utz or CT scan

  c. Tx = surgical resection, may be curative if liver function is normal; in presence of cirrhosis, usually not effective

XII. Gallbladder

A. CHOLELITHIASIS = GALLSTONES

1. Epid = higher incidence in women, multiple pregnancies, obesity **(the 4 Fs = female, forty, fertile, fat)**

2. 10% of US population has gallstones, complications of the disorder are what necessitate intervention

3. Pts ≤20 yr with gallstones should be worked up for congenital spherocytosis or hemoglobinopathy

4. Si/Sx = asymptomatic by definition

5. Dx = Utz, often incidental finding that does not require therapy

6. Tx

  a. Asymptomatic pts with gallstones do not require cholecystectomy unless there is an ↑ risk for developing cancer

  b. Pts with a porcelain gallbladder (calcified gallbladder walls) & those of Native American descent with gallstones are at ↑ risk of developing gallbladder cancer & should receive a cholecystectomy

B. BILIARY COLIC

1. Due to gallstone impaction in cystic or common bile duct

2. **The vast majority of people who have asymptomatic gallstones WILL NEVER progress to biliary colic** (2–3% progress per year, lifelong risk = 20%)

3. Sx = sharp colicky pain made worse by eating, particularly fats

4. May have multiple episodes that resolve, but eventually this condition will lead to further complications so surgical resection of the gallbladder is required

5. Dx = Utz, ERCP

6. Tx = cholecystectomy to prevent future complications

C. CHOLECYSTITIS

1. Cholecystitis is due to 2° infection of obstructed gallbladder

  a. The EEEK! bugs: *Escherichia coli, Enterobacter cloacae, Enterococcus, Klebsiella spp.*

  b. Si/Sx = sudden onset, severe, steady pain in RUQ/epigastrium; muscle guarding/rebound; ⊕ **Murphy's sign** (RUQ palpation during inspiration causes sharp pain & sudden cessation of inspiration)

  c. Labs → leukocytosis (may be over 20,000 in emphysematous cholecystitis = presence of gas in gallbladder wall), ↑ AST/ALT, ↑ bilirubin

   d. Dx = Utz → gallstones, pericholecystic fluid & thickened gallbladder wall,
      if results equivocal can confirm with radionuclide cholescintigraphy (e.g.,
      HIDA scan)—CT scan is usually not the test of choice to diagnose
      cholecystitis
   e. Tx
      1) NPO, IV hydration & third-generation cephalosporins or mezlocillin +/−
         aminoglycoside & Flagyl
      2) Demerol better for pain as morphine causes spasm of the sphincter of Oddi
      3) Surgical resection if unresponsive or worsening

D. CHOLEDOCHOLITHIASIS
   1. Passage of stone through the cystic duct, can obstruct common bile duct (CBD)
   2. Si/Sx = obstructive jaundice, ↑ conjugated bilirubin, hypercholesterolemia, ↑ alkaline
      phosphatase
   3. Dx = ultrasound (Utz) → CBD > 9-mm diameter (Utz first line for Dx)
   4. **Passage of stone to CBD can cause acute pancreatitis if the ampulla of Vater is
      obstructed by the stone**
   5. Tx = laparoscopic cholecystectomy + ERCP or CBD exp-

E. ASCENDING CHOLANGITIS
   1. Results from 2° bacterial infection of obstructed CBD, facilitated by obstructed bile
      flow
   2. Obstruction usually due to choledocholithiasis, but can be 2° to strictures, foreign
      bodies (e.g., surgical clips from prior abdominal surgery) & parasites
   3. **Charcot's triad = jaundice, RUQ pain, fever (85% sensitive for cholangitis)—for
      Reynold's pentad add altered mental status & hypotension** (shock)
   4. Dx = Utz or CT → common bile duct dilation, definitive Dx requires endoscopic ret-
      rograde pancreaticoduodenoscopy (ERCP) or percutaneous transhepatic cholangiog-
      raphy (PTC)
   5. This is a life-threatening emergency!
   6. Tx
      a. NPO, IV hydration, IV ampicillin/gentamicin/Flagyl or mezlocillin/Flagyl
      b. ERCP or PTC to decompress the biliary tree & remove obstructing stones

F. CANCER
   1. Very rare, usually occurs in seventh decade of life
   2. More commonly seen in females, gallstones are risk factors for developing cancer
   3. Most common 1° tumor of gallbladder is adenocarcinoma
   4. Frequently seen in Far East, associated with *Clonorchis sinensis* (liver fluke)
      infestation
   5. When the tumor occurs at the confluence of the hepatic ducts forming the common
      duct, the tumor is called **"Klatskin's tumor"** (mean survival = 9–12 mo, no Tx, invari-
      ably lethal)
   6. **Courvoisier's law** = gallbladder enlarges when CBD is obstructed by pancreatic CA
      but not enlarged when CBD is obstructed by stone
   7. Courvoisier's sign is a palpable gallbladder
   8. Si/Sx = as for biliary colic but persistent
   9. Dx = Utz or CT to show tumor, but preoperative Dx of gallbladder CA is often
      incorrect

10. Tx = palliative stenting of bile ducts, can consider surgical resection for palliation only
11. Px = terminal, almost all pts are dead within 1 yr of Dx

XIII. Exocrine Pancreas

A. ACUTE PANCREATITIS

1. Pancreatic enzymes autodigest pancreas → hemorrhagic fat necrosis, calcium deposition & sometimes formation of pseudocysts (cysts not lined with ductal epithelium)
2. Most common causes in US = gallstones & alcohol
3. Other causes include infection, trauma, radiation, drug (thiazides, AZT, protease inhibitors), hyperlipidemia, hypercalcemia, vascular events, tumors, scorpion sting
4. Si/Sx = severe abdominal pain, prostration (fetal position opens up retroperitoneal space & allows more room for swollen pancreas), hypotension (due to retroperitoneal fluid sequestration), tachycardia, fever, ↑ serum amylase (90% sensitive)/lipase, hyperglycemia, hypocalcemia
5. Dx = clinically &/ or abdominal CT, **classic x-ray finding = sentinel loop or colon cut-off sign** (loop of distended bowel adjacent to pancreas)
6. **Classic physical findings = Grey Turner's sign (discoloration of flank) & Cullen's sign (periumbilical discoloration)**
7. Tx is aimed at decreasing stress to pancreas
   a. NPO until symptoms/amylase subside; TPN if NPO for >7–10 days
   b. Demerol to control pain
   c. IV fluid resuscitation
   d. Alcohol withdrawal prophylaxis
   e. May require ICU admission if severe
8. Complications = abscess, pseudocysts, duodenal obstruction, shock lung & acute renal failure
9. Repeated bouts of pancreatitis cause chronic pancreatitis, resulting in fibrosis & atrophy of the organ with early exocrine & later endocrine insufficiency
10. Prognosis of acute pancreatitis determined by **Ranson's criteria:**

TABLE 2-11   Ranson's Criteria

ON ADMISSION	WITHIN 24–48 HRS
Age > 55, WBCs > 16,000/mL, AST > 250 IU/dL, LDH > 350, blood glucose > 200, base deficit > 4 mEq/L	↓ HCT > 10%, BUN rise > 5 mg/dL, serum calcium < 8 mg/dL, arterial pO$_2$ < 60 mm Hg, fluid sequestration > 6 L
Risk of mortality: 20% if 3–4 signs, 40% if 5–6 signs, 100% if 7 or more signs	

B. PANCREATIC PSEUDOCYST

1. Collection of fluid in pancreas surrounded by a fibrous capsule, no communication with fibrous ducts
2. **Suspect anytime a patient is readmitted with pancreatitis complaints within several weeks of being discharged after a bout of pancreatitis**
3. 2° to pancreatitis or trauma as in steering wheel injury
4. Dx = Abd Utz/CT (See Figure 2-4)

let mature >6wks then drain if don't resolve

5. Tx = percutaneous surgical drainage or pancreaticogastrostomy (creation of surgical fistula to drain cyst into the stomach), but small cysts will resorb on their own
6. New cysts contain blood, necrotic debris, leukocytes; old cysts contain straw-colored fluid
7. Can become infected with purulent contents, causing peritonitis after rupture

C. PANCREATIC CANCER (See Figure 2-5)

1. Epid = 90% are adenocarcinoma with 60% of these arising in the head of pancreas
2. More common in African Americans, cigarette smokers & males, linked to chronic pancreatitis & diabetes mellitus
3. Si/Sx = jaundice, weight loss, abdominal pain, **classic sign is Trousseau's syndrome = migratory thrombophlebitis, occurs in 10% of patients**   *usually painless Jaundice*
4. Frequently invades duodenum, ampulla of Vater, common bile duct & can also cause biliary obstruction
5. Dx = Labs: ↑ bilirubin, ↑ alk phos, ↑ CA 19-9 (not diagnostic), **CT scan** (See Figure 2-6)
6. Tx = Whipple's procedure, resection of pancreas, part of small bowel, stomach, gallbladder
7. Site of cancer & extent of disease at time of diagnosis determines Px: usually very poor, 5-yr survival rate after palliative resection is 5%

head can resect
body/tail unresectable

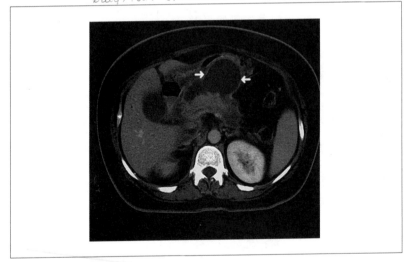

FIGURE 2-4   CT scan showing a well-defined, low-density pseudocyst (arrows).

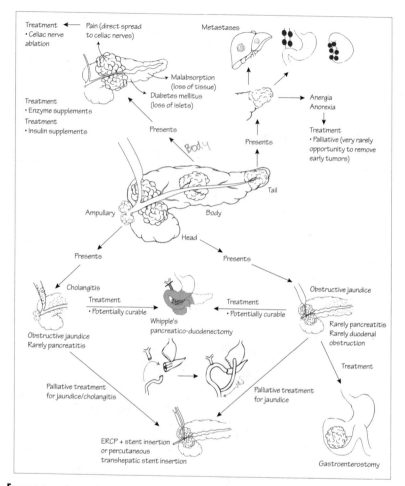

Treatment
• Celiac nerve ablation

Pain (direct spread to celiac nerves)

Metastases

Malabsorption (loss of tissue)
Diabetes mellitus (loss of islets)

Anergia
Anorexia

Treatment
• Enzyme supplements
Treatment
• Insulin supplements

Presents

Presents

Treatment
• Palliative (very rarely opportunity to remove early tumors)

Body

Presents

Tail

Ampullary

Body

Head

Tail

Presents

Presents

Cholangitis

Obstructive jaundice

Treatment
• Potentially curable

Treatment
• Potentially curable

Obstructive jaundice
Rarely pancreatitis

Whipple's
pancreatico-duodenectomy

Rarely pancreatitis
Rarely duodenal obstruction

Treatment

Palliative treatment for jaundice/cholangitis

Palliative treatment for jaundice

ERCP + stent insertion
or percutaneous transhepatic stent insertion

Gastroenterostomy

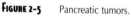

FIGURE 2-5   Pancreatic tumors.

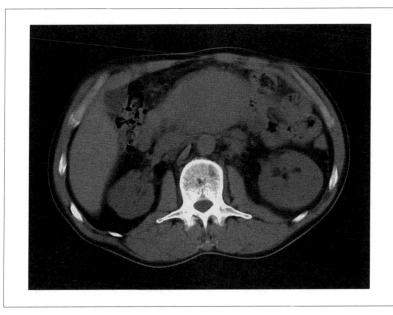

FIGURE 2-6   CT scan showing an upper abdominal mass: pancreatic carcinoma.

D. ENDOCRINE PANCREATIC NEOPLASM

1. Insulinoma due to hyperplasia of insulin producing β-cells
2. Hyperglucagonemia = α cell tumor → hyperglycemia & exfoliative dermatitis
3. Zollinger-Ellison syndrome   ulcers
   a. Dx = clinically, elevated serum levels of insulin, glucagon, or gastrin
   b. Tx = surgical resection of the tumor

secretin → ↑ gastrin ZES

XIV. Small Intestine

Panc ? check ca (screen MEN I)
Tumors ?

A. SMALL BOWEL OBSTRUCTION (SBO)

1. **Most common surgical condition of the small bowel**
2. Causes = peritoneal adhesions, hernias & neoplasms in order of occurrence in the adult population
3. Other causes include Crohn's, Meckel's, radiation enteritis, gallstone ileus & inflammation
4. Si/Sx = crampy abdominal pain, nausea, vomiting, lack of flatus, abdominal tenderness, abdominal distention & hyperactive, high-pitched bowel sounds
5. DDx = paralytic ileus (similar Si/Sx)
6. Numerous etiologies including abdominal surgery, hypokalemia, narcotics, anticholinergics, acute pancreatitis, gastroenteritis & cholecystitis
7. Dx = abdominal series → distended loops of small bowel proximal to the obstruction, upright film → air–fluid levels or free air beneath the diaphragm on a PA chest film

8. Tx
   a. Conservative Tx = IV fluids, NG tube decompression & Foley catheter, partial obstructions may be successfully treated with conservative therapy
   b. Surgical candidates receive antibiotics to include both anaerobic & gram-negative coverage
   c. Objective of surgery is to remove obstruction & resect nonviable bowel

B. SMALL BOWEL NEOPLASMS
1. Leiomyoma is most common benign tumor of the small bowel.
2. Si/Sx = pain, anemia, weight loss, nausea & emesis, common complication is obstruction that is caused primarily by leiomyomas
3. Carcinoid tumors (small bowel is the second most common location, appendix is first) → cutaneous flushing, diarrhea & respiratory distress.
4. Malignant neoplasms in order of decreasing incidence: **adenocarcinoma, carcinoid, lymphoma & sarcomas**
5. Dx = biopsy, not necessarily reliable
6. Tx = surgical resection of primary tumor along with lymph nodes & liver metastases if possible

XV. Colon

A. COLONIC POLYPS
1. Classified as **neoplastic, hamartomas, inflammatory, or miscellaneous**
2. Neoplastic polyps are most commonly adenomas & can be classified as either tubular adenoma (smallest malignant potential), tubulovillous adenoma, or villous adenoma (greatest malignant potential)
3. The mean age of patients with polyps is 55, incidence ↑ with age
4. 50% of polyps occur in the sigmoid or rectum
5. Si/Sx = intermittent rectal **bleeding** is most common presenting complaint
6. Dx = colonoscopy, sigmoidoscopy, always consider family Hx
7. Tx
   a. Colonoscopic polypectomy or laparotomy
   b. If invasive adenocarcinoma is found, a colectomy is not mandatory if gross & microscopic margins are clear, if tissue is well-differentiated without lymphatic or venous drainage & polyp stalk does not invade

B. FAMILIAL POLYPOSIS SYNDROMES [SEE APPENDIX A FOR MORE]
1. Familial adenomatous polyposis (FAP)
   a. Si/Sx = autosomal dominant inheritance of APC gene, abundant polyps throughout the colon & rectum beginning at puberty
   b. Gardner's syndrome consists of polyposis, desmoid tumors, osteomas of mandible or skull, & sebaceous cysts
   c. Turcot's syndrome is polyposis with medulloblastoma or glioma
   d. Dx = family Hx, colonoscopy, presence of congenital hypertrophy of retinal pigment epithelium predicts FAP with 97% sensitivity
   e. Tx = colectomy & upper GI endoscopy to rule out gastroduodenal lesions—a favored operation is an abdominal colectomy, mucosal proctectomy & ileoanal anastomosis
2. Peutz-Jeghers syndrome

a. Si/Sx = autosomal dominant inheritance, nonneoplastic hamartomatous polyps in stomach, small intestine & colon, skin & mucous membrane hyperpigmentation, **particularly freckles on lips**
b. ↑ **risk of developing CA in other tissues** (e.g., breast, pancreas)
c. Dx = clinical & family Hx
d. Tx = careful, regular monitoring for malignancy
3. Juvenile polyposis syndromes
   a. Examples include juvenile polyposis coli, generalized juvenile gastrointestinal polyposis & Cronkhite-Canada syndrome
   b. Si/Sx = hamartomatous polyps & thus carry decreased malignant potential, similar to Peutz-Jeghers, patients with familial juvenile polyposis carry increased risk of gastrointestinal cancer
   c. Dx = clinical & family Hx
   d. Tx = polypectomy is generally reserved for symptomatic polyps

C. DIVERTICULAR DISEASE
1. General characteristics
   a. ≅ 50% of people will have diverticula, ↑ incidence between fifth & eighth decade of life in Western countries, but **only 10–20% cause Sx**
   b. True diverticula = herniations involving the full bowel wall thickness
   c. True diverticula are rare, often found in cecum & ascending colon
   d. False diverticula = only mucosal herniations through muscular wall *weakness where*
   e. False diverticula are common, >90% found in sigmoid colon *blood vessels enter*
   f. It is believed that ↑ intraluminal pressure (perhaps promoted by ↓ fiber diet) causes herniation
2. Diverticulosis
   a. Presence of multiple false (acquired) diverticula
   b. Si/Sx = 80% are aSx & are found incidentally, can cause recurrent abdominal pain in left lower quadrant & changes in bowel habits, 5–10% of pts present with lower GI hemorrhage that can be massive
   c. Dx = colonoscopy or barium enema to reveal herniations
   d. Tx
      1) aSx pts should ↑ fiber content of diet, ↓ fatty food intake & avoid foods that exacerbate diverticular obstruction (e.g., seeds)
      2) Surgical therapy for uncomplicated diverticulosis is **rare**
      3) See below for management of GI hemorrhage
3. Diverticulitis
   a. Diverticular infxn & macroperforation resulting in inflammation
   b. The inflammation may be limited to the bowel, extend to pericolic tissues, form an abscess, or result in peritonitis
   c. Si/Sx
      1) Left lower quadrant pain, diarrhea or constipation, fever, anorexia & leukocytosis—**bleeding is more consistent with diverticulosis, not diverticulitis**
      2) **Life-threatening complications from diverticulitis include large perforations, abscess or fistula formation & obstruction**
      3) The most common fistula associated with diverticular dz is colovesicular (presenting with recurrent urinary tract infections)

CXR

d. Dx AXR to r/o free air

1) CT scan may demonstrate edema of the bowel wall & the presence/location of formed abscesses
2) Barium enema & colonoscopy are generally contraindicated for the acute pt, but if the pt's Sx point to obstruction or to the presence of a fistula, a contrast enema is warranted

e. Tx

1) Majority of pts respond to conservative Tx with IV hydration, antibiotics with anaerobic coverage & NPO orders
2) Abscess requires CT- or Utz-guided percutaneous drainage
3) If pt suffers recurrent bouts after acute resolution, a sigmoid colectomy is usually considered on an elective basis   1° anastomosis
4) Perforation or obstruction → resection of affected bowel & construction of a temporary diverting colostomy & a Hartman pouch—reanastomosis performed 2–3 months postop

D. GI HEMORRHAGE

1. **Bright-red blood per rectum** (BRBPR) usually points to bleeding in the **distal small bowel or colon**, although a proximal bleeding site must be considered
2. Massive lower GI hemorrhage is usually caused by diverticular disease, angiodysplasia, ulcerative colitis, ischemic colitis, or a solitary ulcer
3. Chronic rectal bleed is usually due to hemorrhoids, fissures, CA, or polyps
4. Dx
   a. Digital rectal exam (DRE) & visualization with an anoscope & sigmoidoscope to locate & Tx obvious bleeding site
   b. Endoscopy to evaluate for an upper gastrointestinal bleed
   c. Angiography if pt continues to bleed despite r/o upper GI source
   d. If bleeding is minimal/stopped or angiography is indeterminate & the pt is stable, the bowel should be prepped & colonoscopy performed
   e. Tagged RBC scan or barium enema if colonoscopy is non-Dx
5. Tx
   a. IV fluids & transfusions as needed to maintain hemodynamic stability
   b. Surgery is fortunately rarely required & should be considered only if bleeding persists (over 90% of bleeding ceases spontaneously) despite intervention

E. LARGE INTESTINE OBSTRUCTION

1. Accounts for 15% of obstructions—most common site is sigmoid colon
2. 3 most common causes are **adenocarcinoma, scarring 2° to diverticulitis & volvulus—consider adhesions if pt had previous abdominal surgery**
3. Other causes are fecal impaction, inflammatory disorders, foreign bodies & other benign tumors
4. Si/Sx = abdominal distention, crampy abdominal pain, nausea/vomiting
5. **X-ray → distended proximal colon, air–fluid levels, no gas in rectum**
6. Dx = clinical + x-ray, consider barium enema if x-rays are equivocal—**DO NOT GIVE BARIUM ORALLY WITH SUSPECTED OBSTRUCTION**
7. Tx = emergency laparotomy if cecal diameter >12 cm or for severe tenderness, peritonitis, sepsis, free air
8. Pseudo-obstruction (**Ogilvie's syndrome**)

a) The presence of massive right-sided colon dilatation with no evidence of obstruction

b) Tx = colonoscopy & rectal tube for decompression

F. VOLVULUS

1. Rotation of the large intestine along its mesenteric axis—twisting can promote ischemic bowel, gangrene & subsequent perforation

2. Most common site is **sigmoid** (70%) followed by **cecum** (30%)

3. **Commonly occurs in elderly individuals**

4. Si/Sx = obstructive symptoms, including distention, tympany, rushes & high-pitched bowel sounds

5. Dx = clinical, confirmed by radiographic studies

   a. X-ray → dilated loops of bowel with loss of haustra with **a kidney bean appearance**

   b. Barium enema → a narrowing mimicking a **"bird's beak" or "ace of spades"** picture, with point of beak pointing to site of bowel rotation

   sigmoid → omega appearance

6. Tx

   a. Sigmoidoscopy or colonoscopy for decompression

   b. If not successful, laparotomy with a two-stage resection & anastomosis is necessary

   c. Cecal volvulus is treated with cecopexy (attachment of mobile cecum to peritoneal membrane) or right hemicolectomy

G. COLON CANCER

1. Epidemiology

   a. Second leading cause of cancer deaths

   b. Low-fiber, high-fat diet may contribute to risk of development—**while this has been classically taught it remains controversial & recent data suggest otherwise [see New Engl J Med 1999, 340:169–76]**

   c. Genetic influences include tumor suppressor & proto-oncogenes

   d. Lynch syndromes I & II or hereditary nonpolyposis colorectal cancer (HNPCC)

      1) **Lynch syndrome I** is an autosomal dominant predisposition to colorectal cancer with right-sided predominance (70% proximal to the splenic flexure)

      2) **Lynch syndrome II** shows all of the features of Lynch syndrome I & also causes extracolonic cancers, particularly endometrial carcinoma, carcinoma of the ovary, small bowel, stomach & pancreas, & transitional cell CA of the ureter & renal pelvis

2. Screening

   a. >40 yr of age without risk factors (strong family Hx, ulcerative colitis, etc.) → yearly stool occult blood tests, flexible sigmoidoscopy q 3–5 yr or colonoscopy q 10 yr or barium enema q 5–10 yr

   b. Colonoscopy/barium enema if polyps found

   c. Pts with risk factors require more frequent & full colonoscopies

3. Dx

   apple core lesion

   a. Endoscopy or barium enema—biopsy not essential

   b. Obtain preoperative carcinoembryonic antigen (CEA) to follow disease, these levels will be elevated before any physical evidence of disease

4. Surgical = resection and regional lymph node dissection

5. Adjuvant Tx for metastatic dz = 5-fluorouracil ⊕ leucovorin or levamisole → 30% improvement in survival
6. Follow-up
   a. Hx & physical & CEA level q 3 mo for 3 yr then follow up every 6 mo for 2 yr
   b. Colonoscopy at 6 mo, 12 mo & yearly for 5 yr
   c. CT & MRI for suspected recurrences

XVI. Rectum and Anus (See Figure 2-7)

A. HEMORRHOIDS
1. A varicosity in the lower rectum or anus caused by congestion in the veins of the hemorrhoidal plexus
2. Si/Sx = anal mass, bleeding, itching, discomfort
3. The presence or absence of pain depends on the location of the hemorrhoid: internal hemorrhoid is generally not painful whereas an external hemorrhoid can be extremely painful
4. **Thrombosed external hemorrhoid**
   a. Not a true hemorrhoid, but subcutaneous external hemorrhoidal veins of the anal canal
   b. It is classically **painful**, tense, bluish elevation beneath the skin or anoderm
5. Hemorrhoids are classified by degrees
   a. 1° = no prolapse
   b. 2° = prolapse with defecation, but returns on its own
   c. 3° = prolapse with defecation or straining, require manual reduction
   d. 4° = not capable of being reduced
6. Dx = H&P, inspection of the perianal area, digital rectal exam, anoscopy & sigmoidoscopy
7. Tx = conservative therapy consists of a high-fiber diet, Sitz baths, stool bulking agents, stool softeners, cortisone cream, astringent medicated pads
8. Definitive Tx = sclerotherapy, cryosurgery, rubber band ligation & surgical hemorrhoidectomy

B. FISTULA-IN-ANO
1. Communication between the rectum to the perianal skin, usually secondary to anal crypt infection
2. Infection in the crypt forms abscess then ruptures & a fistulous tract is formed, can be seen in Crohn's disease
3. Si/Sx = intermittent or constant discharge, may exude pus, incontinence
4. Dx = physical exam
5. Tx = fistulotomy
6. Factors that predispose to maintenance of fistula patency = **FRIEND** = Foreign body, Radiation, Infection, Epithelialization, Neoplasm, Distal obstruction

C. ANAL FISSURE
1. Epithelium in the anal canal denuded 2° to passage of irritating diarrhea & a tightening of the anal canal related to nervous tension
2. Si/Sx = **classic** presentation, a severely painful bowel movement associated with bright-red bleeding
3. Dx = anoscopy

4. Tx = stool softeners, dietary modifications & bulking agents

5. Surgical Tx = lateral internal sphincterotomy if pain is unbearable & fissure persists

D. RECTAL CANCER

1. More common in males

2. Si/Sx = **rectal bleeding**, obstruction, altered bowel habits & tenesmus

3. Dx = colonoscopy, sigmoidoscopy, biopsy, barium enema

4. Tx = sphincter-saving surgery, adjuvant Tx for rectal cancer with positive nodal metastasis or transmural involvement includes radiation therapy & 5-FU chemotherapy

E. ANAL CANCER

1. Most commonly squamous cell CA, others include transitional cell, adenocarcinoma, melanoma & mucoepidermal

2. Risk factors include fistulas, abscess, infections & Crohn's disease   HPV.

3. Si/Sx = **anal bleeding**, pain & mucus evacuation

4. Dx = biopsy

5. Tx = chemotherapy & radiation

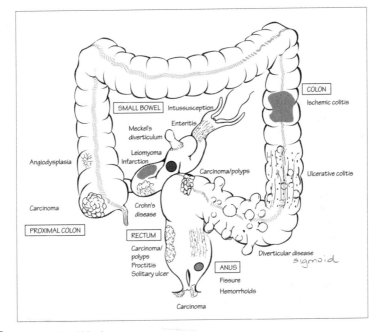

FIGURE 2-7   Rectal bleeding.

XVII. Breast

A. CANCER RISKS

1. Risk increased by

a. #1 factor is gender (1% of breast cancers are in men)

b. Age (#1 factor in women)
c. Young first menarche (<11 yr)
d. Old first pregnancy (>30 yr)
e. Late menopause (>50 yr)
f. Family history defined as 1° relatives with cancer at a young age (95% of cancers are not familial)
2. Risk NOT increased by caffeine, sexual orientation (lesbian)
3. Vitamin E does NOT protect against breast cancer
4. While breast cancers can be asymptomatic, others can present with nipple discharge (unilateral), pain, nipple retraction, dimpling & nipple rash
5. Remember, **most breast cancers develop in the upper outer quadrants**
6. Most common types of cancer are invasive ductal carcinoma (majority), invasive lobular CA & inflammatory CA

B. MASTALGIA

1. Cyclical or noncyclical breast pain NOT due to lumps
2. Pain worse with respiration may be due to Tietze syndrome (costochondritis)
3. Mondor's disease = thoracoepigastric vein phlebitis → skin retraction along vein course
4. Dx = clinical   vit e, evening primrose oil
5. Tx = danazol, works by inducing amenorrhea (hirsutism & weight gain side effects) (androgen)

C. FIBROADENOMA (FA)

1. Most common tumor in teens & young women (peak in 20s)
2. FAs grow rapidly, no increased risk for developing CA
3. Dx = clinical
4. Tx NOT required, often will resorb within several weeks, reevaluation after a month is standard

D. CYSTS

1. Most common tumor in 35–50-yr-olds, rarely postmenopausal, arise in terminal ductal lobular unit
2. Cysts can arise overnight
3. No clinical significance, can be easily drained
4. Si/Sx = pain & tenderness that varies with the menstrual cycle
5. Dx = history, breast exam & aspiration of any suspected cystic lesions, fluid that is drawn from a cyst is usually straw- or green-colored
6. If aspirated fluid is bloody, send for cytology to rule out cystic malignancy
7. Tx = drainage of cyst

E. DUCTAL CARCINOMA IN SITU (DCIS)

1. Usually nonpalpable, seen as irregularly shaped ductal calcifications on mammography
2. This is a true premalignancy, will lead to invasive ductal CA
3. Dx = core or excisional biopsy
4. Tx = excision of mass, ensure clean margins on excision (if not, excise again with wider margins) & add postop radiation that reduces rate of recurrence

CA in ipsilateral breast

F. INVASIVE DUCTAL CARCINOMA (IDC)

1. Most common breast cancer, occurs commonly in mid-30s to late 50s, forms solid tumors

2. **Tumor size is the most important Px factor**, node involvement is also important for Px
3. Dx = core or excisional biopsy—all breast masses in women >35 yr require a tissue diagnosis, regardless of mammographic findings (i.e., even if mammography is not suspicious)
4. Tx = **either** modified radical mastectomy or lumpectomy with postop radiation, both give equivalent outcomes *⊂ axillary node dissection*
5. Adjuvant tamoxifen or raloxifene can be added to reduce the risk of metastasis depending on the size of the primary tumor

G. INVASIVE LOBULAR CARCINOMA

1. Only 3–5% of invasive CA is lobular, present at age 45–56, vague appearance on mammogram *CA in either breast*
2. Patients have increased frequency of bilateral cancer
3. Dx = core or excisional biopsy
4. Tx = **either** prophylactic bilateral mastectomy at time of diagnosis, or *unilateral* mastectomy plus very close follow-up

H. PAGET'S BREAST DISEASE (NOT BONE DISEASE!)

1. Presents with dermatitis/macular rash over nipple or areola
2. Underlying ductal CA almost always present
3. Dx = biopsy
4. Tx = excision + radiation

I. INFLAMMATORY CARCINOMA

1. Breast has classic Sx of inflammation: redness, pain & heat *peau d'orange*
2. Rapidly progressive breast cancer, almost always widely metastatic at presentation
3. Dx = physical exam & biopsy
4. Tx = chemotherapy + radiation, Px poor

J. MAMMOGRAPHY

1. Highly effective screening tool in all but young women
2. Dense breast tissue found in young women interferes with the test's sensitivity & specificity
3. All women over age 50 should have yearly mammograms (proven to ↓ mortality in these patients)
4. Women over age 40 recommended to have yearly or biannual mammograms (efficacy less clear in this group)
5. Women with 1° relatives who have cancer should begin mammogram screenings **10 yr prior to the age at which the relative developed cancer**

WORK-UP OF A BREAST MASS

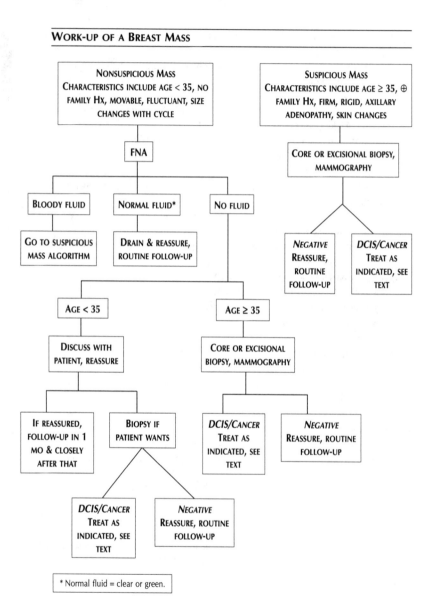

* Normal fluid = clear or green.

XVIII. Urology

A. SCROTAL EMERGENCIES

1. Testicular torsion
   a. Usually peripubertal patient
   b. Si/Sx = acute onset testicular pain & edema, nausea & vomiting, tender, swollen testicle with transverse lie, **absent cremasteric reflex on affected side**
   c. Dx = Doppler Utz to assess testicular artery flow
   d. Tx = emergent surgical decompression, with excision of testicle if it infarcts
2. Epididymitis
   a. Si/Sx = unilateral testicular pain, dysuria, occasional urethral discharge, fever, leukocytosis in severe cases, painful & swollen epididymis
   b. Dx = history & physical, labs → UA can be negative or show pyuria, urine Cx should be obtained, swab for *N. gonorrhoeae* & *Chlamydia*
   c. Tx = antibiotics & NSAIDs
3. Appendix testis (torsion of testicular appendage)
   a. Si/Sx = similar to testicular torsion, severe tenderness over superior pole of testicle, **"blue dot" sign** of ischemic appendage, normal position & lie, **cremasteric reflex present,** testicle & epididymis not tender
   b. Dx = Utz, perfusion confirmed with nuclear medicine scan
   c. Tx = supportive, should resolve in 2 wk
4. Fournier's gangrene
   a. Necrotizing fasciitis of the genital area
   b. Si/Sx = acute pruritus, rapidly progressing edema, erythema, tenderness, fever, chills, malaise, necrosis of skin & subcutaneous tissues, crepitus caused by gas-forming organisms
   c. Dx = history of diabetes mellitus, or immunocompromise, physical exam, labs → leukocytosis, positive blood & wound cultures (polymicrobial); x-ray → subcutaneous gas
   d. Tx emergently with wide surgical débridement & antibiotics

B. PROSTATE CANCER

1. Si/Sx = advanced dz causes obstructive Sx, UTI, urinary retention, pts may also present with Sx due to metastases (bone pain, weight loss & anemia), rock-hard nodule in prostate
2. Dx = labs → anemia, azotemia, elevated serum acid phosphatase & PSA—note that use of these tests for screening is controversial due to relatively low sensitivity & specificity
3. Transrectal Utz, CT scan, MRI, plain films for metastatic work-up, biopsy to confirm Dx
4. Bone scan helpful to detect bony metastases (See Figure 2-8)
5. Tx
   a. May not require Tx, most are indolent cancers, but note that some are very aggressive & may warrant Tx depending on pt's wishes
   b. Modalities include finasteride, local irradiation, nerve sparing or radical prostatectomy—risks of surgery include impotence & incontinence
   c. Aggressiveness of Tx depends on extent of disease & age of patient

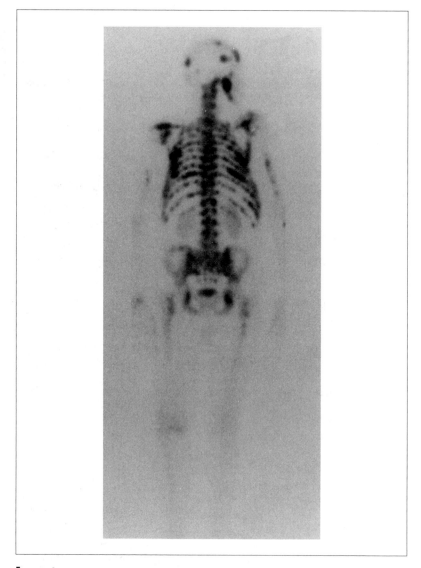

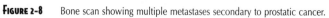

FIGURE 2-8   Bone scan showing multiple metastases secondary to prostatic cancer.

XIX. Orthopedics

A. WRIST INJURIES
1. Fractures
   a. Distal radius fracture (**Colles'**) occurs after fall on outstretched hand (See Figure 2-9)
   b. Ulnar fracture occurs after direct blow, commonly seen in hockey, lacrosse or martial arts
   c. Dx = x-rays, history & physical
   d. Tx for both = cast immobilization for 2–4 wk followed by bracing
   e. Scaphoid fracture
      1) Usually 2° to falls, commonly misdiagnosed as a "wrist sprain"
      2) Dx = clinical (pain in anatomical **snuffbox**), x-rays to confirm, bone scan or MRI for athletes that require early definitive diagnosis (See Figure 2-10)
      3) Tx = thumb splint for 10 wk (↑ risk of avascular necrosis)
2. Carpal tunnel syndrome
   a. Si/Sx = pain & paresthesias in fingers worse at night
   b. Dx = **Tinel's sign** (pathognomonic) = tapping median nerve on palmar aspect of wrist producing "shooting" sensation to fingers & **Phalen's test** = wrist flexion to 60° for 30–60 sec reproduces pt's Sx
   c. Tx = avoid causative activities, splint wrist in slight extension, consider steroid injection into carpal canal; surgery for refractory dz
   d. Px = may require up to 1 yr before Sx resolve even after surgery

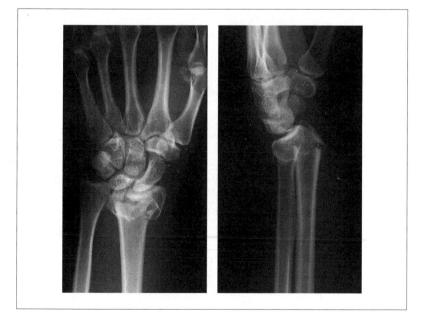

FIGURE 2-9   Colles' fracture.

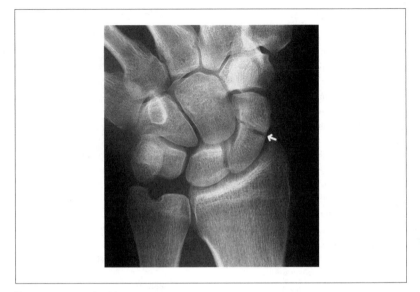

FIGURE 2-10 Scaphoid fracture (arrow).

B. SHOULDER INJURIES

1. Rotator cuff injury (impingement syndrome)
   a. Typically develops over time in pts >45 yr
   b. Si/Sx = pain/tenderness at deltoid & over anterior humeral head, difficulty lying on shoulder, ↓ internal rotation, crepitation, **Neer's sign** (pain elicited with forcible forward elevation of arm), lidocaine injection into subacromial space alleviates pain
   c. Dx = clinical, confirm with MRI
   d. Tx = NSAIDs & stretching, consider steroid injection for refractory dz, arthroscopic surgery for severe dz refractory to steroids
2. Shoulder dislocation
   a. Subluxation = symptomatic translation of humeral head relative to glenoid articular surface
   b. Dislocation = complete displacement out of the glenoid fossa
   c. Anterior instability (about 95% of cases) usually due to subcoracoid dislocation is the most common form of shoulder dislocation (See Figure 2-11)
   d. Si/Sx = pain, joint immobility, arm "goes dead" with overhead motion
   e. Dx = clinical, assess axillary nerve function in neuro exam, look for signs of rotator cuff injury, confirm with x-rays if necessary
   f. Tx = initial reduction of dislocation by various traction–countertraction techniques, 2- to 6-wk period of immobilization (longer for younger patients), intense rehabilitation; rarely is surgery required

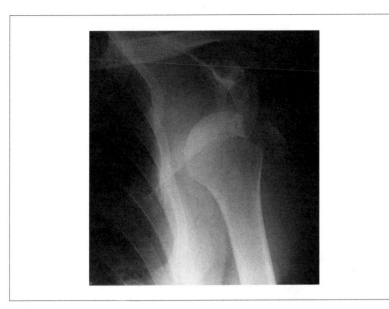

FIGURE 2-11   Anterior dislocation with a fracture of the greater tuberosity.

C. HIP & THIGH INJURIES
1. Dislocations
   a. Requires significant trauma, usually posterior, occur in children
   b. Sciatic nerve injury may be present—do a careful neurologic exam
   c. Dx = x-rays, consider CT scan to assess any associated fractures
   d. Tx
      1) **Orthopedic emergency requiring reduction under sedation (open reduction may be required)**
      2) Light traction for 5 days or longer is strongly recommended
      3) No weight bearing for 3 wk minimum, followed by 3–4 wk of light weight-bearing activities
      4) Follow-up imaging studies required every 3–6 mo for 2 yr
   e. Major complication is avascular necrosis of femoral head
2. Femoral neck fracture (See Figure 2-12)
   a. Like hip dislocation, requires significant force
   b. Si/Sx = severe hip & groin pain worse with movement, leg may be externally rotated
   c. Dx = radiograph is definitive diagnosis
   d. Tx = operative reduction with internal fixation

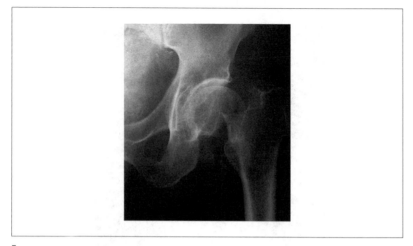

FIGURE 2-12   Femoral neck fracture.

D. KNEE INJURIES

TABLE 2-12   Knee Injuries

INJURY	CHARACTERISTICS	TX
Anterior cruciate ligament tear (ACL)	• Si/Sx = **presents with a "pop" in the knee**, pt may also complain of **knee instability or giving way** • **Lachman test** &/or anterior drawer finds pathologic anterior tibial translation & can Dx without imaging • MRI is most helpful to determine full extent of injury	Conservative or arthroscopic repair of tear
Posterior cruciate ligament tear (PCL)	• Tear seen during falls on flexed knee & dashboard injuries in motor vehicle accidents (MVAs) • X-rays to rule out associated injury or fracture • MRI useful to determine full extent of injury	Conservative or arthroscopic repair of tear
Collateral ligament tear	• **Medial collateral is the most commonly injured knee ligament** (lateral collateral is least commonly injured) • Seen after direct blow to lateral knee • **Commonly pt also injures ACL or PCL** • X-rays to rule out associated injury or fracture • MRI useful to determine full extent of injury	Hinge brace
Meniscus tear	• Acute trauma or more commonly due to degeneration seen with aging • Medial menisci injured 3× more often, male > female • Dx = **McMurray test** = pt supine with hips flexed 90° & knee fully flexed, maneuver foot into abduction-adduction & external-internal rotation while palpating joint line for a click. • MRI is standard diagnostic test (See Figure 2-13)	Rest (fails > 50% of time), consider arthroscopy

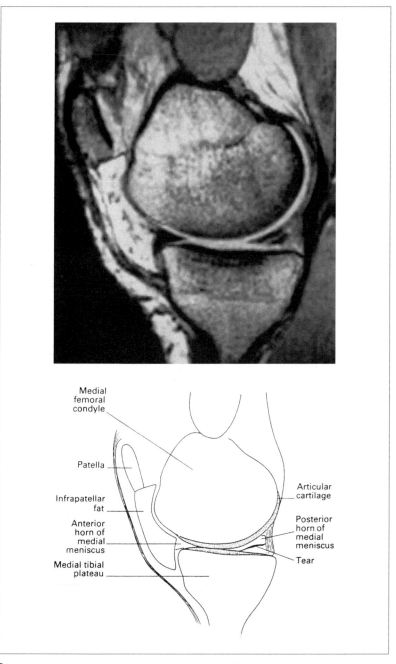

Tear of medial meniscus. Sagittal MRI through the medial part of the knee joint showing a tear in the posterior horn of the medial meniscus. The anterior horn appears normal.

XX. Neurosurgery

A. HEAD INJURY
1.

TABLE 2-13 Intracranial Hemorrhage

TYPE	BLEEDING SITE	CHARACTERISTICS	TREATMENT
Epidural	Middle meningeal artery	• **Dx = CT → biconcave disk not crossing sutures** • This is a medical emergency!!! (See Figure 2-14)	Evacuate hematoma via burr holes
Subdural	Cortical bridging veins	• Causes = trauma, coagulopathy, common in elderly • Sx may start 1–2 weeks after trauma • **Dx = CT → crescentic pattern extends across suture lines** • Px worse than epidural due to ↑ risk of concurrent brain injury	Evacuate hematoma via burr holes
Subarachnoid	Circle of Willis, often at MCA branch	• Causes = AV malformation, berry aneurysm, trauma • Berry aneurysms → severe sudden headache, **CN III palsy** • CSF xanthochromia (also seen any time CSF protein > 150 mg/dL or serum bilirubin > 6 mg/dL) • Dx berry aneurysm with cerebral angiogram	Berry aneurysm = surgical excision or fill with metal coil (See Figure 2-15) Nimodipine to prevent vasospasm & resultant 2° infarcts
Parenchymal	Basal ganglia, internal capsule, thalamus	• Causes = hypertension, trauma, AV malformation, coagulopathy • CT/MRI → focal edema, hypodensity	↑ ICP → mannitol, hyperventilate, steroids &/or ventricular shunt

2. General treatment
   a. Establish ABCs, intubate & ventilate unconscious patients
   b. Maintain cervical spine precautions
   c. ↑ ICP → mannitol, hyperventilate, steroids &/or ventricular shunt

B. FACIAL FRACTURES
1. LeFort fractures are the classic facial trauma fractures
2. Look for mobile palate, fractures always involve the pterygoid plates
3. Dx = clinical + CT
4. Tx = surgical repair & stabilization

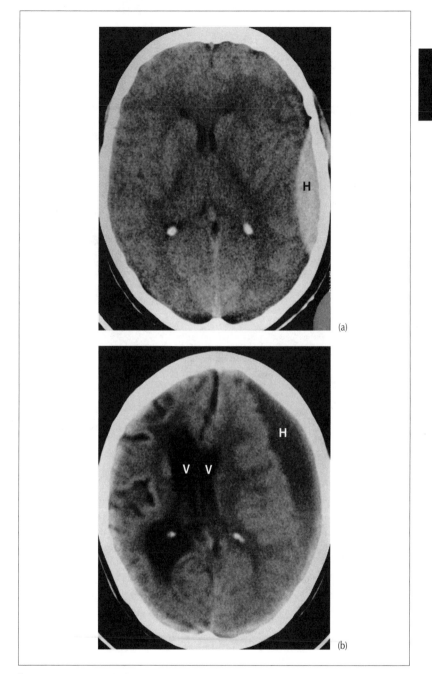

Figure 2-14   Extracerebral hematoma. (a) CT scan showing a high-density lentiform area typical of an acute epidural hematoma (H). (b) CT scan in another patient taken a month after injury showing a subdural hematoma (H) as a low-density area. Note the substantial ventricular displacement. V = ventricles.

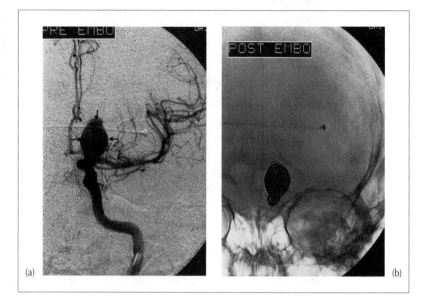

FIGURE 2-15 Aneurysm occlusion. (a) Carotid angiogram showing a large aneurysm (arrows) arising at the termination of the internal carotid artery. (b) Plain film after embolization of the aneurysm that is occluded with metal coils.

C. BASILAR SKULL FRACTURES

1. **Present with 4 classic physical findings: "raccoon's eyes" & Battle's sign, hemotympanum, CSF rhinorrhea & otorrhea**
2. "Raccoon's eyes" are dark circles (bruising) about the eyes, signifying orbital fractures
3. Battle's sign is ecchymoses over the mastoid process, indicating a fracture there
4. Dx = clinical + x-ray or CT
5. Tx = supportive

D. TUMORS

1. Si/Sx
   a. Headache awakening pt at night or is worse in morning after waking
   b. ↑ ICP → nausea/vomit, **bradycardia with hypertension & Cheyne-Stokes respirations (Cushing's triad)** & papilledema
   c. ⊕ focal deficits, frequently of CN III → fixed, dilated pupil
2. DDx

TABLE 2-14   CNS Malignancy

TYPE	CHARACTERISTICS
Metastatic	Small circular lesion, often multiple, at gray/white jnxn—**most common CNS neoplasm**: 1° = lung, breast, melanoma, renal cell, colon, thyroid
Glioblastoma multiforme	Large, irregular, ring enhancing due to central infarction (outgrows blood supply)—**most common 1° CNS neoplasm**
Meningioma	Second most common 1° CNS neoplasm, slow growing & benign
Retinoblastoma	Occurs in children, 60% sporadic, 40% familial (often bilateral)
Craniopharyngioma	Compresses optic chiasm (visual loss) & hypothalamus
Prolactinoma	The most common pituitary tumor, Sx = **bilateral gynecomastia, amenorrhea, galactorrhea, impotence, bilateral hemianopsia**
Lymphoma	The most common CNS tumor in AIDS pts (100× ↑ incidence), **MRI → ring-enhancing lesion difficult to distinguish from toxoplasmosis**
Schwannoma	Usually affects CN VIII (acoustic neuroma) → tinnitus, deafness & ↑ ICP

    3. Dx
      a. Bx → definitive diagnosis
      b. Clinical suspicion + CT/MRI can diagnose lymphoma, prolactinoma, meningioma
      c. Demographics important for retinoblastoma
    4. Tx = excision for all 1° tumors except prolactinoma & lymphoma
      a. First-line Tx for prolactinoma = bromocriptine (D_2 agonist inhibits prolactin secretion), second line = surgery
      b. Tx for lymphoma is radiation therapy, poor Px
      c. Tx for metastases is generally radiation therapy & support

E. HYDROCEPHALUS
    1. Definition = ↑ CSF → enlarged ventricles
    2. Si/Sx = ↑ ICP, ↓ cognition, headache, focal findings, in children separation of cranial bones leads to grossly enlarged calvarium
    3. **Dx made by finding dilated ventricles on CT/MRI** (See Figure 2-16)
    4. Lumbar puncture opening pressure & CT appearance are crucial to determine type of hydrocephalus
    5. Normal ICP is always communicating
      a. Hydrocephalus ex vacuo
        1) Ventricle dilation after neuron loss (e.g., stroke, CNS dz)
        2) Sx due to neuron loss, not ventricular dilation in this case
        3) Tx = none indicated
      b. Normal pressure hydrocephalus
        1) Si/Sx = classic triad: bladder incontinence, dementia, ataxia ("wet, wacky, wobbly")
        2) Causes: 50% idiopathic, also meningitis, cerebral hemorrhage, trauma, atherosclerosis
        3) Due to ↓ CSF resorption across arachnoid villi
        4) Dx = clinically, or radionucleotide CSF studies
        5) Tx = diuretic therapy, repeated spinal taps, consider shunt placement
    6. ↑ ICP can be communicating or noncommunicating
      a. Pseudotumor cerebri
        1) Communicating spontaneous ↑ ICP

2) **Commonly seen in obese, young females**, can be idiopathic, massive quantities of vitamin A can cause it
3) **CT → no ventricle dilation (may even be shrunken)**
4) Tx = symptomatic (acetazolamide or surgical lumboperitoneal shunt), dz is typically self-limiting
  b. Noncommunicating
   1) Due to block between ventricles & subarachnoid space → CSF outflow obstruction at fourth ventricle, foramina of Luschka/Magendie/Munro/Magnum
   2) Causes = congenital (e.g., Arnold-Chiari syndrome), tumor effacing outflow path, or scarring 2° meningitis or subarachnoid hemorrhage
   3) Dx = CT
   4) Tx = treat underlying cause if possible

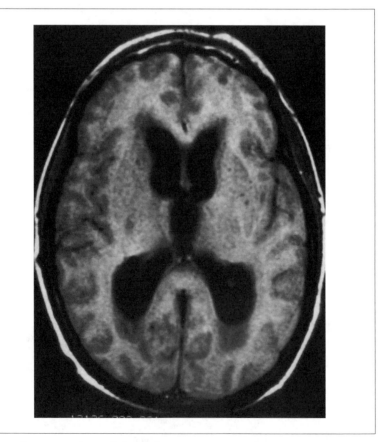

FIGURE 2-16   CT scan showing hydrocephalus.

XXI. Vascular Diseases

A. ANEURYSMS

1. Abnormal dilatation of an artery to **more than twice** its normal diameter
2. Most common cause is atherosclerosis
3. Common sites include abdominal aorta aneurysms (AAAs) & peripheral vessels including femoral & popliteal arteries
4. True aneurysms involve all 3 layers of the vessel wall—caused by atherosclerosis & congenital defects such as Marfan's syndrome
5. False aneurysms are "pulsatile hematomas" covered only by a thickened fibrous capsule (adventitia)—usually caused by traumatic disruption of the vessel wall or at an anastomotic site
6. Si/Sx = mostly asymptomatic; however, patients can present with rupture, thrombosis & embolization, some patients may complain of referred back pain &/or epigastric discomfort
7. Rupture of AAA
   a. **A ruptured AAA is a surgical emergency** & the patient may present with **classic** abdominal pain, pulsatile abdominal mass & hypotension
   b. The rate of rupture for a 5-cm diameter AAA is 6% per yr, rate for 6-cm diameter AAA is 10% per yr
   c. A patient's risk of rupture is increased by large diameter (Laplace's law), recent expansion, hypertension & COPD; as a result, regular follow-up & control of hypertension are critical
8. Dx
   a. Palpation of a pulsatile mass in the abdomen on physical exam, confirmed with abdominal Utz or CT (See Figures 2-17 and 2-18)
   b. CT is the best modality to determine the size of the aneurysm in a stable patient (See Figure 2-19)
   c. A plain film of the abdomen may demonstrate a calcified wall (See Figure 2-20)
   d. Aortogram most definitive diagnosis, also reveals size & extent
9. Tx
   a. BP control & decrease risk factors, or surgical intervention
   b. Surgical intervention usually involves the placement of a synthetic graft within the dilated wall of the AAA; surgery is recommended for **aneurysms > 5 cm** in diameter in a good surgical candidate
10. Complications
    a. MI, renal failure (due to proximity of renal vasculature off of aorta) & colonic ischemia (AAAs usually involve the inferior mesenteric artery [IMA])
    b. Be aware of formation of **aortoduodenal fistula** in patients who have had a synthetic graft placed for AAA disease & present with GI bleeding

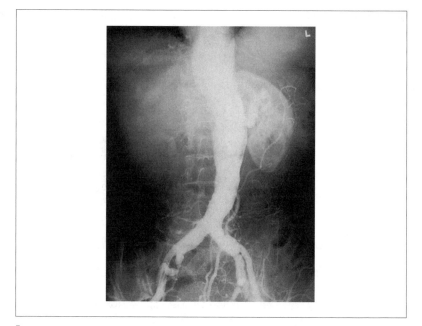

FIGURE 2-17   Suprarenal abdominal aortic aneurysm seen on angiography.

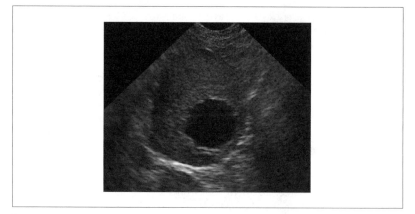

FIGURE 2-18   Transverse ultrasound of the abdomen showing the lumen (black) surrounded by thrombosis.

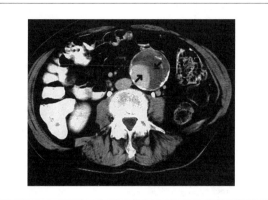

FIGURE 2-19   CT abdomen after contrast shows filling of the lumen (↑) and thrombus in an aneurysm (↓).

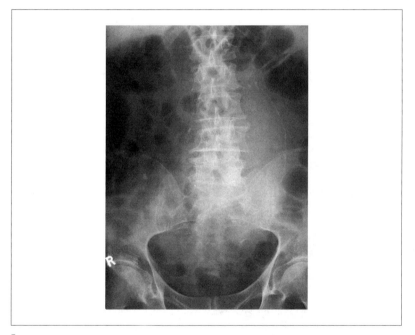

FIGURE 2-20   Plain abdomen film showing curvilinear calcification in a large abdominal aortic aneurysm.

11. **Peripheral aneurysms**
   a. Most commonly in the popliteal artery
   b. 50% of popliteal aneurysms are bilateral & 33% of patients with a popliteal aneurysm will have an AAA
   c. Si/Sx = rupture is rare, & pts usually present with thrombosis, embolization, or claudication
   d. Tx = surgical if patient is symptomatic

B. AORTIC DISSECTION

1. An intimal tear through which blood can flow, creating a plane between the intima & remainder of vessel wall
2. Usually confined to thoracic aorta (e.g., syphilis)
3. These planes can progress proximally & distally to disrupt blood supply to intestines, spinal cord, kidneys & even the coronary vessels
4. In general type A affects ascending aorta only, type B can affect both ascending & descending aorta
5. Si/Sx = **Classic severe tearing (ripping) chest pain in hypertensive patients that radiates toward the back**
6. Dx = clinical, confirm with CT or aortogram, but if pt unstable take immediately to OR
7. Tx
   a. Descending aortic dissection is usually medical (e.g., control of HTN) unless life-threatening complications arise
   b. In contrast, ascending dissection → immediate surgical intervention with graft placement

C. PERIPHERAL VASCULAR DISEASE (PVD)

1. Caused by atherosclerotic dz in the lower extremities
2. Si/Sx = intermittent claudication, rest pain, ulceration, gangrene, reduced femoral, popliteal & pedal pulses, dependent rubor, muscular atrophy, trophic changes & skin blanching on foot elevation
3. Dry gangrene is the result of a chronic ischemic state & necrosis of tissue without signs of active infection
4. Wet gangrene is the superimposition of cellulitis & active infection to necrotic tissue
5. Leriche's syndrome
   a. Aortoiliac disease → claudication in hip, gluteal muscles & impotence
   b. 5% have limb loss at 5 yr with rest pain (represents more severe ischemia) & if not treated almost 50% of patients will need amputation 2° to gangrene
6. Dx
   a. Complete H&P, important to assess risk factors for atherosclerosis & limitations of lifestyle from PVD
   b. Noninvasive testing includes but is not limited to measurement of the ankle brachial index (ABI) & duplex examination
      1) ABI is the ratio of BP in the ankle to the BP in the arm
      2) Patients without disease have ABIs > 1.0 given the higher absolute pressure in the ankle

3) Patients with severe occlusive disease (e.g., rest pain) will generally have indices < 0.4; patients with claudication generally have indices < 0.7

4) The exercise ABI most useful diagnostically; ABI may drop with exercise in a patient with PVD

5) Duplex (Utz) examination combines ultrasound & Doppler instruments, & can provide information regarding blood flow velocity (related to stenosis) & display blood flow as a waveform; **normal waveform is triphasic, moderate occlusive disease demonstrates biphasic, & severe disease shows a monophasic pattern**

6) Preoperative angiograms are classically done to confirm the Dx & to establish distal vessel run-off, or "road-map" vessels for the surgeon

7. Tx
   a. Lifestyle modifications including smoking cessation & increasing moderate exercise
   b. Pharmacotherapy is pentoxifylline
   c. Minimally invasive therapy includes percutaneous balloon angioplasty (PTA) &/or atherectomy—best results for isolated lesions of high grade stenosis in the iliac & superior femoral arteries (SFA) vessels
   d. Treatment of iliac disease now involves PTA plus the placement of endoluminal stents
   e. Indications for surgical intervention are severe **rest pain, tissue necrosis, nonhealing infection & intractable claudication**
   f. Surgical treatment includes local endarterectomy with or without patch angioplasty & bypass procedures
   g. Results are better with autologous vein grafts; common operation for aortoiliac disease is the aortobifemoral bypass graft, while disease of the SFA is commonly treated with a femoral-popliteal bypass graft

8. Potential complication = **thrombosis**, must be addressed with either thrombolytic agents, balloon thrombectomy, or revision of graft

D. VESSEL DISEASE

1. Varicose veins
   a. Dilated, prominent tortuous superficial veins in the lower limbs
   b. Commonly seen in pregnancy (progesterone causes dilation of veins) & prolonged standing professions, may have an inherited predisposition
   c. Si/Sx = may be asymptomatic or cause itching, may also have dull aching & heaviness in legs, especially at the end of the day
   d. Dx = clinically
   e. Tx = support hose, elevate limbs, avoid prolonged standing, sclerotherapy or surgical ablation may be indicated

2. Venous ulcers
   a. 2° to venous hypertension, DVT, or varicose veins, usually located on the medial ankle & calf
   b. Si/Sx = **painless ulcers**, large, shallow & contain bleeding granulation tissue
   c. Phlegmasia alba dolens (milk leg)
      1) Venous thrombosis usually occurring in postpartum women
      2) Si/Sx = cool, pale swollen leg with impalpable pulses
      3) Tx = heparin & elevation
   d. Phlegmasia cerulea dolens (venous gangrene)
      1) Venous thrombosis with complete obstruction of arterial inflow
      2) Si/Sx = sudden intense pain, massive edema & cyanosis
      3) Tx = heparin, elevation, venous thrombectomy if unresolved
   e. Dx = clinical, Doppler studies of extremities
   f. Tx = reduction of swelling by elevation, compression stockings & Unna's boots (zinc oxide paste impregnated bandage), skin grafting is rarely indicated
3. Arterial ulcers
   a. 2° to occlusive arterial disease
   b. Si/Sx = **painful by contrast to venous ulcers**, usually found on lower leg & lateral ankle, particularly on dorsum of the foot, toes & heel, absent pulses, pallor, claudication, & may have "blue toes"
   c. Dx = clinical, work-up of PVD
   d. Tx = conservative management or bypass surgery

E. CAROTID VASCULAR DISEASE
1. Atherosclerotic plaques in carotid arteries (most commonly at carotid bifurcation)
2. DDx of carotid insufficiency = trauma, anatomic kinking, fibromuscular dysplasia & Takayasu's arteritis
3. Si/Sx = Carotid bruit, TIAs (neurologic changes that reverse in less than 24 hr), amaurosis fugax (transient monocular blindness), reversible ischemic neurologic deficits (lasting up to 3 days with no permanent changes) & CVAs that result in permanent neurologic changes
4. Dx = angiography; however, duplex scanning is noninvasive & is able to determine location, percent stenosis & assess the plaque characteristics (e.g., soft vs. calcified)
5. Tx = modification of risk factors important, anticoagulation & use of antiplatelet agents (aspirin, dipyridamole) intended to prevent thrombosis
6. Surgical therapy is carotid endarterectomy (CEA), pts are usually placed on postop aspirin therapy
7. **Surgical indications: symptomatic patient** = 1) carotid stenosis > 70%, 2) multiple TIAs (risk of stroke is 10%/year), 3) patients who have suffered a CVA & have lesion amenable to surgery (stroke recurrence is as high as 50% without surgery); **asymptomatic patient** = endarterectomy is controversial, but stenosis > 75% is an accepted indication (AHA Consensus Statement, *Stroke* 1995, 26:188–201)
8. Mortality rate of operation is very low (1%), & risk of stroke after CEA is reduced to 0.5–2%

F. SUBCLAVIAN STEAL SYNDROME
1. Caused by occlusive lesion in subclavian artery or innominate artery, causing decreased blood flow distal to the obstruction

2. This results in the "stealing" of blood from vertebral artery via retrograde flow
3. Si/Sx = arm claudication, syncope, vertigo, nausea, confusion & supraclavicular bruits
4. Dx = angiogram, Doppler, MRI
5. Tx = **carotid-subclavian bypass**

G. RENOVASCULAR HYPERTENSION

1. Caused by renal artery stenosis & subsequent activation of the renin-angiotensin pathway
2. Commonly due to atherosclerotic lesions
3. Can also be 2° to fibromuscular dysplasia, subintimal dissections & hypoplasia of renal artery
4. Si/Sx = most patients are asymptomatic, some will present with headache, abdominal bruits, or cardiac, cerebrovascular, or renal dysfunction related to hypertension; a sudden onset of hypertension is more consistent with a dysplastic process when compared to the slower evolving atherosclerosis
5. Surgically correctable HTN = **renal artery stenosis (most common)**, pheochromocytoma, unilateral renal parenchymal disease, Cushing's syndrome, primary hyperaldosteronism, hyperthyroidism, hyperparathyroidism, coarctation of the aorta, cancer & increased ICP
6. Dx = definitive Dx obtained by **angiography (string of beads appearance)**, others include IVP, renal scans & renal vein renin ratios
7. Tx = BP control & consider balloon catheter dilation of stenosis—results better with fibromuscular dysplasia vs. atherosclerotic lesions, surgical correction involves endarterectomy, bypass, or resection

H. MESENTERIC ISCHEMIA

1. **Chronic intestinal ischemia**
   a. 2° to atherosclerotic lesions of at least two of the three major vessels supplying the bowel
   b. Si/Sx = **weight loss & postprandial pain & abdominal bruit**
   c. Dx = definitive diagnosis is made with aortogram
   d. Tx = surgical intervention (endarterectomy, bypass from aorta to involved graft) is **indicated** in absence of malignancy (particularly pancreatic cancer must be ruled out)
2. **Acute intestinal ischemia**
   a. Acute thrombosis of a mesenteric vessel secondary to atherosclerotic changes or emboli from the heart
   b. Si/Sx = rapid onset of pain that is out of proportion to exam, vomiting, diarrhea & history of heart condition predisposing to emboli formation (e.g., atrial fibrillation)
   c. Dx = angiogram should be performed immediately to confirm or rule out diagnosis
   d. Tx = embolectomy/thrombectomy, resection of necrotic bowel & bypass

Surgery Case Scenarios

A 73-year-old right-handed female is brought to the emergency room by her husband after she slipped in the bathtub and banged her head. The fall was not witnessed and it is unclear whether or not the patient lost consciousness. She is quite agitated and speaks in long strings of nonsensical words. On exam you find no evidence of focal neurologic disease other than her impressive aphasia. However, you note bilateral carotid bruits as well as an irregularly irregular pulse. The CT scan reveals a crescentic collection of blood extending across suture lines. Also, a focal hypodense area is noted in the left temporal lobe indicating edema from an acute infarct. It has now been 45 minutes since the patient was found down by her husband.

1. The diagnosis and preferred treatment for this patient are:

   a) Epidural hemorrhage, Wernicke's aphasia, tPA thrombolysis

   b) Subdural hemorrhage, Broca's aphasia, tPA thrombolysis

   c) Epidural hemorrhage, Broca's aphasia, tPA thrombolysis

   d) Subdural hemorrhage, Wernicke's aphasia, supportive treatment

   e) Subdural hemorrhage, Wernicke's aphasia, nimodipine

2. If the CT scanner had instead found a biconcave-shaped blood collection that did not cross suture lines, the patient's long-term prognosis would be:

   a) Improved

   b) Worse

You are the surgical resident on call in the emergency department when a 17-year-old male s/p MVA (motorcycle vs. truck) arrives in your emergency room. The patient is unresponsive, has C-collar in place, and is having labored respiration. His trachea is deviated to the right, he has an oral airway in place, and oxygen via face mask is being provided. One peripheral IV has been placed in the left antecubital fossa. The patient has blood oozing from ears, nose, and chest. Vital signs are BP 110/50, HR 110, resp 32, oxygen saturation 91%, temp 97.0. Type and cross, CBC, Chem 7, PT/PTT, and UA are all pending.

3. What are the most important measures that need to be taken in this patient at this time?

   a) Get a thorough history from family members before beginning any treatment

   b) Maintain oral airway, apply pressure to oozing blood, and maintain IV

   c) Protect airway with ET tube, maintain C-spine precautions, insert needle into second intercostal space midclavicular line to evacuate potential pneumothorax; start two large bore IVs

   d) Perform pericardial centesis, insert ET tube, turn victim's head to one side to prevent aspiration of blood

During the secondary survey you notice that the patient has ecchymosis surrounding his eyes and behind his ears. Pupils are asymmetrical and sluggish. The patient also has a swollen abdomen; no blood is noted to be draining from his urethra or rectum, and he has a swollen right thigh. The Glasgow coma score is 8. Diagnostic peritoneal lavage reveals blood-tinged fluid. A Foley catheter is placed with clear-yellow urine noted. Head CT, CXR, lateral C-spine, pelvic and right thigh x-rays are obtained and results are pending. Tox screen is pending. The patient's helmet is noted to be cracked. Vital signs are now BP 80/50, HR 130. Respirations are manually ventilated without resistance and the patient has lung sounds bilaterally. Oxygen saturation is 100%.

4. What are the most important measures to be taken at this time?

a) Observe, hyperventilate, administering mannitol and steroids to decrease ICP; call orthopedics

b) Discontinue ventilation and remove ET tube since patient is now at 100% oxygen saturation; call neurosurgery

c) Observe patient, splint right thigh; call neurosurgery; give O-negative blood; call urology

d) Hyperventilate, slightly elevate head of bed maintaining C-spine precautions; call neurosurgery and orthopedics, informing them that the patient is currently on his way to the OR for possible internal abdominal bleeding; the patient will need his femur stabilized and O-negative blood if cross-match is unavailable

A 32-year-old male presents to the general surgery clinic for preoperative evaluation prior to an elective hernia repair. Upon entering your office you notice multiple bruises on his arms and legs. You also notice that he has a bandage on his left knee.

5. In order to assess this patient's operative risk for a bleeding diathesis, what is the first thing you must obtain?

a) History and physical

b) Prothrombin time

c) Activated partial thromboplastin time

d) Bleeding time test

6. If the patient above is found to have hemophilia A, which of the following laboratory tests will yield the most relevant information with respect to predicting intraoperative bleeding in this patient?

a) Complete blood count

b) Bleeding time

c) Prothrombin time

d) Activated partial thromboplastin time

e) Electrolyte panel

A 63-year-old male presents to his physician with a recent change in bowel habits. The patient states that his stools have become smaller, with occasional minimal gross blood found in the toilet bowel. The patient also admits that he has been experiencing severe, intermittent, crampy abdominal pain, and he has had constipation recently.

7. Which of the following conditions is most consistent with this clinical presentation?

a) Diverticular disease

b) Right-sided colon cancer

    c) Left-sided colon cancer

    d) Carcinoid tumor

    e) Second-degree hemorrhoid

A 46-year-old woman presents to your office with a chief complaint of a breast lump she found while performing her monthly self-examination. Her history reveals that she is a G_0 female who began menarche at age 9. Her last menstrual period was 9 days ago. Her family history is significant for a sister who died of breast cancer at the age of 42. On physical exam, you observe symmetrical breasts with no dimpling, nipple retraction, skin color changes, or nipple discharge. You are able to feel an isolated, firm mass in the left breast.

    8. What are the next steps in the work-up of this patient?

        a) Mammogram, FNA/core biopsy, if nondiagnostic then reassurance

        b) Mammogram, ductography, breast cancer genetic testing, reassurance if nondiagnostic

        c) Open biopsy, simple mastectomy, and reassurance

        d) Core biopsy or open biopsy

A 43-year-old Hispanic female presents to the ER with a 2-day history of vomiting and intermittent abdominal cramping. She has not passed any stool over the past 2 days, but she is able to pass flatus. Her last menstrual period was 7 days ago. Her past medical history includes type II diabetes mellitus and cholecystitis, which was treated with an open cholecystectomy 6 months prior to her current presentation. Her vital signs reveal a temperature of 38.4, a blood pressure of 128/88, pulse of 96, and a respiration rate of 22. CBC, chemistry panel, and glucose are within normal limits.

    9. The most likely diagnosis is:

        a) Incarcerated incisional hernia

        b) Small bowel obstruction secondary to adhesions

        c) Diverticulitis

        d) Appendicitis

A 27-year-old male presents to the ER with purulent discharge from a site several centimeters from the anus. You are able to place a probe into the site of discharge and reach all the way into the rectal lumen.

    10. All of the following will prolong his condition **except**:

        a) Foreign body

        b) Infection

        c) Inadequate vascularization

        d) Radiation

        e) Neoplasm

A 12-year-old African-American boy has burns over 40% of his body from a house fire. While the child survives, the affected limbs are subjected to extensive rehabilitation and remain limited in range of motion and function. Ten years after the accident, a chronic ulcer in the scarred region of his arm is biopsied and is determined to be malignant.

11. Which of the following is the most likely histologic diagnosis?

a) Keloidal formation

b) Melanoma

c) Squamous cell carcinoma

d) Basal cell carcinoma

e) Transitional cell carcinoma

A 67-year-old female presents with a 4-month history of worsening calf cramping with walking. She admits to smoking one-and-a-half packs per day and her current medications include captopril and Premarin. She denies any foot pain while sleeping. Physical exam reveals a morbidly obese woman in no acute distress. Her exam is unremarkable except for a moderate lateral shift in her cardiac point of maximum impulse.

12. An ankle-arm index would most likely reveal which of the following?

a) ABI = 1.0

b) ABI = 0.6

c) ABI = 0.4

d) ABI = 0.2

e) ABI = 0.1

13. The most appropriate intervention for the above described patient includes:

a) Observation only

b) Lifestyle modifications including smoking cessation and exercise

c) Percutaneous transluminal angioplasty of the occluded artery

d) Femoral to popliteal bypass using a PTFE conduit

e) Directional atherectomy of the occluded artery

A 65-year-old male is referred to a gastroenterologist for episodes of dysphagia, reflux of food that is undigested, and putrid breath odor. On physical exam, a cervical mass is noted.

14. This condition is best treated via:

a) Myotomy of thyropharyngeus muscle

b) Myotomy of cricopharyngeus muscle

c) Myotomy of sternothyroid muscle

d) Myotomy of thyrohyoid muscle

e) Myotomy of the omohyoid muscle

Answers

1. **d)** The crescentic collection of blood extending across suture lines is the characteristic description of subdural hemorrhage. The patient's aphasia is receptive

rather than expressive and her temporal lobe lesion is consistent with a diagnosis of a Wernicke's. The bilateral carotid bruits are indications of generalized atherosclerosis and the irregularly irregular pulse is indicative of atrial fibrillation, both of which increase the risk of thromboembolic disease. The focal hypodensity in the temporal lobe on CT is thus likely indicative of a thromboembolic stroke that may be hypothesized to have caused the patient to fall and bang her head. Regardless, despite the fact that the patient is within the time frame for tPA thrombolysis (3–6 hours at the longest, within 1 hour preferred), the presence of the hemorrhage is an absolute contraindication to administration of tPA.

2. **a)** Subdural hemorrhages are associated with concurrent parenchymal brain injury and therefore portend a worse longer term prognosis than epidural hemorrhage, despite the fact that the blood loss is arterial in the epidural hemorrhage.

3. **c)** The ABCs of trauma must always be adhered to, in that order. Although a thorough history of events—**A**llergies, **M**edications, **P**ast medical history, **L**ast meal, **E**xposure to toxins (**AMPLE**)—is useful, this information can be obtained from someone else in the emergency department and relayed to you. Your first priority in the unconscious patient is to maintain the airway with an ET tube while maintaining C-spine precautions. In order to prevent aspiration of gastric contents or of blood, you can insert an orogastric tube to suction the stomach and any blood in the mouth. The deviated trachea is most likely caused by a pneumothorax. The quickest thing to do is to insert a large-gauge needle. If this does not relieve deviation or if a hemothorax is suspected, then chest tube placement is indicated. A pericardiocentesis is recommended if the patient has pericardial tamponade, indicated by distant heart sounds, JVD, and tracheal deviation. Two large-bore IVs are standard trauma therapy in order to maintain blood volume.

4. **d)** This patient is hemodynamically unstable. He must be stabilized in the operating room. Neurosurgery, orthopedics, and general surgery must all be involved. Urology is mentioned to remind you of possible pelvic fractures and the importance of assessing blood at the urethra before Foley catheter placement. A GCS < 8 requires immediate attention, and depending on the cause steps might need to be taken to evacuate blood in the emergency department. Hyperventilation will decrease CO_2, which is known to cause vasodilation of cerebral vessels further increasing the ICP. O-negative blood should be used until cross-matched blood is available.

5. **a)** The most important preoperative information predictive of unexpected bleeding complications is a thorough history, including a complete family history, and a physical exam. The history itself will be of higher yield than any laboratory tests or the physical exam.

6. **d)** A patient carrying a diagnosis of hemophilia A is deficient to some degree in factor VIII. As a result, the PTT laboratory test, which evaluates the intrinsic coagulation pathway, is the most appropriate test. Therapy consists of administering recombinant factor VIII protein.

7. **c)** The left side of the colon has a smaller luminal diameter than the right side. As a result, obstructive-like symptoms and changes in bowel habits are more common in left-sided colon cancer. Right-sided colon cancer is more consistent with a presentation of microcytic anemia and melena, and obstruction is less common in right-sided cancers. Eighty percent of diverticular disease is asymptomatic and found incidentally, but it can cause recurrent abdominal pain in left lower quadrant and changes in bowel habits, and 5–10% of patients present with lower GI hemorrhage that can be massive. Carcinoid tumors occur most frequently in the appendix, and patients usually present with flushing, watery diarrhea and abdominal cramps, and elevated levels of urine 5-HIAA. Second degree hemorrhoids are those that occasionally prolapse into the anal canal and reduce spontaneously without manual manipulation; these patients also complain of blood-tinged stools.

8. **d)** See the algorithm illustrating a breast mass work-up. Every solid lump in a woman over 40 requires a tissue diagnosis. An open biopsy is warranted in this dominant lump, which based on exam and her history should be considered suspicious. A core biopsy can be performed prior to open biopsy, thereby sparing the patient from the invasive open biopsy if the results are negative. A nondiagnostic finding in a high-risk patient such as this is never acceptable, so an inconclusive core biopsy must be followed by an excisional, open biopsy.

9. **b)** This clinical presentation for small bowel obstruction is rather straightforward. Remember, do not get confused regarding the passage of flatus, which can still happen in a complete bowel obstruction. The most common cause of small bowel obstruction in the adult population is adhesions (postabdominal surgery), followed by hernias and neoplasms. Incarcerated incisional hernias are usually visible, unlike in this patient where no such physical finding is mentioned. Patients with diverticulitis commonly present with left lower quadrant pain, diarrhea or constipation, fever, anorexia, and leukocytosis. Appendicitis will normally present with pain in the periumbilical area, which then localizes to McBurney's point.

10. **c)** The clinical vignette describes a patient with a fistula, which is an abnormal communication between two organs. Of all the factors listed, only inadequate vascularization does NOT predispose to fistula. Therefore, all the factors listed except for inadequate vascularization will prevent the patient's fistula from healing.

11. **c)** The description given above is classic for a Marjolin ulcer, a squamous cell carcinoma that occurs in a burn scar.

12. **b)** The clinical description paints the picture of a person with claudication secondary to atherosclerosis, most likely affecting the superficial femoral artery given her symptomatology. The fact that she denies foot pain while sleeping makes rest pain a less likely component of her disease presentation. As a result, the ABI would be greater than 0.4 and most likely less than 0.7. Those patients with rest pain generally have ABIs less than 0.4.

13. **b)** The majority of claudicants will not progress to limb-threatening ischemia. Therefore, appropriate therapy is conservative, not surgical. This includes an aggressive smoking cessation regimen plus exercise despite the limitations imposed by the claudication.

14. **b)** This is the classical presentation of a Zenker's diverticulum, which is a false diverticulum above the cricopharyngeus muscle. A Zenker's diverticulum is found between the thyropharyngeus and the cricopharyngeus muscles and is treated by excision of the diverticulum and myotomy of the cricopharyngeus muscle.

3. Obstetrics and Gynecology

Griselda Gutierrez

Obstetrics

I. Terminology

1. Gravidity ≡ total number of pregnancies
2. Parity ≡ number of pregnancies carried to viability—can also express parity as 4 numbers: term pregnancies, preterm, abortions & living children (TPAL)
3. Term delivery ≡ delivery of infant after 37-wk gestation
4. Premature delivery ≡ delivery of infant weighing between 500 and 2500 g & delivery between 20 and 37 wk

II. Prenatal Care

A. THE FIRST VISIT

1. Pregnancy diagnosis
   a. Si/Sx = amenorrhea, ↑ urinary frequency, breast engorgement & tenderness, nausea, fatigue, **bluish discoloration of vagina due to vascular congestion (Chadwick's sign) & softening of cervix (Hegar's sign)**
   b. Pregnancy test
      1) Detects human chorionic gonadotropin (hCG) or its β subunit
      2) Rapidly dividing fertilized egg produces hCG even before implantation occurs
      3) Commercial kits detect pregnancy 12–15 days after conception
      4) Home tests have low false-positive rate but high false-negative rate
   c. Ultrasound (Utz)
      1) Gestational sac identified at 5 wk, fetal image detected by 6–7 wk, cardiac activity first noted at 8 wk
      2) Utz is most accurate method to determine gestational age
2. Obstetrical Hx
   a. Duration of previous gestations
   b. Mode of delivery (e.g., normal spontaneous vaginal delivery vs. C-section vs. vacuum assisted)
   c. Duration of labor, maternal, postpartum & neonatal complications, newborn weight, newborn sex
3. Menstrual Hx including last menstrual period (LMP), regularity of cycles, age at menarche
4. Contraceptive Hx (important for risk assessment, oral contraceptive pills [OCPs] have been associated with birth defects)
5. Medical Hx
   a. Medicines, consider potential teratogens

TABLE 3-1   Teratogens

DRUG	BIRTH DEFECT
Lithium	Ebstein's anomaly (single-chambered right side of heart)
Carbamazepine & valproate	Neural tube defects
Retinoic acid	CNS defects, craniofacial defects, cardiovascular effects
ACE inhibitors	Renal failure in neonates, renal tubule dysgenesis, ↓ skull ossification
Oral hypoglycemics	Neonatal hypoglycemia
Coumadin	Skeletal & CNS defects
NSAIDs	Constriction of ductus arteriosis, necrotizing enterocolitis

    b. FHx, social Hx including tobacco ETOH, drug use, type of work, exposure to animals

    c. Diabetes & hypertension

6. Estimated date of confinement (EDC)

    a. **Nägele's rule = LMP + 7 days − 3 mo + 1 yr**: e.g., if LMP began 5/20/99, delivery due 2/27/2000

    b. This calculation depends on regular 28-day cycles (only 20–25% of women), adjustments must be made for longer or shorter cycles

7. Complete physical exam with pelvic examination including PAP smear & cultures for gonorrhea & chlamydia & estimation of uterine size

8. Labs include CBC, blood type with Rh status, urinalysis with culture, RPR test for syphilis, Rubella titer, TB skin testing, can offer HIV antibody test

9. If pt is not already immune to Rubella, do NOT vaccinate, as the vaccine is live virus

10. Genetic testing as indicated by history (e.g., hemoglobin electrophoresis in African American pt to determine sickle cell anemia likelihood)

11. Recommend 25–35 pound weight gain during pregnancy

12. Consider folate, iron & multivitamin supplements

B. FIRST TRIMESTER VISITS

1. Visit every 4 wk

2. Assess weight gain/loss, BP, pedal edema, fundal height, urine dip for glucosuria & proteinuria (**trace glucosuria is normal because of ↑ GFR, anything more than trace protein should be evaluated**)

3. Estimation of gestational age by uterine size

    a. Normal uterus is 3 × 4 × 7 cm

    b. Gravid uterus begins to enlarge & soften by 5–6 wk

TABLE 3-2   Height of Uterus by Gestational Week

12 WEEKS	16 WEEKS	20 WEEKS	20–36 WEEKS
At pubic symphysis	Midway from symphysis to umbilicus	At umbilicus	Height (cm) correlates with weeks of gestation*

*If uterine size (cm) > gestational age (wk) by more than 3 wk, consider multiple gestations, molar pregnancy, or MOST COMMONLY inaccurate dating.

C. SECOND TRIMESTER VISITS
1. Continue every 4 wk
2. After 12 wk, use Doppler Utz to evaluate fetal heartbeat at each visit
3. Offer triple marker screen (hCG, estriol, AFP) at 15–18 wk
   a. α-fetoprotein (αFP) ↓ in Down's syndrome
   b. α-fetoprotein ↑ in multiple gestation, neural tube deficit & duodenal atresia
4. At 17–19 wk (quickening) & beyond, document fetal movement
5. Amniocentesis if >35 years old or if history indicates (e.g., recurrent miscarriages, previous child with chromosomal or single gene defect, abnormal triple marker screen)
6. Glucose screening at 24 wk (1-hr Glucola)
7. Repeat hematocrit at 25–28 wk

D. THIRD TRIMESTER VISITS
1. Every 4 wk until week 3̶2̶ 28, every 2 wk from weeks 3̶2̶ 28–36, every wk until delivery
2. Inquire about preterm labor Sx: **vaginal bleeding, contractions, rupture of membranes**
3. Inquire about pregnancy-induced hypertension (PIH) (see below)
4. Screen for *Streptococcus agalactiae* (group B Strep) at 35–37 wk
5. Give RhoGAM at 28–30 wk if indicated (see below)

III. Physiologic Changes in Pregnancy

A. HEMATOLOGIC
1. Pregnancy is a **hypercoagulable** state
   a. ↑ clotting factor levels
   b. Venous stasis due to uterine pressure on lower extremity great veins
2. Anemia of pregnancy
   a. Plasma volume increases about 50% from sixth wk to week 30–34
   b. Red cell mass increases later & to a smaller degree, causing a relative anemia of about 15% due to dilution
3. Slight leukocytosis due to granulocyte demargination
4. Platelets decrease slightly, but remain within normal limits

B. CARDIAC
1. Cardiac output increases 50% (increase in both HR & stroke volume)
2. Because of ↑ flow, increased S2 split with inspiration, distended neck veins, systolic ejection murmur & S3 gallop are normal findings
3. **Diastolic murmurs are not normal findings in pregnancy**
4. ↓ peripheral vascular resistance due to progesterone-mediated smooth muscle relaxation
5. BP decreases during first 24 wk of pregnancy with gradual return to nonpregnant levels by term

C. PULMONARY
1. Nasal stuffiness & ↑ nasal secretions due to mucosal hyperemia
2. 4-cm elevation of diaphragm due to expanding uterus
3. Tidal volume & minute ventilation ↑ 30–40% (progesterone mediated)
4. Functional residual capacity & residual volume ↓ 20%

5. Hyperventilation $\rightarrow\uparrow PO_2$, $\downarrow PCO_2$—this allows the fetal PCO_2 to remain near 40 & still be able to give off CO_2 to maternal blood (sets up a CO_2 concentration gradient across maternal–fetal circulation & PO_2 gradient allowing maternal to fetal O_2 transfer)
6. Respiratory rate, vital capacity & inspiratory reserve do not change, total lung capacity decreases about 5%

D. GASTROINTESTINAL
1. $\downarrow$ GI motility due to progesterone
2. $\downarrow$ esophageal sphincter tone $\rightarrow$ gastric reflux also due to progesterone
3. $\uparrow$ alkaline phosphatase
4. Hemorrhoids due to constipation & $\uparrow$ venous pressure due to enlarging uterus compressing inferior vena cava

E. RENAL
1. $\downarrow$ bladder tone due to progesterone predisposes pregnant women to urinary stasis & UTIs/pyelonephritis
2. GFR increases 50% trace
   a. $\uparrow$ GFR $\rightarrow$ glucose excretion occurs in nearly all pregnant women
   b. Thus urine dipsticks are not useful in managing pts with diabetes
   c. **However, there should be no significant increase in protein loss**
3. Serum creatinine & blood urea nitrogen decrease

F. ENDOCRINE
1. $\downarrow$ fasting blood glucose in mother due to fetal utilization
2. $\uparrow$ postprandial glucose in mother due to $\uparrow$ insulin resistance
3. Fetus produces its own insulin starting at 9–11 wk
4. $\uparrow$ maternal thyroid bonding globulin (TBG) due to $\uparrow$ estrogen, $\uparrow$ total T3 & T4 due to $\uparrow$ TBG
5. Free T3 & T4 remain the same so pregnant women are euthyroid
6. $\uparrow$ cortisol & cortisol-binding globulin

G. SKIN
1. Normal skin changes in pregnancy mimic liver disease due to $\uparrow$ estrogen
2. Can see spider angiomas, palmar erythema
3. Hyperpigmentation occurs from $\uparrow$ estrogen & melanocyte stimulating hormone, affects umbilicus, perineum, face (chloasma) & linea nigra

IV. Medical Conditions in Pregnancy

A. GESTATIONAL DIABETES MELLITUS (GDM)
1. GDM = glucose intolerance or DM first recognized during pregnancy
2. **#1 medical complication of pregnancy, occurs in 2% of pregnancies**
3. GDM risk factors = previous history of GDM, maternal age $\geq$30 yr, obesity, family history of DM, previous history of infant weighing 4000 g at birth, history of repeated spontaneous abortions or unexplained stillbirths
4. GDM caused by placental-released hormone, human placental lactogen (HPL), which antagonizes insulin
5. GDM worsens as pregnancy progresses because increasing amounts of HPL are produced as placenta enlarges

6. Maternal complications = hyperglycemia, ketoacidosis, ↑ risk of UTIs, **2-fold ↑ in pregnancy induced hypertension (PIH)**, retinopathy (can occur very quickly & dramatically)
7. Fetal complications
    a. Macrosomia (≥4500 g), neonatal hypoglycemia due to abrupt separation from maternal supply of glucose, hyperbilirubinemia, polycythemia, polyhydramnios (amniotic fluid volume ≥2000 mL)
    b. **Abruption & preterm labor** due to ↑ uterine size & postpartum uterine atony, **3- to 4-fold ↑ in congenital anomalies** (often cardiac & limb deformities), spontaneous abortion & respiratory distress
8. Dx = 1-hr Glucola screening test at 24–28 wk or at onset of prenatal care in pt with known risk factors, confirm with 3-hr glucose tolerance test
9. Tx = strict glucose control, which significantly decreases complications
    a. Insulin is not required if the pt can adhere to a proper diet
    b. **Oral hypoglycemics are contraindicated** because they cross the placenta & can result in fetal & neonatal hypoglycemia
10. Delivery
    a. Route of delivery determined by estimated fetal weight
    b. If 4500 g consider C-section, if 5000 g C-section recommended
    c. Postpartum 95% of GDM patients return to normal glucose levels
    d. Glucose tolerance screening recommended 2–4 mo postpartum to pick up those few women who will remain diabetic & require Tx

B. THROMBOEMBOLIC DISEASE

1. Incidence during pregnancy is 1–2%, usually occurs postpartum (80%)
2. Si/Sx for superficial thrombophlebitis = swelling, tenderness, erythema, warmth (4 cardinal signs of inflammation), may be a palpable cord
3. Deep vein thrombosis (DVT) occurs postpartum due to spread of uterine infection to ovarian veins
4. Si/Sx of DVT = persistent fever, uterine tenderness, palpable mass, but often aSx,
5. Dx
    a. Doppler ultrasound is first line, sensitivity & specificity >90%
    b. Gold standard is venography but this is invasive
6. Tx
    a. Superficial thrombophlebitis → leg elevation, rest, heat, NSAIDs
    b. DVTs → heparin to maintain PTT 1.5–2.5x baseline
    c. **Coumadin contraindicated in pregnancy** because it crosses the placenta, is teratogenic early & causes fetal bleeding later
7. Px
    a. 25% of untreated DVTs progress to pulmonary embolism (PE)
    b. Anticoagulation decreases progression to 5%
    c. PEs in pregnancy are treated identically to DVTs

C. PREGNANCY-INDUCED HYPERTENSION (PIH)

1. Epidemiology
    a. Develops in 5–10% of pregnancies, 30% of multiple gestations
    b. Causes 15% of maternal deaths

    c. Risk factors = nulliparity, age >40 years, family history of PIH, chronic hypertension, chronic renal disease, diabetes, twin gestation
2.

TABLE 3-3   Types of Pregnancy-Induced Hypertension

DISEASE	CHARACTERISTICS
Preeclampsia	• Hypertension (>140/90 or ↑ in SBP of > 30 mm Hg or DBP of >15 mm Hg compared to previous) • New onset proteinuria &/or edema • Generally occurring at ≥ 20 wk
Severe preeclampsia	• SBP > 160 mm Hg or DBP > 110 mm Hg • Marked proteinuria (>1 g/24-hr collection or > 1+ on dip), oliguria, ↑ creatinine • CNS disturbances (e.g., headaches or scotomata) • Pulmonary edema or cyanosis • Epigastric or RUQ pain, hepatic dysfunction
Eclampsia	• **Convulsions** in a woman with preeclampsia • 25% occur before labor, 50% during labor & 25% occur in first 72 hr postpartum

3. Other Si/Sx seen in preeclampsia or eclampsia
    a. Pts have rapid weight gain (2° to edema)
    b. Peripheral lower extremity edema is common in pregnancy; however, persistent edema unresponsive to rest & leg elevation, or edema involving the upper extremities or face is not normal
    c. Hyperreflexia & clonus are also noted
4. Tx
    a. The only cure for PIH is delivery of the baby, decision to do so depends on severity of preeclampsia & maturity of fetus
    b. Mild preeclampsia + immature fetus → bed rest, preferably in left lateral decubitus position to maximize blood flow to uterus, close monitoring, tell pt to return to ER if preeclampsia worsens
    c. Severe preeclampsia / eclampsia → delivery when possible, magnesium sulfate to prevent seizure, antihypertensives to maintain BP < 140/100
5. Complication of severe PIH = HELLP syndrome
    a. **HELLP** = **H**emolysis, **E**levated **L**iver enzymes, **L**ow **P**latelets
    b. Occurs in 5–10% of women with severe preeclampsia or eclampsia, more frequently in multiparous, older pts
    c. Tx = delivery (the only cure), transfuse blood, platelets, fresh frozen plasma as needed, IV fluids & pressors as needed to maintain BP

D. CARDIAC DISEASE
1. Pts with congenital heart disease have a ↑ risk (1–5%) of having a fetus with a congenital heart disease
2. Pts with pulmonary hypertension & ↑ right-sided pressures (e.g., Eisenmenger's complex) have poor Px with pregnancy
3. Tx of preexisting cardiac disease = supportive, e.g., prevention &/or prompt correction of anemia, aggressive Tx of infections, ↓ physical activity/strenuous work, adherence to a low-sodium diet & proper weight gain

4. Peripartum cardiomyopathy
   a. Rare but severe pregnancy-associated condition
   b. Occurs in last month of pregnancy or first 6 mo postpartum
   c. Risk factors = African American, multiparous, age >30 yr, twin gestation, or preeclampsia
   d. Tx = bed rest, digoxin, diuretics, possible anticoagulation, consider postdelivery heart transplant especially in those whose cardiomegaly has not resolved 6 mo after Dx

E. GROUP B STREPTOCOCCUS (GBS = STREPTOCOCCUS AGALACTIAE)

1. Asymptomatic cervical colonization occurs in up to 30% of women
2. 50% of infants become colonized, clinical infection in <1%
3. Intrapartum prophylaxis with penicillin is reserved for the following situations:
   a. Preterm labor (<37 wk) or prolonged rupture of membranes (ROM) (>18 hours) or fever in labor regardless of colonization status
   b. Women identified as colonized with GBS through screening at 35–37 wk gestation
   c. Women with GBS bacteriuria or with a previous infant with GBS disease

F. HYPEREMESIS GRAVIDARUM

1. Increased nausea & vomiting that, unlike "morning sickness," persists past the sixteenth week of pregnancy
2. Causes = ↑ hCG levels, thyroid or GI hormones
3. Si/Sx = excessive vomiting, dehydration, hypochloremic metabolic alkalosis
4. Dx = clinical, rule out other cause
5. Tx = fluids, electrolyte repletion, antiemetics (IV, IM, or suppositories)
6. Some pts require feeding tubes & parenteral nutrition

V. Fetal Assessment and Intrapartum Surveillance

A. FETAL GROWTH

1. Measure by fundal height, if 2-cm deviation from expected fundal height during weeks 18–36 → repeat measurement &/or Utz
2. Utz is most reliable tool for assessing fetal growth
3. In early pregnancy measurement of gestational sac & crown-rump length correlate very well with gestational age
4. Later in pregnancy 4 measurements are done because of wide deviation in normal range = biparietal diameter of skull, abdominal circumference, femur length & cerebellar diameter

B. FETAL WELL-BEING

1. ≥4 fetal movements per hr generally indicate fetal well-being
2. Nonstress test (NST)
   a. Measures response of fetal heart rate to movement
   b. Normal (i.e., reactive) NST occurs when fetal heart rate ↑ by 15 beats/min (bpm) for 15 sec following fetal movement
   c. 2 such accelerations with 20 min are considered normal
   d. A nonreactive NST → further assessment of fetal well-being

e. Test has a high false-positive rate (test suggests fetus is in trouble, but fetus is actually healthy), so it must be interpreted in the context of other tests & is often repeated within 24 hr to verify results

3. Biophysical profile (BPP)
   a. 5 measures of fetal well-being, each rated on a scale of 0–2
   b. Fetal breathing → ≥1 fetal breathing movement in 30 min lasting at least 30 sec
   c. Gross body movement → ≥3 discrete movements in 30 min
   d. Fetal tone → ≥1 episode of extension with return to flexion of fetal limbs/trunk OR opening/closing of hand
   e. Qualitative amniotic fluid volume → ≥1 pocket of amniotic fluid at least 1 cm in 2 perpendicular planes
   f. Reactive fetal heart rate → reactive NST
   g. Final score of 8–10 is normal, score of 6 is equivocal & requires further evaluation, score of 4 or less is abnormal & usually requires immediate intervention

C. TESTS OF FETAL MATURITY
1. Respiratory system is last fetal system to mature, so decisions regarding when to deliver a premature infant often depend on tests that assess the maturity of this system
2. Phospholipid production (collectively known as "surfactant") remains low until 32–33 wk of gestation, but this is highly variable
3. Lack of surfactant → neonatal respiratory distress syndrome (RDS)
4. Phospholipids enter amniotic fluid from fetal breathing & are obtained by amniocentesis & tested for maturity
5. Tests for fetal maturity
   a. Lecithin-sphingomyelin (L:S) ratio
      1) Lecithin is major phospholipid found in surfactant & increases as fetal lungs become mature
      2) Sphingomyelin production remains constant throughout pregnancy
      3) Ratio >2.0 is considered mature
   b. Phosphatidylglycerol (PG) appears late in pregnancy, its presence generally indicates maturity

D. INTRAPARTUM FETAL ASSESSMENT
1. Causes of nonreassuring fetal status
   a. Uteroplacental insufficiency
      1) Placenta impaired or unable to provide oxygen & nutrients while removing products of metabolism & waste
      2) Causes = placenta previa or abruption, placental edema from hydrops fetalis or Rh isoimmunization, postterm pregnancy, intrauterine growth retardation (IUGR), uterine hyperstimulation
      3) Fetal response to hypoxia → shunting of blood to brain, heart & adrenal glands
      4) If unrecognized can progress to metabolic acidosis with accumulation of lactic acid & damage to vital organs
   b. Umbilical cord compression due to oligohydramnios, cord prolapse or knot, anomalous cord, or abnormal cord insertion

c. Fetal anomalies include IUGR, prematurity, postterm, sepsis, congenital anomalies

2. Fetal heart rate (FHR) monitoring
   a. Normal FHR is 120–160 bpm
   b. Tachycardia = FHR >160 bpm for 10 min or more
      1) Most common cause is maternal fever (which may signal chorioamnionitis)
      2) Other causes = fetal hypoxia, immaturity, tachyarrhythmias, anemia, infection, or maternal thyrotoxicosis or treatment with sympathomimetics
   c. Bradycardia = FHR <120 bpm for 10 min or more, caused by congenital heart block, fetal anoxia (e.g., from placental separation) & maternal treatment with β-blockers
   d. FHR variability
      1) A reliable indicator of fetal well-being, suggesting sufficient CNS oxygenation
      2) ↓ variability associated with fetal hypoxia/acidosis, depressant drugs, fetal tachycardia, CNS or cardiac anomalies, prolonged uterine contractions, prematurity & fetal sleep

3. Accelerations
   a. Types & patterns of accelerations play a role in intrapartum evaluation of the fetus
   b. Accelerations
      1) ↑ FHR of at least 15 bpm above baseline for 15–20 sec
      2) This pattern indicates a fetus unstressed by hypoxia or acidemia → reassuring & suggests fetal well-being
   c. Early decelerations (See Figure 3-1)
      1) ↓ FHR (not below 100 bpm) that mirrors a uterine contraction (i.e., begins with onset of contraction, dips at peak of contraction, returns to baseline with end of contraction)
      2) Results from pressure on fetal head → vagus nerve stimulated reflex response to release acetylcholine at fetal SA node
      3) Considered physiologic & not harmful to fetus
   d. Variable decelerations (See Figure 3-1)
      1) Do not necessarily coincide with uterine contraction
      2) Characterized by rapid dip in FHR, often <100 bpm with rapid return to baseline
      3) Also reflex-mediated, due to umbilical cord compression
      4) Can be corrected by shifting maternal position, or amnioinfusion if membranes have ruptured & cord compression is secondary to oligohydramnios
   e. Late decelerations (See Figure 3-1)
      1) Begin after contraction has already started, dip after peak of contraction, returns to baseline after contraction is over
      2) Viewed as potentially dangerous, associated with uteroplacental insufficiency
      3) Causes include placental abruption, PIH, maternal diabetes, maternal anemia, maternal sepsis, postterm pregnancy & hyperstimulated uterus
      4) Repetitive late decelerations require intervention

OB/GYN

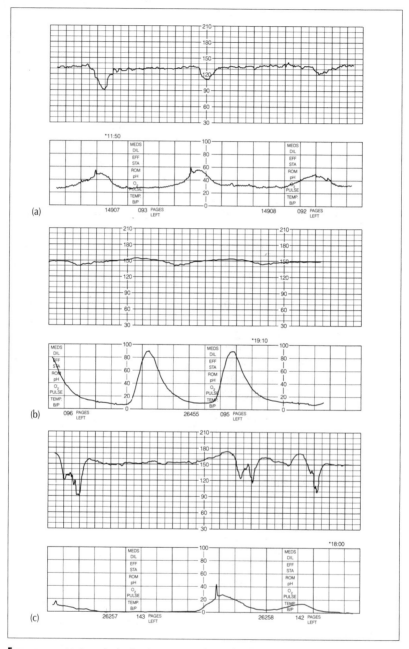

FIGURE 3-1   (a) An early deceleration pattern is depicted in this fetal heart rate (FHR) tracing. Note that each deceleration returns to baseline before the completion of the contraction. The remainder of the fetal heart rate tracing is reassuring. (b) Repetitive late decelerations in conjunction with decreased variability. (c) Variable decelerations are the most common periodic change of the fetal heart rate during labor. Repetitive mild-to-moderate variable decelerations are present. The baseline is normal.

E. ISOIMMUNIZATION

1. Development of maternal IgG antibodies following exposure to fetal red blood cell antigens
2. Exposure commonly occurs at delivery, but can occur during pregnancy as well
3. In subsequent pregnancies (rarely late in the same pregnancy) these antibodies can cross the placenta → attach to fetal RBC cells & hemolyze them → fetal anemia
4. Can occur with any blood group, but most often occurs when mother is Rh-negative & fetus is Rh-positive
5. Extent to which fetus is affected depends on amount of IgG antibodies crossing placenta & ability of fetus to replenish destroyed RBCs
6. Worst case scenario is hydrops fetalis
   a. Significant transfer of antibodies across placenta → fetal anemia
   b. Liver attempts to make new RBCs (fetal hematopoiesis occurs in liver & bone marrow) at the expense of other necessary proteins →↓ oncotic pressure → fetal ascites & edema
   c. High-output cardiac failure associated with severe anemia
7. Maternal IgG titer ≥ 1:16 is high enough to pose risk to the fetus
8. Tx = RhoGAM
   a. Administration of antibody to the Rh antigen (Rh immune globulin = RhoGAM) within 72 hr of delivery prevents active antibody response by the mother in most cases
   b. Risk of subsequent sensitization ↓ from 15% to 2%
   c. When RhoGAM is also given at 28 wk of gestation, risk of sensitization is further reduced to 0.2%
9. RhoGAM given to Rh-negative mothers if the father is Rh-positive
   a. At 28 wks gestation
   b. Within 72 hr of delivery of Rh-positive infant
   c. Other times maternal-fetal blood mixing can occur
      1) At time of amniocentesis
      2) After an abortion
      3) After an ectopic pregnancy
      4) ⊕ Kleihauer-Betke test (identifies fetal RBCs in maternal blood)

F. GENETIC TESTING

1. Chromosomal abnormalities account for 50–60% of spontaneous abortion, 5% of stillbirths, 2–3% of couples with multiple miscarriages
2. 0.6% of all live births have a chromosomal abnormality
3. Indications for prenatal genetic testing
   a. Most common is advanced maternal age (AMA)
      1) Trisomy 21 (Down's syndrome) incidence ↑ 10-fold from age 35 to age 45, other polysomies ↑ similarly
      2) Amniocentesis routinely offered to all women who will be >35 yr old at estimated time of delivery
   b. Prior child with chromosome or single gene abnormality
   c. Known chromosomal abnormality such as a balanced translocation or single gene disorder in parent(s)
   d. Abnormal results from screening tests such as the triple marker screen

VI. Labor and Delivery

A. INITIAL PRESENTATION
1. Labor = progressive effacement & dilation of uterine cervix resulting from contractions of uterus
2. **Braxton Hicks contractions** (false labor) = uterine contractions without effacement & dilation of cervix
3. 85% of patients undergo spontaneous labor & delivery between 37 and 42 wk gestation
4. Pts are told to come to hospital for regular contractions q 5 min for at least 1 hr, rupture of membranes, significant bleeding, ↓ in fetal movement
5. Initial exam upon arrival
   a. Auscultation of fetal heart tones
   b. Leopold maneuvers help determine fetal lie (relation of long axis of fetus with maternal long axis), determine fetal presentation (i.e., breech vs. cephalic) & position of presenting part with respect to right or left side of maternal pelvis
   c. Vaginal examination
      1) Check for rupture of membranes, cervical effacement & cervical dilation (in cm)
      2) Fetal station (level of fetal presenting part relative to ischial spines) measured from −3 (presenting part palpable at pelvic inlet) to +3 (presenting part palpable beyond pelvic outlet)
      3) 0 station = presenting part palpable at ischial spines, significance of 0 station is that biparietal diameter (biggest diameter of fetal head) has negotiated pelvic inlet (smallest part of pelvis)

B. STAGES OF LABOR
1. Labor divided into 3 stages (See Figure 3-2)
2. Stage 1
   a. Interval between onset of labor & full cervical dilation (10 cm)
   b. Further subdivided into:
      1) Latent phase = cervical effacement & early dilation
      2) Active phase = more rapid cervical dilation occurs, usually beginning at 3–4 cm
3. Stage 2 = interval between complete cervical dilation & delivery of infant
4. Stage 3 = interval between delivery of infant & delivery of placenta
5. Stage 4 = immediate postpartum period lasting 2 hr during which pt undergoes significant physiologic changes

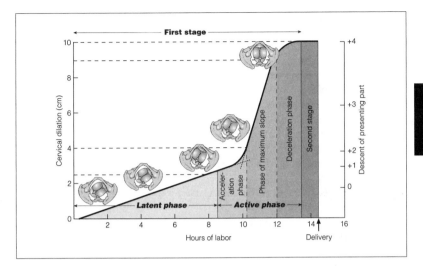

FIGURE 3-2   Schematic illustration of progress of rotation of occipitoanterior presentation in the successive stages of labor. Note relationship between changes in cervical dilation and phases of labor.

C. MANAGEMENT OF LABOR

1. First stage
   a. Continuous monitoring of fetal heart rate, either external monitoring via Doppler, or internal monitoring via fetal scalp electrode (FSE) that allows for more detailed evaluation of fetal heart rate pattern
   b. Monitoring of uterine activity
      1) External tocodynamometer measures frequency & duration of contractions, but not intensity
      2) Internal uterine pressure catheter (IUPC) measures intensity by measuring intrauterine pressure
   c. Analgesic (typically meperidine) &/or anesthetic (typically an epidural block that provides both continuous analgesia & anesthesia) can be given—agents usually not given until active stage of labor
2. Second stage
   a. Maternal effort (i.e., pushing) accelerates delivery of fetus (↑ in intra-abdominal pressure assists fetal descent down birth canal)
   b. Delivery should be well controlled with protection of the perineum
   c. If used, episiotomies are usually cut midline
   d. After head is delivered, bulb suction of nose & mouth is performed & neck is evaluated for presence of nuchal cord
   e. Shoulders are delivered by applying gentle downward pressure on head to deliver anterior shoulder followed by easy upward force to deliver posterior shoulder
   f. Delivery of body follows, cord is clamped & cut, & infant given to mother or to warmer

g. Blood from umbilical cord sent for ABO & Rh testing as well as arterial blood gases
3. Third stage
  a. 3 signs of placenta separation
    1) Uterus rises in abdomen signaling that placenta has separated
    2) Gush of blood
    3) Lengthening of umbilical cord
  b. Excessive pulling on placenta should be avoided because of risk of uterus inversion with associated profound hemorrhage & retained placenta
  c. Gentle traction should be applied at all times
  d. May take up to 30 min for placenta to be expulsed
4. Fourth stage
  a. Systemic evaluation of cervix, vagina, vulva, perineum & periurethral area for lacerations
  b. Likelihood of serious postpartum complications is greatest in first 1–2 hr postpartum

D. ABNORMAL LABOR
1. Dystocia = difficult labor
  a. Cause detected by evaluating the **3 Ps**
    1) **Power**
      a) Refers to strength, duration & frequency of contractions
      b) Measured by using tocodynamometer or IUPC
      c) For cervical dilation to occur ≥3 contractions in 10 min must be generated
      d) During active labor maternal effort comes into play, as maternal exhaustion, effects of analgesia/anesthesia, or underlying disease may prolong labor
    2) **Passenger**
      a) Refers to estimates of fetal weight + evaluation of fetal lie, presentation & position
      b) Occiput posterior presentation, face presentation & hydrocephalus are associated with dystocia
    3) **Passage**
      a) Difficult to measure pelvic diameters
      b) Adequacy of pelvis often unknown until progress (or no progress) is made during labor
      c) Distended bladder, adnexal or colon masses & uterine fibroids can all contribute to dystocia
  b. Dystocia divided into prolongation disorders
    1) Prolonged latent phase
      a) Latent phase >20 hr in primigravid or >14 hr in multigravid patient is prolonged & abnormal
      b) Causes include ineffective uterine contractions, fetopelvic disproportion & excess anesthesia
      c) Prolonged latent phase → no harm to mother or fetus
    2) Prolonged active phase

a) Active phase >12 hr or rate of cervical dilation <1.2 cm/hr in primigravid or <1.5 cm/hr in multigravid

b) Causes include excess anesthesia, ineffective contractions, fetopelvic disproportion, fetal malposition, rupture of membranes before onset of active labor

c) Prolonged active phase → ↑ risk of intrauterine infection & increased risk of cesarean section

2. Arrest disorders
   a. 2° arrest occurs when cervical dilation during active phase ceases for ≥2 hr
   b. Suggests either cephalopelvic disproportion or ineffective uterine contractions
3. Management of abnormal labor
   a. Labor induction = stimulation of uterine contractions before spontaneous onset of labor
   b. Augmentation of labor = stimulation of uterine contractions that began spontaneously but have become infrequent, weak, or both
   c. Induction trial should occur only if cervix is prepared or "ripe"
   d. Bishop score used to try to quantify cervical readiness for induction

TABLE 3-4   Bishop Score

FACTOR	POINTS			
	0	1	2	3
Dilation	Closed	1–2 cm	3–4 cm	≥5 cm
Effacement	0–30%	40–50%	60–70%	≥80%
Station	−3	−2, −1	0	≥+1
Position		Posterior	Mid	Anterior

Score: 9–13 associated with highest likelihood of successful induction.
0–4 associated with highest likelihood of failed induction.

4. Indications for induction = suspected fetal compromise, fetal death, PIH, premature ROM, chorioamnionitis, postdates pregnancy, maternal medical complication
5. Contraindications for induction include placenta previa, active genital herpes, abnormal fetal lie, cord presentation
6. If cervix not "ripe," prostaglandin E2 gel can be used to attempt to ripen cervix, biggest risk is uterine hyperstimulation → uteroplacental insufficiency
7. Another method is insertion of laminaria or rods inserted into the internal os that absorb moisture & expand, slowly dilating cervix, risks include failure to dilate, laceration, rupture of membranes & infection
8. Prolonged latent phase can be managed with rest, augmentation of labor with oxytocin, &/or amniotomy that may allow for fetal head to provide greater dilating force
9. During active phase of labor fetal malposition & cephalopelvic disproportion must be considered & may warrant cesarean section vs. augmentation
10. If fetus has descended far enough, forceps or vacuum can be used, if not cesarean section is carried out
11. Risks of prolonged labor include infection, exhaustion, lacerations, uterine atony with hemorrhage

12. Breech presentation occurs in 2–4% of pregnancies & risk ↑ in cases of multiple gestations, polyhydramnios, hydrocephaly, anencephaly & uterine anomalies (See Figure 3-3)

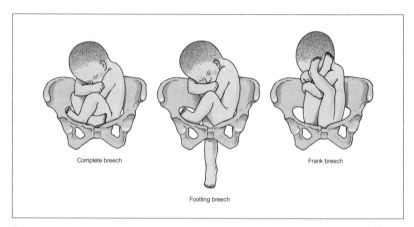

Complete breech   Frank breech

Footling breech

FIGURE 3-3   Different breech presentations.

E. POSTPARTUM HEMORRHAGE
1. Defined as blood loss >500 mL associated with delivery
2. Causes = uterine atony (most common), lacerations, retained placenta
3. Uterine atony
   a. Normally uterus quickly contracts following delivery of placenta, muscle contraction compresses down on spiral arteries & prevents excessive bleeding
   b. If contraction does not occur → postpartum hemorrhage
   c. Risk factors for uterine atony = multiple gestations, hydramnios, multiparity, macrosomia, previous history of postpartum hemorrhage, fibroids, magnesium sulfate, general anesthesia, prolonged labor, amnionitis
   d. Dx based on clinical exam of soft, "boggy" uterus
   e. Tx
      1) Start with uterine massage to stimulate contractions
      2) IV fluids & transfusions as needed, cervix & vagina visualized for lacerations
      3) Medical Tx = oxytocin, methergine (potent uterotonic always given IM—if given IV can cause severe hypertension), or prostaglandins →uterine contractions
      4) If these measures are unsuccessful, surgical interventions are used & include ligation of uterine arteries, ligation of internal iliac arteries, selective arterial embolization or hysterectomy as last resort
4. Retained placenta
   a. Occurs when separation of placenta from uterine wall or expulsion of placenta is incomplete
   b. Risk factors include previous cesarean section, fibroids & prior uterine curettage
   c. Placental tissue that abnormally implants into uterus can also result in retention
   d. Placenta accreta: placental villi abnormally adhere to superficial lining of uterine wall

  e. Placenta increta: placental villi penetrate into uterine muscle layer
  f. Placenta percreta: placental villi completely invade uterine muscle layer
5. Disseminated intravascular coagulation (DIC)
  a. A rare cause of postpartum hemorrhage
  b. Severe preeclampsia, amniotic fluid embolism & placental abruption are associated with DIC
  c. Tx aimed at correcting coagulopathy

VII. Postpartum Care

A. LACTATION & BREAST FEEDING
1. Engorgement occurs about 3 days postpartum
2. 3 causes of tender enlarged breasts postpartum are engorgement, mastitis & plugged duct
3. Tx engorgement with continued breast feeding, mastitis with antibiotics (nursing can be continued) & plugged duct with warm packs
4. Advantages of breast feeding = ↑ bonding between mother & child, convenience, ↓ cost, protection against infection & allergies
5. Breast milk provides all vitamins except vitamin K

B. CONTRACEPTION
1. Contraception should be discussed with all patients prior to discharge
2. About 15% of women are fertile 6wk postpartum
3. OCPs are not contraindicated in breast-feeding & postpartum tubal ligation should be discussed as well

C. POSTPARTUM IMMUNIZATIONS
1. Rubella nonimmune women should be immunized (they can continue to breast feed)
2. Rh-negative woman who has given birth to an Rh-positive baby should receive RhoGAM

D. POSTPARTUM DEPRESSION
1. Recurrence rate for patients with previous postpartum depression is 25%
2. Postpartum depression ranges from the "blues" that affects 50% of women & typically occurs about day 2–3, resolving in 1–2wk, to postpartum depression that affects 10% of women, to suicidal ideation that occurs more rarely
3. Especially worrisome is a mother who has estranged herself from her newborn or has become indifferent
4. Tx depends on severity of Sx & may range from simple telephone contact to psychotherapy & medication to inpatient hospitalization

E. POSTPARTUM UTERINE INFECTION
1. Incidence of infection ranges from 10–50% depending on population, mode of delivery (C-section > vaginal delivery) & risk factors
2. Risk factors = maternal obesity, immunosuppression, chronic disease, vaginal infection, amnionitis, prolonged labor, prolonged ROM, multiple pelvic examinations during labor, internal fetal monitoring or intrauterine pressure catheter, C-section
3. **Most common infection post C-section is metritis** (uterine infection)

4. Si/Sx = fever on first or second postpartum day, uterine tenderness, ↓ bowel sounds, leukocytosis (difficult to interpret because of normal leukocytosis in puerperium)
5. DDx
   a. First day postpartum: think *lungs (wind)* → atelectasis, especially if general anesthesia was used, or pneumonia
   b. Second day postpartum: think *urinary tract (water)* → UTI, pyelonephritis
   c. Third day postpartum: think *wound*
   d. Fourth day postpartum: think *extremities (walking)* → thrombophlebitis
6. Metritis usually polymicrobial with aerobic & anaerobic organisms present
7. Dx = clinical
8. Tx = first generation cephalosporin, add coverage (mezlocillin + aminoglycoside) if no response within 48–72 hr
9. Prophylactic antibiotic therapy (one-time dose) at time of C-section delivery significantly reduces incidence of postpartum infection

VIII. Obstetrical Complications

A. ABORTION
1. Termination of a pregnancy before viability, usually at 20 wk or less, occurs spontaneously in 15% of all pregnancies
2. Risk factors = ↑ parity, advanced maternal age, ↑ paternal age, conception within 3 mo of a live birth
3. Single pregnancy loss does not significantly increase risk of future loss
4. Chromosomal abnormalities cause 50% of early spontaneous abortion, mostly trisomies (the longer a pregnancy goes before undergoing spontaneous abortion less likely that fetus is chromosomally abnormal)
5. Other causes = endocrine dz (e.g., thyroid), structural abnormalities (e.g., fibroids, incompetent cervix), infection (e.g., *Listeria*, *Mycoplasma*, ToRCHS), chronic dz (e.g., DM, SLE, renal or cardiac dz), environmental factors (e.g., toxins, radiation, smoking, alcohol)
6. Vaginal bleeding in first half of any pregnancy is presumed to be a threatened abortion unless another diagnosis such as ectopic pregnancy, cervical polyps, cervicitis, or molar pregnancy can be made
7.

TABLE 3-5   Types of Abortion

Threatened	• Si/Sx = vaginal bleeding in first 20 wk of pregnancy without passage of tissue or ROM, with cervix closed • Occurs in 25% of pregnancies ($^1/_2$ go on to spontaneously abort) • ↑ risk preterm labor & delivery, low birth weight, perinatal mortality • Dx = Utz to confirm early pregnancy is intact • If no cardiac activity by 9 wk → consider D&C procedure • HCG levels are also used to identify viable pregnancies at various stages of development
Inevitable	• Si/Sx = threatened abortion with dilated cervical os &/or ROM, usually accompanied by cramping with expulsion of products of conception (POC) • Pregnancy loss is unavoidable • Tx = surgical evacuation of uterine contents & RhoGAM if mother is Rh-negative

TABLE 3-5   *Continued*

Completed	• Si/Sx = documented pregnancy that spontaneously aborts all POCs • POCs should be grossly examined & submitted to pathology to confirm fetal tissue &/or placental villi, if none is observed must rule out ectopic pregnancy • Pts may require curettage because of ↑ likelihood that abortion was incomplete (suspected if β-hCG levels plateau or fail to decline to zero) • RhoGAM given to Rh-negative women
Incomplete	• Si/Sx = cramping, bleeding, passage of tissue, with dilated cervix & visible tissue in vagina or endocervical canal • Curettage usually needed to remove remaining POCs & to control bleeding • Again Rh-negative patients are given RhoGAM • Hemodynamic stabilization may be required if bleeding is very heavy
Missed	• Failure to expel POC • Si/Sx = lack of uterine growth, lack of fetal heart tones & cessation of pregnancy symptoms • Evacuation of uterus required after fetal death has been confirmed, suction curettage recommended for first-trimester pregnancy, dilation & evacuation (D&E) recommended for second-trimester pregnancies • Serious but rare complication is DIC • Rh-negative patients receive RhoGAM
Recurrent	• Si/Sx = ≥2 consecutive or total of 3 spontaneous abortions • If early, often due to chromosomal abnormalities → karyotyping for both parents to determine if they carry a chromosomal abnormality • Examine mother for uterine abnormalities • Incompetent cervix is suspected by history of painless dilation of cervix with delivery of normal fetus between 18 and 32 weeks of gestation • Tx = surgical cerclage procedures to suture cervix closed until labor or rupture of membranes occurs

B. ECTOPIC PREGNANCY

1. Implantation outside of uterine cavity
2. ↑ incidence recently because of ↑ in PID, second leading cause of maternal mortality
3. Risk factors = previous ectopic pregnancy, previous history of salpingitis (scarring & adhesions impede transport of ovum down tube), age ≥35 yr old, >3 prior pregnancies, sterilization failure
4. Si/Sx = abdominal/pelvic pain, referred shoulder pain from hemoperitoneal irritation of diaphragm, amenorrhea, vaginal bleeding, cervical motion or adnexal tenderness, nausea, vomiting, orthostatic changes
5. DDx = surgical abdomen (see Surgery), abortion, salpingitis, endometriosis, ruptured ovarian cyst, ovarian torsion
6. Ectopic pregnancy should be suspected in any reproductive age woman who presents with abdominal/pelvic pain, irregular bleeding & amenorrhea—lag in treatment is a significant cause of mortality
7. Dx
   a. ⊕ pregnancy test with Utz to determine intrauterine vs. extrauterine pregnancy
   b. Very low progesterone level strongly suggests nonviable pregnancy that may be located outside the uterine cavity while higher levels suggest viable pregnancy
8. Tx

a. Surgical removal now commonly done via laparoscopy with maximum preservation of reproductive organs

b. Methotrexate can be used early, especially if pregnancy is <3.5 cm in diameter, with no cardiac activity on Utz

c. Regardless of technique used, posttreatment serial β-hCG levels must be followed to ensure proper falloff in level

d. Rh-negative women should receive RhoGAM to avoid Rh sensitization

C. THIRD-TRIMESTER BLEEDING

1. Occurs in about 5% of all pregnancies
2. Half of these are due to placenta previa or placental abruption, others due to vaginal/vulvar lacerations, cervical polyps, cervicitis, cervical cancer
3. In many cases no cause for bleeding is found
4.

TABLE 3-6   Comparison of Placenta Previa and Placental Abruption

	PLACENTA PREVIA	PLACENTAL ABRUPTION
Abnormality	Placenta implanted over internal cervical os (completely or partially)	Premature separation (complete or partial) of normally implanted placenta from decidua
Epidemiology	↑ risk grand multiparas & prior C-section	↑ risk preeclampsia, previous history of abruption, rupture of membranes in a patient with hydramnios, cocaine use, cigarette smoking & trauma
Time of onset	20–30 wk	Any time after 20 wk
Si/Sx	Sudden, **painless** bleeding	**Painful** bleeding, can be heavy, painful & frequent uterine contractions
Dx	Utz → placenta abnormal location	Clinical, based on presentation of painful vaginal bleeding, frequent contractions & fetal distress. **Utz not useful**
Tx	Hemodynamic support, expectant management, deliver by C-section when fetus mature enough	Hemodynamic support, urgent C-section or vaginal induction if pt is stable & fetus is not in distress
Complications	Associated with 2-fold ↑ in congenital malformations so evaluation for fetal anomalies should be undertaken at Dx	↑ risk of fetal hypoxia/death, DIC may occur as a result of intravascular & retroplacental coagulation

D. PRETERM LABOR (PTL)

1. Regular uterine contractions at ≤10 min intervals, lasting ≥30 sec, between 20 and 36 wk gestation & accompanied by cervical effacement, dilation &/or descent of fetus into the pelvis
2. It is a major cause of preterm birth → significant perinatal morbidity & mortality
3. Risk factors = premature rupture of membranes (PROM), infection (UTI, vaginal, amniotic), dehydration, incompetent cervix, smoking, fibroids, placenta previa, placental abruption, many cases are idiopathic

4. Si/Sx = cramps, dull low back pain, abdominal/pelvic pressure, vaginal discharge (mucous, water, or bloody) & contractions (often painless)
5. Dx = external fetal monitoring to quantify frequency & duration of contractions, vaginal exam → extent of cervical dilation/effacement
6. Utz to confirm gestational age, amniotic fluid volume (helps to determine if rupture of membranes has occurred), fetal presentation & placental location
7. Tx focused on delaying delivery if possible until fetus is mature
   a. 50% of patients have spontaneous resolution of preterm uterine contractions
   b. IV hydration important because dehydration is well known to cause uterine irritability
   c. Empiric antibiotic therapy is given for suspected chorioamnionitis or vaginal infection
   d. Tocolytic regimens
      1) Magnesium sulfate, β-2 agonists like terbutaline & ritodrine, Ca^{2+}-blockers like nifedipine, or indomethacin may be instituted although they have never been shown to substantially prolong delivery more than several days
      2) Contraindications to tocolysis = advanced labor (cervical dilation >3 cm), mature fetus, chorioamnionitis, significant vaginal bleeding, anomalous fetus, acute fetal distress, severe preeclampsia or eclampsia
   e. From 24 to 34 wk steroids such as betamethasone are generally used to enhance pulmonary maturity
   f. Management of infants at 34–37 wk is individualized; survival rates for infants born at 34 wk is within 1% of the survival rate for infants born at 37 wk & beyond; assessment of fetal lung maturity may help decide who to deliver between 34 and 37 wk
8. Common complications include death, respiratory distress syndrome & subsequent bronchopulmonary dysplasia, sepsis, intraventricular hemorrhage, necrotizing entero-colitis, developmental delays & seizures

E. Premature Rupture of Membranes (PROM)

1. Rupture of chorioamniotic membrane before onset of labor, occurs in 10–15% of all pregnancies
2. Labor usually follows PROM; 90% of patients & 50% of preterm patients go into labor within 24 hr after rupture
3. Biggest risk is labor & delivery of preterm infant with associated morbidities/mortality, second biggest complication is infection (chorioamnionitis)
4. PROM at 26 wk of gestation or less is associated with pulmonary hypoplasia
5. Dx = vaginal exam with testing of nonbloody fluid from the vagina
   a. Nitrazine test: uses pH to distinguish alkaline amniotic fluid (pH > 7.0) with more acidic urine & vaginal secretions (note false-positive seen with semen, cervical mucus, trichomonas infection, blood, unusually basic urine)
   b. Fern test: amniotic fluid placed on slide that is allowed to dry in room (up to 30 min); the branching fern leaf pattern that results when the slide is completely dry is caused from sodium chloride precipitates from amniotic fluid

     c. Utz confirms Dx by noting oligohydramnios, labor is less likely to occur if sufficient fluid remains

  6. Tx

     a. If intrauterine infection is suspected, empiric broad spectrum antibiotics are started

     b. Otherwise treat as for preterm labor above

F. MULTIPLE GESTATIONS

1. 1 in 90 incidence in US (slightly higher in black women, slightly lower in white women)

2. **Dizygotic twins occur when 2 separate ova are fertilized by 2 separate sperm, incidence ↑ with ↑ age & parity**

3. Monozygotic twins represent division of the fertilized ovum at various times after conception

4. Multiple gestations are considered high-risk pregnancies because of the disproportionate increase in perinatal morbidity & mortality as compared with a singleton gestation

     a. **Spontaneous abortions & congenital anomalies occur more frequently in multiple pregnancies as compared with singleton pregnancies**

     b. Maternal complications = anemia, hydramnios, eclampsia, PTL, postpartum uterine atony & hemorrhage, increased risk for C-section

     c. Fetal complications: congenital anomalies, spontaneous abortion, IUGR, prematurity, PROM, umbilical cord prolapse, placental abruption, placenta previa & malpresentation

5. Average duration of gestation ↓ with ↑ number of fetuses (twins deliver at 37 wk, triplets deliver at 33 wk, quadruplets deliver at 29 wk)

6. Twin-twin transfusion syndrome

     a. Occurs in 10% of twins sharing a chorionic membrane

     b. Occurs when blood flow is interrupted by a vascular anastomoses such that one twin becomes the donor twin & can have impaired growth, anemia, hypovolemia, & the other twin (recipient twin) can develop hypervolemia, hypertension, polycythemia & congestive heart failure as a result of the increased blood flow from one twin to the other

7. Dx of twins usually suspected when uterine size exceeds calculated gestational age & can be confirmed with ultrasound

8. DDx = incorrect dates, fibroids, polyhydramnios & molar pregnancy

9. Delivery method largely depends on presentation of twins; usually if first fetus is in vertex presentation, vaginal delivery is attempted; if not C-section is often performed

10. Important to watch for uterine atony & postpartum hemorrhage because overdistended uterus may not clamp down normally

Gynecology

I. Benign Gynecology

A. MENSTRUAL CYCLE (See Figure 3-4)

1. Due to hypothalamic pulses of gonadotropin releasing hormone (GnRH), pituitary release of follicle stimulating hormone (FSH) & luteinizing hormone (LH), & ovarian sex steroids estradiol & progesterone

2. ↑ or ↓ of any of these hormones → irregular menses or amenorrhea

3. At birth, the human ovary contains approximately 1 million primordial follicles each with an oocyte arrested in the prophase stage of meiosis

4. Process of ovulation begins in puberty = follicular maturation

    a. After ovulation the dominant follicle released becomes the corpus luteum, which secretes progesterone to prepare the endometrium for possible implantation

    b. If the ovum is not fertilized the corpus luteum undergoes involution, menstruation begins & cycle repeats

5. Phases of the menstrual cycle

    a. First day of menstrual bleeding is day 1 of the cycle

    b.

TABLE 3-7 Phases of the Menstrual Cycle (See Figure 3-4)

FOLLICULAR PHASE (PROLIFERATIVE PHASE)	OVULATORY PHASE	LUTEAL PHASE (SECRETORY PHASE)
Day 1–13 of cycle: estradiol-induced negative feedback on FSH & ⊕ feedback on LH in anterior pituitary leads to LH surge on day 11–13	**Day 13–17 of cycle:** dominant follicle secretion of estradiol → ⊕ feedback to anterior pituitary FSH & LH, ovulation occurs 30–36 hr after the LH surge, small FSH surge also occurs at time of LH surge	**Day 15 to first day of menses:** marked by change from estradiol to progesterone predominance, corpus luteal progesterone causing negative feedback on FSH & LH, progesterone acts on hypothalamus, resulting in ↓ to basal levels prior to next cycle, if fertilization & implantation do not occur → rapid ↓ in progesterone

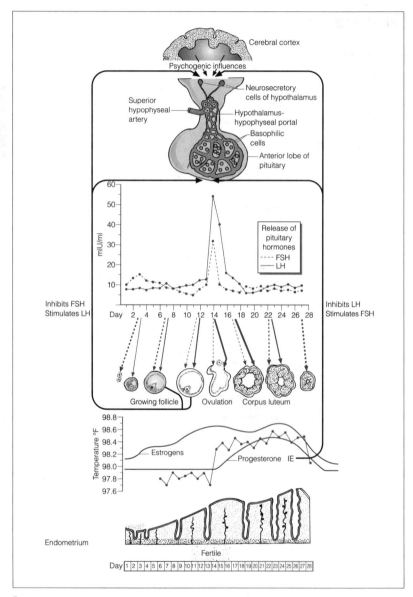

Figure 3-4   Normal menstrual cycle. Note the suprahypothalamic (cerebral, pineal), hypothalamic, pituitary, ovarian, and endometrial interrelations.

B. CONTRACEPTION

1. Oral contraceptive pills (OCPs) = combination estrogen & progestin

   a. Progestin is major contraceptive by suppressing LH & thus ovulation, also thickens cervical mucus so it is less favorable to semen

   b. Estrogen participates by suppressing FSH thereby preventing selection & maturation of a dominant follicle

   c. Estrogen & progesterone together inhibit implantation by thinning endometrial lining, also resulting in light or missed menses

   d. Monophasic pills deliver a constant dose of estrogen & progestin

   e. Phasic OCPs alter this ratio (usually by varying the dose of progestin) that slightly ↓ the total dose of hormone per month, but also has slightly ↑ rate of breakthrough bleeding between periods

   f. Pts usually resume fertility once OCPs are discontinued; however, **3% may have prolonged postpill amenorrhea**

   g.

TABLE 3-8   Risks and Benefits of OCPs

ADVANTAGES	DISADVANTAGES

• Highly reliable, failure rate <1% (failure usually related to missing pills)
• Protect against endometrial & ovarian CA
• ↓ incidence of pelvic infections & ectopic pregnancies
• Menses are more predictable, lighter, less painful
	• Require daily compliance
	• Does not protect against STDs
	• 10–30% have breakthrough bleeding
	• Side effects:
	  ◊ Estrogen → bloating, weight gain, breast tenderness, nausea, headaches
	  ◊ Progestin → depression, acne, HTN*

*Try lower progesterone pill, if hypertension doesn't resolve, D/C OCP—pts with preexisting hypertension can try OCPs if they are ≤35 yr old & in good medical control.

   h. Absolute contraindications to use of OCPs = pregnancy, DVT or thromboembolic dz, endometrial CA, cerebrovascular or coronary artery dz, breast CA, cigarette smoking in women > 35 yr old, hepatic dz/neoplasm, abnormal vaginal bleeding, hyperlipidemia

TABLE 3-9   Alternatives to OCPs

METHOD	INDICATION	ADVANTAGE	DISADVANTAGE
Progestin only pills ("Mini-pills")	• **Lactating women**	• Can start immediately postpartum • No impact on milk production or the baby	• ↑ failure rate than OCP (ovulation continues in 40%) • Requires strict compliance—low dose of progesterone requires that pill be taken at same time each day
Depo-Provera (Medroxy-progesterone)	• Contraception for ≥1 yr • Noncompliance with daily OCPs • Breast feeding	• **IM injection** maintained for 14 wk	• Irregular vaginal bleed[a] • 50% pts infertile for 10 mo after last injection • Risk of abortion[b]

OB/GYN

TABLE 3-9   *Continued*

METHOD	INDICATION	ADVANTAGE	DISADVANTAGE
Norplant	• Long-term contraception	• Subcutaneous implants provide **contraception for 5 yr** • Prompt fertility when DC'd	• 30% of breakthrough pregnancies are ectopic
Intrauterine device	• For those at low risk for STDs	• Inserted into endometrial cavity, left in place for several years	• Contraindicated in cervical or vaginal infxn, Hx of PID or infertility • Spontaneous expulsion, menstrual pain, ↑ rate of ectopic pregnancy, septic abortion & pelvic infxns
Postcoital	• Emergency contraception	• **Ovral** taken **within 72 hr of intercourse,** repeat in 12 hr • Allows for early termination of unwanted pregnancy	• Follow pt to ensure withdrawal bleeding occurs within 5 days • Nausea

[a] Oral estrogen or NSAIDs can ↓ bleeding, bleeding ↓ with each use, 50% pts are amenorrheic in 1 yr.
[b] Injection given within first 5 days of menses (ensuring pt not pregnant).

C. PAP SMEAR

1. First Pap smear should be done when woman becomes sexually active or by age 18, then yearly thereafter
2. In pts with 1 sexual partner, 3 consecutive normal pap smears & onset of sexual activity after age 25, may be able to screen less frequently
3. Reliability depends on presence/absence of cervical inflammation, adequacy of specimen & prompt fixation of specimen to avoid artifact
4. If Pap → mild- or low-grade atypia → repeat Pap—atypia may spontaneously regress
5. Recurrent mild atypia or high-grade atypia → more intensive evaluation
   a. Colposcopy
      1) Allows for magnification of cervix allowing subtle areas of dysplastic change to be visualized, optimizing selection of biopsy sites
      2) Cervix washed with acetic acid solution, white areas, abnormally vascularized areas & punctate lesions are selected for biopsy
   b. Endocervical curettage (ECC) → sample of endocervix obtained at same time of colposcopy so that disease further up in endocervical canal may be detected
   c. Cone biopsy
      1) Cone-shaped specimen encompassing squamocolumnar junction (SCJ) & any lesions on ectocervix removed from cervix by knife, laser, or wire loop
      2) Allows for more complete ascertainment of extent of disease & in many cases is therapeutic as well as diagnostic
      3) Indications = ⊕ ECC, unsatisfactory colposcopy meaning that entire scquamocolumnar junction was not visualized, & discrepancy between Pap smear & colposcopy biopsy
6. Tx = excision of premalignant or malignant lesions—if cancer, see Section VIII below for appropriate adjunctive modalities

D. VAGINITIS

1. 50% of cases due to *Gardnerella* ("bacterial vaginosis"), 25% due to *Trichomonas*, 25% due to *Candida* (↑ frequency in diabetics, in pregnancy & in HIV)
2. Most common presenting symptom in vaginitis is discharge
3. Rule out noninfectious causes, including chemical or allergic sources
4. Dx by pelvic examination with microscopic examination of discharge
5. DDx of vaginitis

TABLE 3-10   Differential Diagnosis of Vaginitis

	CANDIDA	TRICHOMONAS	GARDNERELLA
Vaginal pH	4–5	>6	>5
Odor	None	Rancid	"Fishy" on KOH prep
Discharge	Cheesy white	Green, frothy	Variable
Si/Sx	Itchy, burning erythema	Severe itching	Variable to none
Microscopy	Pseudohyphae, more pronounced on 10% KOH prep (See Figure 3-5)	Motile organisms (See Figures 3-6 and 3-7)	Clue cells (large epithelial cells covered with dozens of small dots)
Treatment	Fluconazole	Metronidazole—treat partner also	Metronidazole

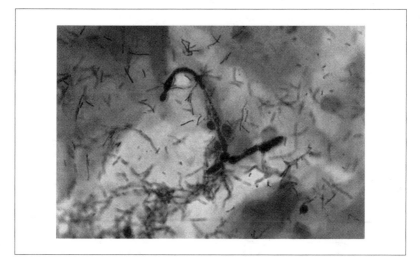

FIGURE 3-5   Gram's-stain appearance of candidal pseudohyphae and cells.

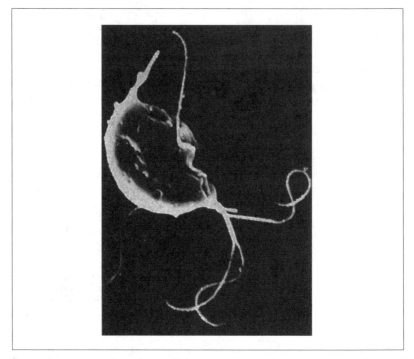

Figure 3-6 Scanning electronmicrograph of *Trichomonas vaginalis*. The undulating membrane and flagellae of *Trichomonas* are its characteristic features.

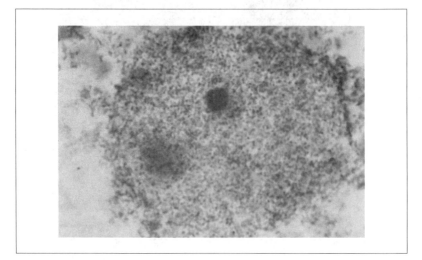

Figure 3-7 Gram's-stain appearance of a "clue cell"—a vaginal epithelial cell covered with bacteria. No lactobacilli are present.

E. ENDOMETRIOSIS
1. Affects 1–2% of women (up to 50% in infertile women), peak age = 20s–30s
2. Endometrial tissue in extrauterine locations, most commonly ovaries (60%), but can be anywhere in the peritoneum & rarely extraperitoneal
3. Adenomyosis = endometrial implants within the uterine wall
4. Endometrioma = endometriosis involving an ovary with implants large enough to be considered a tumor, filled with chocolate-appearing fluid (old blood) that gives them their name of "chocolate cysts"
5. Si/Sx = **the 3 D's = dysmenorrhea, dyspareunia, dyschezia** (painful defecation), pelvic pain, infertility, uterosacral nodularity palpable on rectovaginal exam, severity of Sx often do not correlate with extent of dz
6. Dx requires direct visualization via laparoscopy or laparotomy with histologic confirmation
7. Tx
   a. Start with NSAIDs, can add combined estrogen & progestin pills, allowing maintenance without withdrawal bleeding & dysmenorrhea
   b. Can use progestin-only pills, drawback is breakthrough bleeding
   c. GnRH agonists inhibit ovarian function → hypoestrogen state
   d. Danazol inhibits LH & FSH midcycle surges, side effects include hypoestrogenic & androgenic (hirsutism, acne) states
   e. Conservative surgery involves excision, cauterization, or ablation of endometrial implants with preservation of ovaries & uterus
   f. Recurrence after cessation of medical Tx is common, definitive Tx requires hysterectomy, ⊕ oophorectomy (TAH/BSO), lysis of adhesions & removal of endometrial implants
   g. Pts can take estrogen replacement therapy following definitive surgery, risk of reactivation of endometriosis is very small compared to risk of prolonged estrogen deficiency

II. Reproductive Endocrinology and Infertility

A. AMENORRHEA
1. Amenorrhea ≡ absence of menstruation, primary amenorrhea = a woman who has never menstruated, secondary amenorrhea = a menstrual-aged woman who has not menstruated in 6 mo
2. Causes of amenorrhea
   a. **Pregnancy = most common cause**, thus every evaluation should begin with an exclusion of pregnancy before any further work-up
   b. Asherman's syndrome
      1) Scarring of the uterine cavity after a D&C procedure
      2) **The most common anatomic cause of 2° amenorrhea**
   c. Hypothalamic deficiency due to weight loss, excessive exercise (e.g., marathon runner), obesity, drug induced (e.g., marijuana, tranquilizers), malignancy (prolactinoma, craniopharyngioma), psychogenic (chronic anxiety, anorexia)
   d. Pituitary dysfunction results from either ↓ hypothalamic pulsatile release of GnRH or ↓ pituitary release of FSH or LH
   e. Ovarian dysfunction

1) Ovarian follicles are either exhausted or resistant to stimulation by FSH & LH
2) Si/Sx = those of estrogen deficiency = hot flashes, mood swings, vaginal dryness, dyspareunia, sleep disturbances, skin thinning
3) **Note that estrogen deficiency 2° to hypothalamic-pituitary failure does not cause hot flashes, while ovarian failure does**
4) Causes = inherited (e.g., Turner's syndrome), premature natural menopause, autoimmune ovarian failure (Blizzard's syndrome), alkylating chemotherapies
  f. Genital outflow tract alteration, usually the result of congenital abnormalities (e.g., imperforate hymen or agenesis of uterus/vagina)
3. Tx
  a. Hypothalamic → reversal of underlying cause & induction of ovulation with gonadotropins
  b. Tumors → excision or bromocriptine for prolactinoma
  c. Genital tract obstruction → surgery if possible
  d. Ovarian dysfunction → exogenous estrogen replacement

B. DYSFUNCTIONAL UTERINE BLEEDING
1. Irregular menstruation without anatomic lesions of the uterus
2. **Usually due to chronic estrogen stimulation** (vs. amenorrhea, an estrogen deficient state), more rarely to genital outflow tract obstruction
3. Abnormal bleeding = bleeding at intervals <21 days or >36 days, lasting longer than 7 days, or blood loss > 80 mL
4. Menorrhagia (excessive bleeding) is usually due to anovulation
5. Dx
  a. Rule out anatomic causes of bleeding including uterine fibroids, cervical or vaginal lesions or infection, cervical & endometrial cancer
  b. Evaluate stress, exercise, weight changes, systemic disease such as thyroid, renal or hepatic disease & coagulopathies, & pregnancy
6. Tx
  a. Convert proliferative endometrium into secretory endometrium by administration of a progestational agent for 10 days
  b. Alternative is to give OCPs that suppress the endometrium & establish regular, predictable cycles
  c. NSAIDs ⊕ iron used in pts who want to preserve fertility
  d. **Postmenopausal bleeding is cancer until proven otherwise**

C. HIRSUTISM & VIRILIZATION (See Figure 3-8)
1. Hirsutism ≡ excess body hair, usually associated with acne, most commonly due to polycystic ovarian dz or adrenal hyperplasia
2. Virilization ≡ masculinization of a woman, associated with marked ↑ testosterone, clitoromegaly, temporal balding, voice deepening, breast involution, limb-shoulder girdle remodeling

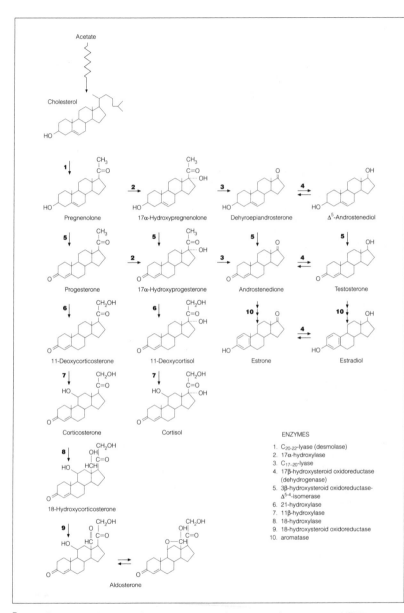

FIGURE 3-8   Biosynthesis of androgens, estrogens, and corticosteroids.

TABLE 3-11   Differential Diagnosis of Hirsutism and Virilization

DISEASE	CHARACTERISTICS	TREATMENT
Polycystic ovarian disease	• **#1 cause of androgen excess & hirsutism** • Etiology likely related to LH overproduction • Si/Sx = oligo- or amenorrhea, anovulation, infertility, hirsutism, acne • Labs → ↑ **LH/FSH**, ↑ **testosterone**	• Break feedback cycle with OCPs → ↓ LH production • Weight loss may allow ovulation, sparing fertility • Refractory pts may require clomiphene to ⊕ ovulation
Sertoli-Leydig cell tumors	• Ovarian tumors secreting testosterone, usually in women aged 20–40 • Si/Sx = **rapid onset** of hirsutism, acne, amenorrhea, virilization • Labs → ↓ **LH/FSH**, ↑↑↑ **testosterone**	• Removal of involved ovary (tumors usually unilateral) • 10-yr survival = 90–95%
Congenital adrenal hyperplasia	• Usually due to 21-α-hydroxylase defect • Autosomal recessive, variable penetrance • When severe → virilized newborn, milder forms can present at puberty or later • Labs → ↑ **LH/FSH**, ↑**DHEA**	• Glucocorticoids to suppress adrenal androgen production

D. MENOPAUSE

1. Defined as the cessation of menses, **average age in US is 51 yr**
2. Suspect when menstrual cycles are not regular & predictable & when cycles are not associated with any premenstrual symptoms
3. Si/Sx = rapid onset hot flashes & sweating with resolution in 3 min, mood changes, sleep disturbances, vaginal dryness/atrophy, dyspareunia (painful intercourse) & osteoporosis
4. Dx = irregular menstrual cycles, hot flashes & ↑ FSH level (> 30 mIU/mL)
5. Depending on clinical scenario other laboratory tests should be conducted to exclude other diagnoses that can cause amenorrhea such as thyroid disease, hyperprolactinemia, pregnancy
6. Tx
   a. **First line is estrogen hormone replacement therapy (HRT)**
   b. HRT can be via continuous estrogen with cyclic progestin to allow controlled withdrawal bleeding or via daily administration of both estrogen & progestin, which does not cause withdrawal bleeding
   c. There are risks & benefits of HRT

TABLE 3-12   Risks and Benefits of Hormone Replacement Therapy

RISKS	BENEFITS
Endometrial CA ↑ risk with HRT, but risk significantly ↓ by addition of ≥10 days of progesterone to induce uterine wall sloughing	Relief of menopause Sx
Breast CA • Very controversial, studies equivocal, some show that prolonged HRT (≥5–10 yr) → ↑ relative risk of breast CA • Regardless, breast CA or heavy risk factors for its development are contraindications to HRT	↓ risk of heart dz or stroke, ↑ HDL, ↓ LDL
DVT/PE Only seen with oral estrogen (not transdermal)	↓ osteoporosis
Breast pain Due to constant estrogen stimulation	↓ risk of dementia

 d. Raloxifene
  1) Second-generation tamoxifen-like drug = mixed estrogen agonist/antagonist, FDA approved to prevent osteoporosis
  2) So far Raloxifene shown to act like estrogen in bones (good), ↓ serum LDL (good) but does not stimulate endometrial growth (good) (unlike tamoxifen & estrogen alone), effects on breast are not yet known
 e. **Calcium supplements are not a substitute for estrogen replacement**

E. INFERTILITY
 1. Defined as failure to conceive after 1 yr of unprotected sex
 2. Affects 10–15% of reproductive-age couples in the US
 3. Causes = abnormal spermatogenesis (40%), anovulation (30%), anatomic defects of the female reproductive tract (20%), unknown (10%)
 4. Dx
  a. **Start work-up with male partner not only because it is the most common cause**, but because the work-up is simpler, noninvasive & more cost-effective than work-up of infertility in the female
  b. **Normal semen excludes male cause in > 90% of couples**
  c. Work-up of female partner should include measurement of basal body temperature, which is an excellent screening test for ovulation
   1) Temperature drops at time of menses, then rises 2 days after LH surge at the time of progesterone rise
   2) Ovulation probably occurs 1 day before first temperature elevation & temperature remains elevated for 13–14 days
   3) A temperature elevation of > 16 days suggests pregnancy

d. Anovulation
1) Hx of regular menses with premenstrual Sx (breast fullness, ↓ vaginal secretions, abdominal bloating, mood changes) strongly suggests ovulation
2) Sx such as irregular menses, amenorrhea episodes, hirsutism, acne, galactorrhea, suggest anovulation
3) FSH measured at day 2–3 is best predictor of fertility potential in women, FSH > 25 IU/L correlated with a poor prognosis
4) Dx confirm with basal body temperature, serum progesterone (↑ postovulation, >10 ng/mL → ovulation), endometrial Bx

e. Anatomic disorder
1) **Most commonly results from an acquired disorder, especially acute salpingitis 2° to *N. gonorrhoeae* & *C. trachomatis***
2) Endometriosis, scarring, adhesions from pelvic inflammation or previous surgeries, tumors & trauma can also disrupt normal reproductive tract anatomy
3) Less commonly a congenital anomaly such as septate uterus or reduplication of the uterus, cervix, or vagina is responsible
4) **Dx with hysterosalpingogram**

5. Tx
a. Anovulation → restore ovulation with use of ovulation-inducing drugs
1) First line = clomiphene, an estrogen antagonist that relieves negative feedback on FSH, allowing follicle development
2) Anovulatory women who bleed in response to progesterone are candidates for clomiphene, as are women with irregular menses or midluteal progesterone levels <10 ng/mL
3) 40% get pregnant, 8–10% ↑ rate of multiple births, mostly twins
4) If no response, FSH can be given directly → pregnancy rates of 60–80%, multiple births occur at an ↑ rate of 20%
b. Anatomic abnormalities → surgical lysis of pelvic adhesions
c. If endosalpinx is not intact & transport of the ovum is not possible, an assisted fertilization technique, such as in vitro fertilization, may be used with 15–25% success

III. Urogynecology

A. PELVIC RELAXATION & URINARY INCONTINENCE
1. ↑ incidence with age, also with birth trauma, obesity, chronic cough

2. Si/Sx = prolapse of urethra (urethrocele), uterus, bladder (cystocele), or rectum (rectocele), pelvic pressure & pain, dyspareunia, bowel & bladder dysfunction, & urinary incontinence
3. Types of urinary incontinence (See Figure 3-9)
    a. Stress incontinence = bladder pressure exceeds urethral pressure briefly at times of strain or stress such as coughing or laughing
    b. Urge incontinence & overflow incontinence result from ↓ innervation & control of bladder function resulting in involuntary bladder contraction (urge) or bladder atony (overflow)
4. Dx = urodynamic testing, assess for underlying medical conditions such as diabetes, neurologic dz, genitourinary surgery, pelvic irradiation, trauma & medications that may account for Sx
5. Tx = correct underlying cause
    a. Kegel exercises to tone pelvic floor
    b. Insertion of pessary devices to add structural support
    c. Useful drugs = anticholinergics, Ditropan/Detrol, β-agonists
    d. Surgical repair aimed at restoring structures to original anatomic position

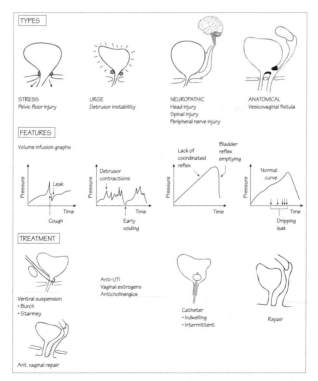

FIGURE 3-9   Urinary incontinence.

IV. Gynecology Oncology

A. ENDOMETRIAL CANCER

1. Most common reproductive tract cancer with approximately 35,000 new cases per year
2. "Estrogen-dependent" cancer
   a. Estrogen source can be glandular from the ovary
   b. Extraglandular from peripheral conversion of androstenedione to estrone or from a granulosa cell tumor
   c. Exogenous from oral estrogen, cutaneous patches, vaginal creams & now tamoxifen (reduces risk of breast cancer by 50%, but associated with 3x ↑ incidence of endometrial cancer)
3. Risk factors
   a. Unopposed postmenopausal estrogen replacement therapy
   b. Menopause after 52 yr
   c. Obesity, nulliparity, feminizing ovarian tumors (e.g., ovarian granulosa cell tumors), chronic anovulation, polycystic ovarian syndrome, postmenopausal (75% of patients), diabetes
4. Si/Sx = abnormal uterine bleeding, especially postmenopausal—any woman over age 35 yr with abnormal uterine bleeding should have a sample of endometrium taken for histologic evaluation
5. DDx = endometrial hyperplasia
   a. Abnormal proliferation of both glandular & stromal elements, can be simple or complex
   b. Atypical hyperplasia
      1) Significant numbers of glandular elements that exhibit cytological atypia & disordered maturation
      2) Analogous to carcinoma in situ → 20–30% risk for malignancy
6. Dx
   a. **Pap smear IS NOT reliable in Dx of endometrial cancer; however, if atypical glandular cells of undetermined significance (AGCUS) are found on the smear then endometrial evaluation is mandatory**
   b. Bimanual exam for masses, nodularity, induration & immobility
   c. Endometrial biopsy by endocervical curettage, D&C, hysteroscopy with directed biopsies
7. Tx
   a. Simple or complex hyperplasia → progesterone to reverse hyperplastic process promoted by estrogen (e.g., Provera × 10 d)
   b. Atypical hyperplasia → hysterectomy because of likelihood that it will become invasive endometrial carcinoma
   c. Endometrial carcinoma
      1) Total abdominal hysterectomy with bilateral salpingo-oophorectomy (TAH/BSO), lymph node dissection
      2) Adjuvant Tx may include external-beam radiation
      3) Tx for recurrence is high-dose progestins (e.g., Depo-Provera)
8. Px
   a. **Most important prognostic factor is histological grade**

b. G1 is highly differentiated, G2 is moderately differentiated, G3 is predominantly solid or entirely undifferentiated carcinoma

c. **Depth of myometrial invasion is second most important Px factor**

d. Pt with G1 tumor that does not invade the myometrium has a 95% 5-yr survival, pt with G3 tumor with deep myometrial invasion has 5-yr survival rate closer to 20%

B. UTERINE LEIOMYOMAS = FIBROIDS

1. Benign tumors, growth related to estrogen production, usually most rapid growth occurs perimenopausally
2. Most common indication for hysterectomy (30% of cases)
3. Si/Sx = bleeding (usually menorrhagia or ↑ amount & duration of flow), pelvic pressure, pelvic pain often manifested as dysmenorrhea
4. Dx = Utz, confirm with tissue sample by either D&C or biopsy (especially in post-menopausal pts)
5. Tx
   a. If Sx are mild → reassurance & observation
   b. Medical Tx → estrogen inhibitors such as GnRH agonists shrink uterus, resulting in a simpler surgical procedure or can be used as a temporizing measure until natural menopause occurs
   c. Surgery → myomectomy indicated in young pts who want to preserve fertility (risk of intraoperative & postoperative hemorrhage ↑ compared to hysterectomy); hysterectomy is considered definitive treatment, but should be reserved for symptomatic women who have completed childbearing

C. LEIOMYOSARCOMA

1. Rare malignancy accounting for only 3% of cancers involving uterine corpus
2. ↑ suspicion for postmenopausal uterine enlargement
3. Si/Sx suggestive of sarcoma = postmenopausal bleeding, pelvic pain & ↑ vaginal discharge
4. Tx = hysterectomy with intraoperative lymph node biopsies
5. Surgical staging same as that for endometrial adenocarcinoma
6. Survival rate is much lower than that for endometrial cancer, only 50% of patients survive 5 yr
7. Adjunctive therapies are of minimal benefit

D. CERVICAL CANCER

1. Annual Pap smear is most important screening tool available to detect disease
2. Risk factors = early sexual intercourse, multiple sexual partners, HPV infection (especially types 16, 18), cigarette smoking, early childbearing & immunocompromised patients
3. Average age of Dx = 50 yr, but can occur much earlier
4. 85% are of squamous cell origin, 15% are adenocarcinomas arising from endocervical glands
5. Si/Sx = postcoital bleeding, but there is no classic presentation for cervical cancer
6. Dx = Pap screening, any visible cervical lesion should be biopsied
7. Tx
   a. Local dz → hysterectomy + lymph node dissection—ovaries may remain → survival >70% at 5 yr
   b. Extensive or metastatic dz → pelvic irradiation → survival <40% at 5 yr

E. OVARIAN NEOPLASMS

TABLE 3-13   Ovarian Neoplasms

NEOPLASM	CHARACTERISTICS	TX
Benign cysts	• Functional growth resulting from failure of normal follicle to rupture • Si/Sx = pelvic pain or pressure, rupture of cyst → acute, severe pain & hemorrhage mimicking acute abdomen • Confirm cyst with Utz	• Typically self-limiting • Rupture may require laparotomy to stop bleeding
Benign Tumors: more common than malignant, but risk of malignancy ↑ with age		
Epithelial	• Serous cystadenocarcinoma most common type, almost always benign unless bilateral → ↑ risk of malignancy • Other types = mucinous, endometrioid, Brenner tumors, all rarely malignant • Dx = clinical, can see on CT/MRI	• Surgical excision
Germ cell	• Teratoma is most common (also called "dermoid cyst") • Very rarely malignant, contain differentiated tissue from all 3 embryologic germ layers • Si/Sx = unilateral cystic, mobile, nontender adnexal mass, often aSx • Dx confirmed with Utz	• Excision to prevent ovarian torsion or rupture
Stromal cell	• Functional tumors secreting hormones • Granulosa tumor makes estrogens → gynecomastia, loss of body hair, etc. • Sertoli-Leydig cells make androgens, virilize females	• Excision

Malignant Tumors
• Usually occur in women >50 yr old
• Risk factors = low parity, ↓ fertility, delayed childbearing—**OCP use is a protective factor**
• Most lethal gynecologic cancer due to lack of early detection → ↑ rate of metastasis (60% at Dx)
• Dz are typically asymptomatic until extensive metastasis has occurred
• Can follow dz with Ca-125 marker, not specific enough for screening
• Yearly pelvic exams remain most effective screening tool
• Si/Sx = vague abdominal/pelvic complaints, e.g., distension, early satiety, constipation, pelvic pain, urinary frequency—shortness of breath due to pleural effusion may be only presenting Sx
• Tx = debulking surgery with chemo- & radiotherapy

SUBTYPES	CHARACTERISTICS	TREATMENT
Epithelial cell	• Cause 90% of all ovarian malignancies • Serous cystadenocarcinoma is most common, often originate from benign precursors • Others = endometrioma & mucinous cystadenocarcinoma	• Excision
Germ cell	• Most common ovarian cancers in women <20 years old • Can produce HCG or α-fetoprotein, useful as tumor markers • Subtypes = dysgerminoma, which is very radiosensitive, & immature teratoma	• Radiation first line • Chemotherapy second line • 5-yr survival >80% for both
Stromal	• Granulosa cell makes estrogen, can result in 2° endometriosis or endometrial carcinoma • Sertoli-Leydig tumor makes androgens	• Total hysterectomy with oophorectomy

F. VULVAR & VAGINAL CANCER
   1. Vulvar intraepithelial neoplasia (VIN)
      a. VIN I & II = mild & moderate dysplasia, ↑ risk progressing to advanced stages & then carcinoma
      b. VIN III = carcinoma in situ
      c. Si/Sx = pruritus, irritation, presence of raised lesion
      d. Dx = biopsy for definitive diagnosis
      e. DDx includes Paget's disease, malignant melanoma
      f. Tx = excision, local for VIN I & II & wide for VIN III
   2. Vulvar cancer
      a. 90% are squamous
      b. Usually presents postmenopausally
      c. Si/Sx = pruritus, with or without presence of ulcerative lesion
      d. Tx = excision
      e. 5-yr survival rate is 70–90% depending on nodal status, if deep pelvic nodes are involved survival is a dismal 20%
   3. Vaginal CIS & carcinoma are very rare
      a. 70% of patients with vaginal CIS have either previous or coexistent genital tract neoplasm
      b. Tx = radiation, surgery reserved for women with extensive dz

G. GESTATIONAL TROPHOBLASTIC NEOPLASIA (GTN) = HYDATIFORM MOLE OR MOLAR PREGNANCY
   1. Rare variation of pregnancy in which a neoplasm is derived from abnormal placental tissue (trophoblastic) proliferation
   2. Usually a benign disease called a "molar pregnancy" that is further subdivided into complete mole (90%) in which there is no fetus & incomplete mole in which there is a fetus & molar degeneration
   3. Persistent or malignant disease develops in 20% of pts (mostly in complete moles)
   4. Complete moles are 46 XX, do not form fetus
   5. Partial moles are 69 XXY triploids, often form partial fetus
   6. Si/Sx = exaggerated pregnancy Sx, with missing fetal heart tones & enlarged uterus (size > dates), painless bleeding commonly occurs in early second trimester
   7. Pts can also present with PIH
   8. Utz → characteristic "snowstorm" pattern
   9. Dx = Utz + ↑↑↑ hCG levels (See Figures 3-10 and 3-11)
   10. Tx = removal of uterine contents by D&C & suction curettage
   11. Nonmetastatic persistent GTN is treated with methotrexate
   12. Follow-up = check that hCG levels are appropriately dropping
   13. Contraception is recommended during first yr of follow-up

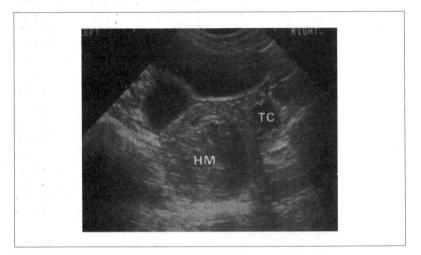

Figure 3-10   Ultrasound scan of a hydatidiform mole (HM) with a theca-luteal cyst (TC) in the ovary.

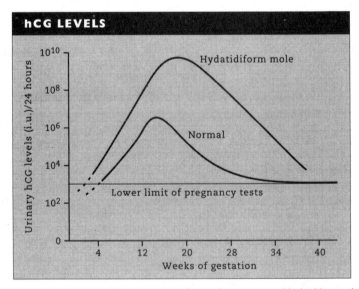

Figure 3-11   Means of levels of hCG in women with normal pregnancies and hydatidiform moles.

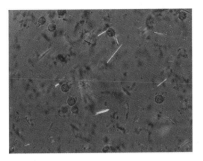

PLATE 2 Gout. Synovial fluid microscopy under compensated polarized light showing the slender needle-shaped and negatively birefringent urate crystals. The axis of slow vibration is from bottom left to top right.

PLATE 1 Café au lait patch (polyostotic fibrous dysplasia, neurofibromatosis can appear similarly).

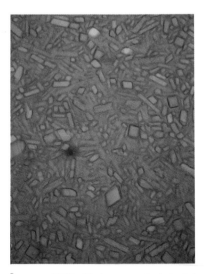

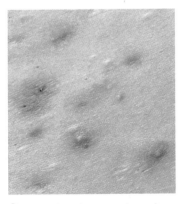

PLATE 4 Comedones, pustules, and scars (acne vulgaris).

PLATE 3 CPPD dihydrate crystals (extracted from synovial fluid). These are pleomorphic, rectangular, and weakly positively birefringent. The axis of slow vibration is from bottom left to top right.

PLATE 5   Impetigo

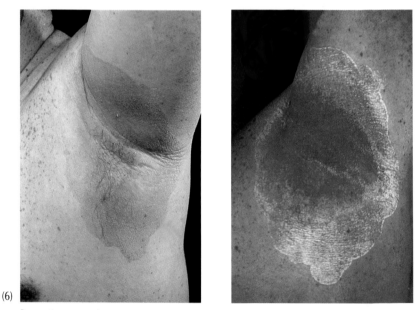

(6)   (7)

PLATES 6 & 7   Erythrasma: (6) normal light; (7) coral-red axillary fluorescent, due to proporphyria III
elaborated by *Corynebacterium minutissimum* in erythrasma, under Wood's lamp.

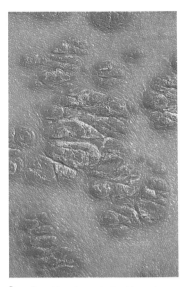

PLATE 8   Hyperkeratotic (scaly), erythematous plaques (psoriasis).

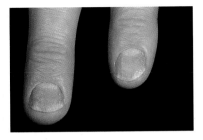

PLATE 9   Nail involvement in psoriasis. Note dystrophy, pits, and irregular yellowing onychylosis.

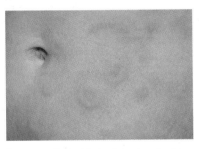

PLATE 11   Urticarial wheals (acute urticaria).

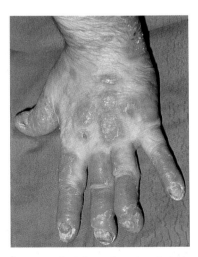

PLATE 10   Psoriatic arthropathy (arthritis mutilans); severe nail dystrophy.

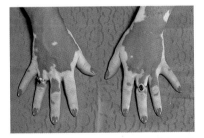

PLATE 12   Macules and patches of hypopigmentation (vitiligo).

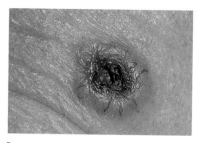

PLATE 13 Classic crateriform basal cell carcinoma. Ulcerating nodule.

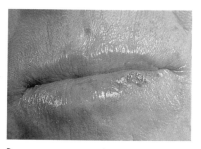

PLATE 14 Squamous cell carcinoma of the lip (early ulcer).

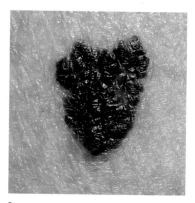

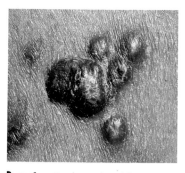

PLATE 16 Papules and nodules (Kaposis sarcoma–AIDS).

PLATE 15 Superficial spreading melanoma.

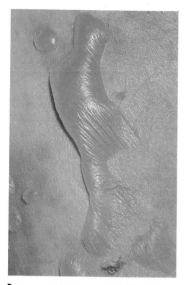

PLATE 17 Vesicles and bulla (bullous pemphigoid).

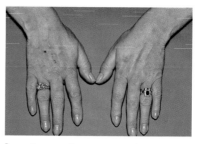

PLATE 18 Porphyria cutanea tarda.

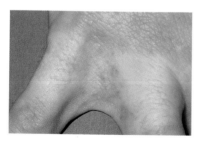

PLATE 19 Scabies.

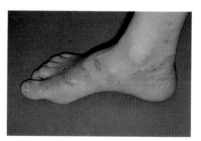

PLATE 20 Tinea pedis. Well-marginated erythematous scaly eruption (moccasin pattern).

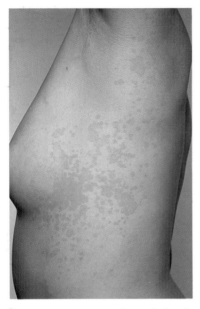

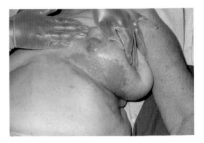

PLATE 22   Candidiasis. Erythematous, almost eroded intertrigo.

PLATE 21   Pityriasis versicolor. Petaloid, scaly macules.

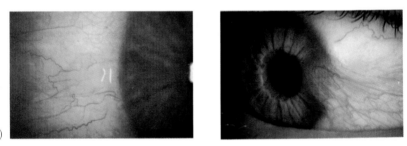

(23)

(24)

PLATES 23 & 24   The clinical apearance of (23) a pingueculum; (24) a pterygium.

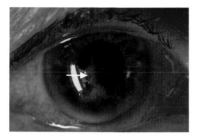

PLATE 25   A dendritic ulcer seen in herpes simplex infection.

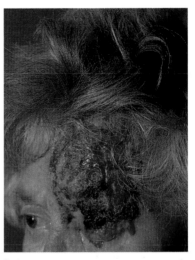

PLATE 26   The clinical appearance of herpes zoster ophthalmicus.

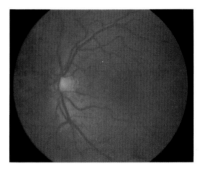

PLATE 27   A normal left fundus. note the optic disc with retinal veins and arteries passing from it to branch over the retina. The large temporal vessels are termed *arcades*. The macula lies temporal to the disc with the fovea at its center.

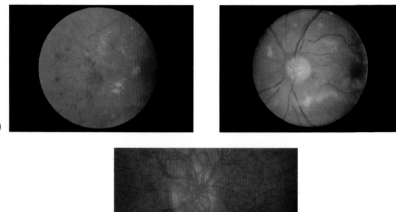

(28)

(29)

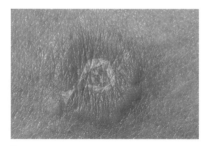

(30)

PLATES 28, 29 & 30   The signs of retinal vascular disease: (28) hemorrage and exudate; (29) cotton wool spots; (30) new vessels, here particularly florid arising at the disc. Note the yellowish nature and distinct margin to the exudates compared to the less distinct and white appearance of the cottom wool spot.

PLATE 31   Sweet's syndrome.

Obstetrics and Gynecology Case Scenario

A 24-year-old woman presents to your office because of amenorrhea for 8 weeks. Menarche was at age 12 and cycles have always been irregular. Three months ago she was started on a low-dose combination OCP in an attempt to regulate her cycles. She had withdrawal bleeding following the first cycle, but no vaginal bleeding since. The patient also reports some nausea and breast tenderness. She would like to discuss a switch to another OCP. Physical exam is unremarkable. Labs show normal FSH, increased LH.

1. What is your next course of action?

   a) Measure serum androstenedione

   b) Measure serum β hCG

   c) Change OCP to a higher dose preparation

   d) Begin evaluation to determine underlying cause of patient's ovarian failure

A couple in their early 30s seek treatment for infertility. The couple has been having unprotected intercourse for 18 months and have been unable to conceive. Semen analysis in the man is normal. The woman's history includes a previous elective abortion at age 18, as well as two episodes of salpingitis in her 20s. She reports irregular menstrual cycles with heavy bleeding and dysmenorrhea. Her last menstrual period was about 6 weeks ago. Pelvic exam is remarkable for a retroverted uterus that is somewhat fixed, moderate cervical motion tenderness, and some bilateral adnexal fullness.

2. The most likely diagnosis and course of treatment for this patient is:

   a) Acute PID with hospitalization for intravenous antibiotic administration

   b) Endometriosis—start patient on GnRH agonist

   c) Pelvic adhesions with need for diagnostic laparoscopy

   d) Anovulation with recommendation for in vitro fertilization

A 42-year-old female complains of vaginal burning and a malodorous discharge. She also has itching. After placing the speculum, you obtain a sample of the discharge and run tests on it. The pH of the discharge is 5.3, and upon addition of 10% potassium hydroxide you detect the unmistakable odor of fish.

3. What other finding is present?

   a) The discharge is thick and white

   b) The discharge is green and frothy

   c) The wet mount prep contains epithelial cells covered in bacteria

   d) The wet mount prep contains motile organisms

   e) The wet mount prep contains hyphae

4. What is the proper treatment?

   a) Fluconazole

   b) Cefotetan

   c) Vancomycin

d) Metronidazole

e) Doxycycline

A 33-year-old G1P0 obese female has been coming to you for prenatal care. The patient has a history of hypertension, which runs in her family. She also has a family history of diabetes mellitus, although she has never been diagnosed with it. When she told you what medication she had been taking to control her hypertension, you told her to stop taking the drug because it causes birth defects.

5. Which class of antihypertensive drugs is teratogenic?

a) Beta blocker

b) ACE inhibitor

c) Calcium channel blocker

d) Alpha blocker

e) Thiazide diuretic

At 24 weeks you perform a standard Glucola screening to detect pregnancy-induced diabetes. The screening test is positive, and you confirm the result with a 3-hour glucose tolerance test. You place the patient on a calorie-restricted diet and teach her how to record her daily glucose levels. A week later the patient returns, and you realize that the diet is not sufficiently controlling the patient's glucose levels.

6. The most appropriate agent to start the patient on for improved glucose control is:

a) Metformin

b) Glyburide

c) Troglitazone

d) Insulin

e) Beta blocker

At 30 weeks, the patient comes to your office complaining of some abdominal discomfort and fatigue. She has gained 10 pounds over the past week and feels slightly uncomfortable. Her blood pressure is 150/90, which is increased by 30/10 from the prior week, despite the antihypertensive to which you switched her. On exam, you find 1+ pitting edema in the ankles, and the patient has 3 + deep tendon patellar and Achilles' reflexes bilaterally. Urinalysis is positive for glucose but negative for protein.

7. Your management for this patient is:

a) Increase the dose of the antihypertensive medication

b) Start furosemide

c) Emergent delivery of the baby

d) Water restriction

e) Bed rest

At 36 weeks the patient's blood pressure has again increased and she is now complaining of severe headache. It is now 170/90, and she has developed 2 + protein on urine dipstick. She has 2 + pitting edema on exam and marked abdominal discomfort. The patient's hemoglobin has fallen 2 g/dL since the prior week, and her indirect bilirubin is elevated. Her platelet count is 95,000. Transaminases are elevated.

8. The treatment for this patient is:
   a) Increase the dose of the antihypertensive medication(s)
   b) Start IV magnesium
   c) Emergent delivery of the baby
   d) Water restriction
   e) Bed rest

During the evaluation of a 28-year-old G0P0 female who had complained of months of pelvic pain, you discover a uterine fibroid on pelvic examination and confirm the diagnosis with ultrasound. The pain is only partially controlled with NSAIDs. The patient tells you that she wishes to have children.

9. What is the next step in the treatment of this patient?
   a) Morphine
   b) Hysterectomy
   c) Referral to pain clinic
   d) GnRH analogue + myomectomy if the pain does not abate
   e) Exploratory laparotomy

A 26-year-old female comes into your office complaining of painful menses over the past few months. Her menses used to be regular, starting every 5 weeks and lasting for 5 days. The last 3 cycles have started after 3 weeks, 6 weeks, and then 4 weeks, and have been accompanied by significant pelvic discomfort. The patient also says that bowel movements and intercourse with her husband are particularly painful during menstruation, but have never before been uncomfortable. She has tried taking NSAIDs for her discomfort without any appreciable effect. On pelvic exam you palpate several nodular masses along the uterosacral ligament.

10. What is your diagnosis?
   a) Endometrial carcinoma
   b) Pelvic inflammatory disease
   c) Endometriosis
   d) Cervical cancer
   e) Uterine fibroid

A 28-year-old G2P1 female rushes to the ER at 31 weeks of pregnancy with sudden onset of vaginal bleeding. The patient had developed mild pregnancy-induced hypertension 3 weeks earlier, for which bed rest had been prescribed. She had been feeling well until this morning when a sharp pain developed in her belly. Quickly thereafter she noticed blood running down her leg. She immediately came to the hospital. The patient is in considerable pain, described as a 7 out of 10 in intensity. She has also begun to have contractions, which are somewhat irregular but coming about every 10 minutes. An ultrasound is unrevealing.

11. What is your diagnosis?

   a) Placenta accreta

   b) Placenta previa

   c) Severe preeclampsia

   d) Premature rupture of membranes

   e) Placental abruption

Answers

1. **b)** This question illustrates the importance of always suspecting pregnancy in an amenorrheic patient. This patient's amenorrhea could be due to pregnancy or could be due to too low of a dose of OCPs. Nausea and breast tenderness are nonspecific and could point toward pregnancy or could be a side effect of the OCPs. It is not unusual for physical exam to not show any signs of pregnancy this early in gestation. However, the increase in LH with no increase in FSH is highly suggestive of pregnancy (most assays do not distinguish between LH and β-hCG). The history and physical are not consistent with polycystic ovary disease, which would be associated with elevated androstenedione; therefore, there is no reason to pursue option a. A patient with ovarian failure would experience symptoms of estrogen deficiency (hot flashes, mood swings, vaginal dryness, etc.) and labs would show increases in both FSH and LH.

2. **c)** The patient's history is consistent with scarring from PID, a common cause of infertility because of structural abnormality. Other than moderate cervical motion tenderness the patient has no signs of acute PID (fever, malaise, severe pain, discharge). Endometriosis is a possibility; however, a diagnosis can only be made by direct observation during laparoscopy. Also a GnRH agonist would induce a chemical menopause and would likely not be an option for a woman desiring fertility. A suspicion of anovulation would warrant a work-up to confirm the diagnosis, not an immediate leap to IVF.

3. **c)** The pH of greater than 4.5 indicates that *Candida* is not likely the responsible organism, and the positive whiff test (fishy smell on KOH prep) is indicative of bacterial vaginosis. The pathognomonic wet mount finding are "clue cells," which are epithelial cells covered with tiny blue dots (stained bacteria). Motile organisms would indicate *Trichomonas*, as would the green and frothy discharge.

4. **d)** Metronidazole is first-line therapy for both bacterial vaginosis and trichomoniasis

5. **b)** ACE inhibitors are known to cause fetal cardiac defects.

6. **d)** Oral hypoglycemic agents are contraindicated in pregnancy because they cross the placenta and can cause fetal or neonatal hypoglycemia. Insulin should be

administered for glucose control in all diabetic pregnant women for whom diet is insufficient.

7. **e)** This patient is at an increased risk for pregnancy-induced hypertension. She is nulliparous, had prepregnancy hypertension, and developed pregnancy-induced diabetes, all of which are risk factors. The rapid weight gain and pedal edema are consistent with the diagnosis of PIH, as is the hyperreflexia. The blood pressure of greater than 140/90, with a 30-point increase in systolic BP compared to baseline, confirms the diagnosis. However, the patient is not severely ill. First-line treatment for PIH for women who are not in extremis is bed rest, particularly if the fetus is relatively immature and therefore at increased risk if delivery is induced.

8. **c)** In the past six weeks, the patient's PIH has worsened. She now has severe preeclampsia (but not eclampsia since she is not seizing), and has developed the HELLP syndrome of hemolysis, elevated liver enzymes, and low platelets. The severity of her illness necessitates delivery of the fetus, either by induced vaginal delivery or by C-section.

9. **d)** With failure of NSAIDs, estrogen inhibitors such as GnRH can be helpful in controlling symptoms by shrinking the estrogen-dependent fibroids. This can allow either symptom abatement or reduction in the size of the fibroid so that it can be extracted while sparing the rest of the uterus (myomectomy).

10. **c)** This patient has the 3 Ds: **d**ysmenorrhea, **d**yspareunia, and **d**yschezia, which are classic for endometriosis. The nodules appreciated on the uterosacral ligament are also consistent.

11. **e)** Painful bleeding in the third trimester accompanied by contractions is the usual presentation of placental abruption. The main differential diagnosis is placenta previa, which is usually painless and is effectively ruled out in this patient by the normal ultrasound (which would show the fetus implanted over the cervical os in placenta previa).

4. Pediatrics

Beatriz Mares

I. Development

A.

TABLE 4-1   Development Milestones

AGE	GROSS MOTOR	FINE MOTOR	LANGUAGE	SOCIAL/ COGNITION
Newborn	Head side to side, **Moro & grasp reflex**			
2 mos	Holds head up	Swipes at object	Coos	Social smile
4 mos	Rolls front to back	**Grasps object**	Orients to voice	Laughs
6 mos	Rolls back to front, **sits upright**	Transfers object	Babbles	**Stranger anxiety, sleeps all night**
9 mos	Crawl, pull to stand	**Pincer grasp,** eats with fingers	**Mama-dada (nonspecific)**	Waves bye-bye, responds to name
12 mos	**Stands**	**Mature pincer**	**Mama-dada (specific)**	Picture book
15 mos	**Walks**	Uses cup	4–6 words	**Temper tantrum**
18 mos	Throws ball, walks upstairs	Uses spoon for solids	Names common objects	**Toilet training may begin**
24 mos	Runs, up/down stairs	Uses spoon for semisolids	**2-word sentence** (2 word at 2 yr)	Follows 2-step command
36 mos	Rides tricycle	Eats neatly with utensils	**3-word sentence** (3 word at 3 yr)	Knows first & last name

B. PUBERTY

TABLE 4-2   Tanner Stages

BOYS	GIRLS
Testicular enlargement at 11.5 yr*	Breast buds at 10.5 yr*
Increase in genital size	Pubic hair
Pubic hair	Linear growth spurt at 12 yr
Peak growth spurt at 13.5 yr*	Menarche at 12.5 yr*

*Years represent population averages.

II. Infections

A. ToRCHS

TABLE 4-3 The ToRCHS

DISEASE	CHARACTERISTICS
Toxoplasmosis	• Acquired in mothers via ingestion of poorly cooked meat or through contact with cat feces • Carriers common (10–30%) in population, only causes neonatal dz if acquired during pregnancy (1%) • 1/3 of women who acquire during pregnancy transmit infection to fetus, & 1/3 of fetuses are clinically affected • Sequelae = intracerebral calcifications, hydrocephalus, chorioretinitis, microcephaly, severe mental retardation, epilepsy, intrauterine growth retardation (IUGR), hepatosplenomegaly • Screening is useless since acquisition prior to infection is common & clinically irrelevant • Pregnant women should be told to avoid undercooked meat, wash hands after handling cat, do not change litter box • If fetal infection established → Utz to determine major anomalies & provide counseling regarding termination if indicated
Rubella	• First trimester maternal Rubella infxn → 80% chance of fetal transmission • Second trimester → 50% chance of transmission to fetus, third trimester → 5% • Si/Sx of fetus = intrauterine growth retardation, cataracts, glaucoma, chorioretinitis, patent ductus arteriosus, pulmonary stenosis, atrial or ventricular septal defect, myocarditis, microcephaly, **hearing loss, "blueberry muffin rash,"** mental retardation • Dx confirmed with IgM Rubella Ab in neonate's serum, or viral culture • Tx = prevention by universal immunization of all children against Rubella, there is no effective therapy for active infection
Cytomegalovirus (CMV)	• # 1 congenital infection, affecting 1% of births • Transmitted through bodily fluids/secretions, infection often asymptomatic • 1° seroconversion during pregnancy → ↑ risk of severely affected infant, but congenital infection can occur if mother reinfected during pregnancy • About 1% risk of transplacental transmission of infection, about 10% of infected infants manifest congenital defects of varying severity • Congenital defects = microcephaly, intracranial calcifications, severe mental retardation, chorioretinitis, IUGR • 10–15% of asymptomatic but exposed infants will develop later neurologic sequelae
Herpes simplex virus	• **C-section delivery for pregnant women with active herpes** • Vaginal → 50% chance that the baby will acquire the infection & is associated with significant morbidity & morality • Si/Sx = vesicles, seizures, respiratory distress, can cause pneumonia, meningitis, encephalitis → impaired neurologic development after resolution • Tx = acyclovir (markedly decreases mortality)
Syphilis	• Transmission from infected mother to infant during pregnancy nearly 100%, **occurs after the first trimester in the vast majority of cases** • Fetal/perinatal deaths in 40% of affected infants • Early manifestations in first 2 years, later manifestations in next 2 decades • Si/Sx of early dz = jaundice, ↑ liver function tests, hepatosplenomegaly, hemolytic anemia, rash followed by desquamation of hands & feet, wart-like lesions of mucous membranes, **blood-tinged nasal secretions (snuffles), diffuse osteochondritis, saddle nose (2° to syphilitic rhinitis)** • Si/Sx of late dz = **Hutchinson teeth** (notching of permanent upper 2 incisors), mulberry molars (both at 6 yr), bone thickening (frontal bossing), **anterior bowing of tibia (saber shins)** • Dx = RPR/VDRL & FTA serologies in mother with clinical findings in infant • Tx = procaine penicillin G for 10–14 days

B. INFANT BOTULISM

1. Acute, flaccid paralysis caused by *Clostridium botulinum* neurotoxin that irreversibly blocks acetylcholine release from peripheral neurons
2. Dz acquired via **ingestion of spores in honey** or via inhalation of spores
3. 95% cases in infants 3 wk to 6 mo old, peak 2–4 mo
4. Si/Sx = constipation, lethargy, poor feeding, weak cry, ↓ spontaneous movement, hypotonia, drooling, ↓ gag & suck reflexes, as dz progresses → **loss of head control & respiratory arrest**
5. Dx = clinical, **based on acute onset of flaccid descending paralysis with clear sensorium, without fever or paresthesias,** can confirm by demonstrating botulinum toxin in serum or toxin/organism in feces
6. Tx = intubate, supportive care, no antibiotics or antitoxin needed in infants

C. EXANTHEMS

TABLE 4-4   Viral Exanthems

DISEASE/*VIRUS*	SI/SX
Measles (Rubeola) Paramyxovirus	• Erythematous maculopapular rash, **erupts 5 days after onset of prodromal Sx, begins on head & spreads to body, lasting 4–5 days,** resolving from head downward • Koplik spots (white spots on buccal mucosa) are pathognomonic, but leave before rash starts so often not found when pt presents • **Dx = fever & Hx of the 3 C's: cough, coryza, conjunctivitis**
Rubella (German measles) Togavirus	• **Suboccipital lymphadenopathy** (very few dzs do this) • Maculopapular rash begins on face then generalizes • Rash lasts 5 days, fever may accompany rash on first day only • May find reddish spots of various sizes on soft palate
Hand, foot & mouth disease Coxsackie A virus	• Vesicular rash on hands & feet with ulcerations in mouth • Rash clears in about 1 wk • Contagious by contact
Roseola infantum (Exanthem subitum) (HHV6)*	• **Abrupt high fever persisting for 1–5 days even though child has no physical Sx to account for fever & does not feel ill** • When fever drops, macular or maculopapular rash appears on trunk & then spreads peripherally over entire body, lasts 24 hr
Erythema infectiosum (Fifth disease) Parvovirus B-19	• Classic sign = "slapped cheeks," erythema of the cheeks • Subsequently an erythematous maculopapular rash spreads from arms to trunk & legs forming a reticular pattern • **Dz is dangerous in sickle cell pts (& other anemias) due to parvovirus B-19's tendency to cause aplastic crises**
Varicella (Chicken pox) Varicella Zoster Virus (VZV)	• Highly contagious, pruritic "tear drop" vesicles that break & crust over, start on face or trunk (centripetal) & spread to extremities • New lesions appear for 3–5 days & typically take 3 days to crust over, so rash persists for about 1 wk • **Lesions are contagious until they crust over** • Zoster (shingles) = reactivation of old varicella infxn, painful skin eruptions are seen along the distribution of dermatomes that correspond to the affected dorsal root ganglia

Dx = clinical for all, Tx = supportive for all.
*HHV6 = human herpes virus 6.

D. VACCINATIONS

TABLE 4-5 Recommended Childhood Immunization Schedule[a]

AGE	VACCINE			
Newborn	Hepatitis B (1)			
2 mo	Hepatitis B (2)	DTaP (rotavirus[b])	Hib	Polio[c]
4 mo		DTaP (rotavirus[b])	Hib	Polio[c]
6 mo	Hepatitis B (3)	DtaP (rotavirus[b])	Hib	
12 mo	MMR	Varicella	Hib	Polio[c]
15 mo		DtaP (may combine with Hib at 12 mo)		
4–6 yr	MMR	DtaP		Polio[c]
11–12 yr	MMR (if second dose not yet given)	Varicella	Td	

[a] The immunization schedule above is one example of a schedule that is frequently revised as new immunization findings are released. Always refer to the appropriate current, updated guidelines for pediatrics immunization schedules.
[b] New vaccine, standard guidelines not yet available.
[c] First 3 doses IM; others can be oral.

III. Respiratory Disorders

A. OTITIS MEDIA
1. Usually in children, precipitated by a viral URI
2. Congenital disorders (e.g., Down's syndrome, cleft palate) that prevent eustachian tube drainage ↑ risk of infection
3. Si/Sx = ear pressure, ↓ hearing, fever, **erythema & ↓ mobility of tympanic membrane** (TM), TM bulging & a meniscus of fluid behind the TM (effusion)
4. Caused by *S. pneumoniae, H. influenzae, Moraxella,* or viral infection such as respiratory syncytial virus (RSV)
5. Tx = amoxicillin (first line), Augmentin (second line)
6. Surgical tube placement may be required for chronic effusions to prevent developmental delay secondary to hearing loss

B. BRONCHIOLITIS (See Figure 4–1)
1. Commonly seen in children under 2 yr, peak incidence at 6 mo
2. **>50% due to RSV**, others include parainfluenzae & adenovirus
3. Si/Sx = mild rhinorrhea & fever progress to cough, wheezing with crackles, tachypnea, nasal flaring, decreased appetite
4. Dx by culture or antigen detection of nasopharyngeal secretions
5. Tx = bronchodilators, oxygen as needed

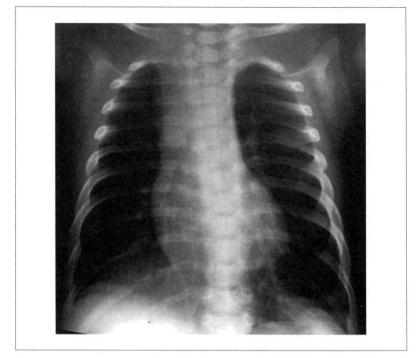

FIGURE 4-1   Chest x-ray of an 8-week-old baby with bronchiolitis. The x-ray shows gross overinflation of the lungs clearly seen by the level of the diaphragm and the intercostal spaces. There is also some bronchial wall thickening.

C. UPPER RESPIRATORY DISEASES

TABLE 4-6   Pediatric Upper Respiratory Disorders

DISEASE	CAUSE	SI/SX	LABS	TX
Croup (Laryngotracheobronchitis)	Parainfluenza, influenza, RSV, Mycoplasma	**Presents in fall & winter, 3mo—3yr old, with barking cough, inspiratory stridor, Sx worse at night,** hoarse voice, preceded by URI	Neck x-ray → "steeple sign"	O₂, cool mist, racemic Epi & steroids if severe, ribavirin may be used for immunocompromised
Epiglottitis	H. influenzae type B	**Medical emergency!!! Fulminant inspiratory stridor, drooling, sits leaning forward,** dysphagia, "hot potato" voice	"Thumb print" sign on lateral neck film, cherry-red epiglottitis on endoscopy	**Examine pt in OR,** Intubate as needed, ceftriaxone
Bacterial tracheitis	*Staph. & Strep. spp.*	Inspiratory stridor, high fever, toxic appearing	Leukocytosis	Nafcillin or ceftriaxone

TABLE 4-6   *Continued*

DISEASE	CAUSE	SI/SX	LABS	TX
Foreign body aspiration		**Usually presents after 6 mo old** (need to grasp object to inhale it) with **inspiratory stridor** (chronic), wheeze, ↓ breath sounds, dysphagia & unresolved pneumonia	CXR → hyperinflation on affected side, ENT consult (See Figure 4-2)	Endoscopic or surgical removal

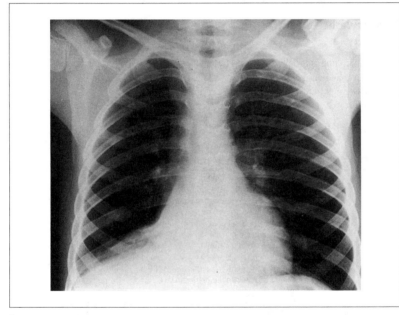

FIGURE 4-2   X-ray of a child admitted with fever and cough that failed to respond to treatment. At bronchoscopy a toy car steering wheel was found in the right intermediate bronchus. The chest x-ray shows collapse of the right middle and lower lobe with loss of definition of the right hemidiaphragm and right heart border.

D. PNEUMONIA

1. Common etiologies vary with age
    a. Newborns get *S. agalactiae* (group B Strep), gram-negative rod, *Chlamydia trachomatis*
    b. Infants get *S. pneumoniae, H. influenzae, Chlamydia, S. aureus, Listeria monocytogenes* & viral
    c. Preschoolers get RSV, other viruses & *Mycoplasma*
    d. Adolescents get *S. pneumoniae, Mycoplasma* & *Chlamydia*

2. Si/Sx = cough (productive in older children), fevers, nausea/vomiting, diarrhea, tachypnea, grunting, retractions, crackles
3. Pertussis presents with 3 stages
   a. Catarrhal stage = 1–2 weeks of cough, rhinorrhea, wheezing
   b. Paroxysmal stage = 2–4 weeks of paroxysmal cough with "whoops"
   c. Convalescent stage = 1–2 weeks of persistent chronic cough
4. *Chlamydia* causes classic "staccato cough" & conjunctivitis, pts afebrile
5. RSV causes wet cough, often with audible wheezes
6. *Staphylococcus* infections may be associated with skin lesions as well
7. Dx = rapid antigen detection or culture of secretions, CXR → infiltrates
8. Tx = infants get hospitalized, bronchodilators & O_2 for RSV, erythromycin for atypical dz (e.g., *Chlamydia*, *Mycoplasma*), cefuroxime for bacteria

IV. Musculoskeletal

A. LIMP

1. Painful limp is usually acute onset, may be associated with fever & irritability, toddlers may refuse to walk
2. DDx painful limp

TABLE 4-7   Pediatric Painful Limp

DISEASE	CHARACTERISTICS	TX
Septic arthritis	• **#1 cause of painful limp in 1–3-yr-old** • Usually monoarticular → hip, knee, or ankle • Causes = *S. aureus* (**most common**), *H. influenzae*, *N. gonorrhoeae* • Si/Sx = **acute onset pain**, arthritis, fever, ↓ range of motion, child may lie still & refuse to walk or crawl, ↑ **WBC**, ↑ **ESR** • X-ray → joint space widening, soft tissue swelling • Dx = joint aspiration → turbid gray, **WBC ≥ 10,000 with neutrophil predominance,** low glucose	Tx = drainage, antibiotics appropriate to Gram's stain or cultures
Toxic synovitis	• Most common in males 5–10 yr old, may precede viral URI • Si/Sx = **insidious onset pain**, low grade fever, **WBC & ESR normal** • **Typically no tenderness, warmth, or joint swelling** • X-ray → usually normal • Dx → technetium scan → ↑ **uptake of epiphysis**	Rest & analgesics for 3–5 days
Aseptic avascular necrosis	• Legg-Calve-Perthes dz = head of femur, Osgood-Schlatter = tibial tubercle, Kohler's bone dz = navicular bone • Legg-Calve-Perthes → usually 4–9 yr old (boys-girls = 5:1), bilateral in 10–20% of cases, ↑ incidence with delayed growth & ↓ birth weight • Si/Sx = **afebrile, insidious onset** hip pain, inner thigh, or knee, ↑ pain with movement, ↓ with rest, antalgic gait, **normal WBC & ESR** • X-ray → **femoral head sclerosis** & ↑ width of femoral neck (See Figure 4-3) • Dx → technetium scan → ↓ **uptake in epiphysis**	↓ weight bearing on affected side over long time

TABLE 4-7   *Continued*

DISEASE	CHARACTERISTICS	TX
Slipped capital femoral epiphysis	• Often in **obese male adolescents** (8–17 yr old), 20–30% bilateral • 80% → slow, progressive, 20% → acute, associated with trauma • Si/Sx → **dull, aching pain** in hip or knee, ↑ pain with activity • X-ray → lateral movement of femur shaft in relation to femoral head, looks like **"ice-cream scoop falling off cone"** • Dx = clinical	Surgical pinning
Osteomyelitis	• Neonates → *S. aureus* (50%), *S. agalactiae, E. coli* • Children → *Staph. & Strep., Salmonella* (sickle cell), *P. aeruginosa* • Si/Sx young infants → fever may be only symptom • Si/Sx older children → fever, malaise, ↓ extremity movement, edema • X-ray lags changes by 3–4 weeks • Dx → neutrophilic leukocytosis, ↑ ESR (50%), blood cultures, bone scan (90% sensitive), **MRI is the gold standard**	IV antibiotics for 4–6 wk

3. Painless limp usually has insidious onset, may be due to weakness or deformity of limb 2° to developmental hip dysplasia, cerebral palsy, or leg length discrepancy

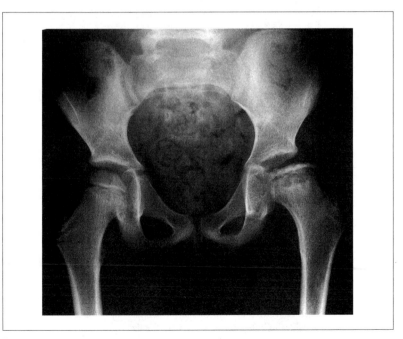

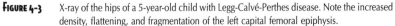

FIGURE 4-3   X-ray of the hips of a 5-year-old child with Legg-Calvé-Perthes disease. Note the increased density, flattening, and fragmentation of the left capital femoral epiphysis.

B. COLLAGEN VASCULAR DISEASES

1. Juvenile rheumatoid arthritis
   a. Chronic inflammation of ≥1 joints in pt ≤ 16 yr old
   b. Most commonly in children 1–4 yr old, females > males
   c. 3 categories = systemic, pauciarticular, polyarticular

TABLE 4-8   Types of Juvenile Rheumatoid Arthritis

Systemic (10–20%)	• High, **spiking fevers** with return to normal daily, generalized lymphadenopathy • **Rash of small, pale pink macules with central pallor on trunk & proximal extremities with possible involvement of palms & soles** • Joint involvement may not occur for weeks to months after fever • 1/3 have disabling chronic arthritis

Pauciarticular (40–60%)	• Involves ≤ 4 joints, large joints primarily affected (knees, ankles, elbows, asymmetric)
	• Other Si/Sx = fever, malaise, anemia, lymphadenopathy, **chronic joint dz is unusual**
	• Divided into 2 types
	  ◊ *Type 1* (most common) → females < 4 yr, ↑ risk for chronic iridocyclitis, 90% ANA+
	  ◊ *Type 2* → males > 8 yr, ANA –, 75% HLA-B27+, ↑ risk of ankylosing spondylitis or Reiter's later in life

Polyarticular	• ≥5 joints involved, small & large, insidious onset, fever, lethargy, anemia • 2 types depending on if rheumatoid factor is present or not • Rheumatoid factor⊕ → 80% females, late onset, more severe, rheumatoid nodules present, 75% ANA+ • Rheumatoid factor – → occurs any time during childhood, mild, rarely associated with rheumatoid nodules, 25% ANA+

   d. Dx = Sx persists for 3 consecutive mo with exclusion of other causes of acute/chronic arthritis or collagen vascular diseases
   e. Tx = NSAIDs, low-dose methotrexate, prednisone only in acute febrile onset
2. Kawasaki's disease (mucocutaneous lymph node syndrome)
   a. Large & medium vessel vasculitis in children < 5 yr old, predilection for Japanese children
   b. Dx = fever > 104° for > 5 days, unresponsive to antibiotics ⊕ 4 out of 5 of the following criteria (**mnemonic: CRASH**)
      1) **C**onjunctivitis
      2) **R**ash, primarily truncal, protean
      3) **A**neurysms of coronary arteries
      4) **S**trawberry tongue, crusting of lips, fissuring of mouth & oropharyngeal erythema
      5) **H**ands & feet show induration, erythema of palms & soles, desquamation of fingers & toes
   c. Complications = cardiac involvement, 10–40% of untreated cases show evidence of coronary vasculitis (dilation/aneurysm) within first weeks of illness
   d. Tx = immediate IVIG to prevent coronary vasculitis, **high-dose aspirin—prednisone is contraindicated & will exacerbate the dz!**
   e. Px
      1) Response to IVIG & aspirin is rapid, 2/3 pts afebrile within 24 hr

2) Evaluate pts one week after discharge, repeat echocardiography 3–6 wk after onset of fever, if baseline & repeat echo do not detect any coronary abnormalities, further imaging is unnecessary

3. Henoch-Schönlein purpura
   a. IgA small vessel vasculitis, related to IgA nephropathy (Berger's disease)
   b. Si/Sx = **pathognomonic palpable purpura** on legs & buttocks (in children), abdominal pain, may cause intussusception
   c. Tx = self-limited, rarely progresses to glomerulonephritis

C. **HISTIOCYTOSIS X**
   1. Proliferation of histiocytic cells resembling Langerhans skin cells
   2. 3 common variants
      a. Letterer-Siwe disease
         1) Acute, aggressive, disseminated variant, usually fatal in infants
         2) Si/Sx = hepatosplenomegaly, lymphadenopathy, pancytopenia, lung involvement, recurrent infections
      b. Hand-Schuller-Christian
         1) Chronic progressive variant, presents prior to 5 yr old
         2) **Classic triad = skull lesions, diabetes insipidus, exophthalmus**
      c. Eosinophilic granuloma
         1) Extraskeletal involvement generally limited to lung
         2) Has the best Px, rarely fatal, sometimes spontaneously regresses

V. Metabolic

A. **CONGENITAL HYPOTHYROIDISM**
   1. Due to 2° agenesis of thyroid or defect in enzymes
   2. **T4 is crucial during first 2 yr of life for normal brain development**
   3. Birth Hx → normal Apgars, prolonged jaundice (↑ indirect bilirubin)
   4. Si/Sx = presents at 6–12 wk old with poor feeding, lethargy, **hypotonia, coarse facial features, large protruding tongue,** hoarse cry, constipation, developmental delay
   5. Dx = ↓ T4, ↑ TSH
   6. Tx = levothyroxine replacement
   7. **If Dx delayed beyond 6 wk, child will be mentally retarded**
   8. Newborn screening is mandatory by law

B. **NEWBORN JAUNDICE**
   1. Physiologic jaundice is clinically benign, occurs 24–48 hr after birth
      a. Characterized by unconjugated hyperbilirubinemia
      b. 50% of neonates have jaundice during first wk of life
      c. Results from increased bilirubin production & relative deficiency in glucuronyl transferase in the immature liver
      d. Requires no Tx
   2. **Jaundice present AT birth is ALWAYS pathologic**
   3. Unconjugated hyperbilirubinemia
      a. Caused by hemolytic anemia or congenital deficiency of glucuronyl transferase (e.g., Crigler-Najjar & Gilbert's syndromes)
      b. Hemolytic anemia can be congenital or acquired
         1) Congenital due to spherocytosis, G6PD, pyruvate kinase deficiency

2) Acquired due to ABO/Rh isoimmunization, infection, drugs, twin-twin transfusion, chronic fetal hypoxia, delayed cord clamping, maternal diabetes
4. Conjugated hyperbilirubinemia
   a. Infectious causes = sepsis, the ToRCH group, syphilis, *Listeria monocytogenes*, hepatitis
   b. Metabolic causes = galactosemia, α-1-antitrypsin deficiency
   c. Congenital causes = extrahepatic biliary atresia, Dubin-Johnson & Rotor syndromes

TABLE 4-9   Differential Diagnosis of Neonatal Jaundice by Time of Onset

Within 24 hr of birth	• Hemolysis (ABO/Rh isoimmunization, hereditary spherocytosis) • Sepsis
Within 48 hr of birth	• Hemolysis • Infection • Physiologic
After 48 hr	• Infection • Hemolysis • Breast milk (liver not mature to handle lipids of breast milk) • Congenital malformation (biliary atresia) • Hepatitis

5. Tx = UV light to break down bilirubin pigments & Tx underlying cause
6. Complications of UV light = retinal damage, dehydration, dermatitis, diarrhea
7. Tx urgently to prevent mental retardation 2° to kernicterus (biliary precipitation in basal ganglia)

C. REYE SYNDROME

1. Acute encephalopathy & fatty degeneration of the liver associated with **use of salicylates in children with varicella or influenza-like illness**
2. Most cases in children 4–12 yr old
3. Si/Sx = biphasic course with prodromal fever → aSx interval → abrupt onset vomiting, delirium, stupor, hepatomegaly with abnormal liver function tests, may rapidly progress to seizures, coma & death
4. Dx = clinical ⊕ ↑↑ liver enzymes, normal CSF
5. Tx = control of ↑ intracranial pressure due to cerebral edema (major cause of death) with mannitol, fluid restriction, give glucose because glycogen stores are commonly depleted
6. Px = ↑ chance to progress into coma if ≥3-fold ↑ in serum ammonia level, ↓ prothrombin not responsive to vitamin K
7. Recovery rapid in mild dz, severe dz may → neuropsychologic defects

D. FEBRILE SEIZURES

1. Usually occurs between 3 mo & 5 yr, associated with a fever without evidence of infection (intracranial) or defined cause
2. It is the most common convulsive order in young children, rarely develops into epilepsy
3. Risk = very high fever (≥39°C) & family history, seizure occurs during rise in temperature, not at the peak of temperature

4. Si/Sx = commonly tonic-clonic seizure with most lasting < 10 min with a drowsy postictal period
5. **Note:** if seizure lasts > 15 min, most likely due to infection or toxic process and careful work-up should follow
6. Dx = clinical, routine lab tests should only be performed to evaluate fever source, EEG not indicated unless febrile seizure is atypical (complex febrile seizure)
7. Consider lumbar puncture to rule out meningitis
8. Tx = careful evaluation for source of fever, control of fever with antipyretics, parental counseling & reassurance to decrease anxiety
9. Px = 33–50% of children experience recurrence of seizure

VI. Genetic and Congenital Disorders

A. FAILURE TO THRIVE (FTT)
1. Failure of children to grow & develop at an appropriate rate
2. Due to inadequate calorie intake or inadequate calorie absorption
3. Can be idiopathic or due to gastroesophageal reflux, urinary tract infections, cardiac disease, cystic fibrosis, hypothyroidism, congenital syndromes, lead poisoning, malignancy
4. Additional factors include poverty, family discord, neonatal problems, maternal depression
5. Dx requires 3 criteria
    a. Child < 2 yr old with weight < third to fifth percentile for age on more than one occasion
    b. Child < 2 yr old whose weight is < 80% of ideal weight for age
    c. Child < 2 yr old whose weight crosses 2 major percentiles downward on a standardized growth chart
    d. Exceptions = children of genetically short stature, small-for-gestational-age infants, preterm infants, normally lean infants, "overweight" infants whose rate of height gain increases while rate of weight gain decreases
6. Tx
    a. Organic causes → treat underlying condition & provide sufficient caloric supplementation
    b. Idiopathic → observe the parent feeding the infant & educate parents on appropriate formulas, foods & liquids that are appropriate for the infant
    c. In older infants & children it is important to offer solid foods before liquids, decrease distractions during meal times, & child should eat with others & not be force-fed
    d. Monitor closely for progressive weight gain in response to adequate calorie feeding
7. Px poor in first year of life due to maximal postnatal brain growth during the first 6 mo of life—1/3 of children with nonorganic FTT are developmentally delayed

B. CRANIOFACIAL ABNORMALITIES
1. Mildest form is bifid uvula, no clinical significance
2. Cleft lip
    a. Can occur unilaterally or bilaterally, due to failure of fusion of maxillary prominences

b. **Unilateral cleft lip is the most common malformation of the head & neck**

c. Does not interfere with feeding

d. Tx = surgical repair

3. Cleft palate

a. Can be anterior or posterior (determined by position relative to incisive foramen)

b. Anterior cleft palate due to failure of palatine shelves to fuse with primary palate

c. Posterior cleft palate due to failure of palatine shelves to fuse with nasal septum

d. **Interferes with feeding, requiring a special nipple for the baby to feed**

e. Tx = surgical repair

4. Macroglossia

a. Congenitally enlarged tongue seen in Down's syndrome, gigantism, hypothyroidism

b. Can also be acquired in amyloidosis & acromegaly

c. This is different from glossitis (redness & swelling, with burning sensation) that is seen in vitamin B deficiencies

d. Tx is directed at underlying cause

C. DOWN'S SYNDROME

1. **Invariably caused by trisomy 21, ↑ risk if maternal age > 35 yr**

2. Si/Sx → cardiac septal defects, psychomotor retardation, classic Down's facies, ↑ risk of leukemia, premature Alzheimer's dz

3. Down's facies = flattened occiput (brachycephaly), **epicanthal folds, up-slanted palpebral fissures, speckled irises (Brushfield spots)**, protruding tongue, small ears, redundant skin at posterior neck, **hypotonia, simian crease in palms (50%)**

4. Px = typically death in 30s–40s

D. TURNER'S SYNDROME

1. **#1 cause of 1° amenorrhea**, due to XO genotype

2. Si/Sx = newborns have ↑ skin at dorsum of neck (**neck webbing**), lymphedema in hands & feet, as develop → short stature, ptosis, **coarctation of aorta, amenorrhea but uterus is present**, juvenile external genitalia, bleeding due to GI telangiectasias, no mental retardation

3. Tx = hormone replacement to allow 2° sex characteristics to develop

E. FRAGILE X SYNDROME

1. X-linked dominant trinucleotide repeat expansion disorder

2. **#1 cause of mental retardation in boys**

3. Si/Sx = long face, prominent jaw, large ears, enlarged testes (postpubertal), developmental delay, mental retardation

4. Tx = none

F. ARNOLD-CHIARI MALFORMATION

1. Congenital disorder

2. Si/Sx = caudally displaced cerebellum, elongated medulla passing into foramen magnum, flat skull base, hydrocephalus, meningomyelocele & aqueductal stenosis

3. Px = death as neonate or toddler

G. NEURAL TUBE DEFECTS

1. Associated with ↑ α-fetoprotein levels in maternal serum

2. **Preventable by folic acid supplements during pregnancy**

3. Si/Sx = spina bifida (posterior vertebral arches don't close) & meningocele (no vertebrae cover lumbar cord)

4. Tx = prevention, neurologic deficits often remain after surgical correction

H. FETAL ALCOHOL SYNDROME

1. Seen in children born to alcoholic mothers
2. Si/Sx = characterized by facial abnormalities & developmental defects (mental & growth retardation), **smooth filtrum of lip,** microcephaly, atrial septal defect
3. Tx = prevention

I. CONGENITAL PYLORIC STENOSIS

1. Causes projectile vomiting in first **2 wk–2 mo of life**
2. More common in males & in first-born children
3. **Pathognomonic physical finding is palpable "olive" nodule in midepigastrium**, representing hypertrophied pyloric sphincter
4. If olive is not present, diagnosis made by ultrasound
5. Tx = longitudinal surgical incision in hypertrophied muscle

J. CONGENITAL HEART DISEASE

1. Atrial septal defect (ASD)
   a. Usually aSx, often found on routine preschool physicals
   b. Predispose to CHF in second & third decades, also predispose to stroke due to embolus bypass tract (Eisenmenger's complex)
   c. Si/Sx = loud S_1, **wide fixed-split S_2,** midsystolic ejection murmur
   d. Dx = echocardiography
   e. Tx = surgical patching of bypass, more important for females due to eventual increased cardiovascular stress of pregnancy
2. Ventricular septal defect (VSD)
   a. **Most common congenital heart defect**, 30% of small to medium defects close spontaneously by age 2
   b. Si/Sx = small defects may be completely aSx throughout entire life, large defects → CHF, ↓ development/growth, frequent pulmonary infections, holosystolic murmur over entire precordium, maximally at fourth LICS
   c. Eisenmenger's complex = R → L shunt 2° to pulmonary HTN
      1) RV hypertrophy → flow reversal through the shunt, so that an R → L shunt develops
      2) Causes cyanosis 2° to lack of blood flow to lung
      3) Allows venous thrombi (e.g., DVT) to bypass lung, causing systemic paradoxical embolization
   d. Dx = echocardiography
   e. Tx = complete closure for simple defects
3. Tetralogy of Fallot
   a. 4 physical defects comprising the tetralogy are
      1) Ventricular septal defect
      2) Pulmonary outflow obstruction
      3) Right ventricular hypertrophy
      4) Overriding aorta (aorta inlet spans both ventricles)

    b. Si/Sx = acyanotic at birth, ↑ cyanosis over first 6 mo, **"Tet spell"** = acute cyanosis & panic in child, child adopts a squatting posture to improve blood flow to lungs, **CXR shows classic boot-shaped contour** due to RV enlargement

    c. Dx = echocardiography

    d. Tx = surgical repair of VSD, repair of pulmonary outflow tracts

4. Transposition of the great arteries

    a. Aorta comes off right ventricle, pulmonary artery off left ventricle

    b. Must have persistent arteriovenous communication or dz is incompatible with life (can be via patent ductus arteriosus or persistent foramen ovale)

    c. Si/Sx = marked cyanosis at birth, early digital clubbing, often no murmur, **CXR →
enlarged egg-shaped heart** & ↑ pulmonary vasculature

    d. Dx = echocardiography

    e. Tx = surgical switching of arterial roots to normal positions with repair of communication defect

    f. Px = invariably fatal within several months of birth without Tx

5. Coarctation of the aorta

    a. Congenital aortic narrowing, often aSx in young child

    b. Si/Sx = ↓ BP in legs with normal BP in arms, **continuous murmur over collateral vessels in back, classic CXR sign = rib notching**

    c. Dx confirmed with aortogram or CT

    d. Tx = surgical resection of coarctation & reanastomosis

6. Patent ductus arteriosus (PDA)

    a. ↑ incidence with premature births, predisposes pt to endocarditis & pulmonary vascular disease

    b. Si/Sx = **continuous machinery murmur heard best at second left interspace, wide pulse pressure**, hypoxia

    c. Dx = echocardiography or heart catheterization

    d. Tx = indomethacin (block prostaglandins, induces closure) for infants, surgical repair for older children

VII. Trauma and Intoxication

A. CHILD ABUSE

1. Can be physical trauma, emotional, sexual, or neglect

2. Nutritional neglect is the most common etiology for underweight infants

3. Most common perpetrator of sexual abuse is family member or family friends, 97% of reported offenders are males

4. **Physicians are required by law to report suspected child abuse or neglect (law provides protection to mandated reporters who report in good faith), clinical & lab evaluations are allowed without parental/guardian permission**

5. Epidemiology

    a. 85% of children reported to children's protective services (CPS) are < 5 yr old, 45% are < 1 yr old

    b. 10% of injuries to children < 5 yr old seen in the ER are due to abuse, & 10% of abuse cases involve burns

    c. **High-risk children** = premature infants, children with chronic medical problems, colicky babies, those with behavioral problems, children living in poverty, children of teenage parents, single parents, or substance abusers

6. Si/Sx = injury is unexplainable or not consistent with Hx, bruises are the most common manifestation
   a. Accidental injuries seen on shins, forearms, hips
   b. Less likely to be accidental are bilateral & symmetric, seen on buttocks, genitalia, back, back of hands, different color bruises (repeat injuries over time)
   c. Highly suspicious for abuse are fractures due to pulling or wrenching, causing damage to the metaphysis
7. **Classic findings**
   a. Chip fracture, where the corner of metaphysis of long bone is torn off with damage to epiphysis
   b. Periosteum spiral fracture before infant can walk
   c. Rib fractures
8. Dating fracture can be done by callus formation (callus appears in 10–12 days)
9. Burns
   a. Shape/pattern of burn may be diagnostic
   b. **Cigarette** → circular, punched out lesions of similar size, hands & feet common
   c. **Immersion** → most common in infants, affecting buttocks & perineum (hold thighs against abdomen), or with scalded line clearly demarcated on thighs or waist without splash marks
   d. Stocking-glove burn on hands or feet
10. Injury to head is the most common cause of death from physical abuse, infants can present with convulsions, apnea, increased intracranial pressure, subdural hemorrhages, retinal hemorrhages (marker for acceleration/deceleration injuries), or in a coma
11. Sexual abuse
    a. Child may talk to mother or teacher, friend, relative about situation
    b. Si/Sx = vaginal, penile, or rectal pain, erythema, discharge, bleeding, chronic dysuria, enuresis, constipation, encopresis
    c. Behaviors = sexualized activity with peers or objects, seductive behavior
12. Dx
    a. Labs → PT/PTT & platelets to screen for bleeding diathesis
    b. Consider bone survey in children < 2 yr old, plain films or MRI for severe injuries or refusal/inability to communicate
    c. For sexual abuse collect specimens of offender's sperm, blood & hair, collect victim's nail clipping & clothing, obtain *Chlamydia* & gonorrhea cultures from mouth, anus & genitalia
    d. Dx is tentatively based on H&P, record all information, photograph when appropriate
13. Tx
    a. Medical, surgical, psychiatric treatment for injuries
    b. Report immediately, do not discharge before talking to CPS
    c. Admit pt if injuries are severe enough, if Dx unclear, or if no other safe placement available

B. POISONINGS

1. Accidental seen in younger children left unsupervised momentarily, usually a single agent ingested or inhaled (plants, household products, medications)

2. Intentional seen in adolescents/adults, toxic substances for recreational purposes or overdose taken with intent to produce self-harm
3. Epidemiology
   a. Nearly 50% of cases occur in children < 6 yr old, as a result of an accidental event or as abuse
   b. 92% occur at home, 60% with nonpharmacologic agent, 40% with pharmacologic agent
   c. Ingestion occurs in 75% of cases, 8% dermal, 6% ophthalmic, 6% inhalation
4. Hx is crucial during initial contact with patient or guardian
   a. Evaluation of severity (asymptomatic, symptomatic)
   b. Age & weight
   c. Time, type, amount & route of exposure
   d. Past medical history
5. Si/Sx

TABLE 4-10   Pediatric Toxicology

SI/SX	POSSIBLE TOXIN
Lethargy/Coma	Ethanol, sedative-hypnotics, narcotics, antihistamines, antidepressants, neuroleptic
Seizures	Theophylline, cocaine, amphetamines, antidepressants, antipsychotics, pesticides
Hypotension (with bradycardia)	Organophosphate pesticides, beta blockers
Arrhythmia	Tricyclic antidepressants, cocaine, digitalis, quinidine
Hyperthermia	Salicylates, anticholinergics

6. Tx
   a. Syrup of ipecac followed by clear liquid (water) induces vomiting, should not use in children < 6 mo, those with depressed sensorium, those with seizures or who ingested strong acids or bases
   b. Lavage usually unnecessary in children, may be useful with drugs that decrease gastric motility
   c. Charcoal may be most effective & safest procedure to prevent absorption, repeat doses every 2–6 hr with cathartic for first dose, ineffective in heavy metal or volatile hydrocarbon poisoning

VIII. Adolescence

A. EPIDEMIOLOGY
1. Injuries
   a. 50% of all deaths in adolescents attributed to injuries
   b. Many occur under the influence of alcohol & other drugs
   c. Older adolescents more likely to be killed in motor vehicle accidents while younger adolescents are at risk for drowning & fatal injuries with weapons
   d. Homicide rate is 5x higher for black males than white males
2. Suicide
   a. Second leading cause of adolescent death

b. Females more likely to attempt than males but males are 5x more likely to succeed than females

c. Pts with preexisting psychiatric problems or those who abuse alcohol & drugs more likely to attempt suicide

3. Substance abuse
   a. A major cause of morbidity in adolescents
   b. Average age of first use is 12–14 yr old
   c. 1 of every 2 adolescents have tried an illicit drug by their high school graduation
   d. Survey of high school seniors (1994–1995) noted that 90% had experience with alcohol & ≥40% had tried marijuana

4. Sex
   a. 61% of all male & 47% of all female high school students have had sex
   b. Health risks of early sexual activity are unwanted pregnancies, sexually transmitted diseases (STDs) such as gonorrhea, *Chlamydia* & HIV
   c. 86% of all STDs occur among adolescents & young adults 15–29 yr old
   d. More than 1 million adolescent females become pregnant yearly, 33% are < 15 yr old—this is a second major cause of morbidity in adolescents

5. Eating disorders
   a. Anorexia nervosa occurs in 0.5% of adolescent females & bulimia in 1–3%
   b. Si/Sx = cardiovascular symptoms, fluid & electrolyte abnormalities, amenorrhea, decreased bone density, anemia, parotid gland enlargement, tooth decay, constipation (hallmark of anorexia)
   c. Adolescents with anorexia lose 15% of ideal body weight & appear sick, but those with bulimia may look well nourished
   d. Anorexia nervosa is seen at 2 peak ages, one at 14.5 yr, the next at 18 yr, but 25% of females with anorexia may be < 13 yr old

B. CONFIDENTIALITY
1. Most issues revealed by adolescents to physicians in an interview are confidential
2. **Exceptions** include suicidal or homicidal behavior, sexual or physical abuse
3. It is strongly encouraged for physicians to inform adolescents about confidentiality at the beginning of the interview to help develop a trusting relationship between adolescent & physician

C. SCREENING
1. Annual risk behavior screening in every adolescent is strongly recommended
2. **HEADSSS** assessment allows physicians to evaluate critical areas in each adolescent's life that may be detrimental to growth & development
   a. **H**ome environment → who does adolescent live with?, any recent changes?, quality of parental interaction (if applicable)?, has he/she ever run away from home?
   b. **E**mployment & **E**ducation → is child in school?, favorite subjects?, academic performance?, are friends in school?, any recent changes?, does child have a job?, future plans?
   c. **A**ctivities → what does child like to do in spare time?, who does child spend time with?, involved in any sports/exercise?, hobbies?, attends parties or clubs?

PEDIATRICS

d. **D**rugs → has child ever used tobacco?, alcohol?, marijuana?, other illicit drugs? if so, when was the child's last use?, how often?, do friends or family members use drugs?, who does the child use these substances with?

e. **S**exual activity → sexual orientation?, is child sexually active?, number of sexual partners?, does the child use condoms or other forms of contraception?, any history of STDs or pregnancy?

f. **S**uicide → does the child ever feel sad, tired, or unmotivated?, has the child ever felt that life was not worth living?, any feelings of wanting to harm self?, if so, does the child have a plan?, has the child ever tried to harm self in the past?, does the child know anyone who has attempted suicide?

g. **S**afety → does the child use a seat belt or bike helmet?, does the child enter into high-risk situations?, does the child have access to a firearm?

Pediatric Case Scenario

A 2-year-old immigrant boy presents to your clinic with his mother, who tells you that he has had a fever, cough & runny nose for the past 3 days & that his eyes are slightly red. His mother stated that when this all started she looked in his mouth & saw some white spots on the inside of his cheeks. The next day he developed a rash that started on his head & then began to spread down his body over the next few days.

On exam you notice a maculopapular rash on his trunk. His has some conjunctivitis and coryza. No spots are noted in mouth and there is no lymphadenopathy.

1. What is the most likely diagnosis?

a) Rubella

b) Roseola infantum

c) Erythema infectiosum

d) Measles

The mother also tells you that the child has been very irritable and pulling on his ears occasionally during the day.

2. What is the most likely cause of these associated symptoms?

a) Rubella

b) Erythema infectiosum

c) Eczema

d) Otitis media

You are the senior resident on the pediatric service at a local children's hospital. You are currently working in the pediatric clinic when the wife of the president of the hospital presents to you for her first well-baby check-up. You complete the physical exam on the child and realize he is in perfect health. As you say good-bye to the mother she begins to ask you questions regarding the developmental milestones of her child.

3. She presents you with the following list of questions. Choose the correct response for each of her questions. You may or may not need to use a letter more than once.

(1) When will my child hold his head up?	a) 4 months
(2) When will he be able to use a cup?	b) 2 months
(3) When will he speak 2-word sentences?	c) 12 months
(4) When will stranger anxiety begin?	d) 9 months
(5) When should he begin walking?	e) 6 months
(6) When can he ride his first tricycle?	f) 15 months
(7) When can he begin throwing a ball?	g) 36 months
	h) 24 months
	i) 18 months

You are still the senior resident in pediatrics after having answered the above question correctly. As you walk down the hallway to take a break outside, the chief of pediatrics stops you. He begins to "pimp" you by presenting five different children with musculoskeletal complaints and asking you to correctly identify their diagnosis.

4. The five children are:

(1) 10-year-old boy with fever, and pain in his knees, elbows, and ankles. ANA-negative, HLA-B27-positive	a) Septic arthritis
	b) Pauciarticular juvenile rheumatoid arthritis
(2) 15-year-old obese male with a dull aching pain in his right hip that increases with activity.	c) Osgood-Schlatter
	d) Slipped capital femoral epiphysis
(3) 2-year-old girl with a painful limp, complaining of pain in her knee; the child refuses to walk and has a fever	e) Polyarticular juvenile rheumatoid arthritis
(4) 18-year-old girl with pain in her shoulders, knees, and elbows; rheumatoid factor–positive, ANA-positive	
(5) 6-year-old boy with tenderness and pain in the anterior portion of his tibia; the pain is worse when kneeling; afebrile; normal labs	

You have now completed your pediatric residency and are seeing your first patient as an attending physician. Your patient is a 3-year-old boy with bruises on his back, thigh, and neck, and circular punched-out lesions on his hands and feet. You question the parents about these injuries and the father insists that everything is fine. He states that his son fell down the stairs and he had to discipline him once or twice to make sure he behaves. While examining the child the child automatically clings to you and doesn't want to go with his parents.

5. What should you do next?

a) Do nothing; it's obvious this child has a problem with authority and this seems like a personal family matter

b) Ask the family to return to their previous provider and obtain their medical records so that you can better provide them medical care

c) Consider reporting the family to child protective services if they return on their next visit with the same bruises and burns

d) Report the family to child protective services for suspected child abuse or neglect

Answers

1. **d)** Measles commonly presents with cough, coryza, and conjunctivitis. In addition, these patients have high fevers and Koplik spots often appear on the buccal mucosa prior to the onset of rash. The rash begins on the head and spreads downward, lasting 4–5 days, and Koplik spots typically regress prior to the onset of the rash. Rubella presents with suboccipital lymphadenopathy, and the rash begins on the face and is accompanied by a fever on the first day only. Roseola infantum begins with an abrupt fever with no symptoms, and the rash appears only after the fever resolves. The rash itself resolves within 24 hours. The classic finding in erythema infectiosum is "slapped cheeks" erythema.

2. **d)** Otitis media in children is commonly precipitated by a viral URI. The increased upper respiratory secretions in measles patients may precipitate this condition. Children may commonly only complain of an itchy ear or may have increased fussiness or agitation as their only presenting symptoms. Patients' symptoms usually resolve on their own without medication, although patients are commonly placed on antibiotics to treat or prevent secondary bacterial infection.

3. **1-b, 2-f, 3-h, 4-e, 5-f, 6-g, 7-i.**

4. **1-b, 2-d, 3-a, 4-e, 5-c.**

5. **d)** Physicians are required by law to report suspected child abuse or neglect. If this family leaves and these issues are not addressed, then you may never see them again. These families commonly go from physician to physician trying to avoid anyone noticing any patterns of abuse. Also this child may never live to the next visit.

5. Family Medicine

Pedro Cheung

I. Headache

A. Signs/Symptoms & Differential Diagnosis

Table 5-1 Summary of Headaches

Type	Epidemiology	Characteristics
Tension	Usually after age 20 (rarely > age 50)	• Most common headache type • **Bilateral, band-like, dull in quality** • Worse with stress; not aggravated by activity • Chronic HA associated with depression
Cluster	Male-female = 6:1 Mean age 30 yr	• **Unilateral,** stabbing peri/retro-orbital pain, lasting 15 min to 3 hr • Seasonal attacks occur in series (6x/day) lasting weeks, followed by months of remission • **Associated with ipsilateral lacrimation (85%), ptosis, nasal congestion & rhinorrhea** • Often occurs within 90 min of onset of sleep
Migraine	80% have positive FHx Female-male = 3:1	• Classically, HA is **unilateral (60%)** with **aura (only 15%);** pt looks for quiet place to rest • Visual aura: **scotoma** (blind spots), **teichopsia** (jagged zigzag lines), **photopsias** (shimmering lights), or **rhodopsins** (colors) • Accompanied by **nausea & photophobia** • Triggered by stress, odors, certain foods, alcohol, menstruation, or sleep deprivation
Temporal arteritis (Giant cell)	Female-male = 2:1 Age > 50	• **Unilateral temporal** headache • **Associated with jaw claudication, temporal artery tenderness with palpation, ESR ≥ 50** • 50% also have polymyalgia rheumatica • If not treated leads to optic neuritis & **blindness** • Screen by ESR; Dx with temporal artery Bx
Trigeminal neuralgia	Peak age at 60	• Episodic, severe pain shooting from side of mouth to ipsilateral ear, eye, or nose
Withdrawal headache		• Common cause of frequent headaches • Can be withdrawal from various drugs
SAH*		• Head trauma is most common cause • Spontaneous: usually berry aneurysm rupture • Classically the "worst headache of my life"

*Subarachnoid hemorrhage.

B. Dx Is Made by Clinical History & Physical Except:
1. Temporal arteritis Dx requires temporal artery biopsy
2. **Trigeminal neuralgia** Dx requires head CT or MRI to rule out sinusitis, cerebellopontine angle neoplasm, multiple sclerosis, herpes zoster
3. **Subarachnoid hemorrhage requires** confirmation by CT scan or lumbar puncture to detect CSF xanthochromia (can be detected 6 hr after onset of HA)

4. Suspect intracranial lesion causing headache in **pts > 50 or pts with headaches immediately upon waking up**
5. **Suspect ↑ ICP in pts awakened in middle of night by headache, who have projectile vomiting, or focal neural deficits; obtain head CT**

C. TREATMENT

TABLE 5-2   Treatment of Headache

HEADACHE	TREATMENT
Tension	• Acutely NSAIDs or Midrin® • Prophylaxis with antidepressants or β-blockers
Cluster	• Acutely 100% O_2, sumatriptan* or dihydroergotamine • Prophylaxis with verapamil, lithium, methysergide, or ergotamine
Migraine	• Acutely sumatriptan,* dihydroergotamine, NSAIDs, antiemetics • Prophylaxis with **β-blockers** (first line) or calcium blockers
Temporal arteritis	• High-dose prednisone or cytotoxic drug to prevent blindness
Trigeminal neuralgia	• Carbamazepine (first line) or phenytoin, clonazepam, valproic acid
Withdrawal	• NSAIDs
SAH	• Immediate neurosurgical evaluation & nimodipine to reduce incidence of postrupture vasospasm & ischemia

*Sumatriptan contraindicated with known coronary dz or ergot drugs taken within 24 hr.

II. Ears, Nose, and Throat

A. OTITIS EXTERNA

1. Si/Sx = **pulling on pinna or pushing on tragus causes pain**
2. *Pseudomonas* is usual cause, can be chronic in pts with seborrhea
3. Tx = antibiotic ear drops
4. DDx = Ramsay Hunt syndrome (herpes zoster oticus)
   a. Herpes infection of geniculate ganglia (CN VII)
   b. Si/Sx = painful vesicles in external auditory meatus
   c. Tx = urgent acyclovir to prevent extension to meningitis
5. In diabetics, get CT/MRI of temporal bone to rule out osteomyelitis (**malignant otitis externa**), which requires surgical débridement

B. INNER EAR DISEASE

1. Tinnitus (ringing in the ears)
   a. Objective (heard by observer) or subjective (heard only by patient)
   b. Causes = foreign body in external canal, pulsating vascular tumors, or medications (aspirin), hearing loss
2. Vertigo
   a. Feel as though surroundings are spinning when eyes are open, whereas in dizziness pt feels as if he/she is spinning, not the surroundings

TABLE 5-3   Causes of Vertigo

DISEASE	CHARACTERISTICS	TX
Benign positional vertigo	• Sudden, episodic vertigo with head movement lasting for seconds	Hallpike maneuver
Ménière's disease	• Dilation of membranous labyrinth due to excess endolymph • **Classic triad = hearing loss, tinnitus & episodic vertigo lasting several hours**	Medical (thiazide, anticholinergics, antihistamines) or surgery (labyrinthectomy)
Viral labyrinthitis	• Preceded by viral respiratory illness • Vertigo lasting days to weeks	Meclizine
Acoustic neuroma	• CN VIII schwannoma, commonly affects vestibular portion but can also affect cochlea • Si/Sx = vertigo, sudden deafness, tinnitus • Dx = MRI of cerebellopontine angle	Tx = local radiation or surgical excision

C. EPISTAXIS

1. 90% of bleeds occur at Kiesselbach's plexus (anterior nasal septum)
2. **#1 cause of epistaxis in children is trauma (induced by exploring digits)**
3. Also precipitated by rhinitis, nasal mucosa dryness, septal deviation & bone spurs, alcohol, antiplatelet medication, bleeding diathesis
4. Tx = direct pressure, topical nasal vasoconstrictors (Neo-Synephrine), consider anterior nasal packing if unable to stop, 5% originate in posterior nasal cavity requiring packing to occlude choana

D. SINUSITIS

1. Maxillary sinuses most commonly involved
2. DDx

TABLE 5-4   Sinusitis

	ORGANISMS	SI/SX	TX
Acute bacterial (<4 wk)	S. pneumoniae, H. influenzae, Moraxella catarrhalis	**Purulent rhinorrhea,** headache, **pain on sinus palpation,** fever, **halitosis,** anosmia, **tooth pain**	Bactrim, amoxicillin, decongestants
Chronic bacterial (>3 mo)	Bacteroides, Staph. aureus, Pseudomonas, Streptococcus spp.	Same as for acute but lasts longer, also otitis media in children	Surgical correction of obstruction, nasal steroids
Fungal	Aspergillus—**diabetics get** mucormycosis!	Usually seen in the immunocompromised	Surgery & amphotericin

3. Dx = CT scan showing inflammatory changes or bone destruction (See Figure 5-1)
4. Potential complications of sinusitis include meningitis, abscess formation, orbital infection, osteomyelitis

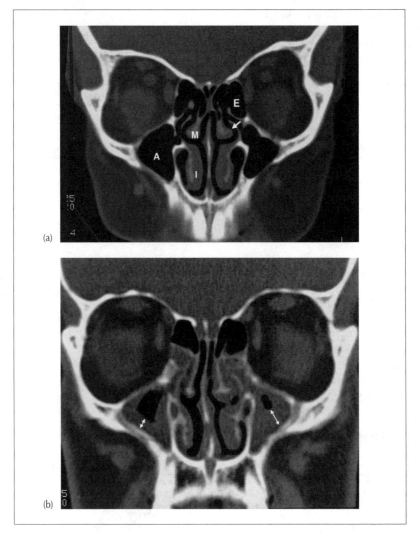

FIGURE 5-1   Coronal CT scan. (a) Normal sinuses. Note the excellent demonstration of the bony margins. The arrow points to the middle meatus into which the maxillary antrum, frontal, anterior, and middle ethmoid sinuses drain. A = maxillary antrum; E = ethmoid sinus; I = inferior turbinate; M = middle turbinate. (b) Sinusitis. Mucosal thickening prevents drainage of the sinuses. Both antra are almost opaque. The arrows indicate mucosal thickening in the antra.

E.

TABLE 5-5   Pharyngitis

DISEASE	SI/SX	DX	TX
Group A Strep throat	High fever, **severe throat pain without cough**, edematous **tonsils with white or yellow exudate, cervical adenopathy**	• H&P 50% accurate • Antigen agglutination kit for screening • Throat swab culture is gold standard	Penicillin to prevent acute rheumatic fever
Membranous (diphtheria)	High fever, dysphagia, drooling, **can cause respiratory failure** (airway occlusion)	**Pathognomonic gray membrane on tonsils extending into throat**	**STAT antitoxin**
Fungal (*Candida*)	Dysphagia, sore throat with white, cheesy patches in oropharynx (oral thrush), **seen in AIDS & small children**	Clinical or endoscopy	Nystatin liquid, swish & swallow
Adenovirus	**Pharyngoconjunctival fever (fever, red eye, sore throat)**	Clinical	Supportive
Mononucleosis (EBV)	Generalized lymphadenopathy, exudative tonsillitis, palatal petechiae & splenomegaly	• ⊕ **heterophile antibody** • **skin rash** occurs in pts given ampicillin	Supportive
Herpangina (coxsackie A)	Fever, pharyngitis, body ache, tender vesicles along tonsils, uvula & soft palate	Clinical	Supportive

III. Outpatient Gastrointestinal Complaints

A. DYSPEPSIA

1. Si/Sx = upper abdominal pain, early satiety, postprandial abdominal bloating or distention, nausea, vomiting, often exacerbated by eating
2. DDx = peptic ulcer, gastroesophageal reflux disease (GERD), cancer, gastroparesis, malabsorption, intestinal parasite, drugs (e.g., NSAIDs), etc.
3. Dx = clinical
4. Tx = empiric for 4 wk, if Sx not relieved → endoscopy
   a. Avoid caffeine, alcohol, cigarettes, NSAIDs, eat frequent small meals, stress reduction, maintain ideal body weight, elevate head of bed
   b. H_2 blockers & antacids, or proton pump inhibitor
   c. **Antibiotics for *H. pylori* are NOT indicated for nonulcer dyspepsia**

B. GASTROESOPHAGEAL REFLUX DISEASE (GERD)

1. Causes = obesity, relaxed lower esophageal sphincter, esophageal dysmotility, hiatal hernia
2. Si/Sx = heartburn occurring 30–60 min postprandial & upon reclining, usually relieved by antacid self-administration, dyspepsia, postprandial burning sensation in esophagus, also regurgitation of gastric contents into the mouth
3. Atypical Si/Sx sometimes seen = asthma, chronic cough/laryngitis, atypical chest pain
4. Upper endoscopy → tissue damage but may be normal in 50% of cases
5. Dx = clinical, can confirm with ambulatory pH monitoring
6. Tx
   a. First line = lifestyle modifications: avoid lying down postprandial, avoid spicy foods & foods that delay gastric emptying, reduction of meal size, weight loss

  b. Second line = H2-receptor antagonists—aim to discontinue in 8–12 wk

  c. Promotility agents may be comparable to H2-antagonists

  d. Third line = proton pump inhibitors, reserve for refractory dz, often will require maintenance Tx since Sx return upon discontinuation

  e. Fourth line = surgical fundoplication, relieves Sx in 90% of pts, may be more cost-effective in younger pts or those with severe dz

 7. Sequelae

  a. Barrett's esophagus

   1) Chronic GERD → metaplasia from squamous to columnar epithelia in lower esophagus

   2) Requires close surveillance with endoscopy & aggressive Tx as 10% progress to adenocarcinoma

  b. Peptic stricture

   1) Results in gradual solid food dysphagia often with concurrent improvement of heartburn symptoms

   2) Endoscopy establishes diagnosis

   3) Requires aggressive proton pump inhibitor Tx & surgical opening if unresponsive

C. DIARRHEA

 1. Diarrhea ≡ stool weight > 300 g/day (normal = 100–300 g/day)

 2. Small bowel dz → stools typically voluminous, watery & fatty

 3. Large bowel dz → stools smaller in volume but more frequent

 4. Prominent vomiting suggests viral enteritis or *Staph. aureus* food poisoning

 5. Malabsorption diarrhea characterized by high fat content

  a. Lose fat soluble vitamins, iron, calcium & B vitamins

  b. Can cause iron deficiency, megaloblastic anemia (B_{12} loss) & hypocalcemia

 6. General Tx = oral rehydration, IV fluids & electrolytes (supportive)

 7. Specific diarrheas

TABLE 5-6 Diarrheas

TYPE	CHARACTERISTICS	DX	TX
Infectious	• #1 cause of acute diarrhea • Si/Sx = vomiting, pain; blood/mucus & fevers/chills suggest invasive dz	• Stool leukocytes, Gram's stain & culture, O & P for parasitic • C. difficile toxin test	• Ciprofloxacin • Metronidazole for C. difficile[a]
Osmotic	• Causes = lactose intolerance, oral Mg, sorbitol/mannitol	• ↑ osmotic gap • Check fecal fat	• Withdraw inciting agent
Secretory	• Causes = toxins (cholera), enteric viruses, ↑ dietary fat	• Normal osmotic gap • Fasting → no change	• Supportive
Exudative	• Mucosal inflammation → plasma & serum leakage • Causes = enteritis, TB, colon CA, inflammatory bowel dz	• ↑ ESR & CRP[b] • Radiologic imaging or colonoscopy to visualize intestine	• Varies by cause—see appropriate section of text
Rapid transit	• Causes = laxatives, surgical excision of intestinal tissue	• Hx of surgery or laxative use	• Supportive
Encopresis	• Oozing around fecal impaction in children or sick elderly	• History of constipation	• Fiber rich diet & laxatives

TABLE 5-6   Continued

TYPE	CHARACTERISTICS	DX	TX
Malabsorption			
Celiac sprue	• Gluten allergy (wheat, barley, rye, oats contain gluten) • Sx/Si = weakness, failure to thrive, growth retardation • Classic rash = **dermatitis herpetiformis** = pruritic, red papulovesicular lesions on shoulders, elbows & knees • 10–15% of pts develop intestinal lymphoma	**Dx by small bowel biopsy → pathognomonic blunting of intestinal villi**	Avoid dietary gluten
Tropical sprue	• Diarrhea probably caused by a tropical infection • Si/Sx = glossitis, diarrhea, weight loss, steatorrhea	Dx = clinical	Tetracycline ⊕ folate
Whipple's disease	• GI infection by *Tropheryma whippelii* • Si/Sx = diarrhea, arthritis, rash, anemia	Dx = biopsy → PAS⊕ macrophages in intestines	Penicillin or tetracycline
Lactase deficiency	• Most of world is lactase deficient as adults, people lose as they emerge from adolescence • Si/Sx = abdominal pain, diarrhea, flatulence after ingestion of any lactose-containing product	Dx = clinical	Avoid lactose or take exogenous lactase
Intestinal lymphan-giectasia	• Seen in children, congenital or acquired dilation of intestinal lymphatics leads to marked GI protein loss • Si/Sx = diarrhea, hypoproteinemia, edema	Dx = jejunal biopsy	Supportive
Pancreas dz	• Typically seen in pancreatitis & cystic fibrosis due to deficiency of pancreatic digestive enzymes • Si/Sx = foul smelling steatorrhea, megaloblastic anemia (folate deficiency), weight loss	Hx of prior pancreatic disease	Pancrease supplementation

[a] Vancomycin reserved for resistance.
[b] CRP = C-reactive protein.

8. Common infectious pathogens for diarrhea

TABLE 5-7   Infectious Causes of Diarrhea

	BACTERIAL	VIRAL	PARASITIC
Etiology	*E. coli, Shigella, Salmonella, Campylobacter jejuni, Vibrio parahaemolyticus, Vibrio cholera, Yersinia enterocolitica*	Rotavirus Norwalk virus	*Giardia lamblia, Cryptosporidium, Entamoeba histolytica*
Tx	Ciprofloxacin, Bactrim	Supportive	Metronidazole

IV. Urogenital Complaints

A. URINARY TRACT INFECTION (UTI)

1. Epidemiology
   a. 40% of females have ≥ 1 UTI, 8% have bacteriuria at a given time
   b. Most common in sexually active young women, elderly, posturethral catheter or instrumentation—rare in males (↑ risk with prostate dz)
   c. Due to *E. coli* (80%), *S. saprophyticus* (15%), other gram-negative rods
2. Si/Sx = **burning during urination**, urgency, sense of incomplete bladder emptying, hematuria, lower abdominal pain, nocturia
3. Systemic Sx = fever, chills, **back pain suggest pyelonephritis**
4. Dx = **UA → pyuria**; ⊕ bacteria on Gram's stain; positive culture results
5. Tx
   a. Lower UTI → Bactrim (first line), fluoroquinolone for refractory dz
   b. Uncomplicated pyelonephritis → same antibiotics given IV or PO depending on severity of pt's illness
   c. Men cured within 7 days of Tx do not warrant further work-up, but **adolescents & men with pyelonephritis or recurrent infxn require renal Utz & intravenous pyelogram to rule out anatomic etiology**
   d. UTI 2° to bacterial prostatitis requires 6–12 wk of antibiotics
   e. Asymptomatic bacteriuria
      1) Defined as urine culture > 100,000 CFU/mL but no Sx
      2) Only Tx in 1) pregnancy (use penicillins or nitrofurantoin), or pts with 2) renal transplant, 3) about to undergo GU procedure, 4) severe vesicular-ureteral reflux & 5) struvite calculi

B. SEXUALLY TRANSMITTED DISEASES (STDs)—SEE SECTION C FOR AIDS

TABLE 5-8   Sexually Transmitted Diseases

DISEASE	CHARACTERISTICS	TX
Herpes simplex virus (HSV)	• Most common cause of genital ulcers (causes 60–70% of cases) • Si/Sx = **painful vesicular & ulcerated** lesions 1–3 mm diameter, onsets 3–7 days after exposure • Lesions generally resolve over 7 days • Primary infection also characterized by malaise, low grade fever & inguinal adenopathy in 40% of patients • Recurrent lesions are similar appearing, but milder in severity & shorter in duration, lasting about 2–5 days • Dx confirmed with direct fluorescent antigen (DFA) staining, Tzanck prep, serology, HSV PCR, or culture	• Tx = acyclovir, famciclovir, or valacyclovir to ↓ duration of viral shedding & shorten initial course

TABLE 5-8 *Continued*

DISEASE	CHARACTERISTICS	TX
Pelvic inflammatory disease	• *Chlamydia trachomatis* & *Neisseria gonorrhoeae* are primary pathogens, but PID is polymicrobial involving both aerobic & anaerobic bacteria • PID includes endometritis, salpingitis, tuboovarian abscess (TOA) & pelvic peritonitis • Infertility occurs in 15% of pts after 1 episode of salpingitis, ↑ to 75% after ≥ 3 episodes • Risk of ectopic pregnancy ↑ 7–10 times in women with history of salpingitis • Dx = abdominal, adnexal & cervical motion tenderness + at least 1 of the following: ⊕ Gram's stain, temp > 38°C, WBC > 10,000, pus on culdocentesis or laparoscopy, tuboovarian abscess on bimanual or Utz	• Toxic pts, ↓ immunity & noncompliant should be Tx as inpatients with IV antibiotics • Use fluoroquinolone + metronidazole or cephalosporin + doxycycline • Start antibiotic as soon as PID is suspected, even before culture results are available
Human papillomavirus (HPV)	• Serotypes 16, 18 most commonly associated with cervical cancer • Incubation period varies from 6 wk to 3 mo, spread by direct skin-to-skin contact • Infection after single contact with an infected individual results in 65% transmission rate • Si/Sx = condyloma acuminata (genital warts) = soft, fleshy growths on vulva, vagina, cervix, perineum & anus • Dx = clinical, confirmed with biopsy	• Topical podophyllin or trichloracetic acid, if refractory → cryosurgery or excision • If pregnant, C-section recommended to avoid vaginal lacerations
Syphilis (*Treponema pallidum*)	• Si/Sx = **painless ulcer** with bilateral inguinal adenopathy, chancre heals in 3–9 wk • Because of lack of Sx, Dx of primary syphilis is often missed • 4–8 wk after appearance of chancre, 2° dz → fever, lymphadenopathy, maculopapular rash affecting palms & soles, condyloma lata in intertriginous areas • Dx = serologies, VDRL & RPR for screening, FTA-ABS to confirm	• Benzathine penicillin G

FAMILY MEDICINE

C. ACQUIRED IMMUNODEFICIENCY SYNDROME (AIDS)

1. Epidemiology
   a. AIDS is a global pandemic (currently the fastest spread is in SE Asia & central Europe)
   b. **Heterosexual transmission is the most common mode worldwide**
   c. In the US, IV drug users & their sex partners are the fastest growing population of HIV⊕ patients
   d. Homosexual transmission is slowing dramatically [see *N Engl J Med* 1999, 341:1046-1050]
2. HIV biology
   a. Retrovirus with the usual *gag, pol* & *env* genes
   b. p24 is a core protein encoded by *gag* gene, can be used clinically to follow disease progression
   c. gp120 & gp41 are envelope glycoproteins that are produced on cleavage of gp160, coded by *env*

    d. Reverse transcriptase (coded by *pol*) converts viral RNA to DNA so it can integrate into the host's DNA

    e. Cellular entry is by binding to both CD4 & an additional ligand (can be CCR4, CCR5, others) that typically is a cytokine receptor

    f. HIV can infect CD4⊕ T cells, macrophages, thymic cells, astrocytes, dendritic cells & others

    g. The mechanisms of T-cell destruction are not well understood but probably include direct cell lysis, induction of CTL responses against infected CD4⊕ cells & exhaustion of bone marrow production (suppression of production of T cells)

    h. In addition, the virus induces alterations in host cytokine patterns rendering surviving lymphocytes ineffective

3. Disease course

    a. In most patients AIDS is relentlessly progressive & death occurs within 10–15 yr of HIV infection

    b. Long-term survivors

      1) Up to 5% of patients are "long-term survivors," meaning the disease does not progress even after 15–20 yr without Tx

      2) This may be due to infection with defective virus, a potent host immune response, or genetic resistance of the host

      3) People with homozygous deletions of CCR5 or other viral coreceptors are highly resistant to infection with HIV, while heterozygotes are less resistant

    c. Although patients can have no clinical evidence of disease for many years, **HIV has no latent phase in its life cycle**; clinical silence in those patients who eventually progress is due to daily, temporarily successful host repopulation of T cells

    d. Death is usually caused by opportunistic infections (OIs)

      1) OIs typically onset after CD4 counts fall below 200

      2) Below 200 CD4 cells, all pts should be on permanent Bactrim prophylaxis against *P. carinii* pneumonia (PCP) & *Toxoplasma encephalitis*

      3) Below 75 CD4 cells, all patients should receive azithromycin prophylaxis against *M. avium-intracellulare* complex (MAC)

      4) Kaposi's sarcoma = common skin cancer found in homosexual HIV patients, thought to be caused by cotransmission of human herpes virus 8 (HHV 8)

      5) Other diseases found in AIDS patients include generalized wasting & dementia

4. Treatment

    a. Triple combination therapy is now the cornerstone

      1) Cocktail includes 2 nucleoside analogues (e.g., AZT, ddl, d4T) ⊕ a protease inhibitor

      2) Protease inhibitors block the splicing of the large *gag* precursor protein into its final components, p24 & p7

      3) Newest addition to arsenal is hydroxyurea

        a) Inhibits host ribonucleotide reductase → decreased concentration of purines

        b) ddl is a purine analogue (competitor), so hydroxyurea ↑ efficacy of ddl

        c) In theory, virus should not be able to become resistant to hydroxyurea, since it acts on a host enzyme & not on the virus

    b. **No patient should ever be on any single drug regimen for HIV—resistance is invariable in monotherapy**

c. Current Tx is able to suppress viral replication to below detectable limits in the majority of patients, but **up to 50% of patients end up "failing" therapy (viral loads rebound)**

d. **Failure of the regimen is associated with poor compliance** (missed doses lead to resistance) & **prior exposure to one or more drugs in the regimen** (the virus is already resistant to the agent)

e. The long-term significance of viral suppression is unclear, but **it is known that the virus is NOT cleared from the body at up to 2 yr after it ceases to be detectable in the blood** (it can be found latent in lymph nodes)

D. HEMATURIA

1. Red/brown urine discoloration $2°$ to RBCs, correlates with presence of >5 RBCs/high-powered field on microanalysis
2. Can be painful or painless
   a. Painless = $1°$ renal dz (tumor, glomerulonephritis), TB infection, vesicular dz (bladder tumor), prostatic dz
   b. Painful = nephrolithiasis, renal infarction, UTI
3. DDx = myoglobinuria or hemoglobinuria, where hemoglobin dipstick is positive but no RBCs are seen on microanalysis
4. Dx = finding of RBCs in urinary sediment
   a. Urinalysis → WBCs (infection) or RBC casts (glomerulonephritis)
   b. CBC → anemia (renal failure), polycythemia (renal cell CA)
   c. Urogram will show nephrolithiasis & tumors (Utz → cystic vs. solid)
   d. Cystoscopy only after UA & IVP; best for lower urinary tract
5. Tx varies by cause

E. PROSTATE

1. Benign Prostatic Hyperplasia
   a. Hyperplasia of the periurethral prostrate causing bladder outlet obstruction
   b. Common after age 45 (autopsy shows that 90% of men over 70 have BPH)
   c. Does not predispose to prostrate cancer
   d. Si/Sx urinary frequency, urgency, nocturia, ↓ size & force of urinary stream leading to hesitancy & intermittency, sensation of incomplete emptying worsening to continuous overflow incontinence or urinary retention, rectal exam → enlarged prostate (classically a rubbery vs. firm, hard gland that may suggest prostate cancer) with loss of median furrow
   e. Labs → PSA elevated in up to 50% of pts, not specific—not useful marker for BPH
   f. Dx based on symptomatic scoring system, i.e., prostate size >30 mL (determined by Utz or exam), maximum urinary flow rate (<10 mL/sec) & postvoid residual urine volume (>50 mL) (see *J Urology* 1992, 148:1549)
   g. Tx = α-blocker (e.g., terazosin), 5-α-reductase inhibitor (e.g., Finasteride); avoid anticholinergics, antihistaminergics, or narcotics
   h. Refractory dz requires surgery = transurethral resection of prostate (TURP); open prostatectomy recommended for larger glands (>75 g)
2. Prostatitis
   a. Si/Sx = fever, chills, low back pain, urinary frequency & urgency, tender, possible fluctuant & swollen prostate

b. Labs → leukocytosis, pyuria, bacteriuria

c. Dx = clinical

d. Tx = systemic antibiotics

F. IMPOTENCE

1. Affects 30 million men in US, strongly associated with age (about 40% among 40-yr-olds & 70% among 70-yr-olds)
2. Causes
   a. 1° erectile dysfunction = never been able to sustain erections
      1) Psychological (sexual guilt, fear of intimacy, depression, anxiety)
      2) ↓ testosterone 2° to hypothalamic-pituitary-gonadal disorder
      3) Hypo- or hyperthyroidism, Cushing's syndrome, ↑ prolactin
   b. 2° erectile dysfunction = acquired, **>90% due to organic cause**
      1) Vascular dz = atherosclerosis of penile arteries &/or venous leaks causing inadequate impedance of venous outflow
      2) Drugs = diuretics, clonidine, CNS depressants, tricyclic antidepressants, high-dose anticholinergics, antipsychotics
      3) Neurologic dz = stroke, temporal lobe seizures, multiple sclerosis, spinal cord injury, autonomic dysfunction 2° to diabetes, post-TURP or open prostatic surgery
3. Dx
   a. Clinical, rule out above organic causes
   b. **Nocturnal penile tumescence** testing differentiates psychogenic from organic—nocturnal tumescence is involuntary, ⊕ in psychogenic but not in organic dz
4. Tx
   a. Sildenafil (Viagra)
      1) Selective inhibitor of cGMP specific phosphodiesterase type 5a → improves relaxation of smooth muscles in corpora cavernosa
      2) Side effects = transient headache, flushing, dyspepsia & rhinitis, transient visual disturbances (blue hue) is very rare, drug may lower blood pressure → **use of nitrates is an absolute contraindication**, deaths have resulted from combo
   b. Vacuum-constriction devices use negative pressure to draw blood into penis with band placed at base of penis to retain erection
   c. Intracavernosal prostaglandin injection has mean duration about 60 min; risks = penile bruising/bleeding & priapism
   d. Surgery = penile prostheses implantation; venous or arterial surgery
   e. Testosterone therapy for hypogonadism
   f. Behavioral therapy & counseling for depression & anxiety

V. Common Sports Medicine Complaints

A. LOW BACK PAIN

1. 80% of people experience low back pain—second most common complaint in 1° care (next to common cold)
2. **50% of cases will recur within the subsequent 3 yr**
3. **Majority cases attributed to muscle strains**, but always consider disk herniation
4. Si/Sx of disk herniation = shooting pain down leg (sciatica), pain on **straight leg raise (>90% sensitive)** & pain on **crossed straight leg raise (>90% specific, not sensitive)**

5. Dx
   a. **Always rule out RED FLAGS** (see below) with Hx & physical exam
   b. If no red flags detected, presume Dx is muscle strain & not serious—**no radiologic testing is warranted**
   c. Dz not remitting after 4 wk of conservative Tx should be further evaluated with repeat Hx & physical; consider radiologic studies
   d. Red Flags

TABLE 5-9   Low Back Pain Red Flags

DIAGNOSIS	SI/SX	DX
Fracture	• Hx of trauma (fall, car accident) • Minor trauma in elderly (e.g., strenuous lifting)	• Spine x-rays
Tumor	• **Pt > 50 yr old** (accounts for >80% of cancer cases) or <20 yr old • Prior Hx of CA • **Constitutional Sx** (fever/chills, weight loss) • Pain worse when supine or at night	• Spinal MRI is gold standard, can get CT also
Infection	• Immunosuppressed pts • Constitutional Sx • Recent bacterial infection or IV drug abuse	• Blood cultures, spinal MRI to rule out abscess
Cauda equina syndrome	• Acute urinary retention, **saddle anesthesia**, lower extremity weakness or paresthesias & ↓ reflexes, ↓ anal sphincter tone	• Spinal MRI
Spinal stenosis	• Si/Sx = **pseudoclaudication** (neurogenic) with pain ↑ with walking **& standing**; relieved by sitting or leaning forward	• Spinal MRI

Radiculopathy (herniation compressing spinal nerves)*	• Sensory loss:
	  (**L5** → **L**arge toe/ medial foot, **S1** → **S**mall toe/ lateral foot)
	• Weakness:
	  (L1–L4 → quadriceps, L5 → foot dorsiflexion, S1 → plantar flexion)
	• ↓ reflexes (L4 → patellar, S1 → achilles)
		• **Clinical**—MRI may confirm clinical Dx but false-positive are common (clinically insignificant disk herniation) (See Figure 5-2)

*Radiculopathy ≠ herniation; radiculopathy indicates evolving spinal nerve impingement & is a more serious Dx than simple herniation indicated by straight leg testing & sciatica.

6. Tx
   a. No red flags → conservative with acetaminophen (safer) or NSAIDs, **muscle relaxants have not been shown to help**; avoid narcotics
   b. **Strict bed rest is NOT warranted** (extended rest shown to be debilitating, especially in older patients)—encourage return to normal activity, low-stress aerobic & back exercises
   c. **90% of cases resolve within 4 wk with conservative Tx**
   d. Red flags:
      1) Fracture → surgical consult
      2) Tumor → urgent radiation/steroid (↓ compression), then excise
      3) Infection → abscess drainage & antibiotics per pathogen
      4) Cauda equina syndrome → emergent surgical decompression
      5) Spinal stenosis → complete laminectomy

6) Radiculopathy → anti-inflammatories, nerve root decompression with laminectomy or microdiscectomy only if (1) sciatica is severe & disabling, (2) Sx persist for 4 wk or worsening progression & (3) strong evidence of specific nerve root damage with MRI correlation of level of disk herniation

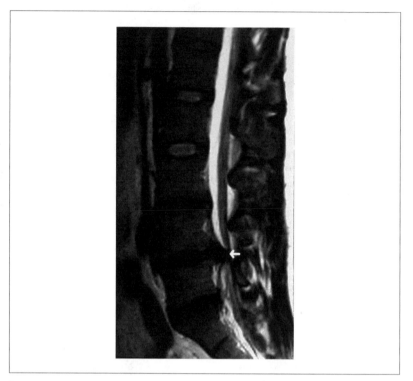

FIGURE 5-2   MRI scan demonstrating a prolapsed disk at L4/L5 with posterior deviation of the theca (arrow).

B. SHOULDER DISLOCATION

1. Subluxation = symptomatic translation of humeral head relative to glenoid articular surface
2. Dislocation = complete displacement out of the glenoid
3. Anterior instability (about 95% of cases) usually due to subcoracoid dislocation is the most common form of shoulder dislocation
4. Si/Sx = pain, joint immobility, arm "goes dead" with overhead motion
5. Dx = clinical, assess axillary nerve function in neuro exam, look for signs of rotator cuff injury, confirm with x-rays if necessary
6. Tx = initial reduction of dislocation by various traction-countertraction techniques, 2–6 wk period of immobilization (longer for younger patients), intense rehabilitation; rarely is surgery required

C. CLAVICLE FRACTURE

1. Occurs primarily due to contact sports in adults
2. Si/Sx = pain & deformity at clavicle
3. Dx = clinical, confirm fracture with standard AP view x-ray
4. Must rule out subclavian artery injury by checking pulses, brachial plexus injury with neuro examination & pneumothorax by checking breath sounds
5. Tx = sling until range of motion is painless (usually 2–4 wk)

D. ELBOW INJURIES

1. Epicondylitis (tendinitis)
   a. Lateral epicondylitis **(tennis elbow)**
      1) Usually in tennis player (>50%), or racquetball, squash, fencing
      2) Si/Sx = pain 2–5 cm distal & anterior to lateral epicondyle reproduced with wrist extension while elbow is extended
   b. Medial epicondylitis **(golfer's elbow)**
      1) Commonly in golf, racquet sports, bowling, baseball, swimming
      2) Si/Sx = acute onset of medial elbow pain & swelling localized 1 or 2 cm area distal to medial epicondyle, pain usually reproduced with wrist flexion & pronation against resistance
   c. Tx for both = ice, rest, NSAIDs, counterforce bracing, rehabilitation
   d. Px for both varies, can become chronic condition; surgery sometimes indicated (débridement & tendon reapproximation)
2. Olecranon fracture
   a. Usually direct blow to elbow with triceps contraction after fall on flexed upper extremity
   b. Tx = long arm cast or splint in 45–90° flexion for ≥ 3 wk
   c. Displaced fracture requires open reduction & internal fixation
3. Dislocation
   a. Elbow joint most commonly dislocated joint in children, second most in adults (next to shoulder)
   b. Fall onto outstretched hand with fully extended elbow (posterolateral dislocation) or direct blow to posterior elbow (anterior dislocation)
   c. May also be seen after jerking child's arm by hurried parent or guardian (**nursemaid's elbow**) (See Figure 5-3)
   d. Key is associated nerve injury (ulnar, median, radial or anterior interosseous nerve), vascular injury (brachial artery) or other structural injury (associated coronoid process fracture common)
   e. Tx = reduce elbow by gently flexing supinated arm, long arm splint or bivalved cast applied at 90° flexion

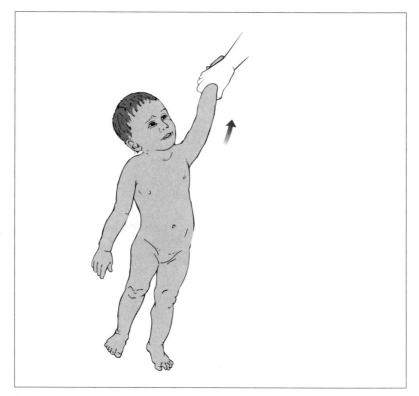

FIGURE 5-3   Nursemaid's elbow. Sudden forceful traction dislocates the elbow joint.

  4. Olecranon bursitis
     a. Inflammation of bursa under olecranon process
     b. Seen with direct blow to elbow by collision or fall on artificial turf
     c. Si/Sx = swollen & painful posterior elbow with restricted motion
     d. Dx = clinical, confirm with bursa aspiration to rule out septic bursitis
     e. Tx = bursa aspiration, compression dressing & pad
E. ANKLE INJURIES
  1. Achilles tendonitis
     a. 2° to overuse, commonly seen in runners, gymnasts, cyclists & volleyball players
     b. Si/Sx = swelling or erythema along area of Achilles tendon with tenderness 2–5 cm proximal to calcaneus
     c. Evaluate for rupture = Thompson test (squeezing leg with passive plantar flexion) positive only with complete tear
     d. Tx = rest, ice, NSAIDs, taping or splinting to ↓ stress & ↑ support
     e. Rupture requires long leg casting × 4 wk, short leg walking cast × 4 wk, then wear heel lift × 4 wk
     f. Open repair speeds recovery & is recommended with complete tears in younger patients

2. Ankle sprains
   a. Lateral sprain occurs when ankle is plantar-flexed (90% of sprains)
   b. Anterior drawer sign is done with foot in 10–15° plantar flexion
   c. Medial sprain is rare (10%) because ligament is stronger
   d. Dx = multiple view x-rays both free & weight bearing
   e. Tx = **RICE** = **R**est (limit activity +/– crutches), **I**ce, **C**ompression (ACE bandage), **E**levation above level of heart to decrease swelling
   f. Severe sprains may benefit from casting, open repair rarely indicated

VI. Preventive Medicine

A. CANCER SCREENING

TABLE 5-10   Cancer Screening

DISEASE	INTERVENTION
Cervical CA	• Annual PS in women ≥ 18 yr or sexually active (ACS) • Perform less often if ≥3 consecutive Paps are nl & pt is monogamous
Breast CA	• Exam & mammogram every 1–2 yr women 50–69 yr (AAFP, USPTF) • Self exams; annual exam & mammogram in women >40 yr (ACS)
Colorectal CA	• Hemoccult annually >50 yr (screen earlier with positive family Hx) • Pt > 50 yr → sigmoidoscopy q 5 yr or colonoscopy q 10 yr (ACS)
Prostate CA	• Annual digital exam & PSA should be offered to all men >50 yr (ACS)
Endometrial CA	• High-risk patients should have biopsy shortly after menopause (ACS)
Other CA	• Annual physical exam for signs of thyroid, skin, oral, testicular or ovarian CA (ACS)

B. ADULT IMMUNIZATION

TABLE 5-11   Adult Immunization

Tetanus	All require primary series & periodic boosters q 10 yr (A)
MMR	All require vaccination if born after 1956 without immunity (A)
Hepatitis B	Recommended for all young adults & ↑ risk pts (A)
Pneumococcal	Give once in immunocompetent pts ≥ 65 yr or to any pt with ↑ risk (B)
Influenza	Annually for all pts ≥ 65 yr or high-risk pts (B)
Hepatitis A	Only for high-risk patients like travelers (B)
Varicella	Adults without Hx of disease or previous vaccination (B)
In HIV pts avoid live preparations, but MMR should be given if CD4 count >500	
In pregnant pts live vaccinations are not recommended (MMR, OPV, VZV)	

A = proven benefit, B = probably benefit.

C. TRAVEL PROPHYLAXIS

TABLE 5-12   Travel Prophylaxis

Traveler's diarrhea	Prevent w/ Pepto-Bismol; Tx w/ ciprofloxacin & loperamide
Malaria	Chloroquine; mefloquine (endemic chloroquine-resistant areas)
Hepatitis A	Most travelers; vaccine requires 4 wk; give IVIG for short-term
Typhoid	Endemic in India, Pakistan, Peru, Chile, Mexico; oral or inject
Yellow fever	Endemic in parts of South America & Africa
Meningococcus	Endemic in meningococcal belt (sub-Saharan Africa)
	Ensure all other routine immunizations are up to date (MMR, polio, Hep B)

Note: current cholera & plague vaccines are not very effective.

D. SMOKING CESSATION
1. 20–50 million US smokers attempt to quit; 6% long-term success rate
2. **Nicotine replacement (gum or patch) increases success about twofold**
3. Support from weekly counseling session, telephone calls, family & other support groups shown ↑ success
4. For best success, set a precise quit date to begin complete abstinence
5. Pts with negative affect (e.g., depression) have more difficulty quitting
6. **Bupropion +/– nicotine replacement** has 12 mo abstinence rate of >30%, **2x better than nicotine replacement alone** [*New Engl J Med* 1999, 340:9, 655]
7. On average, pts who quit successfully will gain weight (mean = 5 lb)

E. OTHER PERIODIC HEALTH EXAMINATION CONCERNS
1. Adolescence (11–24 yr)
   a. Leading cause of death are MVA & injuries & homicide/suicide
   b. BP check, Pap smears, rubella status, drug & STD education, safety
2. HTN: check BP every 2 yr in normotensive pts 21+ yr (USPTF)
3. Hyperlipidemia: check cholesterol & lipids in normal population about every 5 yr in men 35–65 yr & women 45–65 yr (USPTF)
4. Endocarditis: antibiotic prophylaxis (amoxicillin or erythromycin) given before & after dental procedures & certain surgeries; consider prophylaxis for (1) prosthetic values, (2) mitral or aortic valvular dz, (3) congenital heart dz & (4) prior Hx of infectious endocarditis

VII. Biostatistics

A. TABLE OF DEFINITIONS

TABLE 5-13   Biostatistics

SNout
SPin

TERM	DEFINITION
Sensitivity	Probability that test results will be positive in pts with disease
Specificity	Probability that test results will be negative in pts without disease
False-positive	Pt without disease who has a positive test result
False-negative	Pt with disease who has a negative test result
PPV	Positive predictive value: probability pt with positive test actually has disease

TABLE 5-13   *Continued*

TERM	DEFINITION
NPV	Negative predictive value: probability pt with negative test actually has no disease
Incidence	# of newly reported cases of disease divided by total population
Prevalence	# existing cases of disease divided by total population at a given time
Relative risk	From cohort study (prospective)—risk of developing dz for people with known exposure compared to risk of developing dz without exposure
Odds ratio	From case control study (retrospective)—approximates relative risk by comparing odds of developing dz in exposed pts to odds of developing dz in unexposed pts (if dz is rare, odds ratio approaches true relative risk)
Variance	An estimate of the variability of each individual data point from the mean
Std deviation	Square root of the variance
Type I error (α error)	Null hypothesis is rejected even though it is true—e.g., the study says the intervention works but it only appears to work because of random chance
Type II error (β error)	Null hypothesis is not rejected even though it is false—e.g., the study fails to detect a true effect of the intervention
Power ($1 - \beta$)	An estimate of the probability a study will be able to detect a true effect of the intervention—e.g., power of 80% means that if the intervention works, the study has an 80% chance of detecting this but a 20% chance of randomly missing it

B. STUDY TYPES
Prospective is more powerful than retrospective
Interventional is more powerful than observational
1. Clinical trial: **Prospective interventional trial** in which pts are randomized into an intervention group & a control group. **Randomization blunts effect of confounding factors. Blinding both clinician & patient (double-blind) further decreases bias.**
2. Cohort study: Population is divided by exposure status. Requires large population (cannot study rare disease). Can study multiple effects by exposure. Gives **relative risk if prospective**. Can be prospective or retrospective.
3. Case control study: Pts divided by those with dz (cases) & those without dz (controls). Fewer patients are needed (good for rare disease). Can study correlation of multiple exposures. Gives **odds ratio**. **Always retrospective**.

C. CALCULATION OF STATISTICAL VALUES

TABLE 5-14   Sample Calculation of Statistical Values

	PT HAS DZ	PT DOES NOT HAVE DZ
Positive test	a = true-positive	b = false-positive
Negative test	c = false-negative	d = true-negative

PPV = a/a + b
NPV = d/c + d
Sensitivity = a/a + c
Specificity = d/b + d

Sensitivity & specificity are inherent characteristics of the test—they must be given in the question. **Predictive values vary with the prevalence of the disease.** They are NOT inherent characteristics of the test, but rather reflect an interaction of sensitivity & specificity with the frequency of the disease in the population.

EXAMPLE 1: For disease X, a theoretical screening test is **90% sensitive** & **80% specific**. In Africa, where the disease has a **prevalence of 50%**, the test's **PPV = 82%** (a / a + b = 45 / 55), & the **NPV is 89%** (d / c + d = 40 / 45).

	PT HAS DZ	PT DOES NOT HAVE DZ
POSITIVE TEST	45	10
NEGATIVE TEST	5	40

Always fill the table in assuming 100 patients—it's easier to do the math this way. The prevalence of the disease (50%) tells you that 50 patients should be in the first column, because 50% of 100 patients have the disease. Therefore, 50 patients should also be in the second column (if 50 of 100 patients have the disease, 50 patients also do NOT have the disease). The sensitivity tells you that 45 of the patients in the first column should be in the top row because the test will find 90% of the 50 patients who have the disease. The specificity tells you that 40 of the patients in the second column should be in the bottom row because the test will correctly describe 80% of the 50 people who truly don't have the disease (& incorrectly claim that 20% of the 50 patients who truly don't have the disease do have the disease).

EXAMPLE 2: Now study the **same test for the same disease (X)** in America, where the **prevalence of the disease is 10%**. The test characteristics remain the same: **90% sensitive** & **80% specific**. The test's **PPV = 33%** (a / a + b = 9 / 27) & the **NPV = 99%** (d / c + d = 72 / 73). **The same test has drastically different predictive values depending on the disease prevalence!!!**

	PT HAS DZ	PT DOES NOT HAVE DZ
POSITIVE TEST	9	18
NEGATIVE TEST	1	72

Now the disease prevalence tells you that 10 patients should be in the first column (10% of 100 patients have the disease). Therefore, 90 patients should be in the second column (if 10 of 100 patients have the disease, 90 patients do NOT have the disease). The sensitivity tells you that 9 of the patients in the first column should be in the top row because the test will find 90% of the 10 patients who have the disease. The specificity tells you that 72 of the patients in the second column should be in the bottom row because the test will correctly describe 80% of the 90 people who truly don't have the disease (& incorrectly claim that 20% of the 90 patients who don't have the disease do have the disease).

Family Medicine Case Scenario

A 48-year-old female presents to your urgent care clinic complaining of 3 days of severe low back pain, which first began while she was stretching her back before exercising. It is constant, 8 out of 10 in severity, and shoots down her right leg from her buttocks to her feet "like a lightning bolt." She denies fevers, chills, nausea, vomiting, weight loss, or recent trauma. On exam she has a positive straight leg and crossed straight left test, and her patellar reflexes are 2+ on the left and 1– on the right. The Achilles reflexes are 2+ bilaterally. Her right quadriceps is weaker than her left, and she is unable to dorsiflex her right foot with any power. Plantar-flexion seems to be spared.

1. The diagnosis and treatment for this patient are:

   a) Cauda equina syndrome, immediate surgical consult

   b) Spinal stenosis, corticosteroids

    c) Musculoskeletal strain, acetaminophen and restricted activity

    d) Spinal cord tumor, immediate local irradiation

    e) Radiculopathy, anti-inflammatories

The sensitivity and specificity of MRI for diagnosing spinal stenosis in low back pain are 80% and 90%.

2. If spinal stenosis causes 10% of low back pain seen in your clinic, what are the positive predictive value and negative predictive value of MRI in making this diagnosis?

3. What are the PPV and NPV if spinal stenosis causes only 1% of low back pain seen in your clinic?

4. What are the PPV and NPV if spinal stenosis causes 40% of low back pain seen in your clinic?

A 36-year-old male presents to your office complaining of severe abdominal cramps, bloating, and nonbloody diarrhea for 24 hours. He denies fevers, chills, nausea, and vomiting. He has no history of recent travel and has no sick contacts at home. However, the patient has been taking clindamycin, which his dentist prescribed 5 days earlier for a drained dental abscess. You suspect the patient may have developed *C. difficile* colitis.

5. What test will confirm this diagnosis?

    a) Stool culture

    b) Flexible sigmoidoscopy showing a pseudomembrane

    c) Stool toxin test

    d) Fecal leukocyte count

    e) Serology

6. Assuming the diagnosis is confirmed, what is the preferred treatment?

    a) Metronidazole

    b) Kaopectate

    c) Amoxicillin

    d) Vancomycin

    e) Fluconazole

An 18-year-old female presents to the clinic with 2 days of malaise, fevers, and chills. She denies any upper respiratory symptoms, including congestion or cough, and denies nausea, vomiting, or diarrhea. For the last day she has had a stinging pain when she urinates, but she has not noticed a discharge. The patient has a normal physical exam except for her genital area. She has localized inguinal adenopathy with several clusters of vesicles on her introitus. Each vesicle is about 3 mm in diameter. You take a sexual history and learn that the patient recently became sexually active. She has had 1 steady partner for 3 months now, and uses condoms occasionally. She insists that both she and her boyfriend are monogamous. Their last sexual activity was one week earlier, and she is certain that he had no lesions on his genitals, nor has he become ill in the interim.

FAMILY MEDICINE

7. What is your diagnosis?

a) Chlamydia

b) Gonorrhea

c) Syphilis

d) HIV seroconversion syndrome

e) HSV

8. What tests will you order for this patient?

a) HSV culture and direct immunofluorescence

b) Urine PCR for *Chlamydia*

c) HIV serology

d) RPR

e) All the above

9. How can she have contracted this illness if she is in a monogamous relationship with an unaffected male?

a) She is lying to you about having only 1 partner

b) Her partner did have lesions but she did not notice them

c) He is infected with HSV and is shedding infectious virus, but has no overt signs of the disease (i.e., a carrier)

d) He is lying to her and has other sex partners

A 34-year-old male comes to your office because of "heartburn," which particularly disturbs him after eating spicy food (which he loves). He has also noticed that his favorite chocolate ice cream dessert causes this sensation. He describes the sensation as a burning feeling that starts in his chest but then creeps up his throat. On occasion food actually regurgitates up to his mouth. He suffers from heartburn at least 3 times per week and often daily. It usually affects him at night but on occasion he gets it after lunch as well. He has tried over-the-counter antacids, which take some of the sting away but don't relieve the burning. The patient is afraid he has an ulcer. When you ask about his dietary habits, he tells you that he loves spicy Italian food. He typically eats dinner about 9 p.m. and goes to bed about 10 p.m. He often drinks wine with dinner, but on occasion has a soft drink instead.

10. What is your initial management?

a) Endoscopy to rule out ulcer

b) Empiric triple antibiotics for *H. pylori*

c) Omeprazole

d) H$_2$ blocker

e) Lifestyle modifications

A 58-year-old female with a long history of migraine headaches presents to you with complaints of an unremitting, boring, unilateral headache that is not responsive to aspirin or ergotamine. The patient is desperate for pain relief, as this headache has been ongoing for nearly 4 days. She also has terrible muscle aches in her back and shoulders, which have been increasing in intensity for several weeks. She has no aura, but she does not normally get auras before her migraines anyway. The headache is localized to her right temporal area, and it is painful to touch there as well. She has some tearing in both eyes, which she attributes to the pain from the headache. Her eyes are not inflamed, and her pupils are mid-sized and reactive. She has no jaw pain or rhinorrhea. When you touch the temporal area of her scalp she jumps and scolds you, "I told you it hurt there!"

11. What is your initial management?

   a) Prednisone
   b) Nasal lidocaine
   c) Schedule for arterial biopsy and await results
   d) Sumatriptan
   e) Order a head CT

A 38-year-old male presents to your office with complaints of shaking chills, fever, nausea, and burning on urination. The symptoms began 2 days ago with malaise and have since progressed to his current illness. He has no significant past medical history and takes no medications. On exam, he is febrile to 101.5°F, is mildly tachycardic to 102°F, and is normotensive. He has no costovertebral angle tenderness, but his prostate is extremely tender and is somewhat boggy. Urinalysis reveals pyuria, and a Gram's stain reveals too many gram-negative rods to count. The patient has leukocytosis. His BUN and creatinine are normal, as is the rest of his metabolic panel.

12. What is your management?

   a) 5 days of ciprofloxacin
   b) Admit to the hospital for a week of intravenous antibiotics
   c) 6 weeks of ciprofloxacin as an outpatient
   d) Kidney biopsy
   e) Pelvic CT

Answers

1. **e)** Pain shooting from the back down the leg is classic for radiculopathy (sciatica). The loss of reflexes and muscle weakness are also consistent with the diagnosis. In this case, the loss of patellar reflex but normal Achilles reflex isolates the radiculopathy to L4, while the weakness of dorsiflexion indicates that L5 is also involved. S1 is spared (the Achilles reflex and plantar flexion are normal). There is no mention of urinary retention or incontinence, loss of anal tone, or distal paresthesias or loss of sensation that might indicate cauda equina syndrome. Spinal stenosis presents with pseudoclaudication, not acute low back pain. Although spinal cord tumor may cause radiculopathy, the lack of weight loss or other constitutional symptoms, the acute onset, and the association of onset with the patient stretching her back mitigate against this. Anti-inflammatories should be administered for radiculopathy to minimize local cord edema and ease compression. If symptoms become severely disabling, get progressively worse despite treatment, or do not resolve within several weeks, surgical decompression of the radiculopathy should be attempted.

2. PPV = 47%, NPV = 98%

	PT HAS DZ	PT DOES NOT HAVE DZ
POSITIVE TEST	8	9
NEGATIVE TEST	2	81

Fill the table in assuming 100 patients—it's easier to do the math this way. The prevalence of spinal stenosis (10%) tells you that 10 patients should be in the first column, because 10% of 100 patients have the disease. Therefore, 90 patients should be in the second column (if 10 of 100 patients have the disease, 90 patients do NOT have the disease). The sensitivity tells you that 8 of the patients in the first column should be in the top row because the test will find 80% of the 10 patients who have the disease. The specificity tells you that 81 of the patients in the second column should be in the bottom row because the test will correctly describe 90% of the 90 people who truly don't have the disease (and incorrectly claim that 10% of the 90 patients who truly don't have the disease do have the disease).
The PPV = 8 / 8 + 9. The NPV = 81 / 81 + 2.

3. PPV = 7.5%, NPV = 99.8%

	PT HAS DZ	PT DOES NOT HAVE DZ
POSITIVE TEST	8	99
NEGATIVE TEST	2	891

In this case fill the table in assuming 1000 patients because 1% of 100 leaves you with only 1 patient who has the disease, and you need patients in both rows of the first column (you can't split 1 patient up between the top and bottom rows!). The prevalence of spinal stenosis (1%) tells you that 10 patients should be in the first column, because 1% of 1000 patients have the disease. Therefore, 990 patients should also be in the second column (if 10 of 1000 patients have the disease, 990 patients also do NOT have the disease). The sensitivity tells you that 8 of the patients in the first column should be in the top row because the test will find 80% of the 10 patients who have the disease. The specificity tells you that 891 of the patients in the second column should be in the bottom row because the test will correctly describe 90% of the 990 people who truly don't have the disease (and incorrectly claim that 10% of the 990 patients who truly don't have the disease do have the disease).
The PPV = 8 / 8 + 99. The NPV = 891 / 891 + 2.

4. PPV = 84%, NPV = 87%

	PT HAS DZ	PT DOES NOT HAVE DZ
POSITIVE TEST	32	6
NEGATIVE TEST	8	54

In this case fill the table in assuming 100 patients. The prevalence of spinal stenosis (40%) tells you that 40 patients should be in the first column, because 40% of 100 patients have spinal stenosis. Therefore, 60 patients should be in the second column (if 40 of 100 patients have the disease, 60 patients do NOT have the disease). The sensitivity tells you that 32 of the patients in the first column should be in the top row because the test will find 80% of the 40 patients who have the disease. The specificity tells you that 54 of the patients in the second column should be in the bottom row because the test will correctly describe 90% of the 60 people who truly don't have the disease (and incorrectly claim that 10% of the 60 patients who truly don't have the disease do have the disease).
The PPV = 32 / 32 + 6. The NPV = 54 / 54 + 8.

5. **c)** The diagnosis of *C. difficile* colitis is made by stool analysis for clostridial toxin.

6. **a)** Metronidazole is first-line treatment for *C. difficile* colitis, with vancomycin being reserved for resistant cases. The other antibiotics have no efficacy. In general, antimotility agents should not be administered, as they only prolong the contact between the toxin and the sensitive bowel wall.

7. **e)** This is the classic presentation of primary HSV II. The vesicular lesions appear 3 to 7 days after inoculation of the virus, and fevers and chills with local adenopathy are common during primary (but not recurrent) disease. Chlamydia, gonorrhea, and syphilis do not cause vesicular eruptions. HIV seroconversion is consistent with the fevers and chills, but the adenopathy is usually diffuse, and again, by itself HIV does not cause the classic vesicular eruption.

8. **e)** In a patient with 1 sexually transmitted disease, ruling out others is essential since they are often co-transmitted.

9. **c)** Contrary to common lore, transmission of HSV (even male to female) can occur without overt lesions being present. Patients can shed infectious virus even without visible evidence of active desease.

10. **e)** This patient has gastroesophageal reflux disease (GERD), for which the first-line treatment is lifestyle modifications. This patient has several modifications he can make. Eating dinner several hours before lying down in bed, avoiding alcohol with dinner, avoiding chocolate (which contains caffeine) and caffeinated soda will all help his lower esophageal sphincter work better. He should also cut back on the spicy foods. If lifestyle modifications do not work, an H_2 blocker is second-line, with omeprazole third-line. Patients with GERD should never be treated with anti–*H. pylori* antibiotics. GERD and ulcers are completely unrelated, and nonindicated use of antibiotics selects for resistant *H. pylori*.

11. **a)** This patient presents with a history and physical convincing for the presence of temporal arteritis. Aside from the extremely tender temporal area of her scalp, the accompanying muscle aches in her back and shoulder are consistent with polymyalgia rheumatica, a poorly understood inflammatory disorder that often accompanies temporal arteritis. Although biopsy of the artery is necessary to confirm the diagnosis, administration of prednisone *should not wait for the results of the biopsy*! Delay in starting the prednisone can result in blindness.

12. **c)** The patient's prostate exam is strongly suggestive of prostatitis. Although pyelonephritis is a possibility, it is made unlikely by the lack of CVA tenderness. The patient appears stable enough to be cared for as an outpatient (even mild pyelonephritis can be cared for on an outpatient basis). For urinary tract infections secondary to bacterial prostatitis, 6 weeks of antibiotics is required.

6. Psychiatry

Charles Lee

I. Introduction

A. **DSM-IV (DIAGNOSTIC & STATISTICAL MANUAL)**
   1. The DSM-IV lists current US diagnostic criteria for psychiatric conditions
   2. **The USMLE will rely on DSM-IV diagnostic criteria**
   3. **Do not try memorizing all the possible Sx mentioned by the DSM** to define a given condition. It is impossible and not a good use of time. This review will focus on the Sx you are **most likely to see on the exam.**

B. **PRINCIPLES OF PSYCHIATRY FOR THE USMLE (MORE COMPLEX IN REAL LIFE)**
   1. Major psychiatric Dx requires **significant impairment in the pt's life**
   2. **Always rule out drug abuse** (frequent comorbidity in psychiatric dz)
   3. **Combination Tx** (pharmacology & psychotherapy) **is superior** to either alone but **pharmacologic Tx is first line for severe dz in acute setting**
   4. **Criteria for hospitalization (any single criterion is acceptable)**
      a. Danger to self (suicide)
      b. Danger to others
      c. Unable to provide food, clothing, shelter (grave disability)
   5. Psychiatric dz is chronic—if asked about dz course, **"cures" are rare**
   6. Prognosis depends on symptom onset, insight & premorbid function

TABLE 6-1 Prognosis of Psychiatric Disorders

PROGNOSIS	SYMPTOM ONSET	INSIGHT*	PREMORBID FUNCTION
Favorable	Acute	Good	High
Unfavorable	Subacute/Chronic	Poor	Low

*Insight = pt recognizes symptoms as abnormalities & is distressed by them.

II. Mood Disorders

A. **MAJOR DEPRESSIVE DISORDER (MDD)**
   1. A syndrome of **repeated major depressive episodes**
   2. One of the most common psychiatric disorders, with lifetime prevalence of 15–25%, with a greater incidence in women & elderly (often overlooked)
   3. Si/Sx for depression in general
      a. Major Si/Sx = ↓ **mood** &/or **anhedonia** (inability to experience pleasure)
      b. Others = insomnia (less commonly hypersomnia), ↓ appetite/weight loss (less commonly ↑ appetite/weight gain), fatigue, ↓ concentration, guilt or feeling worthless, recurrent thoughts of death & suicide
      c. **Commonly presents with various somatic complaints & ↓ energy level rather than complaints of depression**—beware of clinical scenarios in which pts have multiple unrelated physical complaints

4. DDx = dysthymic disorder, bipolar disorder, medical dz (**classically hypothyroidism**), bereavement
5. Dx requires depressive episode to continue for ≥2 wk, with ≥2 episodes separated by ≥2 mo (**2 episodes of 2 wk, 2 mo apart**)
6. Tx
    a.

TABLE 6-2   Pharmacologic Therapy for Depression[a]

DRUG	EXAMPLES	SIDE EFFECTS
SSRIs[b]	Fluoxetine, paroxetine	Favorable profile: rare impotence
TCAs[b]	Amitriptyline, desipramine, imipramine, nortriptyline	More severe: confusion, sedation, **orthostatic hypotension, prolonged QRS duration** (think autonomic/cholinergic)
MAO[b] Inhibitors	Phenelzine, tranylcypromine	Very severe: classic syndromes • **Serotonin syndrome** = caused by **MAO inhibitor interaction with SSRIs, demerol, or pseudoephedrine** & others, presents with hyperthermia, muscle rigidity, altered mental status • **Hypertensive crisis** = malignant hypertension when ingested with foods rich in **tyramine** (wine & cheese)

[a] Takes 2–6 wk for effect.
[b] SSRIs (selective serotonin reuptake inhibitors) are first line; TCAs (tricyclic antidepressants) are second line; MAO inhibitors (monoamine oxidase inhibitors) are third line.

   b. Psychotherapy = **psychodynamic** (understanding self/inner conflicts), **cognitive-behavioral** (recognizing negative thought or behavior & altering thinking/behavior accordingly), **interpersonal** (examines relation of Sx to negative/absent relationships with others)
   c. **Electroconvulsive therapy (ECT)** is effective for refractory cases, main side effect is short-term memory loss

B. DYSTHYMIC DISORDER
   1. Si/Sx as per major depressive episodes but is continuous
   2. Dx = **steady Sx duration for minimum of 2 yr**—dysthymic disorder is longer but less acute than MDD
   3. If major depressive episode takes place during the 2 yr of dysthymia, then by definition the Dx is MDD rather than dysthymic disorder
   4. Tx as per MDD

C. BEREAVEMENT
   1. **Bereavement** is a commonly asked test question!
   2. Si/Sx = an older adult whose partner has died & who has been feeling sad, losing weight & sleeping poorly (depression symptoms)
   3. Dx: key is **how much time** has elapsed since the partner died—**if Sx persist for >2 mo, Dx is MDD rather than normal bereavement**
   4. Although bereavement is normal behavior, grief management may be helpful.

D. BIPOLAR DISORDER (MANIC-DEPRESSION)
   1. Seen in 1% of population, genders equally affected but **often presents in young people** while **major depression is a dz of middle age (40s)**
   2. Si/Sx = abrupt onset of ↑ **energy**, ↓ **need to sleep, pressured speech** (speaks quickly

to the point of making no sense), ↓ attention span, **hypersexuality, spending large amounts of money**, engaging in outrageous activities (e.g., directing traffic at an intersection while naked)
3. DDx = cocaine & amphetamine use, personality disorders (cluster B, see below, Section V.B), schizophrenia (see below, Section III), hypomania
4. Dx
    a. **Manic episode causes significant disability**, whereas hypomania presents with identical Sx but no significant disability
    b. Episodes **must last ≥1 wk & should be abrupt, not continuous,** which would suggest personality disorder or schizophrenia
    c. **Bipolar I** = manic episode with or without depressive episodes (pts often have depressive episodes before experiencing mania)
    d. **Bipolar II** = depressive episodes **with hypomanic episodes** but, by definition, **the absence of manic episodes**
    e. **Rapid cycling** = 4 episodes (depressive, manic, or mixed) in 12 mo; can be precipitated by antidepressants
5. Tx
    a. Hospitalization, often involuntary since manic pts rarely see the need
    b. **Valproate** or **carbamazepine** are first line, **lithium** second line
    c. Valproate & carbamazepine cause **blood dyscrasias**
    d. Lithium blood levels must be checked due to frequent toxicity, including **tremor** & polyuria due to **nephrogenic diabetes insipidus**
6. Px worse than major depression, episodes more frequent with age

E. DRUG-INDUCED MANIA
1. Cocaine & amphetamines are major culprits
2. Si/Sx = mania as above, also tachycardia, hypertension, dilated pupils, **EKG arrhythmia or ischemia in young people is highly suggestive**
3. Dx = urine or serum toxicology screen
4. Tx = calcium-channel blockers for acute autonomic Sx, drug Tx programs longer term

III. Psychosis

A. SI/SX
1. **Hallucinations & delusions** are hallmark
    a. Hallucination ≡ false sensory perception not based on real stimulus
    b. Delusion ≡ false interpretation of external reality
    c. Can be paranoid, grandiose (thinking one possesses special powers), religious (God is talking to the pt), or ideas of reference (every event in the world somehow involves the pt)

B. DDX

TABLE 6-3   Diagnosis of Psychotic Disorders

DISEASE	CHARACTERISTICS
Schizophrenia	• **Presents in late teens–20s (slightly later in women), very strong genetic predisposition** • Often accompanied by **premorbid** sign, including poor school performance, poor emotional expression & lack of friends • Positive Sx = hallucinations (**more often auditory than visual**) & delusions • Negative Sx = lack of affect, alogia • Other Sx = disorganized behavior &/or speech • **Schizophrenia lasts ≥6 continuous mo** • **Schizophreniform disorder lasts 1–6 mo** • **Brief psychotic disorder lasts 1 day–1 mo**, with full recovery of baseline functioning—look for acute stressor, e.g., the death of a loved one
Other psychoses	• Schizoaffective disorder = meets criteria for mood disorders & schizophrenia • Delusional disorder = **nonbizarre delusions** (they could happen, e.g., pt's spouse is unfaithful, a person who is trying to kill the pt, etc.), without hallucinations, disorganized speech or disorganized behavior
Mood disorders	• Major depression & bipolar disorder can cause delusions & in extreme cases, hallucinations—can be difficult to differentiate from schizophrenia
Delirium	• Seen in pts with underlying illnesses, often in ICU (ICU psychosis) • **Patients are not orientated to person, place, time** • **Severity waxes & wanes even during the course of 1 day** • Resolves with treatment of underlying dz
Drugs	• LSD & PCP → predominantly visual, taste, touch, or olfactory hallucination • Cocaine & amphetamines → paranoid delusions & **classic sensation of bugs crawling on the skin (formication)** • Anabolic steroids → body-builder with bad temper, acne, shrunken testicles • Corticosteroids → psychosis/mood disturbances early in course of therapy
Medical	• Metabolic, endocrine, neoplastic & seizure dz can all cause psychosis • **Look for associated Si/Sx not explained by psychosis**, including focal neurologic findings, seizure, sensory/motor deficits, abnormal lab values

C. Tx
1. Hospitalization if voices tell pts to hurt themselves or others, or if condition is disabling to the point that pts cannot care for themselves
2. Pharmacologic therapy
   a. All antipsychotics act as dopamine-blockers
   b. Differences among agents relate to side-effect profile

TABLE 6-4   Antipsychotic Drugs

DRUG		ADVERSE EFFECTS[a]
Typical Antipsychotics[b]		
Chlorpromazine	Low potency	↑ anticholinergic effects, ↓ movement disorders
Haloperidol	High potency	↓ anticholinergic effects, ↑ movement disorders
Atypical Antipsychotics[b]		
Clozapine	For refractory dz	1% incidence of agranulocytosis mandates weekly CBC
Risperidone	First line	Minimal
Olanzapine	First line	Minimal

[a] Anticholinergic effects = dry mouth, blurry vision (miosis), urinary retention, constipation.
[b] Atypical agents have much lower incidence of movement disorders—see below.

TABLE 6-5   Antipsychotic-Associated Movement Disorders

DISORDER	TIME COURSE	CHARACTERISTICS
Acute dystonia	4 hr → 4 days	• Sustained muscle spasm anywhere in the body but often in neck (torticollis), jaw, or back (opisthotonos) • Tx = immediate IV diphenhydramine
Parkinsonism	4 days → 4 mo	• Cog-wheel rigidity, shuffling gait, resting tremor • Tx = benztropine (anticholinergic)
Tardive dyskinesia	4 mo → 4 yr	• Involuntary, irregular movements of the head, tongue, lips, limbs & trunk • Tx = immediately change medication or ↓ doses because effects are often permanent
Akathisia	Any time	• Subjective sense of discomfort → restlessness: pacing, sitting down & getting up • Tx = lower medication doses
Neuroleptic malignant syndrome	Any time	• Life-threatening muscle rigidity → fever, ↑ BP/HR, rhabdomyolysis appearing over 1–3 days • Can be easily misdiagnosed as ↑ psychotic Sx • Labs → ↑ WBC, ↑ creatine kinase, ↑ transaminases, ↑ plasma myoglobin, as well as myoglobinuria • Tx = supportive: immediately stop drug, give dantrolene (inhibits Ca release into cells), cool pt to prevent hyperpyrexia

    c. Compliance to drugs can be improved with **depot** form of haloperidol, which administers a month's supply of drug in 1 IM injection

  3. Psychotherapy can improve social functioning

    a. Behavioral Tx teaches social skills that allow pts to deal more comfortably with other people

    b. Family-oriented Tx teaches family members to act in more appropriate, positive fashion

D. Px

  1. Schizophrenia is a chronic, episodic dz, recovery from each relapse typically leaves pt below former baseline function

  2. Presence of negative Sx (e.g., flat affect) marks poor Px

  3. High-functioning prior to psychotic break marks better Px

IV. Anxiety Disorders

A. PANIC DISORDER

  1. Si/Sx = mimic MI: chest pain, palpitations, diaphoresis, nausea, marked anxiety, escalate for 10 min, remain for about 30 min (rarely longer than an hour)

  2. Occurs in younger pts (average age 25)—good way to distinguish from MI

  3. DDx = myocardial infarction, drug abuse (e.g., cocaine, amphetamines), phobias (see below)

  4. Dx is by exclusion of true medical condition & drug abuse

  5. Panic attacks are unexpected, so if pt consistently describes panic Sx in a specific setting, phobia is a more likely diagnosis

  6. Tx

a. TCAs (clomipramine & imipramine) are best studied
b. More recently SSRIs have been shown to have efficacy
c. Benzodiazepenes work immediately, have ↑ risk of addiction
d. Therefore, start benzodiazepene for immediate effects, add a TCA or SSRI, taper off the benzodiazepene as the other drugs kick in
e. Cognitive/behavior TX & **respiratory training** (to help patients recognize & overcome desire to hyperventilate) are helpful

B. Agoraphobia
1. Sx = fear of being in situations where it would be very difficult to get out of should a panic attack arise
2. Theorized that pts develop panic disorder because they've had enough unexpected attacks to know that it can come at any time—& wouldn't it be embarrassing if it happened while sitting in the mezzanine watching a sold-out performance of *Tosca*? (It would certainly be more interesting.)
3. Dx = clinical, look for evidence of social/occupational dysfunction
4. Tx (for phobias in general)
   a. β-blockers useful for prophylaxis in phobias related to performance
   b. **Exposure desensitization** = exposure to noxious stimulus in increments, while undergoing concurrent relaxation Tx

C. Obsessive Compulsive Disorder (OCD)
1. **Obsessions ≡ recurrent thought; compulsions ≡ recurrent act**
2. Sx = obsessive thought causes anxiety & the compulsion is a way of temporarily relieving that anxiety (e.g., pt worries whether he/she locked the door & going back to see it's locked relieves the anxiety), but because relief is only temporary the pt performs compulsion repeatedly
3. Obsessions commonly involve **cleanliness/contamination** (washing hands), doubt, symmetry (elaborate rituals for entering doorways, arranging books, etc.) & sex
4. Dx = pt should be disturbed by their obsessions & **should recognize their absurdity** in contrast to obsessive compulsive personality disorder, where pt sees nothing wrong with compulsion
5. Tx = SSRIs (first line) or clomipramine, psychotherapy in which the pt is literally forced to overcome their behavior

D. Posttraumatic Stress Disorder (PTSD)
1. Dx requires a traumatic, violent incident that effectively scars the person involved; the experiences of Vietnam vets are emblematic of this disorder
2. Sx
   a. **Pt relives the initial incident via conscious thoughts or dreams**
   b. Due to resultant subjective & physiologic distress, the pt avoids any precipitating stimuli & **hence often avoids public places & activities**
   c. Pt may suffer restricted emotional involvement/responses & may experience a detachment from others
   d. **Depression is common, look for moodiness, diminished interest in activities & difficulties with sleeping & concentrating**
3. DDx = **acute stress disorder**
   a. Dx also requires a traumatic incident, but Sx are more immediate (within 4 wk of the event) & limited in time (<4 wk)

b. The Sx are different; imagine being so traumatized that you are in a daze, where nothing seems real & you have trouble remembering what has happened (commonly seen in victims of sexual assault)

4. Tx
   a. Use of tricyclics (imipramine & amitriptyline) is well-supported by clinical trials, SSRIs have also been used
   b. **Beware of giving benzodiazepenes due to a high association of substance abuse with PTSD!**
   c. Psychotherapy takes two approaches
      1) Exposure therapy, the idea being to confront one's demons by "reliving" the experience (either step-wise or abruptly)
      2) Relaxation techniques, think of the two modalities as attacking the source vs. controlling the symptoms
5. Px = variable, but the predictive factors are similar to schizophrenia: abrupt Sx & strong premorbid functioning lead to better outcomes

E. GENERALIZED ANXIETY DISORDER

1. Sx = worry for most days for at least 6 mo, irritability, inability to concentrate, insomnia, fatigue, restlessness (just think of a medical student or intern preparing for the USMLE!)
2. DDx = specific anxieties, including separation anxiety disorder, anorexia nervosa, hypochondriasis
3. **Dx requires evidence of social dysfunction** (e.g., poor school grades, job stagnation, or marital strains) to rule out "normal" anxiety
4. Tx = psychotherapy due to chronicity of the problem
   a. Cognitive-behavioral Tx = teaching pt to recognize his/her worrying & find ways to respond to it through behavior & thought patterns
   b. **Biofeedback** & **relaxation** techniques, in particular, can help the pt deal with physical manifestations of anxiety, e.g., heart rate
   c. Pharmacotherapy includes buspirone or β-blockers (works for peripheral Sx, e.g., tachycardia, but not worry itself)

V. Personality Disorders

A. GENERAL CHARACTERISTICS

1. Sx = pervasive pattern of maladaptive behavior causing functional impairment, consistent behavior can often be traced back to childhood
2. Typically present to psychiatrists because behavior is causing significant problems for others, e.g., colleagues at work, spouse at home, **or for the medical staff in the inpatient or clinic setting (typical USMLE question)**
3. **Pts usually see nothing wrong with their behavior (ego-syntonic),** contrast with pts who recognize their hallucinations as abnormal (ego-dystonic)
4. Ego defenses
   a. Unconscious mental process that individuals resort to in order to quell inner conflicts & anxiety that are unacceptable to the ego
   b. Examples include "splitting" & "projection"
5. Tx = psychotherapy, medication used for peripheral Sx (e.g., anxiety)

B. CLUSTERS

1. **Cluster A** = paranoid, schizoid & schizotypal personalities, often thought of as **"weird"** or **"eccentric"**
2. **Cluster B** = borderline, antisocial, histrionic & narcissistic personalities, **"dramatic"** & **"aggressive"** personalities
3. **Cluster C** = avoidant, dependent & obsessive-compulsive personalities, **"shy"** & **"nervous"** personalities

C.

TABLE 6-6   Specific Personality Disorders

DISORDER	CHARACTERISTICS
Paranoid (Cluster A)	• Negatively misinterpret the actions, words, intentions of others • Often utilize **projection** as ego defense (attributing to other people impulses & thoughts that are unacceptable to their own selves) • **Do not hold fixed delusions** (delusional disorder), **nor do they experience hallucinations** (schizophrenia)
Schizoid (Cluster A)	• Socially withdrawn, introverted, with little external affect • Do not form close emotional ties with others (often feel no need) • Are, however, able to recognize reality
Schizotypal (Cluster A)	• **Believe in concepts not considered real by the rest of society (magic, clairvoyance)**, display the prototypal ego defense: **fantasy** • Not necessarily psychotic (can have brief psychotic episodes) • Like schizoids, they are often quite isolated socially • **Often related to schizophrenics (unlike other cluster A disorders)**
Antisocial (Cluster B)	• Violate the rights of others, break the law (e.g., theft, substance abuse) • Can also be quite seductive (particularly with the opposite sex) • **For Dx the pt must have exhibited the behavior by a certain age (15—think truancy) but must be a certain age (at least 18—adult)** • **A popular USLME topic; you may have to differentiate it from conduct disorder (bad behavior, but Dx of children/adolescents)**
Borderline (Cluster B)	• Volatile emotional lives, swing wildly between idealizing & devaluing other people: (**splitting** ego defense = people are very good or bad) • **Also commonly asked on USMLE**, typical scenario is a highly disruptive hospitalized pt; on interview, he (but usually she) says some nurses are incompetent & cruel but wildly praises others (including you) • Exhibit self-destructive behavior (scratching or cutting themselves) • Ability to **disassociate**: they simply "forget" negative affects/experiences by covering them with overly exuberant, seemingly positive behavior
Histrionic (Cluster B)	• Require the attention of everyone, use sexuality & physical appearance to get it, exaggerate their thoughts with dramatic but vague language • Utilize disassociation & **repression** (block feelings unconsciously)—don't confuse with **suppression** (feelings put aside consciously)
Narcissistic (Cluster B)	• Feel entitled—strikingly so—because they are the best & everyone else is inferior, handle criticism very poorly
Dependent (Cluster C)	• Can do little on their own, nor can they be alone
Avoidant (Cluster C)	• Feel inadequate & are extremely sensitive to negative comments • Reluctant to try new things (e.g., making friends) for fear of embarrassment
Obsessive-compulsive (Cluster C)	• Preoccupied with detail: rules, regulations, neatness • Isolation is a common ego-defense: putting up walls of self-restraint & detail-orientation that keep away any sign of emotional affect

D. OTHER EGO DEFENSES

1. Acting out = transforming unacceptable feeling into actions, often loud ones (tantrums)
2. Identification = patterning behavior after someone else's
3. Intellectualization = explaining away the unreasonable in the form of logic
4. Rationalization = making the unreasonable seem acceptable (e.g., upon being fired, you say you wanted to quit anyway)
5. Reaction formation = set aside unconscious feelings & express exact opposite feelings (show extra affection for someone you hate)
6. Regression = resorting to child-like behavior (often seen in the hospital)
7. Sublimation = taking instinctual drives (sex) & funneling that energy into a socially acceptable action (studying)

VI. Somatoform and Factitious Disorders

A. DEFINITIONS

1. Somatoform disorder = **lack of conscious manipulation of somatic Sx**
2. Factitious disorder = **consciously faking** or manipulating Sx for purpose of "assuming the sick role," **but not for material gain**
3. Malingering = consciously faking Sx **for purpose of material gain**

B. FACTITIOUS DISORDER

1. Pt may mimic any Sx, physical or psychological, to assume the sick role
2. **The patient is not trying to avoid work or win a compensation claim**
3. Munchausen syndrome = factitious disorder with predominantly physical (not psychologic) symptoms
4. Munchausen by proxy = pt claiming nonexistent symptoms in someone else under their care, e.g., parents bringing in their "sick" children
5. DDx = malingering
6. **HINT: the USLME will very likely present a scenario involving nurses or other health care workers as the pts (often involving an episode of apparent hypoglycemia), look for evidence of factitious disorder (e.g., low C-peptide levels suggesting insulin self-injection)**
7. Dx is by exclusion of real medical condition
8. Tx is nearly impossible; when confronted pts often become angry, deny everything, tell you how horrible you are & move on to someone else

C. SOMATOFORM DISORDERS

1. Somatization disorder
   a. Often female pts with problems starting before age 30, with history of frequent visits to the doctor for countless procedures & operations (often exploratory), & often history of abusive/failed relationships
   b. Sx = somatic complaints involving different systems, particularly gastrointestinal (nausea, diarrhea), neurologic (weakness) & sexual (irregular menses), with no adequate medical explanation on the basis of exam/lab findings
   c. Dx = rule out medical condition & material or psychologic gain
   d. Tx = **continuity of care**
      1) Schedule regular appointments so pt can express his or her Sx
      2) Perform physical exam but do not order laboratory tests

3) As the therapeutic bond strengthens, strive to establish awareness in the pt that psychologic factors are involved & if successful in doing so, arrange a psychiatric consult—but if done too early or aggressively, pt may be reluctant or resentful

2. Conversion disorder
   a. Sx are neurologic, not multisystem, & are not consciously faked
   b. Sensory deficits often fail to correspond to any known pathway, e.g., a stocking-&-glove sensory deficit that begins precisely at the wrist, studies will reveal intact neurologic pathways, & pts rarely get hurt, e.g., patients who are "blind" will not be colliding into the wall
   c. Dx requires identification of a stressor that precipitated the Sx as well as exclusion of any adequate medical explanation (**NOTE:** in some studies 50% of pts who received this Dx were eventually found to have nonpsychiatric causes of illness, e.g., brain tumors & multiple sclerosis. Bummer!)
   d. Tx = supportive, Sx resolve within days (less than a month), **do not tell pt that they are imagining their Sx, but suggest that psychotherapy may help with their distress**
   e. Px = the more abrupt the symptoms, the more easily identified the stressor & the higher the premorbid function, the better the outcome

3. Hypochondriasis
   a. Sx = preoccupation with disease, pt does not complain of a large number of Sx but misinterprets them as evidence of something serious
   b. Tx = regular visits to MD with every effort not to order lab tests or procedures, psychotherapy should be presented as a way of coping with stress, **again, do not tell patients that they are imagining their Sx**

4. Body dysmorphic disorder
   a. Sx = concern with body, **pt usually picks 1 feature, often on the face, & imagines deficits that other people do not see;** if there are slight imperfections, the pt exaggerates them excessively
   b. Look for a significant amount of emotional & functional impairment
   c. Tx = SSRIs may be helpful in some cases, surgery is not recommended

VII. Child and Adolescent Psychiatry

A. AUTISM & ASPERGER'S SYNDROME

1. Autism is the prototypic **pervasive developmental disorder**, pervasive because the disorder encompasses so many areas of development: language, social interaction, emotional reactivity
2. The expression "living in his own world" captures this tragic disorder; the autistic child fails to develop normal interactions with others & seems to be responding to internal stimuli
3. Si/Sx
   a. Becomes evident before 3 yr old, often much earlier
   b. The baby does not seem to be concerned with the mother's presence or absence & makes no eye contact, as the baby becomes older, deficiencies in language (including repetitive phrases & made-up vocabulary) & abnormal behavior become more obvious

       c. Look for the behavioral aspects; the child often has a strange, persistent fascination with specific, seemingly mundane objects (vacuum cleaners, sprinklers) & may show stereotyped, ritualistic movements (e.g., spinning around)

       d. Autistic children have an inordinate need for constancy

    4. Think of Asperger's syndrome as autism **without** the language impairment

    5. **Contrary to older thought, poor parenting/bonding is not a cause of autism!— parents need reassurance about this**

B. DEPRESSION

    1. Depression may present slightly differently depending on the age group

       a. Preschool children may be hyperactive & aggressive

       b. Adolescents show boredom, irritability, or openly antisocial behaviors

    2. One should still look for the same symptoms as described for adult depression: depressed mood, anhedonia, neurovegetative changes, etc.

    3. Tx

       a. Unlike adult depression, the use of antidepressants is much more controversial, with far less data supporting its effectiveness

       b. **Note:** children's mood disorders are especially sensitive to psychosocial stressors, so family therapy is a major consideration

C. SEPARATION ANXIETY

    1. Look for a child that seems a bit too attached to his parents or any other figures in his life; the child is worried that something will happen to these beloved figures or that some terrible event will separate them

    2. Si/Sx = sleep disturbances (nightmares, inability to fall asleep alone) & somatic Sx during times of separation (headaches, stomach upset at school)

    3. Tx = desensitizing therapy (gradually increasing the hours spent away from Mom & Dad), in some cases imipramine is used

D. OPPOSITIONAL DEFIANT/CONDUCT DISORDER

    1. Differentiate the 2 by words & action

    2. Oppositional defiant disorder Si/Sx ("bark")

       a. Pts are argumentative, temperamental & defiant, more so with people they know well (they may seem harmless to you)

       b. Big surprise that they are often friendless & perform poorly in school

    3. Conduct disorder Si/Sx ("bite")

       a. Pts bully others, start fights, may show physical cruelty to animals, violate/destroy other people's property (fire-setting), steal things & stay out past curfews or run away

       b. They do not feel guilty for any of this

       c. A glimpse into the child's family life often reveals pathology in the form of substance abuse or negligence

    4. Oppositional defiant disorder may lead to conduct disorder, but the two are not synonymous

    5. Tx = providing a setting with strict rules & expected consequences for violations of them

E. ATTENTION-DEFICIT HYPERACTIVITY DISORDER (ADHD)

    1. Si/Sx can be divided into the components suggested by their name

a. Attention-deficit Sx = inability to focus or carry out tasks completely & being easily distracted by random stimuli

b. Hyperactivity Sx are more outwardly motor; the child is unable to sit still, talks excessively & can never "wait his turn" in group games

2. Dx requires that Sx have been present since before 7 yr old
3. Tx = methylphenidate, an amphetamine

a. Parents & teachers notice improvement in the child's behavior

b. Because of concerns about impeding the child's growth, drug holidays are often taken (e.g., no meds over weekends or vacations)

c. Children with ADHD also do better with an extremely structured environment featuring consistent rules & punishments

d. Px is variable, some children show remissions of their hyperactivity, but quite a few continue to show Sx through adolescents & adulthood; children with ADHD have a higher likelihood of developing conduct disorders or antisocial personalities

F. TOURETTE'S DISORDER

1. Tics are involuntary, stereotyped, repetitive movements or vocalizations
2. **Tourette's Dx requires both a motor tic & a vocal tic present for ≥1 yr**
3. **The vocal tics are often obscene or socially unacceptable (copralalia)**, which is a cause of extreme embarrassment to the patient
4. Tx = haloperidol, effective, but not required in mild cases
5. Psychotherapy is unhelpful in treating the tics per se, but can be helpful in dealing with the emotional stress caused by the disorder

G. ANOREXIA & BULEMIA NERVOSA

1. Eating disorders are by no means limited to children—but because they often start in adolescence, they are worth mentioning here
2. In both disorders exists a profound disturbance in body image & its role in the person's sense of self-worth
3. Anorexia Si/Sx

a. **By definition anorexic patients are below their expected body weight** because they do not eat enough, often creating elaborate rituals for disposing of food in meal settings, e.g., cutting meat into tiny pieces & rearranging them constantly on the plate

b. **Amenorrhea occurs 2° to weight loss**

4. Bulemia Si/Sx

a. More common than anorexia, **characterized by binge eating**: consuming huge amounts of food over a short period, with a perceived lack of control

b. This may be accompanied by active purging (vomiting, laxative use)

c. **Unlike anorexics, who by definition have decreased body weight, bulemics often have a normal appearance**

d. **Abrasions over the knuckles** (from jamming the fingers into the mouth to induce vomiting) & **dental erosion** suggest the Dx

5. Tx

a. Hospitalization may be required for anorexia to restore the pt's weight to a safe level, which the pt will often resist

b. Because of vomiting, monitoring serum electrolytes is essential; the most worrisome consequence is cardiac dysfunction—as exemplified by singer Karen Carpenter, whose battle with anorexia led to her untimely death

c. Psychotherapy is the mainstay of Tx for both diseases

6. Overall, anorexia nervosa has a relatively poor prognosis, with persistent preoccupations with food & weight; bulimics fare slightly better

VIII. Drugs of Abuse

A. INTRODUCTION

1. Always consider drug abuse when a pt's life seems to be going down the tubes, e.g., deteriorating family relations, work performance, financial stability

2. Generally (with many exceptions), withdrawal Sx are the opposite of intoxication, dysphoria is characteristic of all of them—**withdrawal is a sign of physiologic dependence**

3. Individual drugs

TABLE 6-7   Drug Intoxications and Withdrawal

DRUG	INTOXICATION SI/SX	WITHDRAWAL
Alcohol	Disinhibition, ↓ cognition Screen for alcoholism with CAGE • C–feeling the need to **cut** down • A–feeling **annoyed** when asked about drinking • G–feeling **guilty** for drinking • E–need a drink in the morning **(eye-opener)**	Tremor, seizures, delirium tremens (high mortality! → prevent with benzo's)
Cocaine/Amphetamine	Agitation, irritability, ↓ appetite, formication, ↑ or ↓ BP & HR, cardiac arrhythmia or infarction, stroke, seizure, nosebleeds	Hypersomnolence, dysphoria ↑ appetite
Heroin (opioids)	Intense, fleeting euphoria, drowsy, slurred speech, ↓ memory, pupillary constriction, ↓ respiration **The triad of ↓ consciousness, pinpoint pupils & respiratory depression should always lead to a suspicion of opioids**	Nausea/vomiting, pupillary dilation & insomnia
Benzodiazepine & barbiturates	Respiratory & cardiac depression	Agitation, anxiety, delirium
Phencyclidine (PCP)	Intense psychosis, violence, rhabdomyolysis, hyperthermia	
LSD	Sensation is enhanced, colors are richer, music more profound, tastes heightened	

IX. Miscellaneous Disorders

A. DISORDERS OF SEXUALITY & GENDER IDENTITY

1. Sexual identity is based on biology, e.g., men have testes

2. Gender identity is based on self-perception, e.g., biological male perceives himself as a male

3. **Children have a firm conception of their gender identity very early (before age 3)**

4. Sexual orientation is who the person is attracted to; **remember that homosexuality is not a psychiatric disorder** (it used to be, until taken off the DSM in the 1970s) & that treating crises of sexual orientation should focus on accepting one's orientation, not changing it to conform to social "norms"

B. DISASSOCIATIVE DISORDER (MULTIPLE PERSONALITY DISORDER)

1. This was a hot diagnosis in the late 1970s (replaced in 1980s by borderline personality) & a perennial favorite of the movies (think: *Three Faces of Eve*, *Sybil*, & more recently, *Primal Fear*). The older name says it all: a patient seemingly possesses different personalities that can each take control at a given time. A patient's history may give some history of childhood trauma, e.g., abuse. Treatment focuses on gradual integration of these personalities.
2. The main differentials are **dissociative amnesia** & **dissociative fugue**. Amnesia is a syndrome of forgetting a great deal of personal information; fugue refers to the syndrome of sudden travel to another place, with inability to remember the past & confusion of present identity. *Neither case involves shifting between different identities.*

C. ADJUSTMENT DISORDER

1. This refers to any behavioral or emotional Sx that occur in response to stressful life events in excess of what is normal
2. Obviously has a catch-all quality to it; **this will be a frequent answer option on the USMLE**
3. **Dx requires the Sx to come within 3 mo of the stressor** (so they do not have to be immediate) & **they must disappear within 6 mo of the disappearance of the stressor**
4. Bereavement may seem to be a type of adjustment disorder (the stressor being death), but they are separate diagnoses
5. Depending on the setting, adjustment disorder may appear as depression or anxiety—so how to tell the difference? It isn't easy, but remember: **axis I disorders such as major depression & generalized anxiety take precedence**

D. IMPULSIVE-CONTROL DISORDERS

1. Pt is unable to resist the drive to perform certain actions **harmful to themselves or others**
2. Note the emotional response: these individuals **feel anxiety before the action & gratification afterward**
3. *Intermittent explosive disorder*
   a. Discrete episodes of aggressive behavior far in excess of any possible stressor
   b. The key term is **episodic**; antisocial personalities also commit aggressive behaviors, but their aggression is present between outbursts of such behavior
4. *Kleptomania*: the impulse to steal
   a. The object of theft is not needed for any reason (monetary or otherwise)
   b. The kleptomaniac often feels guilty after stealing
5. *Pyromania*: purposeful fire-setting
   a. There is often a fascination with fire itself that distinguishes this from the antisocial personality/conduct disorders, where the fire-setting is purposeful, e.g., revenge, & not the failure to resist an impulse
6. *Trichotillomania*: hair-pulling, resulting in observable hair loss

PSYCHIATRY

Psychiatry Case Scenario

A 22-year-old female college student presents with complaints of 3 months of intermittent headaches. History reveals no particular pattern to the headaches and no past medical problems. She denies any medication or drug use. On further questioning, the patient admits having difficulties sleeping for the past month and says she has gone days without eating a full meal. She can find no activity she is able to enjoy these days. She works as an intern in a publishing firm and says she will spend hours reading the same page without remembering any of it. One of her supervisors has recently told her that she had better "get her act together soon."

Physical exam reveals normal body habitus, with appropriate body weight, and no significant abnormalities, including on the skin exam.

1. Given the available information, the most likely diagnosis is:
   a) Adjustment disorder
   b) Bipolar disorder
   c) Major depressive episode
   d) Anorexia nervosa
   e) Heroin abuse

While on the inpatient psychiatry service you are asked to consult on a 30-year-old female with pneumonia who has refused blood draws, engaged in shouting matches with certain nursing staff, and at times yanked out her IVs. When you see the patient, she is enthusiastic and charming. You ask her if she is experiencing any difficulties, and she tells you that the day nurse assigned to her is irrational and cruel and inflicts intentional pain on her when placing IV lines. The night nurse, on the other hand, is "fantastic"; in fact, she plans to write a letter of commendation to human resources. She is eating and sleeping without disruption, except for that "idiotic nurse in the morning who yanks me awake for no reason." When you ask about the scars on her arms, she says vaguely that she was involved in several accidents. Then she takes your hands vigorously and tells you, "I know that you must be really smart and you're going to take good care of me!"

Mental status exam reveals proper orientation to person, place, and time, with no gross cognitive impairments and no impaired reality testing.

2. The patient is exhibiting traits most suggestive of:
   a) Bipolar disorder
   b) Borderline personality disorder
   c) Histrionic personality disorder
   d) Delirium
   e) Schizophrenia

You are evaluating a 32-year-old man in the ER. He is lying on the gurney, in obvious discomfort. He tells you that his neck is stiff and "stuck in this position." You see that his head is turned to his left side and, indeed, appears quite rigid. He denies any history of trauma or headache, and says only it started recently when he began a new medication. He does not know what it was called, but he says that the doctor had given it to him to "stop the voices in my head."

3. What medication would be of most assistance in relieving the patient's symptoms?
   a) Diphenhydramine
   b) Haloperidol
   c) Fluphenazine
   d) Fluoxetine

You are the psychiatry resident covering the ER when an 18-year-old male is brought in by his parents after he began shouting out of his bedroom window late at night. The young man insists that a satellite orbiting over his parents' house has been stealing his brain waves and transmitting them to CIA headquarters. He says that he can hear the CIA agents laughing at him inside his head. Upon discussion with the parents, you find out that although the patient performed very well academically for the first 3 years of high school, frequently garnering honors, this year his grades have been declining for months. He has become more and more reclusive, and for nearly 8 months has been complaining to his parents about this CIA conspiracy to read his thoughts. His parents are at a total loss and are convinced the boy is heavily into drugs, although they have no evidence of this and have never seen him with any drug paraphernalia. You return to the boy's gurney, where you find him shouting obscenities at his nurse. He is unable to answer direct questions, losing himself in long tangents riddled with compound words that make no sense to you. His urine toxicology screen comes back negative.

4. What is your acute treatment?
   a) Haloperidol
   b) Valium
   c) Reassurance to the patient and his parents
   d) Psychotherapy
   e) Clozapine

5. What do you tell the parents about their son's prognosis?
   a) 50% survival at 5 years
   b) Minimal chance of disease control with medications, so long-term hospitalization is required
   c) Prognosis varies with each patient, but symptomatic control with medications and psychotherapy is often achievable
   d) Disease will completely remit on its own

The patient becomes more oriented over a 3-week period on haloperidol. He is now lucid and has reasonable insight into his condition. He is discharged to home and comes back to see you for follow-up over the next several years. Gradually you begin to notice the onset of tardive dyskinesia in the patient.

6. What are the signs of tardive dyskinesia?

   a) Prolonged dystonic reactions

   b) Slowed reaction time and movements

   c) Involuntary limb and facial movements

   d) Shuffling gait, parkinsonian rigidity

   e) Involuntary shouting of obscenities

7. What action should you take now?

   a) Order prn diphenhydramine

   b) Order prn benztropine

   c) Stop all antipsychotic medications

   d) Change from haloperidol to olanzapine

   e) Lower the dose of haloperidol

A 46-year-old female is referred to your rheumatology practice by her primary care physician. She has a history of rheumatoid arthritis, which is being inadequately treated currently. Upon entering the exam room to meet the patient for the first time, you are taken aback when the patient's first words to you are a very dirty limerick. The patient explodes into laughter and then regales you with several other maladjusted jokes. You try, gently at first, to steer the conversation back to her medical problems, but every time you try to speak she hurriedly interrupts you and chatters away on a tangential subject. Suddenly she is telling you about affairs she is currently having with three different married men in her apartment complex. She also says she lost $5,000 at Las Vegas the prior weekend. You slip your hand into your pocket and press a button on your beeper, which causes it to sound. Granted an excuse, you beat a hasty retreat out of the room and hurry to your office phone. You call the referring physician and demand an explanation for this patient's craziness.

8. What diagnosis does the referring physician tell you the patient has?

   a) Schizophrenia

   b) Histrionic personality disorder

   c) Antisocial personality disorder

   d) Habitual marijuana abuser

   e) Bipolar disorder

A 73-year-old female sees you for the first time since her husband of 46 years died about 1 month ago. You note that she moves very slowly and that she appears sad. She has bags under her eyes and her face appears sunken-in. She confirms that she has not been eating well nor sleeping normally recently. She has no energy and admits to feeling depressed. She denies any suicidal ideations or hopelessness.

9. What is your diagnosis?

   a) Major depressive episode

   b) Major depressive disorder

   c) Dysthymic disorder

d) Normal bereavement

e) Dementia

Four months later the patient returns to see you. She has gained 12 pounds in the interim, although she says her appetite is still diminished. She is constantly fatigued and depressed and does not know what to do. She now admits to having suicidal ideations. She doesn't even have the energy to get out of bed on most days. She also complains of constipation. You note that her heart rate is 60 and regular. She moves very slowly, and her voice is husky, as if she has to struggle to bring herself to talk.

10. What is your next step in management?

a) Blood tests

b) Prescribe an antidepressant

c) Refer for psychotherapy

d) Nothing, this is still normal bereavement

e) Prescribe a laxative

Answers

1. **c)** The hallmarks of depression are either a depressed mood—which the patient does not admit to here—and/or anhedonia, which is revealed in her inability to enjoy activities. She also displays neurovegetative signs (problems with sleep and appetite) and inability to concentrate. The tactful intervention of her supervisor suggests impaired occupational function. Adjustment disorder can present with a depression-like picture, but note that there is no identifiable stressor to which the patient could be adjusting. Bipolar disorder cannot be diagnosed without history of manic or hypomanic episodes. Anorexia is ruled out by her normal height and weight. Although chronic heroin use can lead to the symptoms described by the patient, there are no physical exam findings, including weight loss, skin abscesses, or track marks, that would suggest this diagnosis.

2. **b)** The patient is showing the classic behavior of borderline personality, **splitting**, in which certain individuals are either idealized (the night nurse) or devalued (day nurse). Bipolar disorder is unlikely due to the lack of sleep disturbance, and the absence of elated mood, increased energy, or racing thoughts. Histrionic personality disorder is the major differential here, and the key to choosing borderline personality disorder is the splitting. **Splitting is not entirely specific to borderline personalities, but in the USMLE setting, it is.** Delirium is ruled out by the patient's orientation to person, place, and time. Schizophrenic patients must show impaired reality testing, which our patient does not.

3. **a)** The patient is exhibiting torticollis, one form of an acute dystonic reaction that occurs in certain individuals who are starting antipsychotic medication. The last thing he needs is more antipsychotic medication. Fluoxetine is an antidepres-

sant—not much help here. Diphenhydramine is an anticholinergic that is most often used to treat this condition.

4. **a)** This patient is clearly having a psychotic break. The only other possible explanation, that of drug abuse, is ruled out by the negative tox screen. The boy is at the right age (late teens), has had premorbid indications (gradual isolation and diminishment of performance in school), and has delusions (e.g., conspiracy theory and brain-wave stealing satellite) and hallucinations (CIA agents laughing in his head). Valium will do little aside from sedation, and reassurance and psychotherapy are inappropriate for an acute psychotic episode. Because of the risk of agranulocytosis, clozapine should be reserved as a second-line agent for schizophrenia refractory to other agents.

5. **c)** Because the patient has been exhibiting bizarre symptoms for more than 6 months, schizophrenia, and not brief psychotic disorder, is the appropriate diagnosis. While patients with a brief pyschotic disorder, triggered by an acute, traumatic event, can return to fully functioning baseline without further psychosis, schizophrenia is a nonremitting disorder. However, the course of schizophrenia is variable, and with antipsychotic medications and psychotherapy many patients can live productive lives.

6. **c)** Tardive dyskinesia is an involuntary tic-like motor disturbance often affecting the limbs or face. Classically, these patients involuntarily blink or smack their lips together.

7. **d)** Since the newer, atypical antipsychotics like olanzapine and risperidone have minimal to no movement disorder adverse effects, these drugs should be utilized instead of haloperidol in this patient. Because tardive dyskinesia is irreversible, and there is no cure, the treatment is prevention. Thus, it would have been reasonable to try olanzapine as a first-line agent in this patient rather than haloperidol. Regardless, once tardive dyskinesia has begun, the switch should be made.

8. **e)** This patient has classic signs and symptoms of the mania seen in bipolar disorder. Although to make the diagnosis of bipolar disorder there should be evidence of episodes of depression as well, of the choices given, only bipolar disorder makes sense. In particular, the hypersexuality, the pressured speech, and the throwing away of large sums of money over short periods of time are all classic signs of mania. Although amphetamine abuse can mimic manic signs and symptoms, marijuana certainly does not.

9. **d)** Only time is able to separate the diagnosis of depression from normal bereavement. Within 1 month of a loved one's death, signs of severe depression are considered normal bereavement. If severe depression continues beyond 2 months, the diagnosis must be reconsidered.

10. **a)** The patient's depression is clearly pathologic at this point, 6 months after her husband's death. One's first instinct is to jump at the diagnosis of major

depressive disorder and prescribe medications or therapy. However, before this is done, medical causes of depression should be ruled out. Particularly in an elderly patient, depression, constipation, lack of energy, weight gain, and husky sounding voice should make one think of the possibility of hypothyroidism. Thus, blood work is indicated here.

7. Neurology

Brad Spellberg

I. Infarct

A. TERMINOLOGY
1. Stroke ≡ a sudden, nonconvulsive focal neurologic deficit
2. TIAs ≡ deficit lasting ≤24 hr (usually <1 hr) & resolve completely
3. Emboli sources = **carotid atheroma (most common)**, cardiac & fat emboli, marantic endocarditis (metastasizing cancer cells)
4. Lacunar infarct = small infarct in deep gray matter, strongly associated with hypertension & atherosclerosis
5. Watershed infarcts occur at border of areas supplied by different arteries (e.g., MCA-ACA), often following prolonged hypotension

B. PRESENTATION (See Figures 7-1 and 7-2)
1.

TABLE 7-1   Presentation of Stroke

SIGN/SYMPTOM	ARTERY	REGION (LOBE)
Amaurosis fugax (monocular blind)	Carotid (emboli)	Ophthalmic artery
Drop attack/Vertigo/CN palsy/coma	Vertebrobasilar (emboli)	Brain stem
Aphasia	Middle cerebral	Dominant frontal or temporal[a]
Sensory neglect & apraxia[b]	Middle cerebral	Nondominant frontal or temporal[a]
Hemiplegia	Middle or anterior cerebral	Contralateral parietal
Urinary incontinence & grasp reflex	Middle or anterior cerebral	Frontal
Homonymous hemianopia	Middle or posterior cerebral	Temporal or occipital

[a] Dominant = left in 99% of right-handers & >50% of left-handers.
[b] Apraxia = patient cannot follow command even if it is understood & the pt is physically capable of it.

2. Wernicke's aphasia (temporal lobe lesion) = receptive, pt speaks fluently but words do not make sense: **Wernicke's is wordy**
3. Broca's aphasia (frontal lobe lesion) = expressive, pt is unable to verbalize: **Broca's is broken**
4. Edema occurs 2–4 days postinfarct, watch for this clinically (e.g., ↓ consciousness, projectile vomiting, pupillary changes)
5. Decorticate (cortical lesion) posturing → flexion of arms
6. Decerebrate (midbrain or lower lesion) posturing → arm extension

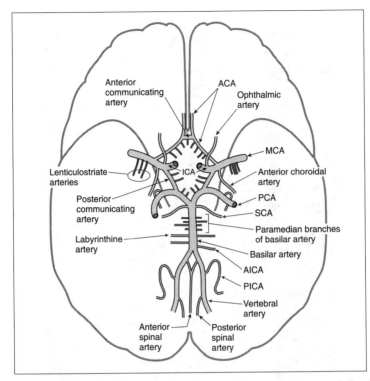

FIGURE 7-1   Circle of Willis. ACA = anterior cerebral artery; AICA = anterior inferior cerebellar artery; ICA = internal carotid artery; MCA = middle cerebral artery; PCA = posterior cerebral artery; PICA = posterior inferior cerebellar artery; SCA = superior cerebellar artery.
(Reproduced with permission from Pritchard TC and Alloway KD. Medical Neuroscience. Madison, Connecticut: Fence Creek Publishing, 1999: 78. © Fence Creek Publishing, LLC.)

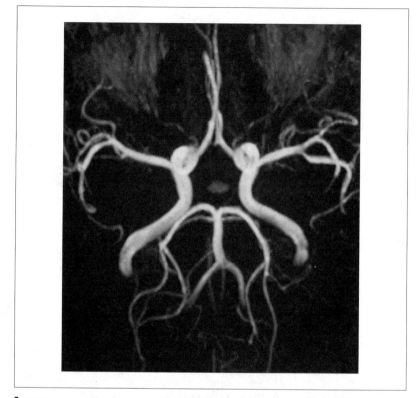

FIGURE 7-2 Magnetic resonance angiography (MRA). The arteries at the base of the brain, the circle of Willis, are very well shown by MRA without the use of any contrast agent.

C. DIFFERENTIAL DIAGNOSIS

1. Stroke, seizure, neoplasm, encephalitis, multiple sclerosis
2. Stroke causes = 35% local atheroembolic, 30% cardiac, 15% lacunar, 10% parenchymal hemorrhage, 10% subarachnoid hemorrhage, ≤1% other (e.g., vasculitis, temporal arteritis, etc.)
3. Dx = CT for acute, MRI for subacute infarct &/or hemorrhage (See Figure 7-3)
4. Rule out seizure → EEG, loss of bowel/bladder control & tongue injury
5. Lumbar puncture to rule out encephalitis & rule in intracranial bleed

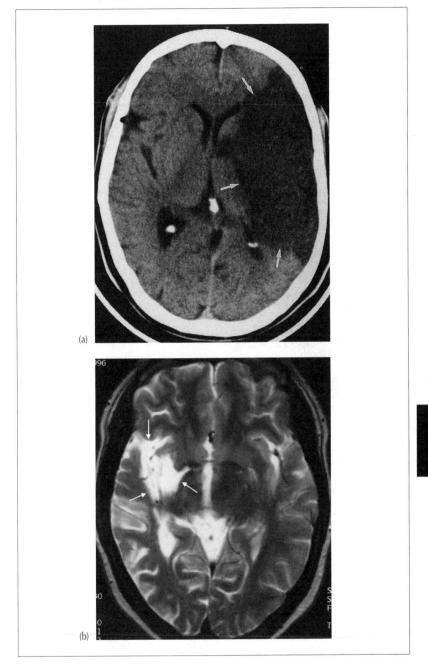

(a)

(b)

FIGURE 7-3 Cerebral infarction. (a) Unenhanced CT scan showing a low-density region of the left cerebral hemisphere conforming to the distribution of the middle cerebral artery (arrows). (b) MRI scan of another patient with a right middle cerebral artery territory infarct. The infarcted area (arrows) shows patchy high-signal intensity on this T2-weighted image. The arrows point to the anterior and posterior extent of the infarcted brain tissue.

D. TREATMENT

1. tPA within 3–6 hours of onset (preferably 1 hr) for occlusive dz only!
2. **Intracranial bleeding is an absolute contraindication to tPA use!**
3. Correct underlying disorder, e.g., hyperlipidemia, hypertension, diabetes, valve abnormality, coagulopathy, atrial fibrillation
4. For embolic strokes give aspirin/warfarin anticoagulation for prophylaxis
5. If carotid is 70% occluded & patient has Sx → endarterectomy

E. PROGNOSIS

1. 20–40% mortality at 30 days (20% atheroemboli, 40% bleed)
2. Less than 1/3 patients achieve full recovery of lifestyle
3. Atheroembolic strokes recur at 10%/yr

II. Infection & Inflammation

A. MENINGITIS

1. Si/Sx = **meningismus** (stiff neck so patient cannot touch chin to chest), fever, headache, no focal neurologic findings (would signify encephalitis)
2. CSF differential for meningitis

TABLE 7-2　CSF Findings in Meningitis

	CELLS	PROTEIN	GLUCOSE
Bacterial	↑ neutrophils	↑↑	↓↓ (≤2/3 serum)
Viral	↑ mononuclear	± ↑	Nml
Subacute	↑ mononuclear	↑	↓

3. Can be acute, subacute, chronic presentations
4. Acute
   a. Send CSF for Gram's stain, bacterial cultures, HSV PCR
   b. Treat all patients empirically by age until specific tests return

TABLE 7-3　Empiric Therapy for Meningitis by Age

AGE	REGIMEN	COMMON ETIOLOGIES
Neonates (≤1 mo)	**Ampicillin + cefotaxime**	Streptococcus agalactiae, Listeria, Escherichia coli
Children to teens	**Cefotaxime ± vancomycin**[a]	Streptococcus pneumoniae, Neisseria meningitidis
Adults	**Cefotaxime ± vancomycin**[a]	S. pneumoniae by far most common

• Add acyclovir to any pt with possible HSV.
[a] Only if resistant Streptococcus common in area.

c. Of viral causes, only HSV (acyclovir) & HIV (AZT) can be treated—otherwise treatment is supportive

d.

TABLE 7-4   Bacterial Meningitis

ORGANISM	PATIENTS	CHARACTERISTICS	TREATMENT
Streptococcus pneumoniae	**#1 cause in adults:** old age, asplenia, poor health predispose	Can progress from otitis media, sinusitis, or bacteremia	Pen G (if susceptible) Second line = cefotaxime, third line = vancomycin
Neisseria meningitidis	≥1 yr old or in adults in epidemics in close populations (military barracks)	**Petechiae on trunk, legs, conjunctivae**—beware of Waterhouse-Friderichsen syndrome (adrenal infarct)	Pen G Rifampin prophylaxis for close contacts
Hemophilus influenzae type B	Formerly #1 cause in children, until vaccine	Now rare, but can cause epiglottitis	Cefotaxime
Streptococcus agalactiae	**#1 cause in neonates**	Acquired at birth	Ampicillin
Escherichia coli	Common in neonates	Acquired at birth	Cefotaxime
Listeria monocytogenes	Elderly/neonates, AIDS, diabetes, steroids	Difficult CSF Gram's stain/ Cx, Dx → blood Cx	Ampicillin
Staphylococcus aureus	Trauma/Neurosurgery	Wound infxn from skin	Oxacillin/Vancomycin

5. Subacute/chronic meningitis
   a. Si/Sx = per acute but evolves over wk → mo, +/– fever
   b. DDx = fungal, mycobacterial, noninfectious, other rare dzs
   c. Send CSF for fungal Cx, cytology, India Ink, TB PCR
   d. Fungal meningitis
      1) DDx = *Cryptococcus, Coccidioides,* other more rare dz
      2) ***Cryptococcus* commonly seen in AIDS**
         a) **India Ink stain will show *Cryptococcus* in CSF**
         b) **Most sensitive test is ↑ LP opening pressure**
      3) ***Coccidioides* blastocysts seen on CSF cytology**
      4) Tx = IV amphotericin B (intrathecal may be necessary)
   e. TB meningitis
      1) Usually occurs in elderly by reactivation, grave Px
      2) Dx is made by TB PCR of the CSF
      3) Tx = **RIPE: R**ifampin + **I**NH + **P**yrazinamide + **E**thambutol
   f. Other causes = sarcoid, cancer, collagen-vascular dz, drug reactions

B. ENCEPHALITIS

1. Si/Sx = similar to meningitis, but focal findings are evident

TABLE 7-5 Encephalitis

ETIOLOGY	DISEASE	SI/SX	TX/PX
Toxoplasmosis	1) Transplacental congenital dz → hydrocephalus/ mental retardation	**Multiple ring enhancing lesions → focal neurologic deficits**	Bactrim
	2) Adults exposed via cat feces get dz if immunosuppressed—**Toxo is the #1 CNS lesion in AIDS**	Toxoplasmosis antibody test very sensitive	Prophylax if CD4 ≤200/μL
HSV	**#1 cause of viral encephalitis**	**Olfactory hallucinations, bloody CSF, personality changes** EEG/MRI → temporal lobe dz	Acyclovir
Syphilis	**Meningovascular disease** Parenchymal disease:	**Argyll-Robertson pupil**[a]	
	1) Tabes dorsalis = bilateral spinal cord demyelination	Pain, hypotonia, ↓ tone, ↓ DTRs ↓ proprioception, incontinence	IV penicillin
	2) Dementia paralytica = cortical atrophy, neuron loss, gliosis	Sx = psychosis, dementia, personality change	
PML[b]	Usually in AIDS, caused by JC virus	Diffuse neurologic dz	None, death inevitable

[a] Pupil accommodates but doesn't react to direct light.
[b] PML = progressive multifocal leukoencephalopathy.

C. ABSCESS

1. Si/Sx = headache, fever, ↑ ICP, focal neurologic findings
2. Risk factors = congenital R-L shunt (lung filtration bypassed), otitis, paranasal sinusitis, metastases, trauma & immunosuppression
3. Anaerobes & aerobes, gram-positive cocci & gram-negative rods can cause
4. Tx = antibiotics ⊕ **surgical drainage if >3 cm or if persists**
5. **Brain abscesses are invariably fatal if untreated**
6. Helminthic infections
   a. Cysticercosis (*Taenia solium*)
      1) Eggs transmitted by fecal-oral route
      2) **Encephalitis in Latin American immigrant is due to neurocysticercosis until proven otherwise**
      3) Tx = praziquantel ⊕ steroids (dead cyst → inflammation)
   b. Hydatid cysts (*Echinococcus*)
      1) Acquired by dog feces, can cause focal Sx & seizure
      2) If cysts rupture they can cause fatal anaphylaxis
      3) Tx = careful surgical excystation, mebendazole

III. Demyelinating Diseases

A. MULTIPLE SCLEROSIS (MS)

1. Unknown etiology, but ⊕ genetic & environmental predispositions, ↑ common in pts who lived first decade of life in northern latitudes

2. Si/Sx = relapsing asymmetric limb weakness, ↑ DTRs, nystagmus, tremor, scanning speech, paresthesias, optic neuritis, ⊕ Babinski sign
3. Dx = history, MRI, lumbar puncture
4. MRI → periventricular plaques, multiple focal demyelination scattered in brain & spinal cord (**lesions disseminated in space & time**)
5. **Lumbar puncture → ↑ CSF immunoglobulins manifested as multiple oligoclonal bands on electrophoresis**
6. Tx = interferon-β, may induce prolonged remissions in some pts
7. Px
   a. Variable types of disease, long remissions sometimes seen
   b. But can progressively decline → death in only a few years

B. **GUILLAIN-BARRÉ SYNDROME**
1. Acute autoimmune demyelinating dz involving peripheral nerves
2. **Si/Sx = muscle weakness & paralysis ascending up from lower limbs, ↓ reflexes, can cause bilateral facial nerve palsy**
3. **Most often preceded by gastroenteritis (classically *Campylobacter jejuni*),** *Mycoplasma* or viral infection, immunization, or allergic reactions
4. Dx = Hx of antecedent stimuli (see above), CSF → **albumin-cytologic dissociation** (CSF protein ↑↑↑ without ↑ in cells seen)
5. Tx = plasmapheresis, IVIG, intubation for respiratory failure
6. Px is excellent for 80–90% of patients, will spontaneously regress
7. Respiratory failure & death can occur in remainder

C. **CENTRAL PONTINE MYELINOLYSIS**
1. Diamond-shaped region of demyelination in basis pontis
2. **Due to rapid correction of hyponatremia & in liver dz**
3. No Tx once condition has begun
4. Coma or death is a common outcome

IV. Metabolic & Nutritional Disorders

A. **CARBON MONOXIDE POISONING**
1. Seen in pts enclosed in burned areas, or during the start of a cold winter (people are using their new gas heaters) → bilateral pallidal necrosis
2. Si/Sx = headache, nausea, vomiting, delirium, cherry-red color of lips
3. Dx = elevated carboxyhemoglobin levels
4. Tx = hyperbaric oxygen (first line) or 100% O_2

B. **THIAMINE DEFICIENCY**
1. Usually 2° to alcoholism
2. Beriberi peripheral neuropathy due to Wallerian degeneration
3. Wernicke's encephalopathy: **Wernicke's triad = confusion (confabulation), ophthalmoplegia, ataxia**
4. Wernicke's is related to lesions of mamillary bodies
5. Tx: give thiamine prior to glucose (e.g., thiamine should be run in IV fluid without glucose) or will exacerbate mamillary body damage

C. **B₁₂ DEFICIENCY**
1. Subacute degeneration of posterior columns & lateral corticospinal tract
2. Si/Sx = weakness & ↓ vibration sense (both worse in legs), paresthesias, hyper-

reflexia, ataxia, personality change, dementia—**note, neurological deficits can occur even if no hematologic abnormalitites are present!**

3. Tx = B_{12} replacement (can use high-dose oral in lieu of injection)

D. WILSON'S DISEASE (HEPATOLENTICULAR DEGENERATION)
1. Defect in copper metabolism → lesions in basal ganglia
2. Si/Sx = extrapyramidal tremors & rigidity, psychosis, & manic-depression
3. **Pathognomonic → Kayser-Fleischer ring around the cornea**
4. Dx = ↓ serum ceruloplasmin
5. Tx = penicillamine or liver transplant if drug fails

E. HEPATIC ENCEPHALOPATHY
1. Seen in cirrhosis, may be due to brain toxicity 2° to excess ammonia & other toxins not degraded by malfunctioning liver
2. Sx = hyperreflexia, **asterixis** (flapping of extended wrists), dementia, seizures, obtundation/coma
3. Tx = lactulose, neomycin & protein restriction to ↓ ammonia-related toxins

F. TAY-SACHS DISEASE
1. Hexosaminidase A defect → ↑ ganglioside GM2
2. Si/Sx = **cherry-red spot on macula**, retardation, paralysis, blind
3. Dx by biopsy of rectum, or enzymatic assay, no Tx

V. Seizures (Sz)

A. TERMINOLOGY
1. Complex sz → loss of consciousness (LOC), simple sz does not
2. Generalized sz = entire brain involved, partial sz = focal area
3. Tonic sz → prolonged contraction, clonic sz → twitches
4. Absence = complex generalized sz → brief LOC
5. Grand mal = complex generalized tonic-clonic sz

B. PRESENTATION
1. Hx of prior head trauma, stroke, or other CNS disease ↑ risk for sz
2. Si/Sx = loss of bowel/bladder control, tongue maceration, postictal confusion/lethargy, focal findings indicate epileptogenic foci
3. If pt has Hx of seizures, always check blood level of medication

C. TREATMENT
1. Tx seizures if they recur or if pt has known epileptic focus

TABLE 7-6   Seizure Therapy

PARTIAL	GRAND MAL	ABSENCE	MYOCLONIC
Phenytoin*	Valproate*	Ethosuximide*	Valproate*
Carbamazepine*	Carbamazepine	Valproate	Clonazepam
Valproate	Phenytoin	Clonazepam	

*First-line choice.

2. Tx underlying cause: electrolyte, infxn, toxic ingestion, trauma, azotemia, stroke/bleed, delerium tremens, hypoglycemia, hypoxia
3. **Phenytoin causes gingival hyperplasia, hirsutism**
4. Carbamazepine causes leukopenia/aplastic anemia, hepatotoxic
5. Valproate causes neutropenia, thrombocytopenia, hepatotoxic
6. Stop Tx if no seizures for 2 yr & normal EEG

D. STATUS EPILEPTICUS
1. Continuous seizing lasting >5 min
2. Tx with benzodiazepines for immediate control, followed by phenytoin loading & phenobarbitol for refractory cases
3. This is a medical emergency!

VI. Degenerative Diseases

A. DEMENTIA VS. DELIRIUM DIFFERENTIAL

TABLE 7-7   Dementia versus Delirium

	DEMENTIA	**DELIRIUM**
Definition	Both cause global decline in cognition, memory, personality, motor, or sensory functions	
Course	Constant, progressive	Sudden onset, waxing/waning daily
Reversible?	Usually not	Almost always
Circadian?	Constant, no daily pattern	Usually worse at night (sun-downing)
Consciousness	Normal	Altered (obtunded)
Hallucination	Usually not	Often, classically visual
Tremor	Often not	Often present (i.e., asterixis)
Causes	Alzheimer's, multi-infarct, Pick's dz, alcohol, brain infxn/tumors, malnutrition (thiamine/B_{12} deficiency)	Systemic infection/neoplasm, drugs (**particularly narcotics & benzodiazepines**), stroke, heart dz, alcoholism, uremia, electrolyte imbalance, hyper/hypoglycemia
Treatment	Supportive—see below for specifics depending on the disease	Treat underlying cause, **control Sx with haloperidol instead of sedatives**—due to agitation pts are often given benzodiazepines or sedatives, but these drugs often exacerbate the delirium as they disorient the pt even more

B. ALZHEIMER'S DISEASE (SENILE DEMENTIA OF ALZHEIMER TYPE)
1. Most common cause of dementia—affects 5% of people over 70
2. Si/Sx = dementia, anxiety, hallucination/delusion, tremor
3. Occurs in Down's syndrome pts at younger ages (age 30–40)
4. Dx = clinical, with definitive diagnosis only possible at autopsy
5. Tx = anticholinesterase inhibitor can slow dementia, antidepressants & antipsychotics can be used for psychosis
6. Px = inevitable decline in function usually over about 10 yr

C. MULTI-INFARCT DEMENTIA
1. Si/Sx = acute, step-wise ↓ in neurologic function, multiple focal deficits on exam, hypertension, old infarcts by CT or MRI

2. Dx = clinical, radiographic
3. Tx = prevent future infarcts by ↓ cardiovascular risks

D. PICK'S DISEASE
1. Clinically resembles Alzheimer's, more in women, younger age onset (50s)
2. Predominates in frontal (more personality changes seen) & temporal lobes
3. Dx = MRI → symmetrical frontal or temporal atrophy, confirm by autopsy
4. Tx/Px = as per Alzheimer's

E. PARKINSON'S DISEASE
1. Parkinson's disease = idiopathic Parkinsonism, mid- to late-age onset
2. Parkinsonism
   a. **Syndrome of tremor, cog-wheel rigidity, bradykinesia, classic shuffling gait, mask-like facies**, ± dementia due to loss of dopaminergic neurons in substantia nigra
   b. DDx = Parkinson's disease, severe depression (bradykinesia & flat affect), intoxication (e.g., manganese, synthetic heroin), phenothiazine side effects, rare neurodegenerative diseases
3. Dx = clinical, rule out other causes
4. Tx
   a. Sinemet (levodopa = carbidopa) best for bradykinesia
   b. Anticholinergics (benztropine/trihexyphenidyl) for tremor
   c. Amantadine → ↑ dopamine release, effective for mild dz
   d. Surgical pallidotomy for refractory cases
5. Px = typically progresses over years despite treatment

F. HUNTINGTON'S CHOREA
1. Si/Sx = progressive choreiform movements of all limbs, ataxic gait, grimacing → dementia, usually in 30s–50s (can be earlier or later)
2. Autosomal CAG triplet repeat expansion in HD gene → atrophy of striatum (especially caudate nucleus), with neuronal loss & gliosis
3. Dx = MRI → atrophy of caudate, ⊕ family history
4. Tx/Px = supportive, death inevitable

G. AMYOTROPHIC LATERAL SCLEROSIS (LOU GEHRIG'S DISEASE, MOTOR NEURON DISEASE)
1. Si/Sx = **upper & lower motor neuron dz** → muscle weakness with fasciculations (anterior motor neurons) progressing to denervation atrophy, hyperreflexia, spasticity, difficulty speaking/swallowing
2. Dx = clinical Hx & physical findings
3. Tx/Px = supportive, death inevitable, usually from respiratory failure

Neurology Case Scenario

A 43-year-old female presents to the emergency room complaining of severe weakness of both legs and tingling and numbness in her fingertips. The symptoms began in her feet with a similar tingling and numbness, and over the course of 3 days developed into lower limb weakness first affecting her calf muscles and then spreading to affect her upper thigh muscles so that she could not stand up. She describes no pain associated with the neuropathy. On examination she is afebrile with normal vital signs. Her cranial nerve exam is normal, her strength is slightly diminished bilaterally in her upper extremities (4/5), and markedly diminished bilaterally in her lower extremities (2/5). She has no loss of fine-point discrimination, but her patellar deep tendon reflexes (DTRs) are +/– bilaterally and her bicep DTRs are 1+ bilaterally. On review of systems you learn that 2 weeks ago she had "the flu," but has felt fine for the past week.

You perform a lumbar puncture.

    1. What is your diagnosis and what should the lumbar puncture show if you are correct?

        a) HIV neuropathy, HIV ELISA is positive in CSF

        b) Multiple sclerosis, oligoclonal bands

        c) Amyotrophic lateral sclerosis, CSF is completely normal despite obvious neurologic disease

        d) Guillain-Barré syndrome, CSF protein is elevated but there are no white cells

        e) Vitamin B_{12} deficiency, level of CSF methylmalonic acid is low

You are the resident on Neuro Consult service, covering for the team over the weekend. On Sunday morning you are called to see a 78-year-old man because of acute onset "confusion" 1-day status-postsurgical repair of a hip fracture. Because the patient has no history of cognitive impairment of psychiatric conditions, the orthopedic surgery team is concerned that the patient might have had a stroke intraoperatively. Overnight he was delusional and kept trying to climb out of bed. He did not know where he was and became agitated and abusive to the nurses. He was given several milligrams of diazepam, but this did not calm him down, and in fact may have made him worse.

When you stop by in the morning to see him, you find a calm, pleasant, elderly gentleman in no acute distress. Other than some pain from the surgery, he is feeling well. You note that he is still connected to his patient-controlled analgesia (PCA), and he says that it helps his pain somewhat. He is afebrile with normal vital signs. His neurologic exam is completely normal. He is A+Ox3, cranial nerves are intact, strength and sensation are normal throughout (except for the right leg, which was surgically repaired). His wife, who came to visit this morning but was not at the hospital last night, tells you that he is acting like his normal self, and "does not know what all the fuss was about last night."

During your examination, the patient tells you he still works as a portfolio manager with a major investment bank. Your eyes alight and you have a very pleasant and cogent conversation with him about the stock market and the world's economy for the next 20 minutes.

    2. What is your diagnosis for his prior night's behavior?

        a) The patient has dementia

        b) The patient is schizophrenic

        c) The patient had a frontal lobe stroke causing personality changes

        d) The patient was delirious

        e) The patient was going through alcohol withdrawal

    3. What is the proper treatment for this diagnosis?

        a) prn antipsychotic medication

b) Decrease narcotic PCA doses as tolerated, switch to non-narcotics if possible

c) prn benzodiazepine

d) 4 point restraints

e) Both a & b

A 60-year-old male has had 1 year of increasingly severe weakness and weight loss. The weakness began in the lower extremities, particularly the ankles, but has gradually spread to affect the thighs and the arms over the past 9 months. The patient has had no fevers, chills, nausea, vomiting, or diarrhea. His facial muscles have not been affected, and he is able to swallow normally. He has no history of major illness nor any significant family history. On exam, you find a generally wasted, pleasant male in no acute distress. His strength is 3–4/5 upper extremities and 2–3/5 lower extremities bilaterally. His DTRs are hyperreflexic diffusely and despite his diffuse wasting, his limbs appear spastic. You note active fasciculations even when the patient is not trying to move his limbs. He has bilateral Babinski signs. Cranial nerves and all sensory functions are intact.

4. What intervention would you make at this point in time?

a) Supportive care

b) Plasmapheresis

c) Antiretroviral agents

d) Prednisone

e) Levodopa/carbidopa

5. What is the likely prognosis?

a) Patient will die with the disease, not of the disease

b) With proper treatment, the disease can be put into remission

c) With or without treatment, the disease will wax and wane in severity, and prognosis is uncertain

d) Inevitable death within several years regardless of treatment

A 41-year-old female presents to the neurologist complaining of several months of stumbling to her right when she walks. She says that she feels unbalanced on occasion, and she also has intermittent paresthesias in her toes. She does not feel weak and she has no pain, but she has been feeling somewhat depressed recently. She has a long history of gastrointestinal symptoms, variably ascribed over the years to reflux disease or cholelithiasis. In fact, 3 months ago a general surgeon found multiple gallstones by ultrasound and removed her gallbladder. However, she says that the discomfort has persisted after the surgery, and she thinks, "my gallbladder may have grown back." On exam you note that the patient appears to be somewhat pale. Her cranial nerves are intact and strength is normal throughout. Her DTRs are normal in the upper extremities; however, she has hyperreflexic ankle jerks. She demonstrates markedly diminished vibration and position sense in her feet, with lesser diminishment in her fingers. She has no tremors, and finger-to-nose testing is normal.

6. What test will confirm the most likely diagnosis?

a) Lead level

b) Antiparietal cell antibodies

c) Head MRI

d) Lumbar puncture

e) Nerve biopsy

A 70-year-old male awoke this morning with new onset of right-sided hemiplegia. He was confused as well, prompting his wife to call their son within an hour of their waking. The son rushed over and brought his father to the ER within 2 hours of his waking. By the time he is seen in the ER, the father's symptoms are beginning to improve slightly. He is no longer confused and is oriented to person and place, although not to time. He has regained slight movement in his arms and legs, but is still very weak. He has no other focal findings. Head CT reveals no evidence of intracranial bleed; however, there is evidence of old lacunar infarcts, and a question of an acute process in the left parietal lobe. His past medical history is significant for an actively bleeding ulcer that recurred 3 weeks ago. He is currently guaiac negative.

7. How would you treat this patient acutely?

a) Nimodipine

b) Heparin

c) tPA

d) Supportive

The patient's weakness entirely resolves within 24 hours. A carotid duplex scan reveals an 80% occlusion of the left carotid artery.

8. How would you treat this patient now?

a) Endarterectomy

b) Aspirin

c) Coumadin

d) Ticlopidine

e) Aspirin plus ticlopidine

A 20-year-old female is brought to the ER by her college roommate. The patient is complaining of severe headache, as well as fevers, chills, nausea, and vomiting that began yesterday afternoon. She lives in a dormitory on campus, but has no sick contacts of which she is aware. The patient is febrile to 102°F, is tachycardic but normotensive, and is breathing normally. She appears very uncomfortable and malaised. On exam you find clear evidence of meningismus. Her fundi are normal, and she is without focal findings on neurological exam. Laboratories are significant for leukocytosis and mild hyponatremia, with a potassium of 5.8. The CT scanner is occupied with a trauma patient and will not be available for 30 minutes to an hour.

9. What is your acute management?

a) Wait for the CT scanner to confirm that the patient has no mass lesion, then perform lumbar puncture

b) Start empiric penicillin for presumed meningitis, do lumbar puncture when CT scan is available

c) Perform lumbar puncture, then start empiric cefotaxime and acyclovir

d) Start empiric vancomycin for presumed meningitis

The patient is admitted to the hospital and you perform a lumbar puncture. Several hours later you receive a page from the ICU nurse informing you that the patient has peaked T waves on her EKG. You give a verbal order for STAT chemistries and rush to see her. Upon examination you note that her blood pressure has fallen from 130/80 to 100/50, and she is tachycardic to 120. She has developed diffuse petechiae on her lower extremities.

10. What is the cause of her peaked T waves on EKG and her hemodynamic instability?

a) Encephalitis

b) Arrhythmia

c) Anaphylactic reaction to the antibiotics you gave her

d) Infarction of the adrenal gland

11. What did the lumbar puncture show?

a) ↑ PMNs, ↑ glucose, ↑ protein

b) ↑ lymphocytes, ↓ glucose, normal protein

c) ↑ PMNs, ↓ glucose, ↑ protein

d) ↑ lymphocytes, ↑ glucose, ↑ protein

e) ↑ PMNs, ↓ glucose, ↓ protein

12. What specific antibiotic should be given to this patient?

a) Rifampin

b) Ceftriaxone

c) Vancomycin

d) Ampicillin

e) Penicillin

13. From a public health perspective, what more needs to be done?

a) Appropriate vaccine administration to all exposed persons

b) Prophylactic cephalosporin administration to all her close contacts

c) Prophylactic penicillin administration to all her close contacts

d) Quarantine of the students on her dormitory floor

e) Prophylactic rifampin administration to all her close contacts

Answers

1. **d)** This patient presents with the classic history, physical, and laboratory findings of Guillain-Barré syndrome. The disease is typically preceded by a mild infection, often *Campylobacter* gastroenteritis, but also any viral or *Mycoplasma*-mediated

upper respiratory infection. It causes a very typical "ascending paralysis," in which the legs are affected earlier and more severely than the arms. Also, there is no sensory loss on exam, but the DTRs are markedly diminished. The CSF will show an "albumin-cytologic" dissociation, in which the protein is elevated but there are no inflammatory cells. Isolated motor weakness, especially in an ascending pattern, is not at all typical of HIV-related neuropathy and certainly would not present in this acute time frame. The age of onset and its acuteness are atypical of multiple sclerosis, and the pattern of involvement, with the ascending paralysis and isolated motor involvement, argues strongly against multiple sclerosis (although it should be included in the differential diagnosis). Amyotrophic lateral sclerosis would not present so acutely, and again the classic ascending nature of the involvement is atypical. B_{12} deficiency does affect predominantly the legs, and this should be included in the differential; however, its onset is more insidious and the methylmalonic acid level is tested in the blood, not the CSF.

2. **d)** This patient clearly has a "waxing and waning" neurologic status, the hallmark of delirium. He also has multiple risk factors for delirium, including major surgery (trauma), high doses of narcotics that increase his disorientation, onset of nightfall ("sun-downing"), and the hospital staff's misguided attempts at calming him down with benzodiazepines, which likely exacerbated his confusion. The patient's obvious intact cognition when you meet him rules out dementia, as well as his lack of history of cognitive impairment; dementia is a chronic, insidious condition. Schizophrenia does not wax and wane over such an acute course, and he would have carried the diagnosis with him coming into the hospital. There are no focal findings on exam indicative of stroke, and such symptoms would not resolve so quickly if they were due to infarction. Although alcohol withdrawal is a cause of delirium, the patient has many other factors that explain his delirium and none of the seizures or autonomic instability you would see in a patient withdrawing from alcohol.

3. **e)** Delirium, particularly that which occurs overnight (i.e., "sun-downing"), is caused by disorientation and lack of sensory input into an elderly person's brain. Benzodiazepines given for acute agitation will often make delirium worse, and agitate the patient more, because the drugs can worsen disorientation. Haloperidol can be effective in calming the patient down without sedating him or her to the point of exacerbating the disorientation and is the drug of choice for prn dosing of delirium-induced agitation. Also, narcotics exacerbate disorientation and agitation, so they should be titrated down as tolerated by the patient.

4. **a)** This patient has amyotrophic lateral sclerosis (ALS). The presence of both upper motor neuron and lower motor neuron findings is virtually pathognomonic for this disorder. Thus, the muscle wasting with weakness and fasciculations in the presence of spasticity and Babinski signs are classic findings. There is no effective treatment for ALS.

5. **d)** The patient will most likely die of respiratory failure. The progression of the disease is inexorable.

6. **b)** The patient's distal paresthesias, loss of position sense, ataxia, depression, and, particularly, loss of vibration sense worse in the lower extremities are all classic findings of vitamin B_{12} deficiency. Her gastrointestinal discomfort is likely due to a long history of atrophic gastritis, and her pale features are likely secondary to pernicious anemia. Thus, antiparietal cell antibodies will confirm the diagnosis.

7. **d)** tPA and heparin are contraindicated if there has been recent internal bleeding, if the signs or symptoms of the neurologic event appear to be resolving on their own, or if the patient's neurologic event occurred more than 3 to 6 hours prior to presentation. Since he awoke with the symptoms, it is impossible to say when the neurologic event occurred. His recent bleeding ulcer is also a contraindication to tPA. Nimodipine is used to prevent vasospasm following intracranial bleeds.

8. **a)** The patient has had a transient ischemic attack. In the presence of a greater than 70% carotid stenosis, a symptomatic patient should be treated with endarterectomy. Coumadin is the preferred treatment for patients without a history of symptoms or with a lesser stenosis, while aspirin or ticlopidine is second line.

9. **c)** Whether the lumbar puncture is performed prior to administration of antibiotics is irrelevant as long as both are done expeditiously. Antibiotics should never be delayed for any significant length of time, and a lumbar puncture performed within an hour of antibiotic administration will not be affected by the drugs. If, for example, there were focal findings on the neurologic exam, and an intracranial mass lesion was suspected, the lumbar puncture should not be performed prior to obtaining a head CT. In this case, antibiotics should be given immediately and the lumbar puncture should be delayed. However, this patient has no evidence of focal neurologic findings. A lumbar puncture can therefore be performed without obtaining a head CT, and the antibiotics can be given afterwards. Cefotaxime is the drug of choice for empiric therapy of bacterial meningitis, and acyclovir can be added because until the lumbar puncture results come back it can be very difficult or impossible to differentiate bacterial from viral meningitis.

10. **d)** The presence of petechiae on the patient's lower extremities, as well as the prior noted hyponatremia and now the peaked T waves that indicate hyperkalemia, are all strongly suggestive of the Waterhouse-Friderichsen syndrome, which is acute adrenal gland infarction seen in patients with *Neisseria meningitidis* meningitis.

11. **c)** Acute bacterial meningitis causes influx of neutrophils, decreased glucose levels, and elevated protein in the CSF.

12. **e)** High dose IV penicillin is the treatment of choice for *Neisseria meningitidis.*

13. **e)** Rifampin prophylaxis is preferred to penicillin prophylaxis, because *Neisseria meningitidis* is spread by respiratory droplets and rifampin has superior salivary penetration. Prophylaxis is necessary because *N. meningitidis* can cause epidemic outbreaks in close populations (e.g., military barracks or college dormitories).

8. Dermatology

Carlos Ayala

I. Terminology

1. Macule = flat discoloration, <1 cm in diameter
2. Papule = elevated skin lesion, <1 cm in diameter
3. Plaque = elevated skin lesion, >1 cm in diameter
4. Vesicle = small fluid-containing lesion <0.5 cm in diameter
5. Wheal = like a vesicle but occurs transiently as in urticaria (hives)
6. Bulla = large fluid-containing lesion, >0.5 cm in diameter
7. Lichenification = accentuated skin markings in thick epidermis due to scratching
8. Keloid = an irregular raised lesion resulting from scar tissue hypertrophy
9. Petechiae = flat, pinhead, nonblanching, red-purple lesion caused by hemorrhage into the skin: seen in any cause of thrombocytopenia
10. Purpura = larger than petechiae
11. Cyst = closed epithelium-lined cavity or sac containing liquid or semi-solid material
12. Hyperkeratosis = ↑ thickness of stratum corneum (seen in chronic dermatitis)
13. Parakeratosis = hyperkeratosis with retention of nuclei in stratum corneum & thinning of stratum granulosum (usually seen in psoriasis)
14. Steroids

TABLE 8-1   Use of Topical Steroids

POTENCY	DRUG	USE FOR DISEASE ON . . .
Low	1% hydrocortisone	Face, genitals, skin folds (prevent atrophy/striae), also use in children for dz on body
Moderate	0.1% triamcinolone	Body/extremities, or ↑ dz on face, genitals, skin folds
High	Fluocinonide (Lidex)	Thick skin (palms/soles), or ↑ body dz, **do not use on face**
Very High	Diflorasone	Thick skin, or if very severe on body

Carrier substance: lotion = low potency; cream = mid potency; ointment = high potency.

II. Infections

A. ACNE

1. Inflammation of pilosebaceous unit caused by secondary *Propionibacterium acnes* infection of blocked pore
2. Si/Sx = open comedones (blackheads) & closed comedones (whiteheads) on face, neck, chest, back, & buttocks, can become inflamed & pustular (See Color Plate 4)
3. Tx = topical antibiotics, Retin-A, benzoyl peroxide, systemic antibiotics, if acne is scarring consider Accutane

B. IMPETIGO

1. Superficial skin infection of epidermis

2. Si/Sx = honey-crusted lesions or vesicles occurring most often in children around the nose & mouth, can be bullous or nonbullous (See Color Plate 5)
3. Common organisms include *Staphylococcus aureus* & *S. pyogenes*
4. Tx = Keflex or oxacillin for 7–10 days

C. FOLLICULITIS
1. Si/Sx = erythematous pustules commonly noted around beard area
2. *S. aureus* most common, *Pseudomonas aeruginosa* causes "hot tub" folliculitis (organism lives in warm water), also fungi & viruses
3. Tx = local wound care, Keflex only if severe

D. SUBCUTANEOUS INFECTIONS
1. Cellulitis
   a. Si/Sx = spreading subcutaneous infxn with classic signs of inflammation: *rubor* (red), *calor* (hot), *dolor* (pain) & *tumor* (swelling)
   b. *Staphylococcus* & *Streptococcus* most common etiologies
   c. Tx = oxacillin or Keflex
2. Abscess
   a. Local collection of pus, often with fever, ↑ white count
   b. Tx = incision & drainage (I&D), can add Keflex
3. Furuncle (boil) & carbuncle
   a. Furuncle = pus collection in 1 hair follicle, often caused by *S. aureus*
   b. Carbuncle = pus collection involving many hair follicles
   c. Tx = I&D, add Keflex or oxacillin if severe
4. Paronychia
   a. Infxn of skin surrounding nail margin that can extend into surrounding skin & into tendons within hand
   b. Commonly caused by *S. aureus*, also *Candida*
   c. Tx = warm compress, I&D if area is purulent, add Keflex if severe
5. Necrotizing fasciitis
   a. Infxn along fascial planes with severe pain, fever, ↑ white count, local inflammation may be deceptively absent but pt will appear very ill
   b. Caused by *S. pyogenes* (group A Strep) or *Clostridium perfringens*
   c. Tx = **immediate, extensive surgical débridement, add penicillin & clindamycin to help prevent further spread**
   d. Px = ↑↑↑ mortality unless débridement is rapid & extensive

E. SCARLET FEVER
1. *S. pyogenes* (group A *Strep* = GAS) is the cause
2. Si/Sx
   a. **"Sunburn with goose bumps"** rash, finely punctate, erythematous but blanches with pressure, initially on trunk, generalizes within hours
   b. Sandpaper rough skin, **strawberry tongue**, beefy-red pharynx, circumoral pallor
   c. **Pastia's lines = rash, most intense in creases of axillae & groin**
   d. Eventual desquamation of hands & feet as rash resolves
   e. Systemic Sx include fever, chills, delirium, sore throat, cervical adenopathy, all of which appear at same time as rash
3. Complications include rheumatic fever & glomerulonephritis
4. Tx = penicillin

F. HIDRADENITIS SUPPURATIVA

1. Si/Sx = plugged apocrine glands presenting as inflamed masses in groin/axilla, become secondarily infected
2. Tx = surgical débridement & antibiotics

G. ROSE SPOTS

1. **Rose spots** = small pink papules in groups of 1–2 dozen on trunk, found in 30% of pts with typhoid fever (*Salmonella typhi*)
2. Typhoid fever Si/Sx
   a. High fever, myalgias, abdominal tenderness, splenomegaly
   b. **Classic pulse-fever dissociation** = high fever with relative bradycardia (also seen in brucellosis)
3. **Tx for chronic aSx typhoid fever (carrier state like "Typhoid Mary") is cholecystectomy because *S. typhi* resides in the gallbladder**

H. ERYTHRASMA

1. Si/Sx = irregular erythematous rash found along major skin folds (axilla, groin, fingers, toes & breasts) (See Color Plates 6 and 7)
2. Commonly seen in adult diabetics, caused by *Corynebacterium spp.*
3. Dx = Wood's lamp of skin → **coral-red fluorescence, KOH prep negative**
4. Tx = erythromycin

III. Common Disorders

A. PSORIASIS

1. Si/Sx = pink plaques with silvery-white scaling **occurring on extensor surfaces such as elbows & knees** (see Color Plate 8) (also scalp, lumbosacral, glans penis, intergluteal cleft), **& fingernail pitting**, can be associated with arthritis (see Color Plates 9 and 10)
2. Classic finding = **Auspitz sign** → removal of overlying scale causes pinpoint bleeding due to thin epidermis above dermal papillae
3. Classic finding = **Koebner's phenomenon** → psoriatic lesions appear at sites of cutaneous physical trauma (skin scratching, rubbing, or wound)
4. Dx = clinical, biopsy is gold standard
5. Tx = topical steroids (first line), PUVA (second line) = **P**soralens + **UVA** light, methotrexate & cyclosporin (third line)

B. ECZEMA (ECZEMATOUS DERMATITIS)

1. Family of superficial, intensely pruritic, erythematous skin lesions
2. Atopic dermatitis
   a. Si/Sx = **an "itch that rashes,"** rash 2° to scratching chronic pruritus, commonly found on the face in infancy, later in childhood can present on the flexor surfaces such as antecubital & popliteal fossa
   b. Atopy = inherited predisposition to asthma, allergies & dermatitis
   c. Dx is clinical
   d. Tx = avoid irritants or triggers, keep skin moist with lotions, use steroids & antihistamines for Sx relief of itching & inflammation
3. Contact dermatitis
   a. Si/Sx = linear pruritic rash at site of contact

b. Caused by delayed type hypersensitivity reaction after exposure to poison ivy, poison oak, nickel, or chemicals

c. Dx is clinical, history of exposure crucial

d. Tx = as per atopic dermatitis

4. Seborrheic dermatitis

a. Si/Sx = erythema, scaling, white flaking (dandruff) in areas of sebaceous glands (face, scalp, groin, axilla & external ear)

b. Called "cradle cap" in infants

c. Dx = clinical & KOH prep to rule out fungal infection

d. Tx = selenium shampoo on face & trunk, steroids for severe dz

C. URTICARIA (HIVES)

1. Common disorder caused by mast cell degranulation & histamine release

2. Si/Sx = transient papular wheals, intensely pruritic, surrounded by erythema, **dermographism** (write word on the skin & it remains imprinted as erythematous wheals) (See Color Plate 11)

3. Most lesions are IgE-mediated (type I hypersensitivity) but exercise, certain chemicals in sensitive pts & inhibitors of prostaglandin synthesis (e.g., aspirin) can also cause IgE-independent reactions

4. Dx = skin testing or aspirin or exercise challenge

5. Tx = avoidance of triggers, antihistamines, steroids, epinephrine

6. Can cause respiratory emergency requiring intubation

D. HYPOPIGMENTATION

1. Vitiligo

a. **Loss of melanocytes** in discrete areas of skin, appearing as sharply demarcated depigmented patches (See Color Plate 12)

b. Occurs in all races but most apparent in darkly pigmented pts

c. Chronic condition that may be autoimmune in nature

d. Associated with thyroid dz in 30% of pts, especially women

e. Tx = mini-grafting or total depigmentation

f. Px = some patients remit over long term, others never do

2. Albinism

a. **Melanocytes are present** but fail to produce pigment due to tyrosinase deficiency

b. Si/Sx = white skin & eyelashes, nystagmus, iris translucency, ↓ visual acuity, decreased retinal pigment & strabismus

c. Tx = avoid sun exposure, sunscreens

d. Px = the oculocutaneous form predisposes to skin cancer

3. Pityriasis alba

a. Nonpathological areas of hypopigmentation on face or upper extremities

b. Can be 2° to prior infection or inflammation, often regress over time

c. Differentiated from tinea versicolor by KOH prep

E. HYPERPIGMENTATION

1. Freckle (ephelis) is caused by normal melanocyte number but ↑ melanin within basal keratinocytes, darkens with sun exposure

2. Lentigo is pigmented macules caused by melanocyte hyperplasia that, unlike freckles, do not darken with sun exposure

3. Nevocellular nevus
   a. Common mole, benign tumor derived from melanocytes
   b. Variations of nevi
      1) Blue nevus = black-blue nodule present at birth, often mistaken for melanoma
      2) Spitz nevus = red-pink nodule, often seen in children, confused with hemangioma or melanoma
      3) Dysplastic nevus = atypical, irregularly pigmented lesion with ↑ risk of transformation into malignant melanoma
      4) Dysplastic nevus syndrome is autosomal dominant inherited dz
   c. Dx = biopsy, Tx = full excision
4. Melasma (chloasma)
   a. A mask-like hyperpigmentation on face seen in pregnancy
   b. Sunlight accentuates pigmentation, which typically fades postpartum
   c. Tx = minimize facial exposure to sun, or hydroquinone cream (works for any hyperpigmentation)
5. Hemangioma
   a. Group of "birthmarks," capillary hemangiomas present at birth
   b. Port-wine stains (purple-red on face or neck)
      1) Can be associated with Sturge-Weber syndrome (See Phakomatoses below, Section V)
      2) Must screen for glaucoma & CNS dz (CT scan)
      3) Tx = laser therapy, will not regress spontaneously
   c. Strawberry hemangiomas (bright raised red lesions) are benign, most disappear on their own
   d. Cherry hemangiomas (benign small red papule) Tx with laser therapy
6. Xanthoma
   a. Yellowish papules, often accumulations of foamy histiocytes
   b. Can be idiopathic or associated with familial hyperlipidemia
   c. If seen on eyelids they are called "xanthelasma"
   d. Tx = ↓ hyperlipidemia, surgically excise papules as needed
7. Pityriasis rosea
   a. Erythematous maculopapular rash with scale apparent in center
   b. Often preceded by a "herald patch" on trunk
   c. **Can appear on back in a Christmas tree distribution**
   d. Tx = sunlight, otherwise spontaneously remits in 6–12 wk
8. Erythema nodosum
   a. Inflammation of subcutaneous fat (panniculitis) & adjacent vessels
   b. Characteristic lesions are **tender red nodules occurring on the lower legs** & sometimes forearms
   c. Usually resolves in 6–8 wk, Tx directed at underlying cause
   d. Common causes
      1) Infections = *Mycoplasma, Chlamydia, Coccidioides immitis, Mycobacterium leprae* & others
      2) Drugs = sulfonamides & contraceptive pills
      3) Inflammatory Bowel Disease, sarcoidosis, rheumatic fever

4) Pregnancy
9. Dermatomyositis
   a. An autoimmune disorder sometimes seen with polymyositis
   b. Presents with **heliotropic (reddish-purple) patches on eyelids** & erythematous scaly rash on hands
   c. Tx = high-dose steroids
10. Seborrheic keratosis
    a. Black or brown benign plaques, appear to be stuck onto skin surface
    b. Commonly seen in elderly & runs in families
    c. Can be mistaken for melanoma
    d. Tx = liquid nitrogen freezing, usually too many to treat
11. Acanthosis nigricans
    a. Black velvety plaques on flexor surfaces & intertriginous areas
    b. Seen in obesity & endocrine disorders (e.g., diabetes)
    c. Can mark underlying malignancy (e.g., GI/GU, lymphoma)
12. Bronze diabetes = 1° hemochromatosis
    a. Familial defect causing intestinal hyperabsorption of iron
    b. **Classic triad: ↑ skin pigmentation, cirrhosis, diabetes mellitus**
    c. Other Sx = cardiomyopathy, pituitary failure & arthropathies
    d. **Clinical pearl: hemochromatosis is the likely Dx in any patient with osteoarthritis involving the MCP joints**
    e. Dx = transferrin saturation (iron/TIBC) ≥ 50%
    f. Tx = phlebotomy, which improves survival if started early

F. Verrucae (Warts)

1. Verruca vulgaris = hand wart
2. Verruca plana (flat wart) smaller than vulgaris, seen on hands & face
3. Human papilloma virus (HPV) types 1–4 cause skin & plantar warts
4. HPV 6 & 11 cause anorectal & genital warts (condyloma acuminatum)
5. HPV 16, 18, 31, 33, 35 cause cervical cancer
6. Condylomata lata are flat warts caused by *Treponema pallidum* (syphilis)

IV. Cancer

Table 8-2   Skin Cancer

Disease	Si/Sx	Tx	Px
Basal cell carcinoma	Most common skin cancer, classic "**rodent ulcer**" seen on face, with **pearly translucent borders & fine telangiectasias**, not usually found on lips (See Color Plate 13)	Excision	Excellent— almost never metastasize
Squamous cell carcinoma	Common in elderly, appears as erythematous nodules on sun-exposed areas that eventually ulcerate & crust, **frequently preceded by actinic keratosis = rough epidermal lesions on sun-exposed areas such as lower lip, ears & nose** (See Color Plate 14)	Excision, radiation	Metastasize more than basal cell but not as much as melanoma

TABLE 8-2 *Continued*

DISEASE	SI/SX	TX	PX
Malignant melanoma	Seen in lightly pigmented individuals with ↑ sun exposure—diagnose with **ABCDEs** (See Color Plate 15) **A**symmetry = malignant, benign = symmetrical **B**order = irregular, benign = smooth **C**olor = multicolored, benign = 1 color **D**iameter >6 mm, benign = <6 mm **E**levation = raised above skin, benign = flat **E**nlargement = growing, benign = not growing	Excision, chemo if mets likely	High rate of metastasis → **#1 skin cancer killer, risk of mets ↑ with depth of invasion on biopsy**
Kaposi's sarcoma	Connective tissue cancer caused by human herpes virus 8, appears as red/purple plaques or nodules on skin & mucosa, frequently affects lungs & GI viscera, almost exclusively seen in AIDS patients (See Color Plate 16)	HIV drugs, chemo	Benign unless damages internal organs
Cutaneous T-cell lymphoma	**"Mycosis fungoides," presents with erythroderma (total body erythematous & pruritic rash), rash can precede malignancy by years,** leukemic phase of disease called "Sézary syndrome"	PUVA, topical chemo, radiation	7–10 yr life expectancy without Tx

V. Neurocutaneous Syndromes (Phakomatoses)

1. Tx is supportive depending upon individual signs & symptoms
2.

TABLE 8-3 Neurocutaneous Syndromes (Phakomatoses)

DISEASE*	CHARACTERISTICS
Tuberous sclerosis	Ash leaf patches (hypopigmented macules), Shagreen spots (leathery cutaneous thickening), adenoma sebaceum of the face, **seizures, mental retardation**
Neurofibromatosis (NF)	Si/Sx = **café-au-lait spots** (see Color Plate 1), neurofibromas, meningiomas, acoustic neuromas, kyphoscoliosis—NF 2 causes bilateral acoustic neuromas
Sturge-Weber syndrome	Si/Sx = **port-wine hemangioma of face** in CN V distribution, mental retardation, seizures
von Hippel-Lindau syndrome	Si/Sx = multiple hemangiomas in various organs, ↑ frequency of renal cell CA & polycythemia (↑ erythropoietin secretion)

*All are autosomal dominant except Sturge-Weber, which has no genetic pattern.

VI. Blistering Disorders

A. PEMPHIGUS VULGARIS (PG)

1. PG is a rare autoimmune disorder, **affecting 20–40-yr-olds**
2. Si/Sx = **flaccid epidermal bullae** that easily slough off leaving large denuded areas of skin (Nikolsky's sign), ↑ risk of 2° infxn

3. DDx = bullous pemphigoid
4. Dx = skin biopsy → **immunofluorescence surrounding epidermal cells** showing "tombstone" fluorescent pattern
5. Tx = high-dose oral steroids, antibiotics for infection
6. Px = **often fatal if not treated**

B. BULLOUS PEMPHIGOID (BP)

1. Common autoimmune disease affecting **mostly the elderly**
2. Resembles PG but much less severe clinically
3. Si/Sx = **hard, tense bullae** that do not rupture easily & usually heal without scarring if uninfected (See Color Plate 17)
4. Dx = skin biopsy → immunofluorescence as a **linear band along the basement membrane, with ↑ eosinophils** in dermis
5. Tx = oral steroids
6. Px = much better than PG

C. ERYTHEMA MULTIFORME

1. A hypersensitivity reaction to drugs, infections, or systemic disorders such as malignancy or collagen vascular disease
2. Si/Sx = **diffuse, erythematous target-like lesions** in many shapes (hence name "multiforme"), often accompanying a herpes eruption
3. **Stevens-Johnson syndrome = a severe febrile form (sometimes fatal) → hemorrhagic crusting also affects lips & oral mucosa**
4. Dx = clinical, hx of herpes infection or drug exposure
5. Tx = stop offending drug, prevent eruption of herpes with acyclovir

D. PORPHYRIA CUTANEA TARDA

1. Autosomal dominant defect in heme synthesis (50% ↓ in uroporphyrinogen decarboxylase activity in RBC & liver)
2. Si/Sx = blisters on sun-exposed areas of face & hands (see Color Plate 18), ↑ hair on temples & cheeks, **no abdominal pain** (differentiates from other porphyrias)
3. Dx = Wood's lamp of urine → **urine fluoresces with distinctive orange-pink color due to ↑ levels of uroporphyrins**
4. Tx = sunscreen, phlebotomy, chloroquine, no alcohol
5. Px = remitting/relapsing, exacerbations due to viral hepatitis, hepatoma, alcohol abuse, estrogen, sunlight

VII. Vector Borne Diseases

A. BACILLARY ANGIOMATOSIS (PELIOSIS HEPATIS)

1. Si/Sx = weight loss, abdominal pain, **rash = red or purple vascular lesions**, from papule to hemangioma-sized, located anywhere on skin & disseminated to any organ
2. DDx = Kaposi's sarcoma, cherry hemangioma
3. **Almost always seen in HIV⊕ patients or homeless population**
4. Caused by *Bartonella spp.*, leading to dysregulated angiogenesis
5. **Cat-scratch disease caused by *B. henselae* transmitted by kitten scratches, trench fever caused by *B. quintana* spread by lice**
6. Dx = histopathology with silver stain, visualization of organisms in lesion, blood culture & PCR can also be done
7. Tx = erythromycin

8. Px = excellent with Tx, some pts require lifelong suppressive Tx

B. LYME DISEASE

1. Si/Sx = fever, chills, headaches, lethargy, photophobia, meningitis, myocarditis, arthralgia & myalgias
2. **Classic rash = erythema chronicum migrans → erythematous annular plaques with a red migrating border & central clearing & induration**
3. Dx = PCR for *Borrelia burgdorferi* DNA, or skin biopsy of migrating edge looking for causative spirochete
4. Tx = spray skin & clothes with DEET or permethrin, wear long pants in woods to prevent tick bite (*Ixodes dammini* & *Ixodes pacificus*)
5. Once infected → high-dose penicillin or ceftriaxone for 2–4 wk

C. ROCKY MOUNTAIN SPOTTED FEVER

1. Si/Sx = acute onset fever, headache, myalgias, classic rash
2. Rash = **erythematous maculopapular, starting on wrists & ankles then moving toward palms, soles & trunk**
3. Rash may lead to cutaneous necrosis due to DIC-induced occlusion of small cutaneous vessels with thrombi
4. Dx = by Hx (exposure to outdoors or tick bite, *Dermacentor spp.*), serologies for *Rickettsia rickettsii*, skin biopsy
5. Doxycycline or chloramphenicol

VIII. Parasitic Infections

A. SCABIES

1. SiSx = erythematous, **markedly pruritic papules & burrows located intertriginous areas** (e.g., finger & toe webs, groin), lesions contagious (See Color Plate 19)
2. Dx = microscopic identification of *Sarcoptes scabiei* mite in skin scrapings (See Figure 8-1)
3. Tx = pt & all close contacts apply Permethrin 5% cream to entire body for 8–10 hr then repeat in 1 wk, wash all bedding in hot water the same day
4. Lindane cream is less effective, associated with adverse effects in kids
5. Symptomatic relief of hypersensitivity reaction to dead mites may be treated with antihistamines & topical steroids

B. PEDICULOSIS CAPITIS (HEAD LOUSE)

1. Si/Sx = can be asymptomatic, or pruritus & erythema of scalp may be noted, common in school-aged children
2. Dx = microscope exam of hair shaft, nits may fluoresce with Wood's lamp
3. Permethrin shampoo or gel to scalp, may need to repeat

C. PEDICULOSIS PUBIS ("CRABS")

1. Si/Sx = very **pruritic papules in pubic area**, axilla, periumbilically in males, along eyelashes, eyebrows & buttocks
2. Dx = microscopic identification of lice, rule out other STDs
3. Tx = apply Permethrin 5% shampoo for 10 min then repeat in 1 wk

D. CUTANEOUS LARVA MIGRANS (CREEPING ERUPTION)

1. Si/Sx = erythematous, pruritic, **serpiginous thread-like lesion** marking burrow of migrating nematode larvae, often on back, hands, feet, buttocks
2. Organism = hookworms: *Ancylostoma*, *Necator* & *Strongyloides*

3. Dx = Hx of unprotected skin lying in moist soil or sand, Bx of lesion
4. Tx = ivermectin orally or thiabendazole topically

IX. Fungal Cutaneous Disorders

TABLE 8-4   Fungal Cutaneous Disorders

DISEASE	SI/SX	DX	TX
Tinea	• Erythematous, pruritic, scaly, well-demarcated plaques (See Color Plate 20) • Black dots may be seen on scalp of patients with tinea capitis	Clinical or KOH prep	Topical antifungal (oral needed for tinea capitis)
Onycho-mycosis	• Fingernails or toenails appear thickened, yellow, degenerating	Clinical or KOH prep	PO itraconazole or fluconizole
Tinea versicolor	• Caused by *Pityrosporum ovale* • Multiple sharply marginated hypopigmented macules on face & trunk noticed in summer because macules will not tan (See Color Plate 21)	KOH prep → yeast & hyphae with classic **spaghetti & meatball appearance**	Selenium sulfide shampoo daily on affected areas for 7 days
Candida	• Erythematous scaling plaques, often in intertriginous areas (groin, breast, buttocks, web of hands) (See Color Plate 22) • Oral thrush → cottage-cheese-like white plaques on mucosal surface • Can extend to esophagus & cause dysphagia & odynophagia	KOH prep → budding yeast & pseudohyphae	Topical Nystatin or oral fluconazole

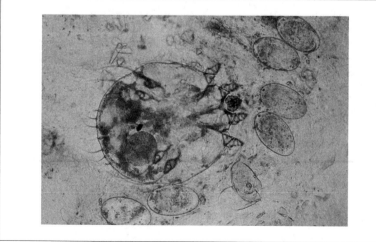

FIGURE 8-1   *Sarcoptes scabiei*, the scabies mite. Female with eggs.

Dermatology Case Scenario

A 43-year-old adult onset diabetic male presents to your outpatient clinic. He states that recently he has started an exercise program to control his weight and maintain his blood glucose. He says that everything was going fine up until 2 days ago, when he started noticing little red bumps on his back and buttocks. He denies any pain, itching, fever, or past history of allergies. He does state that he loves working out on the recumbent bicycle and afterwards he spends at least 30–40 minutes in the hot tub or sauna. He denies any recent changes in detergent, shampoo, or soap. On exam you find erythematous pustules scattered throughout his back and buttocks surrounding hair follicles.

1. The diagnosis and preferred treatment for this patient is:

   a) Necrotizing fascitis, surgical débridement

   b) Henoch-Schönlein purpura, immunosuppressive therapy

   c) Typhoid fever, "Rose spots," cholecystectomy

   d) Folliculitis, supportive treatment and antibiotics

   e) Hidradenitis suppurativa, surgical débridement and antibiotics

During the physical exam you notice an irregular erythematous rash found along major skin folds (axilla, groin, fingers, toes, and chest). You perform a KOH prep and it is negative, and Wood's lamp of skin shows a coral-red fluorescence.

2. What is your diagnosis and treatment?

   a) Tinea, topical antifungal

   b) *Corynebacterium* infection, erythromycin

   c) *Candida* infection, oral azole treatment or nystatin

   d) Eczema, topical steroids

   e) Cellulitis, systemic antibiotics

A 26-year-old male presents to the dermatology clinic complaining of patches of dry, rough skin on his elbows. The skin is dry and scaly to the point of discomfort, and when the young man picks at the scales, the patches of skin tend to bleed easily. He has tried applying moisturizers with limited success. On exam you see 5 × 5 centimeter plaques with silvery scales on an erythematous base covering the extensor surfaces of both elbows.

3. Where else should you look for signs of illness in this patient?

   a) Nail beds and intergluteal clefts

   b) Oral mucosa

   c) Scalp

   d) a & c

   e) b & c

4. What is the first line treatment for this disorder?

   a) Moisturizers

   b) Topical steroids

c) PUVA

d) Tar

e) Cyclosporin

A 56-year-old female is afraid the 5 or 6 dark blotches on her chest and back might be melanomas. She says they have been cropping up for the past several months, although 2 on her back have been present for more than a year. On exam you see 6 dark brown and black, verrucous-like plaques that appear to be "stuck on" the skin, spread over the chest and back.

    5. How will you treat these plaques?

      a) Excision

      b) Topical steroids

      c) Freezing

      d) Laser ablation

A 49-year-old Caucasian male comes to see you, his internist, for a routine physical exam. He is without complaint and in excellent health. He has no significant past medical history and no family history of any serious diseases. During your exam you notice a small, dark spot on the sole of the patient's right foot. The macule is 7mm in diameter, ovoid in shape, with smooth, regular borders. It is brown and black in color, and has a rough surface.

    6. How will you treat this macule?

      a) Excision

      b) Topical steroids

      c) Freezing

      d) Laser ablation

You are the dermatology resident covering the in-patient consult service. You are summoned to see a 44-year-old African-American female with an erythematous nodular rash on her shins. The patient presented to the hospital with fevers, chills, and night sweats of several weeks duration, as well as a chronic cough. The rash on her shins consists of 2- to 4-cm-diameter subcutaneous nodules that are soft but nonfluctuant and mildly tender to the touch. The nodules have erythematous bases. They are not pruritic. The resident who called for the consult tells you that the patient is hypercalcemic and has a CXR that reveals bilateral hilar adenopathy.

    7. Proper management of this rash includes:

      a) Excision of the nodules

      b) Topical steroids

      c) Freezing

      d) Laser ablation

      e) No treatment is warranted

A 63-year-old male presents to your dermatology office complaining of a small ulcer below his right eye. The lesion started as a small bump and has grown into a 2-cm-diameter ulcerating plaque over a several-month period. The lesion is not pruritic, nor is it painful. It has pearly, heaped-up borders with telangiectasias at the rim.

8. Proper management of this lesion is:

a) Excision

b) Topical steroids

c) Freezing

d) Laser ablation

e) Excision plus chemotherapy

9. The patient's prognosis:

a) Depends upon the depth of the lesion

b) Is made bleak by a high likelihood of metastasis

c) Is 50% survival at 5 years

d) Is very good because metastases are very rare

e) Is made bleak by the propensity for recurrence

A 31-year-old habitual drug abuser walks into the ER after lacerating his face and breaking his nose in a fight with his drug dealer. The ER physician orders a Head and Neck consult for the facial injuries but also diagnoses the patient with cellulitis spreading from the site of a recent needle injection. The patient is started on PO Keflex. As he is waiting to be seen by the consulting Head and Neck resident, the patient suddenly spikes a fever to 103 °F and begins complaining of intense pain in his arm, near the site of the cellulitis. He rapidly becomes hypotensive, and the ER physician notices the area of inflammation rapidly spreading up the patient's arm. The patient admits to having injected himself the prior afternoon and to having licked the needle to clean it before injecting himself. The ER physician orders STAT labs and places 2 large bore IVs into the patient's arm. The patient is rapidly becoming hemodynamically unstable. The CBC returns showing a white count of 15,000.

10. What is the principal treatment for this disorder?

a) IV penicillin plus clindamycin

b) IV metronidazole plus ampicillin/sulbactam

c) Surgical débridement

d) Amphotericin B

Answers

1. **d)** The patient presents with classic symptoms of folliculitis. This condition is very common in persons who exercise and wear tight-fitting, sweaty clothing. Although *S. aureus* is the most common organism cultured, *Pseudomonas aeruginosa* is commonly found in "hot tub" folliculitis (organism lives in warm water). Fungi and viruses may also be culprits. In this diabetic patient, we must be especially vigilant to ensure that this infection does not progress to carbuncles, cellulitis, or to a systemic infection. Treatment involves instructing the patient to

stay dry and clean, local wound care, and antibiotics (e.g., Keflex) only if severe. If symptoms do not resolve consider a culture for possible nonbacterial causes. Necrotizing fascitis, although commonly seen in diabetics, usually presents as an infection along fascial plains, with severe pain and erythema rapidly spreading away from the site of infection, fever, and leukocytosis. Also, the patient will appear severely ill. Henoch-Schönlein purpura usually presents with palpable purpura on legs and buttocks, and is accompanied by fever and abdominal distress, and is seen most often in children following an upper respiratory infection. Rose spots are seen in the abdomen of patients infected with *Salmonella*, who typically present with severe gastroenteritis and systemic illness, accompanied by high fever and "pulse-fever dissociation."

2. **b)** This is a classic presentation of erythrasma, a skin infection caused by *Corynebacterium* commonly seen in adult diabetics. Although any of the other choices were possible, the KOH prep makes fungal infections very unlikely, and neither fungal infections nor eczema would show the classic coral-red fluorescence seen on Wood's lamp exam that is characteristic of erythrasma.

3. **d)** Silvery scales on an erythematous base is the classic description of psoriasis, and the Auspitz sign, in which pulling off the scales results in pin-prick bleeding, is a classic physical finding. Psoriasis frequently causes nail pitting and plaques in the intergluteal clefts and the scalp. Mucosal surfaces are not affected.

4. **b)** Although moisturizers can increase patient comfort, they are not sufficient to treat active disease. Topical steroids are the first-line treatment, with PUVA second line and cyclosporin or methotrexate third line. Tar therapy is rarely used.

5. **a) or c)** When you read the phrase "stuck-on" appearance on a case presentation in dermatology, always think of seborrheic keratosis. These plaques are completely harmless and do not require treatment. If they are atypical they can be shave-biopsied to rule out melanoma, but typically they are frozen or excised only if the patient expresses the desire for cosmetic reasons.

6. **a)** This lesion on the sole of the foot is suspicious for melanoma. Remember that melanoma does not only occur in sun-exposed areas, and the sole of the feet, nail-beds, the retina, and oral mucosa are classic occult sites that are commonly missed by clinicians. Despite the fact that it appears to be symmetrical with regular borders, the lesion is >6 mm, has more than 1 color, and is in a suspicious location. It must be excised and sent for pathology.

7. **e)** This patient has erythema nodosum, a panniculitis (inflammation of subcutaneous fat) seen in a variety of inflammatory disorders. Based upon the CXR findings, the chronic cough, the constitutional symptoms, and the hypercalcemia, the patient probably has sarcoidosis as an underlying disorder. The rash itself requires no treatment and should dissipate as the sarcoidosis resolves either spontaneously or with prednisone.

DERMATOLOGY

8. **a)** The words *pearly, heaped-up border* and the finding of telangiectasias in an ulcerating lesion below the eye are all classic descriptors of basal cell carcinoma. The treatment is simple excision.

9. **d)** These malignancies almost never metastasize, and virtually all are cured by excision.

10. **c)** The rapid spread of the infection, the intense pain out of proportion to a simple cellulitis, the fulminant hemodynamic compromise, and the leukocytosis are all indicative of a necrotizing fasciitis. Antibiotics are of limited utility in this disorder, serving only in an adjunctive capacity to extensive and immediate débridement.

9. Ophthalmology

Carlos Ayala

I. Eyes

A. CLASSIC SYNDROMES OR SYMPTOMS

1. Amblyopia
   a. Decreased vision secondary to failure of development of the pathway between the retina & visual cortex before age 7
   b. Usually affects one eye, can be secondary to cataract, severe refractive error, or strabismus
   c. Si/Sx = esotropia (inwardly rotated "crossed eyes") or exotropia (outwardly rotated "walled eyes"), diplopia & refractive error not correctable with lenses
   d. Tx = early correction of cause of visual acuity disturbance
2. Bitemporal hemianopsia (See Figure 9-1)
   a. Unable to see in bilateral temporal fields
   b. Usually caused by a pituitary tumor
3. Internuclear ophthalmoplegia
   a. **Classically found in multiple sclerosis**
   b. Lesion of median longitudinal fasciculus (MLF)
   c. Si/Sx = inability to adduct the ipsilateral eye past midline on lateral gaze (inability to perform conjugate gaze)
   d. Caused by lack of communication between contralateral CN VI nucleus & the ipsilateral CN III nucleus
4. Parinaud's syndrome
   a. Midbrain tectum lesion → bilateral paralysis of upward gaze
   b. Commonly associated with pineal tumor
5. Marcus-Gunn pupil
   a. Due to afferent defect of CN II, pupil will not react to direct light but will react consensually when light is directed at the normal contralateral eye
   b. **Characterized by ⊕ swinging flashlight test**
      1) Swing penlight quickly back & forth between eyes
      2) Denervated pupil will not constrict to direct stimulation & **instead will actually appear to dilate when light is shone in it** because it is dilating back to baseline when consensual light is removed from other eye
6. Argyll-Robertson pupil
   a. **Pathognomonic for 3° syphilis (neurosyphilis)**
   b. Pupils constrict with accommodation but do not constrict to direct light stimulation (pupils accommodate but do not react)
7. Lens dislocation
   a. Occurs in homocystinuria, Marfan's & Alport's syndromes
   b. Lens **dislocates superiorly in Marfan's** (mnemonic: Marfan's patients are tall, their lenses dislocate upward), inferiorly in homocystinuria & variably in Alport's syndrome

295

8. Kayser-Fleischer ring
   a. **Pathognomonic for Wilson's disease**
   b. Finding is a ring of golden pigment around the iris
9. Pterygium
   a. Fleshy growth from conjunctiva onto nasal side of cornea
   b. Associated with exposure to wind, sand, sun & dust
   c. Tx = cosmetic removal unless impairing vision
10. Pinguecula (See Color Plates 23 and 24)
    a. Benign yellowish nodules on either side of the cornea
    b. Commonly seen in patients > 35
    c. Rarely grows & requires no treatment
11. Subconjunctival hemorrhage
    a. Spontaneous onset of a painless, bright red patch on sclera
    b. Benign, self-limited condition usually seen after overexertion
12. Retrobulbar neuritis
    a. Caused by inflammation of the optic nerve, usually unilateral
    b. **Seen in multiple sclerosis, often is the initial sign**
    c. Si/Sx = rapid loss of vision & pain upon moving eye, spontaneously remitting within 2–8 wk, each relapse damages the nerve more, until eventually blindness results
    d. Funduscopic exam is nonrevealing
    e. Tx = corticosteroids
13. Optic neuritis
    a. Inflammation of optic nerve within the eye
    b. Causes include viral infection, multiple sclerosis, vasculitis, methanol, meningitis, syphilis, tumor metastases
    c. Si/Sx = variable vision loss & ↓ pupillary light reflex
    d. **Funduscopic exam reveals disk hyperemia**
    e. If pt is > 60 yr, biopsy temporal artery to rule out temporal arteritis
    f. Tx = corticosteroids

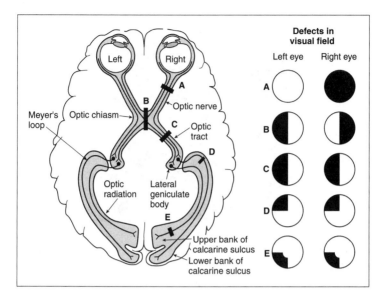

FIGURE 9-1   Visual field deficits. Lesions in the visual system are correlated with specific visual field deficits. (A) Blindness in the right eye. (B) Bitemporal heteronymous hemianopsia. (C) Left homonymous hemianopsia. (D) Superior quadrantic anopia. (E) Inferior quadrantic anopsia with macular sparing. (Reproduced with permission from Pritchard TC and Alloway KD. *Medical Neuroscience.* Madison, Connecticut: Fence Creek Publishing, 1999:307. © Fence Creek Publishing, LLC.)

B. Palpebral Inflammation

TABLE 9-1   Palpebral Inflammation

DISEASE	SI/SX	TX
Chalazion	• Inflammation of internal meibomian sebaceous gland • Presents with swelling on conjunctival surface of eyelid	None, self-limiting
Hordeolum (Stye)	• Infection of external sebaceous glands of Zeiss or Mol • Presents with tender red swelling at lid margin	Hot compress, can add antibiotics
Blepharitis	• Inflammation of eyelids & eyelashes due to infection (*S. aureus*) or secondary to seborrhea • Presents with red, swollen eyelid margins, with dry flakes noted on lashes • **Without Tx can extend along eyelid (cellulitis)**	Wash lid margins daily with baby shampoo, control scalp seborrhea with shampoo
Orbital cellulitis	• Can occur if blepharitis is left untreated (See Figure 9-2) • Also seen as complication of paranasal sinus infection • **Can spread to cavernous sinus leading to deadly thrombosis & meningitis**	Treat emergently with IV nafcillin or cephalosporin

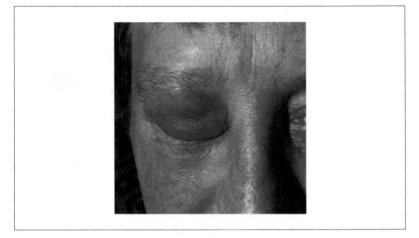

FIGURE 9-2 The appearance of a patient with preseptal cellulitis.

C. RED EYE
1. **Assess pain, visual acuity, type of eye discharge, pupillary abnormalities in all patients**
2. DDx

TABLE 9-2 Red Eye

DISEASE	SI/SX	CAUSE	TX
Bacterial conjunctivitis	• Minimal pain, no vision changes • **Purulent** discharge • No pupillary changes • **Rarely** preauricular adenopathy (only *N. gonorrhoeae*)	*S. pneumoniae, Staph. spp., N. gonorrhoeae, Chlamydia trachomatis* (in neonates, sexually active adults)	Topical sulfacetamide or erythromycin
Viral conjunctivitis	• Minimal pain, no vision changes • **Watery** discharge • No pupillary changes • **Often preauricular adenopathy** • **Often pharyngitis** (adenovirus)	Adenovirus most common, others = HSV, varicella, EBV, influenza, echovirus, coxsackie virus	No treatment required, self-limiting dz
Allergic conjunctivitis	• No pain, vision, or pupil changes • **Marked pruritus** • **Bilateral** watery eyes	Allergy/Hay fever	Antihistamine or steroid drops
Hyphema	• Pain, no vision changes • No discharge, no pupil changes • **Blood in anterior chamber of eye, fluid level noted** (See Figure 9-3)	Blunt ocular trauma	Eye patch to ↓ movement
Xerophthalmia	• Minimal pain, vision blurry, no pupillary changes, no discharge • **Bitot's spots** visible on exam (desquamated, keratinized conjunctival cells)	Sjogren's disease or vitamin A deficiency	Artificial tears, vitamin A

TABLE 9-2 *Continued*

DISEASE	SI/SX	CAUSE	TX
	• **Keratoconjunctivitis sicca** (Sjogren's disease) **Dx by Schirmer test** (place filter paper over eyelid, if not wet in 15 min → Dx)		
Corneal abrasion	• **Painful, with photophobia** • No pupil changes • Watery discharge • Dx by fluorescein stain to detect areas of corneal defect	Direct trauma to eye (finger, stick, etc.)	Antibiotics, eye patch, examine daily
Keratitis	• **Pain**, photophobia, tearing • **Decreased vision** • **Herpes shows classic dendritic branching on fluorescein stain** (See Color Plates 25 and 26) • **Pus in anterior chamber (hypopyon) is a grave sign**	Adenovirus, HSV, *Pseudomonas, S. pneumoniae, Staph., Moraxella* (often in contact lens wearers)	**Emergency, immediate Ophtho consult** Tx = topical vidarabine for herpes
Uveitis	• Inflammation of the iris, ciliary body, &/or choroid • **Pain, miosis**, photophobia • **Flare & cells** seen in aqueous humor **on slit lamp examination** (See Figure 9-4)	Seen in seronegative spondyloarthropathy, inflammatory bowel disease, sarcoidosis, or infxn (CMV, syphilis)	Tx underlying dz
Angle closure glaucoma	• **Severe pain** • ↓ **vision**, halos around lights • **Fixed mid-dilated pupil** • Eyeball firm to pressure (See Figure 9-5)	↓ aqueous humor outflow via canal of Schlemm— mydriatics can also cause	**Emergency,** IV mannitol & acetazolamide, laser iridotomy for cure

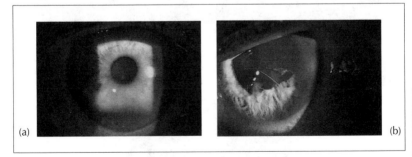

(a) (b)

FIGURE 9-3 (a) A hyphema; (b) penetrating eye injury (notice the eyelashes in the anterior chamber and the distorted iris).

OPHTHAL-MOLOGY

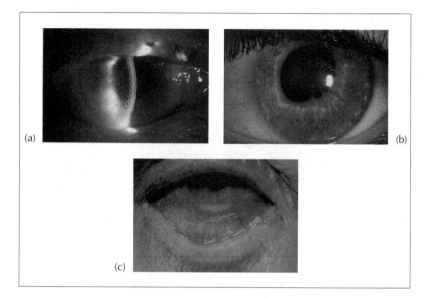

Figure 9-4   Signs of anterior uveitis; (a) keratic precipitates on the corneal endothelium; (b) posterior synechiae (adhesions between the lens and iris) give the pupil an irregular appearance; (c) a hypopyon, white cells have collected as a mass in the inferior anterior chamber.

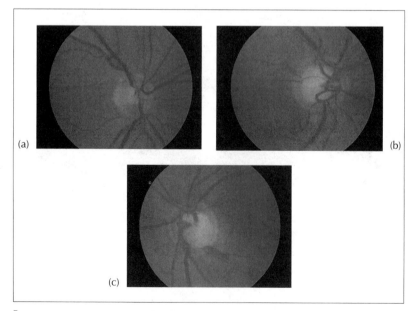

Figure 9-5   Comparison of (a) a normal optic disk; (b) glaucomatous optic disc; (c) a disc hemorrhage is a feature of patients with low-tension glaucoma.

D. DACRYOCYSTITIS (TEAR DUCT INFLAMMATION)

1. Infection of lacrimal sac, usually caused by *Staphylococcus aureus, Streptococcus pneumoniae, Hemophilus influenzae,* or *S. pyogenes*
2. Si/Sx = inflammation & tenderness of nasal aspect of lower lid, purulent discharge may be noted or expressed (See Figure 9-6)
3. Tx = Keflex

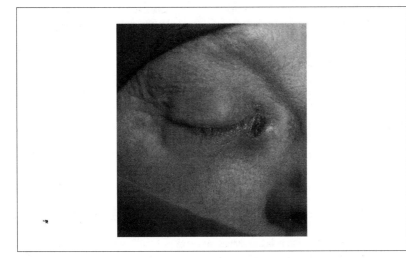

FIGURE 9-6   Dacrocystitis, unusually, in this case, pointing through the skin.

E. EYE COLORS

1. **Yellow eye** (icterus) from bilirubin staining of sclera (jaundice)
2. **Yellow vision** seen in digoxin toxicity
3. **Blue sclera** classically found in osteogenesis imperfecta & Marfan's disease [see Musculoskeletal, Sections II.D & IV.G]
4. **Opaque eye** due to cataract
   a. Opacity of lens severe enough to interfere with vision
   b. Causes = congenital, diabetes (sorbitol precipitation in lens), galactosemia (galactitol precipitation in lens), Hurler's disease [see Appendix A]

F. RETINA (See Color Plate 27)

1. Diabetic retinopathy
   a. Occurs after about 10 yr of diabetes
      1) Background type
         a) Flame hemorrhages, microaneurysms & soft exudates (cotton-wool spots) on retina (See Color Plates 28 and 29)
         b) Tx is strict glucose & hypertension control
      2) Proliferative type
         a) More advanced dz, with neovascularization easily visible around fundus (hyperemia) & hard exudates (See Color Plate 30)

      b) Tx is photocoagulation (laser ablation of blood vessels in the retina) that slows disease progression but is not curative

2. Age-related macular degeneration (AMD)
   a. AMD causes painless loss of visual acuity
   b. Dx by altered pigmentation in macula
   c. No Tx, but pts often retain adequate peripheral vision
3. Retinal detachment
   a. Presents with painless, dark vitreous floaters, flashes of light (photopsias), blurry vision, eventually progressing to a curtain of blindness in vision as detachment worsens
   b. Tx = urgent surgical reattachment
4. Retinitis pigmentosa (See Figure 9-7)
   a. Slowly progressive defect in night vision (often starts in young children) with ring-shaped scotoma (blind-spot) that gradually increases in size to obscure more vision
   b. Disease is hereditary with unclear transmission mode
   c. May be part of the Laurence-Moon-Biedl syndrome
   d. There is no treatment
5. Classic physical findings of retina
   a. **Leukocoria** = absent red reflex, actually appears white, seen in retinoblastoma (See Figure 9-8)
   b. **Roth spots** = small hemorrhagic spots with central clearing in retina associated with endocarditis
   c. **Copper wiring, flame hemorrhages, A-V nicking** seen in subacute hypertension &/or atherosclerosis
   d. **Cotton-wool spots** (soft exudates) seen in chronic HTN
   e. Papilledema appears as disk hyperemia, blurring, & elevation, associated with ↑ intracranial pressure
   f. "Sea fan" neovascularization in sickle cell anemia
   g. Wrinkles on retina seen in retinal detachment
   h. **Cherry-red spot on macula** seen in Tay-Sachs, Niemann-Pick disease, central retinal artery occlusion
   i. Hollenhorst plaque = yellow cholesterol emboli in retinal artery
   j. Brown macule on retina = malignant melanoma (most common intraocular tumor in adults) (See Figure 9-9)

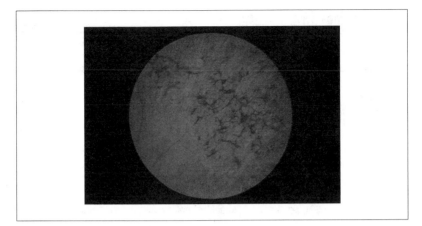

FIGURE 9-7   The clinical appearance of peripheral retina in retinitis pigmentosa.

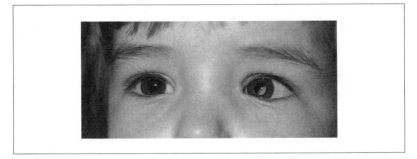

FIGURE 9-8   Left leukocoria.

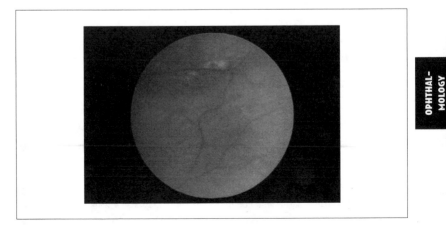

FIGURE 9-9   The clinical appearance of a choroidal melanoma.

Ophthalmology Case Scenario

A 35-year-old male presents to your community outpatient clinic complaining of a week of intermittent episodes of pain and blurry vision in his right eye. Each of these episodes lasts for approximately 1–2 hours. He finds that his pain is usually diminished after taking a nap. The patient denies any pertinent past medical history and until these episodes began he was in his usual state of good health. On physical exam you note that his right eye is red, with a visual acuity of 20/200, and the pupil is fixed and mid-dilated.

1. The most likely diagnosis and preferred treatment for this patient is:

   a) Cluster headache, naproxen, and oxygen therapy

   b) Migraine headache, rest, and NSAIDS

   c) Acute glaucoma, immediate ophthalmology consult, and acetazolamide

   d) Viral conjunctivitis, ophthalmology consult

   e) Uveitis, steroids

A 39-year-old male arrives in your urgent care clinic complaining of a red left eye, accompanied by some discomfort and mildly blurry vision relieved by blinking. His eye does not itch. The patient has just started a gardening job and feels he might be allergic to the roses or other flowers in the garden.

2. Which of the following is the next appropriate step in the work-up and treatment of this patient?

   a) Probably has an allergy to pollen, do vision testing and give the patient steroid eye drops and decongestants, follow up with his primary care provider

   b) Do vision testing, examine eyes with a pen light and assure patient that this is probably a viral infection that will pass with time

   c) Do vision testing, look at eye with a slit lamp, give steroid eye drops to decrease discomfort and inflammation

   d) Do vision testing, apply fluorescein to eye and examine with slit lamp, treat according to findings

Answers

1. **c)** This patient presents with classic signs and symptoms of acute angle-closure glaucoma. The sudden increase in intraocular pressure is commonly accompanied by a hazy cornea and mid-dilated pupils. Patients also commonly complain of seeing halos around lights, nausea, and vomiting. This is an emergency and an ophthalmologist must be immediately notified. The patient has no complaints of headaches, and a viral conjunctivitis would not present with visual and pupillary changes. Furthermore, an ophthalmology consult is not required for the treatment of viral conjunctivitis, which is a benign disorder. Patients with uveitis

commonly present with miosis and other systemic symptoms of inflammatory disorders.

2. **d)** Treating red eye patients with corticosteroid eye drops without properly ruling out herpes keratitis or fungal infections is very dangerous. All these patient must have their vision tested and a slit-lamp examination to rule out foreign bodies and also to magnify fluorescein staining of corneal abrasion or dendritic pattern of herpes keratitis. This patient has no itching, which commonly accompanies allergies. When in doubt get an ophthalmology consult and play it safe.

10. Radiology

Michael Gentry

I. Introduction

1. This section will cover common causes for radiologic findings presented in the clinical vignettes on the USMLE as well as on rounds. Where useful, the causes will be divided into categories using the mnemonic **VINDICATE**

   V = Vascular
   I = Inflammatory/Infectious
   N = Neoplastic
   D = Degenerative
   I = Idiopathic/Intoxication
   C = Congenital
   A = Autoimmune
   T = Trauma
   E = Endocrine

II. Helpful Terms and Concepts

A. LUCENT VS. SCLEROTIC LESIONS

On plain film, a lucency is a focal area of bone or tissue that has a decreased density, usually resulting from a pathological process. A lucent bone lesion may appear like a dark, punched-out hole in the surrounding, normal bone. In contrast, sclerotic bone lesions appear denser than the surrounding bone. Thus, a sclerotic mass presents as whiter and more intense than its surroundings.

B. HYPODENSE VS. HYPERDENSE

Similar to that on plain films, tissue density on CT can be characterized by how light or dark it appears relative to surrounding, normal parenchyma. Hypodense lesions appear darker than normal tissue and hyperdense lesions are brighter. Air- or fluid-filled lesions such as cysts and abscesses are common hypodense lesions.

C. RING-ENHANCEMENT

This refers to a bright intensity that can be observed surrounding many lesions on both CT and MRI. This usually indicates local edema around a mass lesion and in the brain it can indicate breakdown of the blood-brain barrier.

D. RADIOPAQUE

The more radiopaque an object is, the brighter it appears on plain film. Dental fillings, bullets, and metal prostheses are very radiopaque so they appear white on plain film.

E. RADIOLUCENT

The more radiolucent an object is, the darker it appears on plain film.

III. Common Radiologic Studies

TABLE 10-1   Common Radiologic Studies

STUDY	INDICATIONS
CT vs. MRI	• CT → faster, less expensive, greater sensitivity for acute head trauma, better for detection of spinal cord compression • MRI → better visualization of soft tissue, allows multiplanar imaging (axial, coronal, sagittal & obliques), no ionizing radiation
Endoscopic retrograde cholangio-pancreatography (ERCP)	Pancreatitis 2° to choledocholithiasis, cholestatic jaundice
Ultrasound (Utz)*	Abdominal aortic aneurysm, gallbladder disease, renal & adrenal masses, ectopic pregnancy, kidney stones
Carotid doppler Utz	Carotid artery stenosis, assessing flow dynamics
Intravenous pyelogram (IVP)	GU obstruction
Kidney, ureter, bladder (KUB) x-ray*	Kidney stones, solid abdominal masses, abdominal free air
Lateral decubitus chest plain film	To determine whether a suspected pleural effusion will layer

*Note 80/20 rule: gallstones diagnosed 80% of the time & kidney stones 20% of the time by Utz. Kidney stones diagnosed 80% of the time & gallstones only 20% of the time by x-ray.

IV. An Approach to a Chest X-Ray (See Figure 10-1)

A = **A**irway—is trachea midline? & **A**lignment—symmetry of clavicles

B = **B**ones—look for fractures, lytic lesions, or defects

C = **C**ardiac silhouette—normally occupies < $\frac{1}{2}$ chest width

D = **D**iaphragms—flattened (e.g., COPD)?, blunted angles (effusion)?, elevated (airspace consolidation)?

E = **E**xternal soft tissues—lymph nodes (especially axilla), subQ emphysema, other lesions

F = **F**ields of the lung—opacities, nodules, vascularity, bronchial cuffing, etc.

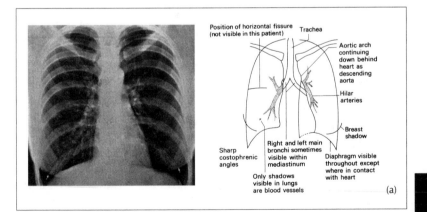

FIGURE 10-1   Normal chest. (a) PA view. The arrows point to the breast shadows of this female patient. (b) Lateral view. Note that the upper retrosternal area is of the same density as the retro-cardiac areas, and the same as over the upper thoracic vertebrae. The vertebrae are more transradiant (i.e., blacker) as the eye travels down the spine, until the diaphragm is reached. Ao = aorta; T = Trachea.

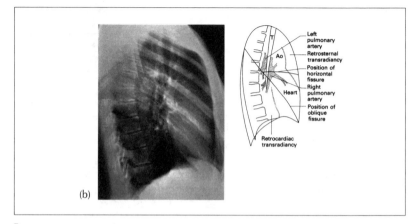

(b)

FIGURE 10-1   *Continued*

V. Common Radiologic Findings

TABLE 10-2   Common Radiologic Findings

FINDING/DESCRIPTION	DIFFERENTIAL DIAGNOSIS	
Hair-on-end skull sign on plain film Caused by new bone formation that occurs perpendicular to the skull table, resulting in a thin, spiked appearance, as if bony hairs growing out of skull (See Figure 10-2)	• Congenital • Sickle cell anemia • Osteosarcoma	
Hypodense cerebral masses on CT (See Figure 10-3)	Neoplastic: • Glioma • Prolactinoma • Craniopharyngiomas	Infectious: • Pyogenic abscess • Tuberculoma • Hydatid cyst
Multiple contrast-enhancing lesions on CT or MRI	Neoplastic: • Metastases (See Figure 10-4) ◊ Breast CA & bronchogenic lung CA most common ◊ Also malignant melanoma, prostate, lymphoma	Infectious: • Bacterial abscess • Toxoplasmosis • Cysticercosis Vascular: • Infarct Degenerative: • Demyelinating disease
Nonsclerotic skull lucency	Infectious: • TB • Syphilis • Osteomyelitis Neoplastic: • Multiple myeloma	• Metastases Trauma: • Burr hole Endocrine: • Hyperparathyroidism

TABLE 10-2   *Continued*

FINDING/DESCRIPTION	DIFFERENTIAL DIAGNOSIS	
Sclerotic bone lesions (See Figures 1-16 and 10-5)	**Infectious:** • Osteomyelitis (presents with periosteal reaction) • Syphilis **Congenital:** • Fibrous dysplasia • Tuberous sclerosis **Vascular:** • Healing fracture callus	**Neoplastic:** • Metastases—primarily prostate & breast • Lymphoma • Multiple myeloma—usually presents with multiple lesions (See Figure 1-17) • Osteosarcoma
"Bone within bone" sign	**Endocrine:** • Growth arrest & recovery • Paget's disease • Osteopetrosis	**Intoxication:** Heavy metal poisoning
Inferior surface rib notching	**Vascular:** • Coarctation of the aorta—**classic finding** • Superior vena cava obstruction	**Congenital:** • Chest wall A-V malformation
Ivory vertebral body Sclerotic change in a single vertebra	**Neoplastic:** • Sclerotic metastases • Lymphoma	**Endocrine:** • Paget's disease
Honeycomb lung Fibrotic replacement of lung parenchyma with thick-walled cysts	**Idiopathic:** • Idiopathic interstitial fibrosis • Histiocytosis X • Sarcoidosis **Congenital:** • Cystic fibrosis • Tuberous sclerosis • Neurofibromatosis	**Autoimmune:** • Scleroderma • Rheumatoid arthritis **Intoxication:** • Allergic alveolitis • Asbestosis • Bleomycin • Nitrofurantoin • Cyclophosphamide
Ground glass opacities on lung CT Hazy, granular increase in density of lung parenchyma that usually implies an acute inflammatory process	**Inflammation:** • Interstitial pneumonia • Hypersensitivity pneumonitis • *Pneumocystic carinii* pneumonia (See Figure 1-9) • Alveolar proteinosis	
Water-bottle-shaped heart on PA plain film	Pericardial effusions with more than 250 mL of fluid	
Pulmonary edema Classically, severe pulmonary edema appears as **a bat's-wing shadow**	**Vascular:** • Congestive heart failure **Inflammatory:** • Adult respiratory distress syndrome (See Figure 1-5) • Mendelson's syndrome	**Intoxication:** Smoke inhalation **Trauma:** Near drowning
Blunting of costophrenic angles 300–500 mL of fluid is needed before blunting of the lateral costophrenic angles becomes apparent (See Figures 10-6 and 10-7)	Pleural effusion	

TABLE 10-2   *Continued*

FINDING/DESCRIPTION	DIFFERENTIAL DIAGNOSIS	
Kerley B lines (See Figure 10-8) Interlobar septa on the peripheral aspects of the lungs that become thickened by disease or fluid accumulation	**Vascular:** • Left ventricular failure • Lymphatic obstruction	**Inflammatory:** • Sarcoidosis Lymphangitis carcinomatosa
Multiple lung small soft tissue Densities <2 mm	**Inflammatory:** • Sarcoidosis • Miliary TB • Fungal infection • Parasites • Extrinsic allergic alveolitis	**Neoplastic:** Metastases **Endocrine:** Hemosiderosis
Lung nodules >2 cm Ghon complex—calcified granuloma classic for TB, found at lung base along hilum (See Figures 10-9 and 1-6)	**Neoplastic:** • Metastases • Primary lung CA • Benign hamartoma **Intoxication:** • Silicosis **Idiopathic:** • Histiocytosis X	**Inflammatory:** • Sarcoidosis • TB • Wegener's • Fungal infections • Abscess
Hilar adenopathy (See Figure 1-24)	**Inflammatory:** • Sarcoidosis (bilateral, eggshell calcification) • Amyloidosis **Intoxication:** • Silicosis	**Neoplastic:** • Bronchogenic CA (unilateral) • Lymphoma
Ring shadow Annular opacity with central lucency (See Figure 10-10)	**Infectious:** • TB (apex) • Lung abscess • Fungal • Amebiasis	**Neoplastic:** • Bronchogenic carcinoma • Metastases • Lymphoma **Autoimmune:** • Rheumatoid lung dz
Unilaterally elevated diaphragm (See Figure 10-11)	**Trauma:** • Phrenic nerve palsy **Congenital:** • Pulmonary hypoplasia scoliosis	**Vascular:** • Pulmonary embolism
Bilaterally elevated diaphragm	• Obesity • Pregnancy • Fibrotic lung dz	
Steeple sign Narrowed area of subglottic trachea	Parainfluenza virus (croup)	
Thumb sign	Epiglottitis classically caused by *Hemophilus influenzae*	
Pneumoperitoneum Free air under the diaphragm on an upright chest film or upright abdomen **Double wall sign on abdominal plain film** The appearance of the outer & inner walls of bowel is almost pathognomonic for pneumoperitoneum	**Inflammatory:** • Perforation ◊ Ulcer ◊ Diverticulitis ◊ Appendicitis ◊ Toxic megacolon ◊ Infarcted bowel	Also can be: • Peritoneal dialysis • Pneumomediastinum that has tracked inferiorly • Diaphragmatic rupture

TABLE 10-2   *Continued*

FINDING/DESCRIPTION	DIFFERENTIAL DIAGNOSIS	
Gasless abdomen on abdominal plain film (See Figure 10-12)	• Obstruction • Severe ascites • Pancreatitis	
Filling defects in stomach on upper GI series	• Gastric ulcer • Gastric cancer	
Dilated small bowel (See Figures 10-12 and 10-13)	• Mechanical obstruction ◊ Postsurgical ◊ Incarcerated hernia ◊ Intussusception	• Paralytic ileus **Inflammatory:** • Celiac sprue • Scleroderma
Coffee bean sigmoid volvulus (See Figure 10-14)	• Large bowel obstruction • Paralytic ileus	
String sign on barium swallow Narrowing of the terminal ileum caused by thickening of the bowel wall	• Crohn's disease	
Lead pipe sign on barium enema Smooth, narrowed colon without haustra	• Inflammatory bowel dz (See Figure 10-15)	
Apple core lesion Circumferential growth in the bowel lumen	• Colon cancer	
Liver calcifications	**Inflammatory:** • Granuloma • Hydatid cyst	**Neoplastic:** • Hepatoma
Gas in portal vein Linear lucencies that reach within 2 cm of liver capsule	**Vascular (seen in adults):** • Mesenteric infarct • Air embolism	**Inflammatory (children):** • Necrotizing enterocolitis
Unilateral cystic renal mass Hypodensities with thin walls	**Inflammatory:** • Renal abscess • Hemodialysis-induced cyst • Hydatid cyst	**Congenital:** • Bilateral renal cysts • Polycystic kidney dz **Neoplastic:** • Renal cell carcinoma
String of beads on renal arteriogram Multiple dilatations alternating with strictures of both renal arteries	• Fibromuscular dysplasia	

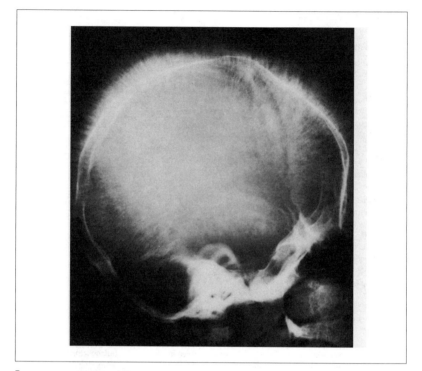

FIGURE 10-2   "Hair-on-end" appearance.

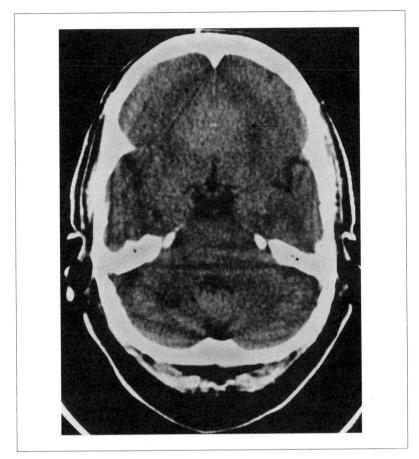

FIGURE 10-3   Hypodense mass on CT.

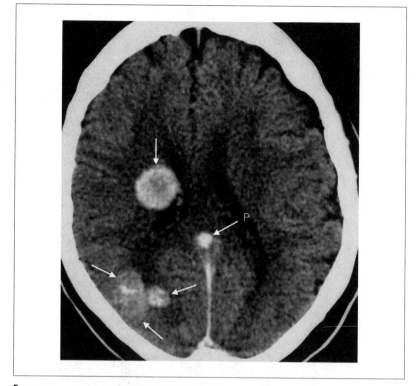

FIGURE 10-4   Metastases (arrows). (P = pineal.)

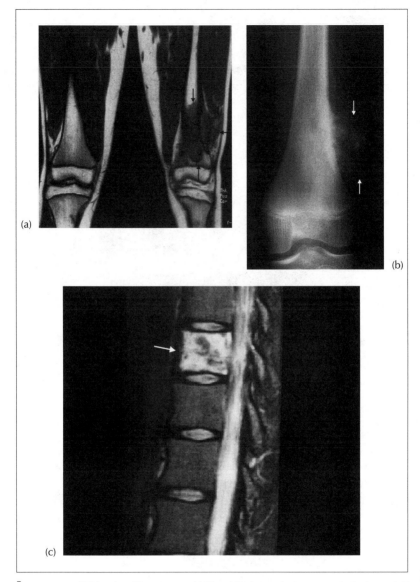

(a)

(b)

(c)

Figure 10-5   MRI imaging of bone tumors. (a) T1-weighted scan of osteosarcoma in the lower shaft and metaphysis of the left femur. The extent of tumor (arrows) within the bone and the soft-tissue extension are both very well shown. This information is not available from the plain film (b), although the plain film provides a more specific diagnosis, because the bone formation within the soft-tissue extension (arrows) is obvious. (c) T2-weighted scan of lymphoma in the T10 vertebral body (arrow). The very high signal of the neoplastic tissue is very evident even though there is no deformity of shape of the vertebral body.

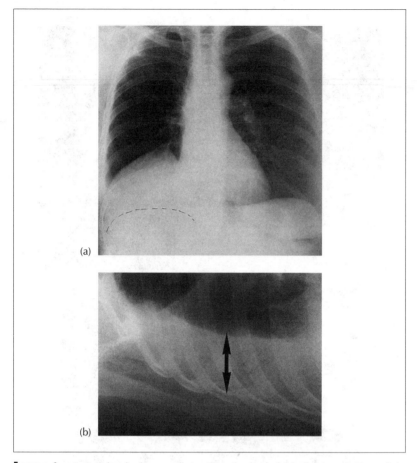

(a)

(b)

FIGURE 10-6   Large right subpulmonary effusion (the patient has had right mastectomy). Almost all the fluid is between the lung and the diaphragm. The right hemidiaphragm cannot be seen. (a) Its estimated position has been penciled in. (b) In the lateral decubitus view, the fluid moves to lie between the lateral chest wall and the lung edge (arrows).

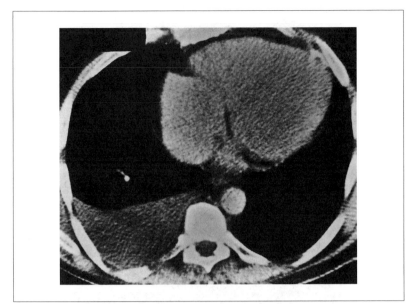

FIGURE 10-7   CT of pleural fluid. The right pleural effusion is of homogeneous density, with a CT number between zero and soft tissue. Its well-defined, meniscus-shaped border with the lung is typical.

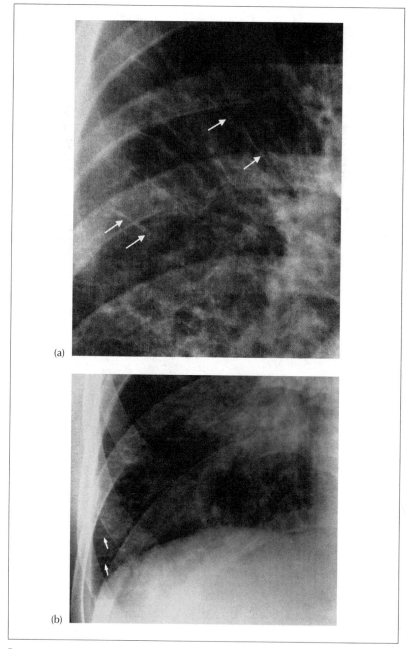

(a)

(b)

FIGURE 10-8   Septal lines. (a) Kerley A lines (arrows) in a patient with lymphangitis carcinomatosa. (b) Kerley B lines in a patient with pulmonary edema. The septal lines (arrows) are thinner than the adjacent blood vessels. The B lines are seen in the outer centimeter of lung where blood vessels are invisible or very difficult to identify.

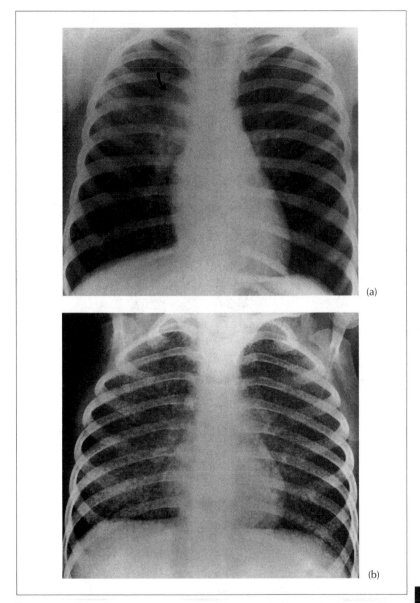

(a)

(b)

FIGURE 10-9   Tuberculosis. (a) The primary complex. This 7-year-old child shows ill-defined consolidation in the right lung together with enlargement of the draining lymph nodes (arrow). (b) Miliary tuberculosis. The innumerable small nodular shadows uniformly distributed throughout the lungs in this young child are typical of miliary tuberculosis. In this instance, no primary focus of infection is visible.

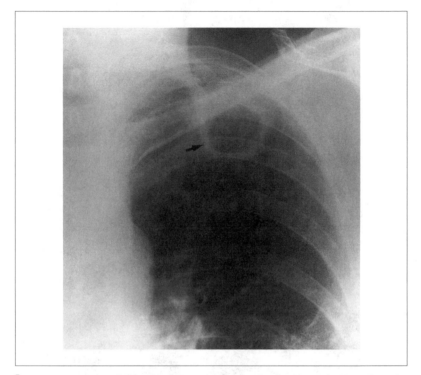

FIGURE 10-10   Fungus infection. The cavity (arrow) in this patient from the southeastern US was due to North American blastomycosis. Note the similarity to tuberculosis. Other fungi, e.g., histoplasmosis, can give an identical appearance.

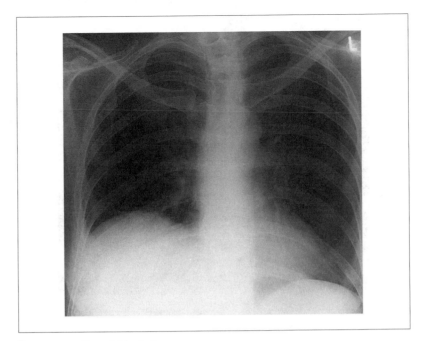

FIGURE 10-11   Elevated right diaphragm.

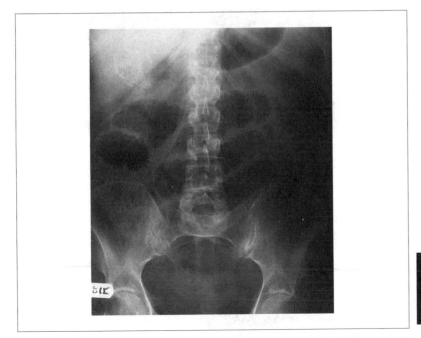

FIGURE 10-12   Small bowel obstruction: distended small bowel and absence of gas shadows in the colon.

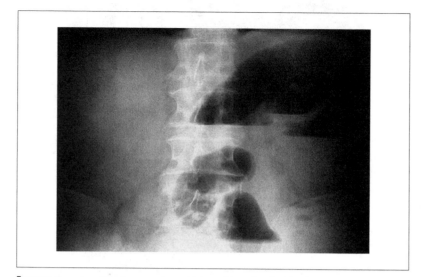

FIGURE 10-13   Erect film demonstrating multiple small bowel air/fluid levels.

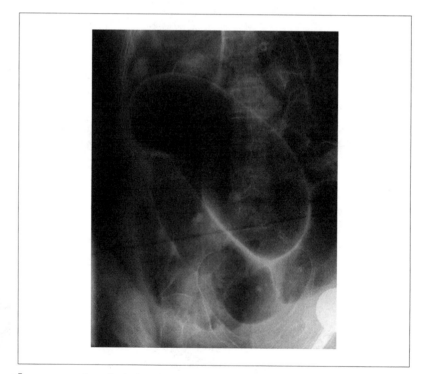

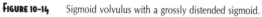

FIGURE 10-14   Sigmoid volvulus with a grossly distended sigmoid.

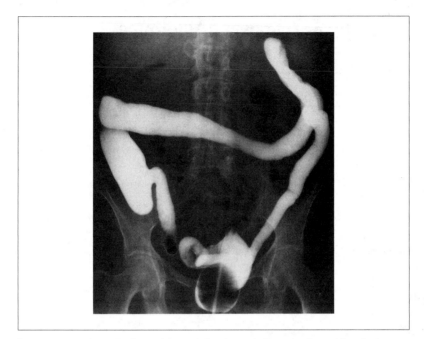

FIGURE 10-15   Ulcerative colitis. With long-standing disease the haustra are lost and the colon becomes narrowed and shortened, coming to resemble a rigid tube. Reflux into the ileum through an incompetent ileocecal valve has occurred.

Appendix A. Zebras and Syndromes

DISEASE	DESCRIPTION/SX
Achondroplasia	Autosomal dominant dwarfism due to early epiphyseal closure → shortening & thickening of bones. Si/Sx = leg bowing, hearing loss, sciatica, infantile hydrocephalus. Patients can live normal lifespans.
Adrenoleuko-dystrophy	X-linked recessive defect in long-chain fatty acid metabolism due to a peroxisomal enzyme deficiency. Causes rapidly progressing central demyelination, adrenal insufficiency, hyperpigmentation of skin, spasticity, seizures & death by age 12.
Albers-Schönberg disease (osteopetrosis)	↑↑ skeletal density due to osteoclastic failure → multiple fractures due to ↓ perfusion of thick bone, also causes anemia due to ↓ marrow space & blindness, deafness & cranial nerve dysfunction due to narrowing & impingement of neural foramina.
Alkaptonuria	Defect of phenylalanine metabolism causing accumulation of homogentisic acid. Presents with black urine, ochronosis (blue-black pigmentation of ear, nose, cheeks) & arthropathy due to cartilage binding homogentisic acid.
Alport's syndrome	X-linked hereditary collagen defect causing sensorineural hearing loss, lens dislocation, hematuria (glomerulonephritis).
Ataxia-Telangiectasia	DNA repair defect affects B & T lymphocytes. Autosomal recessive disease usually appears by age 2. Physical signs include ataxia of gait, telangiectasias of skin & conjunctiva, & recurrent sinus infections.
Banti's syndrome	"Idiopathic portal HTN." Splenomegaly & portal HTN following subclinical portal vein occlusion. Insidious onset, occurring years after initial occlusive event.
Bartter's syndrome	Kidney disease that causes Na, K & Cl wasting. Despite increased levels of renin, the blood pressure remains low.
Beckwith-Wiedemann syndrome	Autosomal dominant fetal overgrowth syndrome of macrosomia, microcephaly, macroglossia, organomegaly, omphalocele, distinctive lateral earlobe fissures, hypoglycemia associated with hyperinsulinemia, ↑ incidence of Wilms' tumor.
Bernard-Soulier syndrome	Autosomal recessive defect of platelet GpIb receptor (binds to vWF), presents with chronic, severe mucosal bleeds & giant platelets on blood smear.
Binswanger's disease	Subacute subcortical dementia caused by small artery infarcts in periventricular white matter. Usually seen in long-standing hypertension, but is rare.
Bruton's agamma-globulinemia	X-linked block of B-cell maturation, causing ↓ B cell levels & immunoglobulin levels. Presents with recurrent bacterial infections in infants >6 mo of age.
Caisson's disease	Decompression sickness ("the bends") caused by rapid ascent from deep-sea diving. Sx occur from 30 min to 1 hr = joint pain, cough, skin burning/mottling.
Caroli's disease	Segmental cystic dilation of intrahepatic bile ducts complicated by stones & cholangitis, can be cancer precursor.
Charcot-Marie-Tooth disease	Autosomal dominant peroneal muscular atrophy causing foot drop & stocking-glove decrease in vibration/pain/temperature sense & DTRs in lower extremities. Histologically → repeated demyelination & remyelination of segmental areas of the nerve. Patients may present as children (type 1) or adults (type 2).
Chediak-Higashi syndrome	Autosomal recessive defect of microtubule function of neutrophils, leads to decreased lysosomal fusion to phagosomes. Presents with recurrent Staphylococcus & Streptococcus infections, albinism, peripheral & cranial neuropathies.
Cheyne-Stokes respirations	A central apnea seen in CHF, ↑ ICP, or cerebral infection/inflammation/trauma: cycles of central apnea followed by regular crescendo-decrescendo breathing (amplitude first waxes & then wanes back to apnea): Biot's is an uncommon variant seen in meningitis in which the cycles consist of central apnea followed by steady amplitude breathing that then shuts back off to apnea.

Disease	Description/Sx
Chronic granulomatous disease	Phagocytes lack respiratory burst or NADPH oxidase, so can engulf bacteria but are unable to kill them. Presents with recurrent infections with *Aspergillus* & *S. aureus* infections. Tx = recombinant interferon-γ.
Cystinuria	Autosomal recessive failure of tubular resorption of cystine & dibasic amino acids (lysine, ornithine, arginine), clinically see cystine stones. Tx = hydration to ↑ urine volume, alkalinization of urine with bicarbonate & acetazolamide.
de Quervain's tenosynovitis	Tenosynovitis causing pain on flexion of thumb (motion of abductor pollicis longus).
Diamond-Blackfan syndrome	"Pure red cell aplasia," a congenital or acquired deficiency in the RBC stem cell. Congenital disorder is sometimes associated with abnormal facies, cardiac & renal abnormalities. Tx = steroids.
DiGeorge's syndrome	Embryologic defect in development of pharyngeal pouches 3 & 4 → thymic aplasia that causes T-cell deficiency, & parathyroid aplasia. Most commonly presents with tetany due to hypocalcemia secondary to hypoparathyroidism, & recurrent severe viral, fungal, or protozoal infections.
Dressler's syndrome	Acute pericarditis, develops within 2–4 wk after acute MI or heart surgery, may be due to autoimmune reaction to myocardial antigens.
Ehlers-Danlos syndrome	Autosomal dominant defect in collagen synthesis, variable expressivity. Si/Sx = loose joints, pathognomonic ↓ skin elasticity, mitral regurgitation, genu recurvatum of knee (fixed in hyperextension), aortic dilation.
Ehrlichiosis	Rickettsial family member, *Ehrlichiosis canis*, causes acute febrile illness, malaise, myalgia, severe headache but with no rash. The protracted illness presents with leukopenia, thrombocytopenia & renal failure. It is contracted by tick bites.
Ellis-van Creveld	Syndrome of polydactyly + single atrium.
Erb's paralysis	Waiter's tip—upper-brachial plexopathy (C5,6).
Evan's syndrome	IgG autoantibody-mediated hemolytic anemia & thrombocytopenia, associated with collagen-vascular dz, TTP, hepatic cirrhosis, leukemia, sarcoidosis, Hashimoto's thyroiditis. Tx = prednisone & intravenous immunoglobulin.
Fabry's disease	X-linked defect in galactosidase, Sx = lower trunk skin lesions, corneal opacity, renal/cardiac/cerebral disease that are invariably lethal in infancy or childhood.
Fanconi's anemia	Autosomal recessive disorder of DNA repair. Presents with pancytopenia, ↑ risk of malignancy, short stature, bird-like facies, café au lait spots, congenital urogenital defects, retardation, absent thumb.
Fanconi syndrome	Dysfunction of proximal renal tubules, congenital or acquired (drugs, multiple myeloma, toxic metals), presenting with ↓ reabsorption of glucose, amino acids, phosphate, & bicarbonate. Associated with RTA type II, clinically see glycosuria, hyperphosphaturia, hypophosphatemia (vitamin D–resistant rickets), aminoaciduria (generalized, not cystine specific), systemic acidosis, polyuria, polydipsia.
Farber's disease	Auto recessive defect in ceramidase, causing ceramide accumulation in nerves, onset within months of birth, death occurs by age 2.
Felty's syndrome	Rheumatoid arthritis plus splenomegaly & neutropenia, often with thrombocytopenia.
Fibrolamellar carcinoma	Variant of hepatocellular carcinoma. Occurs in young people (20–40 yr), is not associated with viral hepatitis or cirrhosis. Has a good Px. Histologically shows nests & cords of malignant hepatocytes separated by dense collagen bundles.
Fitz-Hugh-Curtis syndrome	Chlamydia or gonorrhea perihepatitis as a complication of pelvic inflammatory disease. Presents with right upper quadrant pain & sepsis.
Galactosemia	Deficient galactose-1-phosphate uridyl transferase blocks galactose conversion to glucose for further metabolism, leading to accumulation of galactose in many tissues. Sx = failure to thrive, infantile cataracts, mental retardation, cirrhosis. Rarely due to galactokinase deficiency, blocking the same path at a different step.
Gardner's syndrome	Familial polyposis syndrome with classic triad of desmoid tumors, osteomas of mandible or skull & sebaceous cysts.

DISEASE	DESCRIPTION/Sx
Gaucher's disease	The most frequent cause of lysosomal enzyme deficiency in Ashkenazi Jews. Autosomal recessive deficiency in β-glucocerebrosidase. Accumulation of sphingolipids in liver, spleen & bone marrow. Can be fatal if very expensive enzyme substitute (alglucerase) not administered.
Glanzmann's thrombasthenia	Autosomal recessive defect in GpIIbIIIa platelet receptor that binds fibrinogen, inhibiting platelet aggregation, presents with chronic, severe mucosal bleeds.
Glycogenoses	Genetic defects in metabolic enzymes causing glycogen accumulation. Si/Sx = hepatosplenomegaly, general organomegaly, exertional fatigue, hypoglycemia. Type I = von Gierke's disease, type II = Pompe's disease, type III = Cori's disease, type V = McCardle's disease.
Hartnup's disease	Autosomal recessive defect in tryptophan absorption at renal tubule. Sx mimic pellagra = the 3 D's: Dermatitis, Dementia, Diarrhea (tryptophan is niacin precursor). Rash is on sun-exposed areas, can see cerebellar ataxia, mental retardation & psychosis. Tx = niacin supplements.
Hepatorenal syndrome	Renal failure without intrinsic renal dz, occurring during fulminant hepatitis or cirrhosis, presents with acute oliguria & azotemia, typically progressive & fatal.
Holt-Oram syndrome	Autosomal dominant atrial septal defect in association with finger-like thumb or absent thumb, & cardiac conduction abnormalities & other skeletal defects.
Homocystinuria	Deficiency in cystine metabolism. Sx mimic Marfan's = lens dislocation (downward in homocystinuria as opposed to upward in Marfan's), thin bones, mental retardation, hypercoagulability & premature atherosclerosis → strokes & MIs.
Hunter's disease	X-linked lysosomal iduronidase deficiency, less severe than Hurler's syndrome. Sx = mild mental retardation, cardiac problems, micrognathia, etc.
Hurler's disease	Defect in iduronidase, causing multiorgan mucopolysaccharide accumulation, dwarfism, hepatosplenomegaly, corneal clouding, progressive mental retardation & death by age 10.
Isovalinic acidemia	"Sweaty-foot odor" disease. Caused by a defect in leucine metabolism, leads to buildup of isovaline in the bloodstream, producing characteristic odor.
Job's syndrome	B-cell defect causing hyper-IgE levels but defects in other immunoglobulin & immune functions. Presents with recurrent pulmonary infections, dermatitis, excess teeth (pts unable to shed their baby teeth), frequent bone fractures, classic "gargoyle facies," IgE levels 10- to 100-fold higher than normal.
Kasabach-Merritt	An expanding hemangioma trapping platelets, leading to systemic thrombocytopenia.
Keshan's disease	Childhood cardiomyopathy 2° to selenium deficiency, very common in China.
Klippel-Trénaunay-Weber syndrome	Autosomal dominant chromosomal translocation → prematurity, hydrops fetalis, hypertrophic hemangioma of leg & Kasabach-Merritt thrombocytopenia.
Klumpke's paralysis	Clawed hand—lower brachial-plexopathy (C8, T1) affecting ulnar nerve distributions, often presents with Horner's syndrome as well.
Leigh's disease	Mitochondrially inherited dz → absent or ↓↓ thiamine pyrophosphate. Infants or children present with seizures, ataxia, optic atrophy, ophthalmoplegia, tremor.
Lesch-Nyhan syndrome	Congenital defect in HPRT → gout, urate nephrolithiasis, retardation, choreiform spasticity & self-mutilation (patients bite off their own fingers & lips). Mild deficiency → Kelley-Seegmiller syndrome = gout without nervous system Si/Sx.
Leukocyte adhesion deficiency	Type I due to lack of β2-integrins (LFA-1), type II due to lack of fucosylated glycoproteins (selectin receptors). Both have plenty of neutrophils in blood but can't enter tissues due to problems with adhesion & transmigration. Both present with recurrent bacterial infections, **gingivitis**, **poor wound healing & delayed umbilical cord separation**.
Lhermitte sign	Tingling down the back during neck flexion, occurs in any craniocervical disorder.
Liddle's disease	Disease mimics hyperaldosteronism. Defect is in the renal epithelial transporters. Si/Sx = HTN, hypokalemic metabolic alkalosis.

DISEASE	DESCRIPTION/SX
Li-Fraumeni's syndrome	Autosomal dominant inherited defect of p53 leading to primary cancers of a variety of organ systems presenting at an early age.
Maple syrup urine disease	Disorder of branched chain amino acid metabolism (valine, leucine, isoleucine). Sx include vomiting, acidosis & pathognomonic maple-like odor of urine.
Marchiafava-Bignami syndrome	Overconsumption of red wine → demyelination of corpus callosum, anterior commissure & middle cerebellar peduncles. Possibly anoxic/ischemic phenomenon.
Marfan's disease	Genetic collagen defect → tall, thin body habitus, long & slender digits, pectus excavatum, scoliosis, aortic valve dilation → regurgitation, aortic dissection, mitral valve prolapse & joint laxity, optic lens dislocations & blue sclera. Think about Abe Lincoln when considering this disease, tall & thin.
Melanosis coli	Overzealous use of laxatives causing darkening of colon, but no significant dz.
Mendelson's syndrome	Chemical pneumonitis following aspiration of acidic gastric juice, patient presents with acute dyspnea, tachypnea & tachycardia, with pink & frothy sputum.
Meralgia paresthetica	A condition common to truckers, hikers & overweight individuals who wear heavy backpacks or very tight-fitting belts compressing inguinal area. This causes patients to have a diffuse unilateral pain & paresthesias along anterior portion of upper thigh, corresponding to lateral femoral cutaneous nerve. Typically self-limiting, but can treat with steroids for refractory disease.
Minamata disease	Toxic encephalopathy from mercury poisoning, classically described from fish eaten near Japanese mercury dumping site.
Molluscum contagiosum	Poxvirus skin infection causing umbilicated papules, transmitted by direct contact, often venereal. The central umbilication is filled with semi-solid white material that contains inclusion bodies & is highly characteristic for the disease.
Monckeberg's arteriosclerosis	Calcific sclerosis of the media of medium-sized arteries, usually radial & ulnar. Occurs in people over 50, but it does NOT obstruct arterial flow since intima is not involved. It is unrelated to other atherosclerosis & does not cause dz.
Munchausen's syndrome	A factitious disorder in which the pt derives gratification from feigning a serious or dramatic illness. Munchausen's by proxy is when the pt derives gratification from making someone else ill (often a mother injures her child for attention).
Niemann-Pick's disease	Autosomal recessive defect in sphingomyelinase with variable age onset (↑ severe dz in younger pt) → demyelination/neurologic Sx, hepatosplenomegaly, xanthoma, pancytopenia.
Noonan's syndrome	Autosomal dominant with Sx similar to Turner's syndrome → hyperelastic skin, neck webbing, ptosis, low-set ears, short stature, pulmonary stenosis, AS defect, coarctation of aorta, small testes. Presents in males, X & Y are both present.
Ortner's syndrome	Impingement of recurrent laryngeal nerve by the enlarging atrium in mitral regurgitation, leading to hoarseness.
Osteogenesis imperfecta	Genetic disorder of diffuse bone weakness due to mutations resulting in defective collagen synthesis. Multiple fractures 2° to minimal trauma = brittle bone disease. Classic sign = blue sclera, due to translucent connective tissue over choroid.
Peliosis hepatis	Rare primary dilation of hepatic sinusoids. Associated with exposure to anabolic steroids, oral contraceptives & danazol. Irregular cystic spaces filled with blood develop in the liver. Cessation of drug intake causes reversal of the lesions.
Plummer-Vinson syndrome	Iron deficiency syndrome with classic triad of esophageal web, spoon nail & iron deficiency anemia. Webs produce dysphagia, will regress with iron replacement.
Polycystic kidney disease	Autosomal dominant bilateral dz, Si/Sx = onset in early or middle adult life with hematuria, nephrolithiasis, uremia, 33% of cases have cysts in liver, 10–20% of cases have intracranial aneurysms, hypertension is present in 50% of pts at Dx. Juvenile version is autosomal recessive, much rarer than adult type; almost all cases have cysts in liver & portal bile duct proliferation = "congenital hepatic fibrosis."

DISEASE	DESCRIPTION/SX
Poncet's disease	Polyarthritis that occurs DURING active TB infection but no organisms can be isolated from the affected joints, is thought to be autoimmune-mediated disease.
Pott's disease	Tubercular infection of vertebrae (vertebral osteomyelitis) leading to kyphoscoliosis secondary to pathologic fractures.
Potter's syndrome	Bilateral renal agenesis; incompatible with fetal life, mother has oligohydramnios because fetus normally swallows large quantities of amniotic fluid & then urinates it out, but fetus cannot excrete swallowed fluid because it has no kidneys.
Prinzmetal's angina	Variant angina occurring at rest due to vasospasm, EKG → ST elevation instead of depression. Tx = calcium channel blockers.
Refsum's disease	Autosomal recessive defect in phytanic acid metabolism → peripheral neuropathy, cerebellar ataxia, retinitis pigmentosa, bone disease & ichthyosis (scaly skin).
Rett's syndrome	Congenital retardation secondary to ↑ serum ammonia levels, more common in females. Sx = autism, dementia, ataxia, tremors.
Schafer's disease	Defect in hexosaminidase B, in contrast to the A component of the enzyme that is defective in Tay-Sachs. Px is better for Schafer's.
Schindler's disease	Defect in N-acetylgalactosaminidase.
Schmidt's syndrome	Hashimoto's thyroiditis with diabetes &/or Addison's disease (autoimmune syndrome).
Sweet's syndrome (See Color Plate 31)	Recurrent painful reddish-purple plaques & papules associated with fever, arthralgia & neutrophilia. Occurs more commonly in women, possibly due to hypersensitivity reaction associated with *Yersinia* infection. Can also be seen in following URI or along with leukemia. Tx = prednisone, antibiotics if associated with *Yersinia* infection.
Syndrome X	Angina relieved by rest (typical) with a normal angiogram. Caused by vasospasm of small arterioles, unlike Prinzmetal's angina, which is vasospasm of large arteries.
Tay-Sachs disease	Autosomal recessive defect in hexosaminidase A, causing very early onset, progressive retardation, paralysis, dementia, blindness, cherry-red spot on macula & death by 3–4 yr. Common in Ashkenazi Jews.
Tropical spastic paraparesis	Insidious lower extremity paresis caused by HTLV, which is endemic to Japan & the Caribbean, transmitted like HIV, via placenta, body fluids & sex. Presents with mild sensory deficits, marked lower extremity hyperreflexia, paralysis, urinary incontinence.
Turcot's syndrome	Familial adenomatous polyposis with CNS medulloblastoma or glioma.
Usher syndrome	Most common condition involving both hearing & vision impairment. Autosomal recessive dz → deafness & retinitis pigmentosa (a form of night blindness).
Verner-Morrison syndrome	VIPoma = vasoactive intestinal polypeptide overproduction. Leads to pancreatic cholera, increased watery diarrhea, dehydration, hypokalemia, hypo/achlorhydria.
Von Recklinghausen's disease	Diffuse osteolytic lesions caused by hyperparathyroidism causing characteristic "brown tumor" of bone due to hemorrhage. Can mimic osteoporosis on x-rays.
Wiskott-Aldrich syndrome	X-linked recessive defect in IgM response to capsular polysaccharides like those of *S. pneumoniae*, but pts have ↑ IgA levels. Classic triad = recurrent pyogenic bacteria infections, eczema, thrombocytopenia. Bloody diarrhea is often first Sx, then URIs; leukemia & lymphoma are common in children who survive to age 10.
Xeroderma pigmentosa	Defect in repair of DNA damage caused by UV light (pyrimidine dimers). Patients highly likely to develop skin cancers. Only Tx is avoidance of sunlight.

Appendix B. Toxicology

TOXIN	SI/SX	DX	ANTIDOTE
Acetaminophen	Nausea/vomiting within 2 hr, ↑ liver enzymes, ↑ prothrombin time at 24–48 hr	Blood level	N-acetylcysteine within 8–10 hr
Alkali agents	Derived from batteries, dishwasher detergent, drain cleaners, ingestion causes mucosal burns → dysphagia & drooling	Clinical	Milk or water, then NPO
Anticholinergic	**Dry as a bone, mad as a hatter, blind as a bat, hot as a hare** (delirium, miosis, fever)	Clinical	Physostigmine
Arsenic	**Mees lines** (white horizontal stripes on fingernails), capillary leak, seizures	Blood level	Gastric lavage & dimercaprol
Aspirin	Tinnitus, respiratory alkalosis, **anion gap metabolic acidosis with normal S_{OSM}**[a]	Blood level	Bicarbonate, dialysis
Benzodiazepine	Rapid onset of weakness, ataxia, drowsiness	Blood level	Flumazenil
β-Blockers	Bradycardia, heart block, obtundation, **hyperkalemia, hypoglycemia**	Clinical	Glucagon, IV calcium
Carbon monoxide	Dyspnea, confusion, coma, **cherry-red color of skin**, mucosal cyanosis	Carboxy-Hgb[b]	100% O_2 or hyperbaric O_2
Cyanide	In seconds to minutes → trismus, **almond-scented breath**, coma	Blood level	Amyl nitrite ⊕ Na thiosulfate
Digoxin	**Change in color vision, supraventricular tachycardia with heart block**, vomiting	Blood level[c]	Anti-digoxin Fab-antibodies
Ethylene glycol	**Calcium oxalate crystals in urine, anion gap metabolic acidosis with high S_{OSM}**[a]	Blood level	Ethanol drip, fomepizol[d]
Heparin	Bleeding, thrombocytopenia	Clinical	Protamine
Iron	Vomiting, bloody diarrhea, acidosis, CXR → radiopaque tablets	Blood level	Deferoxamine
Isoniazid	Confusion, peripheral neuropathy	Blood level	Pyridoxine
Lead	**Microcytic anemia with basophilic stippling**, ataxia, retardation, peripheral neuropathy, **purple lines on gums**	Blood level	EDTA, penicillamine
Mercury	**"Erethism" = ↓ memory, insomnia, timidity, delirium (mad as a hatter)**	Blood level	Ipecac, dimercaprol
Methanol	Anion gap metabolic acidosis with high S_{OSM},[a] blindness, **optic disk hyperemia**	Blood level	Ethanol drip, bicarbonate
Opioids	CNS/respiratory depression, miosis	Blood level	Narcan
Organophosphate	Incontinence, cough, wheezing, dyspnea, miosis, bradycardia, heart block, tremor	Blood level	Atropine, pralidoxime
Phenobarbitol	CNS depression, hypothermia, miosis, hypotensions	Blood level	Charcoal, bicarbonate
Quinidine	Torsades des pointes (ventricular tachycardia)	Blood level	IV magnesium
Theophylline	First Sx = hematemesis, then CNS → seizures or coma, cardiac → arrhythmias, hypotension	Blood level[c]	Ipecac, charcoal, cardiac monitor
Tricyclics	Anticholinergic Sx, QRS >100 ms, torsades des pointes	Blood level	Bicarbonate drip
Warfarin	Bleeding	↑ PT	Vitamin K

[a] S_{OSM} = serum osmolality; [b] carboxyhemoglobin; [c] correlates in acute but not chronic toxicity; [d] see *N Engl J Med* 1999, 340:832–838.

Appendix C. Vitamins and Nutrition

NUTRIENT	DEFICIENCY	EXCESS
B₁ (thiamine)	Dry beriberi → neuropathy Wet beriberi → high-output cardiac failure Either → Wernicke-Korsakoff's syndrome	
B₂ (riboflavin)	Cheilosis (mouth fissures)	
B₃ (niacin)	Pellagra → dementia, diarrhea, dermatitis Also seen in Hartnup's disease (dz of tryptophan metabolism)	
B₅ (pantothenate)	Enteritis, dermatitis	
B₆ (pyridoxine)	Neuropathy (frequently caused by isoniazid therapy for TB)	
B₁₂ (cyanocobalamin)	Pernicious anemia (lack of intrinsic factor) → neuropathy, megaloblastic anemia, glossitis	
Biotin	Dermatitis, enteritis (caused by ↑consumption of raw eggs, due to the avidin in the raw eggs blocking biotin absorption)	
Chromium	Glucose intolerance (cofactor for insulin)	
Copper	Leukopenia, bone demineralization	
Folic acid	Neural tube defects, megaloblastic anemia	
Iodine	Hypothyroidism, cretinism, goiter	
Iron	Plummer-Vinson syndrome = esophageal webs, spoon nails	Hemochromatosis → multiorgan failure (bronze diabetes)
Selenium	Myopathy (Keshan's disease, see Appendix A)	
Vitamin A	Metaplasia of respiratory epithelia (seen in cystic fibrosis due to failure of fat-soluble vitamin absorption), xerophthalmia, night blindness (lack of retinal in rod cells), acne, Bitot's spots, frequent respiratory infections (respiratory epithelial defects)	Pseudotumor cerebri (can be caused by consuming polar bear livers), headache, nausea, vomiting, skin peeling
Vitamin C	Scurvy: poor healing, hypertrophic bleeding gums, easy bruising, deficient osteoid mimicking rickets	
Vitamin D	Rickets in kids, osteomalacia in adults	Kidney stones, dementia, constipation, abdominal pain, depression
Vitamin E	Fragile RBCs, sensory & motor peripheral neuropathy	
Vitamin K	Clotting deficiency	
Zinc	Poor wound healing, decreased taste & smell, alopecia, diarrhea, dermatitis, depression (similar to pellagra)	
Calories	**Marasmus** = total calorie malnutrition → pts look deceptively well, but immunosuppressed, poor wound healing, impaired growth	
Protein	**Kwashiorkor** = protein malnutrition → edema/ascites, immunosuppression, poor wound healing, impaired growth & development	

Index

Note: Page numbers followed by *f* refer to figures; page numbers followed by *t* refer to tables.

dilation of, 162
lymphadenitis of, 101*t*
polyps of in abortion, 168
Cesarean section
  with active herpes, 197*t*
  in gestational diabetes
    mellitus, 155
  infection after, 167
  for multiple gestations, 172
Chadwick's sign, 151
Chalazion, 297*t*
Charcoal, 212
Charcot-Marie-Tooth disease,
  324*t*
Charcot's triad, 102*t*, 111
Chediak-Higashi syndrome,
  324*t*
Cheilosis, 330*t*
Chelation, 64
Chemotherapy
  for anal cancer, 121
  for cervical lymphadenitis,
    101*t*
  for cutaneous T-cell
    lymphoma, 286*t*
  for Ewing's sarcoma, 52*t*
  for gastric tumors, 108
  for Hodgkin's lymphoma, 71
  for Kaposi's sarcoma, 286*t*
  for leukemia, 70
  for malignant melanoma,
    286*t*
  for ovarian neoplasms, 188*t*
  for parenchymal lung cancer,
    23
  for rectal cancer, 121
  for Wilms tumor, 43
Cherry hemangioma, 284
Cherry-red spot, 302
Chest pain, tearing, 140
Chest X-ray
  approach to, 307
  lateral decubitus, indications
    for, 307*t*
  normal, 307–308*f*
Cheyne-Stokes respirations
  in CNS tumor, 134
  description of, 324*t*
Chicken pox, 198*t*
Child abuse, 210–211
  diagnosis of, 211
  high-risk children for, 210
  perpetrators of, 210
  signs and symptoms of, 211

treatment of, 211
Child psychiatry, 251–254
Children
  adolescent disorders in,
    212–214
  development of, 196
  genetic and congenital
    disorders of, 207–210
  infections in, 197–199
  metabolic disorders of,
    205–207
  musculoskeletal disorders of,
    202–205
  poisonings in, 211–212
  respiratory disorders of,
    199–202
  trauma in, 210–211
Chlamydia
  pneumonia, 27*t*
  psittaci, 27*t*
  trachomatis, 201, 202
Chloasma, 284
Chloramphenicol, 288
Chloride-responsive alkalosis,
  74*f*
Chloroquine, 287
Chlorpromazine, 245*t*
Cholangitis
  ascending, 111
  characteristics of, 102*t*
Cholecystectomy, 110
  laparoscopic, 111
  for typhoid fever, 282
Cholecystitis, 110–111
  characteristics of, 102*t*
Choledocholithiasis, 32, 111
  characteristics of, 102*t*
Cholelithiasis, 110
Cholestasis
  extrahepatic, 32
  intrahepatic, 31–32
Cholesterol
  drugs to lower, 4
  structure of, 181*f*
Cholesterol-HDL ratio, 2
Chorioamnionitis, 171
Choroidal melanoma, 303*f*
Christmas disease, 68
Chromium, deficiency of, 330*t*
Chromosomal abnormalities
  in abortion, 168
  genetic testing for, 161
Chronic obstructive pulmonary
  disease, 19*t*

Ciprofloxacin, 222*t*, 223*t*
Circinate balanitis, 56
Circulation, assessment of, 97
Cirrhosis
  biliary, 32
  causes of, 33
  signs and symptoms of,
    33–34
  treatment of, 34
Clarithromycin, 29
Claudication, 150
  with atherosclerosis, 147,
    149
Clavicle, fracture of, 231
Cleft lip, 207–208
Cleft palate, 208
Clindamycin
  for bacterial pneumonia, 27*t*
  for necrotizing fasciitis, 281
Clinical trial, 235
Clomiphene
  for anovulation, 184
  for polycystic ovarian
    disease, 182*t*
Clomipramine, 247
Clonazepam
  for seizures, 270*t*
  for trigeminal neuralgia, 218*t*
Clonidine, 228
Clostridium botulinum
  neurotoxin, 198
Clostridium difficile colitis,
  237, 241
Clot lysis, 35
Clotting deficiency, 330*t*
Clozapine, 245*t*
Clue cells, 177*t*, 178*f*
Coagulation, 92
  disorders of, 68–69
Coarctation of aorta. *See* Aortic
  coarctation
Cocaine
  in drug-induced mania, 244
  intoxication and withdrawal
    symptoms of, 254*t*
Coccidioides
  immitis, 27*t*
  meningitis, 267
Codman's triangle, 54*f*
Coffee bean sigmoid volvulus,
  311*t*
Cognitive/behavioral therapy,
  247
Cohort study, 235

P

P waves
 in multifocal atrial
  tachycardia, 7
 in supraventricular
  tachycardia, 7
Pacing, dual-chamber, 11t
Packed red blood cell
  transfusion
 complications of, 93
 viral infections with, 93, 94t
Paget's disease
 of bone, 51
 of breast, 123
Pallidotomy, 272
Palpebral inflammation, 297t,
  298f
Pamidronate, 92t
Pancoast tumor, 23, 24f
Pancreas
 cancer of, 113–115
 carcinoma of, 115f
 disease of, 223t
 endocrine neoplasms of, 115
 exocrine, 112–115
 pseudocysts of, 112–113
  characteristics of, 105t
 tumors of, 114f
Pancreaticogastrostomy, 113
Pancreatitis
 acute, 112
 characteristics of, 105t
Pancreatoma, 50t
Panic disorder, 246–247
Panniculitis, 291, 293
Pantothenate, deficiency of,
  330t
Pap smear, 176
 for cervical cancer, 187
 for endometrial cancer, 186
Papillary muscle dysfunction,
  11
Papilledema, 302
Papule, 280
Paraganglioma, 101t
Parainfluenza
 in bronchiolitis, 199
 characteristics and treatment
  of, 28t
Parakeratosis, 280
Paralysis, ascending, 277
Paralytic ileus, 115
Paramyxovirus, 198t

Paranoid delusions, 244
Paranoid personality, 249t
Parapneumonic effusion, 20t
Parasitic infections, 288–289
Parinaud's syndrome, 295
Parity, 151
Parkinsonism, 272
 characteristics of, 246t
Parkinson's disease, 272
Parkland formula, 100
Paronychia, 281
Paroxetine, 243t
Partial thromboplastin time
  (PTT), 93
 for hemophilia, 145, 148
 preoperative, 94
Parvovirus B-19, 198t
Patent ductus
  arteriosus, 210
 heart murmurs in, 15t
Pediatrics, 196–216
Pediculosis capitis, 288
Pediculosis pubis, 288
Pel-Epstein fever, 71
Peliosis hepatitis, 287–288
 description of, 327t
Pellagra, 330t
Pelvic inflammatory disease
 characteristics and treatment
  of, 225t
 in infertility, 184
Pelvic relaxation, 184–185
Pemphigus vulgaris, 286–287
Penicillamine, 55
Penicillin
 in drug-induced interstitial
  nephritis, 37
 for endocarditis, 14
 for Lyme disease, 288
 for necrotizing fasciitis, 281
 for Neisseria meningitidis,
  276, 279
 for pharyngitis, 221t
 for pneumonia, 27t
 for rheumatic fever, 14
 for scarlet fever, 281
 for Streptococcus agalactiae
  during pregnancy, 157
 for syphilis, 268t
 for urinary tract infections,
  224
 for Whipple's disease, 223t
Penile prosthesis, 228
Pentoxifylline, 141

Peptic stricture, 222
Peptic ulcer, 105t
 characteristics of, 104t
Percutaneous drainage, 118
Pericardial cyst, 24t
Pericardial disease, 14
Pericardial effusion, 14
Pericardiectomy, 14
Pericardiocentesis, 144, 148
 in cardiac tamponade, 14
Pericarditis, 14
Perioperative care, 94–96
Periosteal reactions, 53–54f
Peripheral vascular disease,
  140
 diagnosis of, 140–141
 treatment of, 141
Peritoneal lavage, 98
Peritonitis
 bacterial, 34
 with pancreatic pseudocyst,
  113
Permethrin
 for head lice, 288
 for Lyme disease, 288
 for pediculosis pubis, 288
 for scabies, 288
Personality disorders, 248–250
 characteristics of, 249t
 clusters of, 249
Pertussis, stages of, 202
Pessary devices, 185
Petechiae, 280
Peutz-Jeghers syndrome,
  116–117
Phakomatoses, 286
Phalen's test, 127
Pharyngitis, 221t
Phencyclidine, 254t
Phenelzine, 243t
Phenobarbital
 for Crigler-Najjar syndrome,
  31t
 toxicology of, 329t
Phenoxybenzamine, 48
Phentolamine, 48
Phenylephrine, 1t
Phenytoin
 for seizures, 270t, 271
 for trigeminal neuralgia, 218t
Pheochromocytoma, 47–48
 in hypertension, 1t
 in multiple endocrine
  neoplasia syndromes, 50t

for temporal arteritis, 218*t*,
 238–239, 241
Preeclampsia
 characteristics of, 156
 treatment of, 156
Pregnancy. *See also* Ectopic
 pregnancy
 in amenorrhea, 179
 with amenorrhea, 191, 194
 cardiac disease in, 156–157
 diabetes mellitus in, 154–155
 diagnosis of, 151
 glucose control during, 192,
 194–195
 human chorionic
 gonadotropin levels in,
 190*f*
 hypertension of, 155–156
 medical conditions in,
 154–157   .
 molar, 189
 physiologic changes in,
 153–154
 tests for, 151
Pregnancy-induced
 hypertension, 155
Pregnenolone, 181*f*
Premature delivery, 151
Premature rupture of
 membranes, 171–172
 in preterm labor, 170
Premature ventricular
 contractions, 7
Prenatal care
 first trimester visits in, 152
 first visit in, 151–152
 second trimester visits in,
 153
 third trimester visits in, 153
Prenatal genetic testing, 161
Preoperative care, 94
Presentation
 breech, 166
 during labor, 162
 occipitoanterior, 163*f*
Preterm labor, 170
 abruption of in gestational
 diabetes mellitus, 155
 complications of, 171
 diagnosis of, 171
 risk factors for, 170
 signs and symptoms of, 171
 treatment of, 171
Preventive medicine, 233–234

Primordial follicles, 173
Prinzmetal's angina, 328*t*
Probenecid/sulfinpyrazone, 61
Procainamide
 for atrial fibrillation, 6
 in systemic lupus
 erythematosus, 56
Procarbazine, 71
Proctectomy, 116
Progesterone
 for endometrial cancer, 186
 in oral contraceptives, 175
 release of, 173
 structure of, 181*f*
Progestin
 for endometrial cancer, 186
 for endometriosis, 179
 for menopause, 182
 in oral contraceptives, 175
Progressive multifocal
 leukoencephalopathy, 268*t*
Progressive systemic sclerosis.
 See Scleroderma
Prolactinoma, 43
 in amenorrhea, 180
 characteristics of, 135*t*
 in multiple endocrine
 neoplasia syndromes, 50*t*
 treatment of, 135
Propionibacterium acnes, 280
Propranolol, 35
Propylthiouracil, 49
Prospective studies, 235
Prostaglandins
 for impotence, 228
 for pulmonary hypertension,
 22
 for uterine atony, 166
Prostate
 cancer of, 125
 bone scan of, 126*f*
 screening for, 233*t*
 disorders of, 227–228
Prostatectomy, 125
Prostatitis, 227–228
Protease inhibitors, 226
Protein
 deficiency of, 330*t*
 restriction of in nephrotic
 syndrome, 39
Proteinuria, Bence-Jones, 52
 diagnosis of, 53
Prothrombin time (PT), 92
 preoperative, 94

Prothrombin time/partial
 thromboplastin time
 (PT/PTT), 68*t*
Proton pump inhibitors
 for chronic gastritis, 29
 for dyspepsia, 221
 for gastric ulcers, 29
 for GERD, 222
Proto-oncogenes, 119
Pseudocyst, pancreatic,
 112–113
 characteristics of, 105*t*
 CT scan of, 113*f*
Pseudogout, 61
Pseudohyperkalemia, 79*f*
Pseudohypokalemia, 78*f*
Pseudohyponatremia, 76*f*
*Pseudomonas
 aeruginosa*
 in "hot tub" folliculitis, 281
 in otitis externa, 218
 pneumonia, 27*t*
 in pyogenic osteomyelitis, 51
Pseudotumor cerebri, 135–136,
 330*t*
Psoriasis, 282
Psoriatic arthritis, 58
Psychiatric disorders, prognosis
 of, 242*t*
Psychiatry, 242–265
 principles of, 242
Psychosis, 244–246
Psychotherapy
 for bulimia, 254
 for depression, 243
 for obsessive compulsive
 disorder, 247
 for personality disorders, 248
 for posttraumatic stress
 disorder, 248
 for social functioning, 246
 for Tourette's disorder, 253
Psychotic disorders
 diagnosis of, 245*t*
 drug-induced, 245*t*
 hallmarks of, 244
 medical, 245*t*
PTCA. *See* Angioplasty,
 percutaneous transluminal
 coronary
Pterygium, 296
Pulmonary capillary wedge
 pressure, 21
Pulmonary disease, 16–28

Thyroiditis
  Hashimoto's, 328t
  subacute, 49, 50
Tinea, 289t
Tinea capitis, 289t
Tinea versicolor, 289t
Tinel's sign, 127
Tinnitus, 218
Tissue plasminogen activator
  for infarct, 266
  for pulmonary embolism, 22
  for subdural hemorrhage,
    144, 148
Tocodynamometer, 163
Tocolytics, 171
Togavirus, 198t
Tonic seizures, 270
ToRCH group, 197t
  in conjugated
    hyperbilirubinemia, 206
Torticollis
  differential diagnosis of, 101t
Tourette's disorder, 253
Toxic goiter, 49
Toxic megacolon, 30
Toxic multinodal goiter, 49
Toxic synovitis, 202t
Toxicology, 329t
  pediatric, 212t
Toxoplasmosis, 197t, 268t
Toxoplasmosis encephalitis,
  226
Tracheostomy, 17
Traction, hip, 129
Traction-countertraction
  of dislocated shoulder, 128
  for shoulder dislocation, 230
Tram-track lung markings, 19t
Transfusions, 93–94
  for GI hemorrhage, 118
  packed RBCs, 93
  plasma component, 94
  platelet, 94
  for thalassemia, 64t
  viral infection from, 94t
Transient ischemic attacks
  definition of, 262
Transurethral resection of
  prostate, 227
Tranylcypromine, 243t
Traube's sign, 12
Trauma, 97
  ABCDE survey of, 97–98
  ABCs of, 144, 148

childhood, 210–211
  secondary survey of, 98
  shock with, 98–99
Travel prophylaxis, 234t
Traveler's diarrhea, 234t
Treponema pallidum
  characteristics and treatment
    of, 225t
  warts with, 285
Triamcinolone, 280t
Trichloracetic acid, 225t
Trichomonas vaginalis, 177,
  178f
Trichomoniasis, 191–192, 194
Trichotillomania, 255
Tricuspid valve
  disorders of, 13
  regurgitation of, 13
    heart murmurs in, 15t
  stenosis of, 13
    heart murmurs in, 15t
Tricyclics
  in impotence, 228
  for panic disorder, 247
  for posttraumatic stress
    disorder, 248
  side effects of, 243t
  toxicology of, 329t
Trigeminal neuralgia
  characteristics and
    epidemiology of, 217t
  diagnosis of, 217
  treatment of, 218t
Trihexyphenidyl, 272
Triple combination therapy,
  AIDS, 226
Trisomy 21, 161, 208
Troglitazone, 44
Tropical spastic paraparesis,
  328t
Tropical sprue, 223t
Troponin I levels, 4
Trousseau's syndrome, 113
Tuberculosis
  diagnosis of, 25–26
  manifestations of, 26f
  miliary, 25, 319f
  primary, 25
  radiogram of, 319f
  secondary, 25
  treatment of, 26
Tuberculous meningitis, 267
Tuberous sclerosis, 286t
Tubo-ovarian abscess, 103t

Tumor necrosis factor α, 55
Tumor suppressors, 119
Tumors
  bone, 52–54
  CNS, 134, 135t
  esophageal, 107–108
  gastric, 108
  hepatic, 109–110
  in low back pain, 229
  ovarian, 188t
  pancreatic, 114f
  Sertoli-Leydig cell, 182t
Turcot's syndrome, 116
  description of, 328t
Turner's syndrome, 180, 208
Twins
  dizygotic, 172
  monozygotic, 172
Twin-twin transfusion
  syndrome, 172
Typhoid
  fever, rose spots in, 282
  prophylaxis for, 234t

U

Ulcerative colitis, 30, 31t,
  323f
Ulcers
  arterial, 142
  duodenal, 29–30
  gastric, 29
  Marjolin, 100, 146–147, 149
  peptic, 105t
    characteristics of, 104t
  rodent, 285t
  venous, 142
Ulna, fracture of, 127
Ultrasonography, pregnancy,
  151
Ultraviolet light
  for neonatal jaundice, 206
  for psoriasis, 282
Umbilical cord
  blood testing, 164
  compression of, 158
Unna's boots, 142
Urate crystal deposits, 61
Uremia, 39
Urge incontinence, 185
Uric acid stones, 42
Urinalysis
  for hematuria, 227
  preoperative, 94

von-Willebrand factor
deficiency, 68
V/Q mismatch, 16*t*, 18*f*
Vulva
cancer of, 189
intraepithelial neoplasia of,
189

W

WAGR complex, 43
Warfarin, 266
toxicology of, 329*t*
Warts, 285
Water
extracellular, 90
intracellular, 90
restriction of
for chronic renal failure, 39
for electrolyte disorders,
91*t*
Water deprivation test, 38
Water-bottle-shaped heart, 309*t*
Water-Hammer pulse, 12
Waterhouse-Friderichsen
syndrome, 47

Watershed infarct, 262
Weight loss
for angina, 3*t*
for hypertension, 1
for polycystic ovarian
disease, 182*t*
Wenckebach phenomenon, 8*f*
Wermer's syndrome, 50*t*
Wernicke's aphasia, 262
Wernicke's encephalopathy, 34
Wernicke's triad, 269
Wet gangrene, 140
Wheal, 280
Wheezing, 19*t*
Whipple's disease, 223*t*
Whipple's procedure, 113
Willis, circle of, 263*f*
MRA of, 264*f*
Wilms tumor, 42–43
Wilson's disease, 270
Kayser-Fleischer ring in, 296
Wiskott-Aldrich syndrome,
328*t*
Wolff-Parkinson-White
syndrome, 80, 86
Wrist injuries, 127

X

Xanthoma, 284
Xeroderma pigmentosa, 328*t*
Xerophthalmia, 298–299*t*, 330*t*
Xerostomia, 56
X-ray, KUB, 307*t*
XYY syndrome, 48*t*

Y

Yellow eye, 301
Yellow fever, prophylaxis for,
234*t*
Yellow vision, 301
Yersinia enterocolitis, 103*t*

Z

Zebras, 324–328*t*
Zenker's diverticulum, 107
Zinc, deficiency of, 330*t*
Zinc oxide paste impregnated
bandage, 142
Zollinger-Ellison syndrome,
115
Zoster infection, 198*t*